DATE DUE

The New Religious
Movements Experience
in America

Recent Titles in
The American Religious Experience
Philip Goff, Series Editor

The Buddhist Experience in America
Diane Morgan

The New Religious Movements Experience in America

Eugene V. Gallagher

The American Religious Experience
Philip Goff, Series Editor

GREENWOOD PRESS
Westport, Connecticut • London

Library of Congress Cataloging-in-Publication Data

Gallagher, Eugene V.
   The new religious movements experience in America / Eugene V. Gallagher.
      p.   cm. — (The American religious experience)
   Includes bibliographical references and index.
   ISBN 0-313-32807-2 (alk. paper)
   1. United States—Religion.   I. Title.   II. American religious experience
   (Greenwood Press (Westport, Conn.))
BL2525.G328   2004
200'.973—dc22   2004054365

British Library Cataloguing in Publication Data is available.

Library of Congress Catalog Card Number: 2004054365
ISBN: 0-313-32807-2

First published in 2004

Greenwood Press, 88 Post Road West, Westport, CT 06881
An imprint of Greenwood Publishing Group, Inc.
www.greenwood.com

Printed in the United States of America

The paper used in this book complies with the
Permanent Paper Standard issued by the National
Information Standards Organization (Z39.48–1984).

10   9   8   7   6   5   4   3   2   1

for John S. Grady,
my teacher for thirty-five years

Contents

Series Foreword

Philip Goff

Some years ago, Winthrop Hudson, a leading religious historian, began his survey book on religion in America with a description of a London street. "When Americans walk down the street of an English city," he wrote, "they will be reminded of home."[1]

Few would dispute that for many years this was the case. Multiple faith traditions in today's United States trace their roots to English lineage, most notably the Episcopal, Methodist, and Baptist churches. But that sort of literary device would not hold up under the pressure of today's diversity. Lutherans, Presbyterians, and Dutch Reformed adherents would balk at such oversimplification—and those are just a few among only the Protestant Christians. Add the voices of Jews, Eastern Orthodox, Muslims, Buddhists, and Irish, Italian, and Polish Catholics, and we would have a powerful chorus demanding their stories be told. And their stories do not begin on the streets of London.

Of course, Hudson knew that was the case. His point was not that all significant American religions began in England, but that, "with only a few exceptions, the varied religious groups of America have their roots abroad."[2] But clearly the "abroad" Hudson worked with was predominantly European, even if not entirely English. Today's scholarship has broadened that focus to include African, Asian, Central and South American, as well as Canadian and some "homegrown" traditions that are on their way to becoming worldwide faiths. If ever scholarship in American religion has reflected the lineage of its people, it is in the recent writings that have moved beyond conventional ideas of faith traditions to include non-Anglo peoples who, while often existing off the radar screen of the establishment, have nonetheless formed much of the marrow of American religious life.

Although our studies of American religion have expanded to include more migrating faith groups from more areas of the world, the basic question that divided historians early in the twentieth century remained: namely, are traditions of American life (religion, politics, economics, etc.) transplants from the old world, or did something entirely new and unique form in the New World? That is, should we seek to comprehend America's present religious scene by understanding its roots? Or should we try to understand it by looking at its transformations?

Of course, the truth lies somewhere in between. One cannot understand present-day Methodists or Buddhists by knowing their Old World beginnings in England and China or Japan. Nor can one determine the transformations those faith traditions underwent in America without knowing a good deal about their Old World forms. The American experience, then, is one of constancy of tradition from one angle and continual revision from another. The fact that they may look, think, and sound different than their Old World forms does not negate the fact that they are still recognizably Methodist and Buddhist in their new contexts.

This book series is meant to introduce readers to the basic faith traditions that characterize religious life today by employing that continuum of constancy and change. Each volume traces its topic from its Old World beginnings (when it applies) to its present realities. In doing so, readers will see how many of the original beliefs and practices came to be, as well as how they transformed, remained nearly the same, or were complemented by new ones in the American environment. In some cases—African Americans and Mormons most clearly—the Old World proved important either implicitly or imaginatively rather than explicitly and literally. But even in these cases, development within the context of American culture is still central to the story.

To be sure, each author in this series employed various approaches in writing these books. History, sociology, even anthropology, all play their parts. Each volume, then, may have its idiosyncrasies, as the authors chose which approaches worked best at which moments for their respective topics. These variations of approach resemble the diversity of the groups themselves, as each interacted in various ways at different stages with American society.

Not only do these volumes introduce us to the roots and development of each faith group, they also provide helpful guides to readers who wish to know more about them. By supplying timelines and glossaries, the books give a deeper sense of beliefs, behaviors, and significant figures and moments in those religions. By offering resources for research—including published primary and secondary sources as well as helpful Web sites—the series presents a wealth of helpful information for formal and informal students of religion in America.

Clearly, this is a series conceived and published with the curious reader in mind. It is our hope that it will spur both a deeper understanding of the varieties of religious experience in the United States and better research in the country's many and always changing traditions.

Notes

1. Winthrop Hudson, *Religion in America,* 4th ed. (New York: Macmillan, 1987), p. 11.

2. Ibid., pp. 11–12.

Preface

This book differs from several others in the series because it does not focus on a single religious tradition (e.g., Judaism, Islam, or Buddhism) or a major denomination (e.g., Roman Catholicism or Protestantism). Instead, it addresses a broad category, new religious movements, several of which will also be discussed in other volumes, but in rather different contexts and from different perspectives. Potentially hundreds or even thousands of religious groups could fall within this book's purview. Consequently, choices must be made about which groups to display and discuss. But that is one of the hallmarks of the academic study of religion.[1] Students of religion are always involved in the selection of telling examples that promise to illuminate specific patterns of human action and belief and to clarify pressing issues. In that sense, the study of new religious movements is no different than the study of any other religious movements. It involves the description, analysis, and interpretation of specific religious data both guided by and brought to bear upon prominent theoretical interests. But, as the first chapter demonstrates, virtually everything about new religious movements has been controversial, and not only in the last thirty or forty years.

Nearly every time a new religious movement has surfaced in American history, it has been dogged by opponents who have doubted its truth, sincerity, and motives. This book, then, must necessarily be a guide to difficult and contested terrain. It aims to map the territory occupied by new religious movements throughout American history, investigate their often fractious relations with their surrounding environments, promote an accurate and sophisticated understanding of their distinctive practices and beliefs, and chart the paths along which more detailed research into particular groups or themes might proceed.

While the individual chapters of this book provide a general orientation for further study, an extensive section of annotated resources offers detailed guidance. It lists individual primary sources and collections of them, major treatments of new religious movements in general as well as of specific groups, and substantial audio and visual resources. One noteworthy aspect of the list of resources is the inclusion of important Web sites for the study of new religious movements. New religious movements have a substantial and significant presence on the World Wide Web. Although individual Web sites can be ephemeral, many well-established sites are maintained by scholars, groups themselves, and their critics. In addition there are several sites that maintain impressive electronic archives of both primary and secondary materials, some of which are difficult to obtain by any other means.

Before it proceeds to a discussion of specific new religious movements and identifiable "families" of them, this book provides the reader with a general orientation. It shows how any conversation about new religious movements is necessarily and unavoidably embedded in contemporary controversies about the potential dangers posed by groups described as cults. One of the implications of that social context for study of new religious movements is that any observer must choose to adopt a particular descriptive and analytical vocabulary. The more conscious and articulate the choice, the easier it will be to understand a given observer's particular analysis and interpretation of the general topic of new religious movements and specific cases and themes within it. Moreover, the choice of vocabulary is fraught with significant consequences. To adopt the rhetoric of contemporary opponents of cults, for example, is implicitly to align with a social movement that views with great alarm the purported proliferation of dangerous new religious movements. It is also to adopt specific, negative, views of leadership, processes of affiliation and disaffiliation, and even the potential for violence that are alleged to be characteristic of cults. On the other hand, to adopt what many academic studies of religion claim is a neutral descriptive lexicon of *new religious movements, conversion, myth, ritual,* and related terms is to risk being labeled as a cult apologist or sympathizer, whether that is one's intention or not. There seems to be very little neutral ground. As a result, the choice of a descriptive and analytical vocabulary has consequences beyond its immediate use in the discussion of any group.

In an effort to be clear about the commitments and assumptions that animate this book, the first chapter offers further explanation of fundamental descriptive terms. Because it is the crucial defining term and because many groups express substantial ambivalence about their own novelty, it will consider what is actually new about new religious movements, and what is not. Both because some groups seem to straddle the borders between religion and other cultural domains and because some critics have denied the religious character of certain new religious movements, it will examine what is religious about new religious movements, and what is not. Also, because new religious movements, like all of the other religious traditions addressed in this series, are no respecters of national boundaries, it will try to indicate what is specifically American about new religious movements, and what is not. These sections of the first chapter provide the basis for the analytical focus and organization of the rest of the book.

New religious movements are quicksilver entities. They can dramatically change their beliefs, practices, and organizational structure in the course of a few years or decades. In addition, many of them fade away or vanish after a first generation. Very few stand the test of time.[2] But, as Rodney Stark and William Sims Bainbridge have incisively observed, "in the beginning, all religions are obscure, tiny, deviant cult movements."[3] New religious movements may be interesting in themselves for various reasons, but they are especially interesting for what they can reveal about the formation and growth of religious worlds, the processes by which individuals change their religious orientations by migrating from one group to another, and the interactions between religious dissent and established sources of power and authority. Because of their relatively short life spans and small scale, new religious movements provide compact examples of religious dynamics that are also at work in larger, more complex religious traditions. Study of new religious movements, therefore, may provide a set of fresh questions and materials for comparison that could then be applied to those other traditions. Simply put, the study of new religious movements constitutes an accessible and potentially fruitful point of entry into the study of religion in general.

Given their pronounced dynamism, attempts to categorize new religious movements must respect how they can change and adapt to new circumstances over time. The first chapter offers a typology of new religious movements that is designed to be a rough sorting device that highlights some sets of similarities and differences while relegating others to subsidiary importance. This book, however, is not designed to force readers into using a particular set of classifications; it frequently notes ambiguities and uncertainties and entertains alternative descriptions, analyses, and interpretations.

As a sourcebook, this book aims to introduce readers to a complex and fascinating field of data, provide them with some basic frameworks of orientation, and lead them to the consideration of further sources and issues that will repay their extended attention. Some of the groups considered have settled into more or less stable identities, with relatively durable ways of life, sets of beliefs, and distinctive practices; others are in the process of significant changes even as this book was being written. The fluidity of the situation of new religious movements in the United States today is one of the things that makes the study of them both fascinating and challenging. There are many ways to begin and continue that study. This book adopts an approach that both provides sufficient guidance about crucial issues and allows ample flexibility to pursue multiple ways of understanding new religions. Despite the cacophony of voices that continually surrounds them, this book takes new religious movements seriously *as religions,* as human attempts to provide orientation, direction, and meaning to life by imagining a context of cosmic significance for human actions.[4] Whether the fundamental assumptions and convictions of new religious movements can somehow be shown to be "right" or "true" pales beside their capacity to motivate human activity in this world.

New religious movements have been significant parts of American life because they have been able to secure the loyalties and mobilize the actions of groups of dedicated followers. In doing so, they have had substantial impact on the lives of individuals, families, wider social networks, communities, and the nation itself. In the often exhilarated testimonials of converts to new religious movements, those effects are portrayed as profoundly and positively transformative. The formerly blind claim sight; the lost find both themselves and the communities they have been yearning for; those who thought themselves wretched achieve new identities that give dignity, direction, and importance to their lives.[5] But in the eyes of those who do not experience them, such transformations can seem less amazing than appalling. For some, the practices and beliefs of new religious movements are humorously bizarre but generally unthreatening.[6] But for a vocal minority, new religious movements pose an insidious threat to individuals, families, and the social order. In the following pages their voices will be heard, but only in conversation with members of the groups themselves and authoritative academic analysts—a conversation the alarmists have not often been willing to undertake seriously. It is, however, an interesting and an important conversation—one with substantial religious, social, legal, and moral implications. This book aims to equip readers to become discerning and knowledgeable participants in that continuing conversation.

Notes

1. Jonathan Z. Smith has argued that "for a student of religion . . . choice is everything." See Jonathan Z. Smith, *To Take Place* (Chicago: University of Chicago Press, 1987), xi.

2. For a series of essays on that theme, see Timothy Miller, ed., *When Prophets Die: The Postcharismatic Fate of New Religious Movements* (Albany: State University of New York Press, 1991).

3. Rodney Stark and William Sims Bainbridge, *The Future of Religion: Secularization, Revival, and Cult Formation* (Berkeley: University of California Press, 1985), p. 2.

4. For a sustained attempt to take the religious ideas of new religious movements seriously, see Mary Farrell Bednarowski, *New Religions and the Theological Imagination in America* (Bloomington: University of Indiana Press, 1989).

5. I am employing the familiar terms of the hymn, "Amazing Grace." For the use of that text as an opening into the study of religious conversion, see Eugene V. Gallagher, *Expectation and Experience: Explaining Religious Conversion* (Atlanta: Scholars, 1990), esp. pp. 1–10.

6. For a humorous treatment of recent millennialist groups, see Alex Heard, *Apocalypse Pretty Soon: Travels in End-Time America* (New York: Norton, 1999).

Acknowledgments

Since the early 1980s I have been teaching a course at Connecticut College on new religious movements in the United States. Much of what appears in this book has been developed in conversations with successive groups of students. I am grateful for their inquisitiveness, willingness to investigate what initially appeared to be strange or marginal material, and general feistiness. Several colleagues have contributed to this project in different ways. Roger Brooks remains my most valued conversation partner, and he has reviewed with an unsurpassed critical eye most of the arguments in this book. Lindsey Harlan has given me frequent opportunities to test out my ideas in her classes and in other conversations. Patrice Brodeur has always been willing to help and has been a bottomless source of references to materials on Islam. As chair of our Department of Religious Studies, Garrett Green has unfailingly made it possible for me to teach about at least some of my research interests each year. David Kim was an insightful critic of some of my basic assumptions and a stimulating colleague in the classroom. In the summer of 2003 Michael Reder and Marc Zimmer served as my writing partners and exerted gentle, and sometimes not so gentle, pressure on me to complete this book. Also, in their successive terms as dean of the faculty, both Helen Regan and Fran Hoffman gave welcome tangible and intangible support to my research; so also did Associate Dean William Frasure.

Professor Larry Wills of the Episcopal Divinity School in Cambridge and Professor Naomi Janowitz of the University of California at Davis kindly offered me opportunities to present some of my research at their institutions. Professors Jorunn Buckley, Arthur Droge, and James Tabor all made helpful comments on several aspects of my work. I have learned quite a bit from Professor Catherine Wessinger both in her published writings and in numerous e-mail exchanges over the years.

Several students had a direct hand in the making of this book, including Philip Myers, Yojiro Moro, Steve Reynolds, Taylor Steel, and, most important, Gabe Gold, who read through the entire manuscript and made many important and helpful suggestions. It's been a pleasure to work collaboratively with younger scholars.

Among the many others who supported my work in many ways I also thank Candy and Peter Briggs, especially for their tips about scheduling writing sessions, Sharon Butler, Daniel Curland, Donna Dooley, Sarah Furey, Carol Goodman, David Rezendes, Andrea Rossi, Jack Steel, Kate Steel, and Diane Zimmer. My wife, Jennifer, and daughter, Maggie, both respected my need to work and reminded me frequently and appropriately that there were certainly other things in life.

Finally, I dedicate this book to John S. Grady of La Salle University, who was my undergraduate teacher in the early 1970s and who has remained a trusted friend and colleague ever since.

Chapter 1

Introduction

In 1781 a former member of a tiny millennialist group located near Albany, New York, published a pamphlet that aimed to expose the group's doctrinal errors, deceitful practices, unbridled and unwarranted enthusiasm in worship, and troubling reliance on a charismatic leader.[1] Writing to other "ministers of the gospel" to warn them about "the growing evils and dangerous errors that are prevailing in our land," Valentine Rathbun argued that members of the United Society of Believers in Christ's Second Appearing, commonly known as the Shakers,[2] only feigned to offer hospitality to those who visited their settlement so that they could induce them into membership. Worried about a movement spreading "like a plague," Rathbun took offense at the Shakers' claim that they alone represented the true Christian church and also at their enthusiastic form of worship.[3] He chronicled with disapproval the practices, such as their distinctive manner of speech and the men's short haircuts, that distinguished them from the surrounding populace. But Rathbun reserved particular scorn for the group's claim that one of its leaders, Ann Lee, was actually the woman described in the biblical book of Revelation as being "clothed with the sun, with the moon under her feet, and on her head a crown of twelve stars" (Rev. 12:1). Rathbun found the Shakers' exaltation of "mother" Ann Lee to be theologically offensive and an indication that their millennialist dreams had led them into religious error. Offering his observations as "the public's real friend and humble servant," Rathbun found the little sect to be a product of demonic inspiration or worse. He wrote that "in this new religion, is the whole magazine of error, treasured up in the great mystery of iniquity, in which is found all the power of delusive witchcraft, to blindfold fools, and lead them to hell."[4]

Rathbun was hardly alone in his attacks on the little band of Shakers. Other critics denounced the group for having disrupted families by deluding people into membership.[5] An anonymous broadside published in 1783 attributed to the influence of the devil the convulsive physical movements in worship that had earned the United Society of Believers a nickname that always stuck with them.[6] Further, during her travels through New York, Massachusetts, and Connecticut in the early 1780s, Ann Lee was accused of being a witch and roughly examined to see if any physical signs could prove those suspicions. In less than a decade after their arrival in America, the Shakers had managed to provoke the same sort of opposition that had contributed to their departure from Manchester, England. There, in 1772 and 1773, Ann Lee had several times been arrested for disturbing a church service, presumably with her "enthusiastic" or ecstatic form of worship, which, the Shakers claimed, was prompted by the Holy Spirit. The hostility they experienced in Manchester spurred the coterie of believers to set off for North America in 1774.

The experiences of the founding generation of Shakers were by no means unique. In fact, they outline in compact form a hostile situation often encountered by new religious movements in American history. Whether they are new because they have been transplanted from another culture, as was the case with the Shakers, or because they constitute homegrown religious innovations, such as the Church of Scientology,[7] new religious movements frequently encounter skepticism, suspicion, and hostility from representatives of the status quo. The sincerity and even the mental stability of their leaders are questioned. Members of new religions are portrayed as, in Rathbun's words, "deprived of their reason."[8] Doctrines, when not simply dismissed as absurd, are branded as "damnable heresies, abominable impieties, and horrible blasphemies."[9] Because the ritual practices of new religious movements often appear to be "entirely new and different from all others," they are ridiculed.[10] Throughout American history, opponents of new religious movements, like Valentine Rathbun in 1781, have striven to alert the public about disturbing innovations and spur them to defend the status quo.

Inherent in the message of any new religious movement is an indictment of its predecessors and competitors. From the perspective of a new religious movement, other religious groups can be portrayed as inadequate or wrong because their grasp of the truth is incomplete, their practices are misguided, their ethical codes lack the proper emphases, their understanding of human nature is flawed, or their understanding of history is mistaken, among many other reasons. In contrast, a new religious movement offers a truer doctrine, a more profound grasp of the meaning and direction of history, an unprecedented comprehension of the place of human beings in the cosmos, and an ethical program that will unleash previously untapped human potential, among many other possibilities. In that sense, conflict between a new religious movement and elements of its social environment, such as that experienced by the early Shakers, appears to be virtually inevitable. Many different factors influence the form and intensity of that conflict, but it is an unavoidable feature of the lives of new religious movements. A full appreciation of that context is essential to an understanding of the birth, growth, and history of any new religious movement.

Contemporary Cult Controversies

The last forty years in the United States have been marked by a number of high-profile public controversies about new religious movements. Observers have remarked on the apparent fondness of members of the hippie generation for alternative religions at the end of the 1960s.[11] The increased visibility of alternative religions, especially those imported from the East such as the International Society for Krishna Consciousness and the Transcendental Meditation Movement,[12] can be traced in part to the 1965 rescinding of the Asian Exclusion Act of 1924, which fostered immigration to the United States from Asia.[13] Included in the waves of new immigrants were several gurus, or religious teachers, who would claim significant followings in the United States. But the late 1960s also saw the development of sectarian movements, like the Children of God founded by Moses David Berg, which too seemed to be attracting large numbers of young people to alternative forms of religious life.[14]

Some family members troubled by their loved ones' involvement with innovative groups began to look closely at the communities and their leaders, and they often concluded that their offspring were somehow being exploited. Some banded together with other family members in the same predicament and searched for ways to encourage their children to return to them and conform to their way of life. The first group organized to counteract the influence of a new religious movement addressed the Children of God. In 1972 the Parents Committee to Free Our Sons and Daughters from the Children of God was formed.[15] The mission of the group was clearly encapsulated in its name. FREECOG, as it came to be known, attempted to turn public attention to the claimed abuses in the group by enlisting both the media and the government. For example, they encouraged the attorney general of the state of New York to issue a critical report on the Children of God in 1974 and persuaded Senator Robert Dole (R-Kansas) to hold hearings in 1976. As FREECOG's efforts gained momentum, other groups opposing new religious movements or cults were formed, including the Citizen's Freedom Foundation in California.

At the same time some freelance moral entrepreneurs, most notably a California state employee named Ted Patrick, were developing and executing a radical strategy for removing members from religious groups.[16] They termed their process "deprogramming." Embedded in that description were the assumptions that no person in his or her right mind would join a questionable religious group and that, consequently, those who did join must have been influenced against their better judgment. The practitioners and advocates of deprogramming buttressed their argument with appeals to studies of the brainwashing of American prisoners of war during the Korean War.[17] Especially in their early days deprogrammings often involved deceitful or forcible extractions of the target individuals and intensive attempts to break down their belief systems while they were confined in isolated locations. Although deprogrammers like Patrick claimed many impressive successes, the more extreme elements of the practice soon attracted criticism from some individuals who had experienced deprogramming, groups whose members had been subjected to the process, and proponents of religious and civil liberties. Over time, especially with the influx of professionals trained in psychology and related fields into the anticult movement, strategies for extricating individuals from groups were refined into processes now described as exit counseling or strategic interaction, although they still rely on many of the same assumptions articulated by the early deprogrammers.[18]

Borrowing a term from earlier attempts by evangelical Christians to identify and stigmatize groups they found to be heretical, the secular opponents of new religious movements described them as cults.[19] Although the term *cult* had long been used in both popular and academic discourse to refer to the worship of a specific deity, in the usage of the anticult activists it took on a decidedly pejorative meaning.[20] As its use evolved, it came to refer to three distinctive and interlocking characteristics of the group in question. First, calling a group a cult implied that the leader of the group was suspect because of psychological instability, greed for money and power, sexual voraciousness, religious delusions, or some combination of those factors. Second, defining a group as a cult suggested that its members could not have been thinking clearly when they became followers of the deviant leader; they must therefore have been programmed, brainwashed, or somehow subjected to coercive persuasion. Finally, participation in any group identified as a cult was likely to be damaging to members' mental and physical health, even to the point of costing them their lives.

That negative stereotype of a religious cult received powerful reinforcement in November 1978, when 914 members of a previously obscure group committed suicide in the jungle of Guyana. The Peoples Temple, and its leader the Rev. Jim Jones, quickly became the primary examples of the destructive nature of cults. The impact of the Jonestown tragedy on the anticult movement is succinctly summarized in a statement by Jewish countercult activist, Rabbi Maurice Davis: "the path of segregation leads to lynching every time. The path of anti-Semitism leads to Auschwitz every time. The path of the cults leads to Jonestowns and we watch it at our peril."[21] Several things are notable about his statement. The parallelism asserted between lynching, the Nazi death camps, and "the cults" makes a powerful emotional appeal and provides the basis for a call to dramatic intervention before any more lives are lost. The implicit homogenization of all groups, no matter what their practices or beliefs, into a single category of "the cults" expands the definition of the problem to its fullest possible dimensions; any group that is identified as a cult is correspondingly linked to the carnage at Jonestown. Davis also intends to capitalize on the widespread revulsion at racist violence and Hitler's atrocities by transferring it to what he implies is a burgeoning cult problem. In Davis's understanding, participation in a cult invariably leads to violence and death. As a result, Davis and those who sympathize with his position believe that there is an urgent need first to identify and then to combat any group that falls under his definition.

In the period after Jonestown the anticult argument against new religious movements reached a mature expression that has since varied little in its fundamental propositions. While anticult activists and groups have implemented minor adjustments in self-presentation, terminology, strategies of opposition, and ways of interacting with cult members, the core of the anticult position remains unchanged. Events of the 1990s, including the April 19, 1993 destruction of the Branch Davidians' Mount Carmel Center and the deaths of seventy-four people inside it, the March 20, 1995 release of sarin gas in the Tokyo subway by members of Aum Shinrikyo that killed twelve people and injured thousands, the murder/suicides of members of the Order of the Solar Temple in Quebec, Switzerland, and France in 1994, 1995, and 1997, and the thirty-nine Heaven's Gate suicides in March 1997, added substantial support to the anticult position that cults indeed were "the hidden menace in our everyday lives."[22]

Though the standard anticult argument packs impressive emotional power and makes effective use of specific telling examples, the attempt to portray cults as an urgent social, public health, psychological, and legal problem has not been universally persuasive. Some of its flaws are clearly evident in Maurice Davis's statement that compares cults to lynching and death camps. First, despite the frequent claims of anticult activists that there may be hundreds or even thousands of cults active in the United States at any given time,[23] the composite portrait of cults is based on a rather small and dramatically skewed sample of groups. It therefore ignores overwhelming evidence that by far the majority of cults, even determined on the definition of the anticultists themselves, do not become involved in violence. Second, the stereotype posits a necessary connection between cults and violence; Davis's repetition of "every time" underlines what is seen as the inevitable linkage. Third, the anticult argument takes no account of either social or historical contexts; it relies on what John Hall has called a "cult essentialism" that explains everything by reference to supposedly universal internal dynamics of new religious movements and completely disregards the constantly changing interactions between religious movements and their environments.[24] Far from being an accurate description of new religious movements that it addresses, the characterization of cults proposed by their cultural opponents is a polemical tool. Just like the religious proclamations of individual groups that it stigmatizes, it is designed to influence public perceptions, recruit people to a cause, galvanize them into action, and secure power and status for some actors even as it denies others access to those same scarce resources. It expresses a compelling vision of how society should rightly be ordered in order to achieve both individual fulfillment and the common good, and goads both individuals and institutions toward accomplishing those goals. In short, the cultural opponents of new religious movements advance competing views of the world and the place of individuals within it.

Those alternatives are most clearly expressed in the statements of the religiously motivated countercult movement. For example, in their *Encyclopedia of Cults and New Religions,* John Ankerberg and John Weldon offer this backhanded compliment: "the cults have a positive side. They offer valuable lessons to the Church, something heresy has always accomplished historically. The most important message these religions have for Christianity is to triple underscore the necessity for the dissemination of doctrinal, apologetic and hermeneutical knowledge at the local church level."[25] Similarly, the Christian Research Institute (CRI), a facet of the ministry of evangelist Hank Hanegraaff, offers a wide range of media resources to support its mission of providing "Christians worldwide with carefully researched information and well-reasoned answers that encourage them in their faith and equip them to intelligently represent it to people influenced by ideas and teachings that assault or undermine orthodox, biblical Christianity."[26] Among the groups receiving special attention from CRI are Jehovah's Witnesses, Mormons, and the New Age Movement, all of which are also featured in Ankerberg and Weldon's encyclopedia. The desire to pose alternatives to cults is not limited to evangelical Christians. Dismayed by what he saw as a disproportionate percentage of Jews among the members of new religious movements, Gary Eisenberg undertook a prolonged study of the cult phenomenon. Addressing his coreligionists, he implores that "if we are to prevent more Jews from finding answers outside Judaism, we must ensure that they receive a strong sense of Jewishness from our tradition and that they reap the comfort and security it provides."[27] Similarly, the organization Jews for Judaism describes itself as "the only international, full-time counter-missionary, counter-cult, educational, outreach and counseling organization dedicated to countering the multi-million-dollar efforts of deceptive missionary and cult groups that target the Jewish community for conversion."[28]

In each of these examples, individuals or organizations within a specific religious tradition attempt to protect their members from encroachment by competing religious systems. They aim to shore up the boundaries between their own groups, which are held to be bastions of orthodoxy and correct practice, and upstart, deviant groups that threaten to seduce their members into error. They try to prevent any leakage of membership to the competition by providing members with the intellectual ammunition and emotional support to expose the error of insurgent messages. In classic terms, they are undertaking an apologetic mission. Like Socrates on the eve of his death and like the early Christian apostle Paul speaking in Jerusalem before a crowd of his accusers, they aim not to apologize for their religious commitments but to speak powerfully and persuasively in their defense.[29] Apologetics never takes place in a vacuum. It is always implicated in a situation of conflict, in which claims and counterclaims fill the air. So it is with contemporary countercult responses to new religious movements. As new religious movements strive to identify and redress the perceived inadequacies of their immediate religious environments, they understandably arouse the opposition of the groups that they indict. Being convinced of the truth and righteousness of their own religious commitments, those groups mount a vigorous response. With very few exceptions, the conflict remains an intellectual one. Countercult writers parade proof texts for inspection, advance claims to special revelations or insights, and appeal to unvarying tradition in order to counter pleas made by new religious movements that their audiences should recognize new truths, acknowledge new readings of familiar texts, and conceive of continuity with the past in new ways. In the midst of such religious ferment, new religious movements strive to secure the attention, respect, and even affiliation of individuals who have other, competing commitments, just as more established groups aim to reinforce the commitments of their membership. The movements of individuals back and forth across group boundaries, through conversion and apostasy, for example, is one way of measuring the relative success of those efforts.

If the stake that countercult movements have in defending traditionally constituted communities is relatively clear, the specific values, groups, and institutions that are being championed by the secular anticult movement are more difficult to pin down. On the surface, their claims seem straightforward enough. Steven Hassan, for example, claims simply to empower "the person to gain control of their own mind, rather than just attacking the cult belief system or the cult identity."[30] Hassan's stated goal is to help individuals who have suffered at the hands of destructive cults to return to mental health. He denies that he is in any way antireligious and emphasizes that he is "a human rights activist who very much values my spirituality as the core of my existence."[31] Similarly, anticult entrepreneur Rick Ross argues that "people in cults often develop a distinct new cult identity or personality. This personality will be consistent with the qualities valued by the group and its leader(s) and correspond rigidly to its doctrine."[32] Like Hassan, Ross uses medical metaphors to portray cult members. While in their groups, members suffer from a pathology that virtually erases their genuine or true personalities and replaces them with personae of the cult leader's making. Exiting a cult is consequently depicted as a process of recovery whose symptoms "may include depression, nightmares, anxiety attacks, excessive shame and/or guilt and seemingly unreasonable fears about the future."[33] In describing his own activities, however, Ross abandons the counseling model endorsed by Hassan and other foes of new religious movements. In his view, "cult intervention" is a dialogical educational process, whose goal is "to inform the subject in an effort to affect their continued involvement with a destructive cult, group and/or leader."[34] Later engagement with mental health professionals may speed the process of recovery, but Ross clearly separates what he does from any form of counseling. Ross also stresses that cult intervention should be a completely objective exchange of information and that the "helping professional" should have no personal agenda. He is accordingly critical of any attempts to engage the particular religious ideas of a group or leader. The focus, Ross maintains, should always be on the demonstrably abusive behavior of the cult leader and the attendant suffering, whether they recognize it or not, of the group members.

Margaret Singer, perhaps the most prominent and influential cult opponent until her death in 2003, makes similar points. She sees cults as a consumer issue, a public health issue, a political issue, a matter of freedom, and, ultimately, a matter of life and death.[35] For her, the dimensions of the contemporary "cult problem" are truly staggering because "everyone is vulnerable to the lures of these master manipulators."[36] Most central for Singer, however, is the conviction that "cults" represent an attack on the self, which produces a new and, she argues, counterfeit social identity. Members of cults, in her view, are literally not themselves. Singer expresses her mission in this way: "I am dedicated to individuals' having informed consent over their lives, their choices, and their beliefs."[37] In a more dramatic declaration, referring specifically to the deaths at Jonestown, she proclaims, "I want to be a voice for those children lying beneath the grass who were never allowed to grow up."[38] Undeniably, such statements can have tremendous emotional impact. It is also important to recognize that they depend on the same sorts of assumptions that undergirded Rabbi Maurice Davis's comparison of "the cults" to Nazi death camps and racist lynchings. In Singer's rhetorical formulation, Jonestown stands as the paradigm for any group that is identified as a cult and the specter of violent death haunts any such group. Singer's militance stems from her estimation of the dire seriousness of the problem she confronts.

Hassan, Ross, and Singer are unanimous in their defense of the *status quo ante*. They imply that whatever a person's mental health and social situation may have been before entering a group that they define as a destructive cult, it had to have been better than it was during the period of cult membership. Since destructive cults by definition can do no good, anyone who becomes entrapped by one will suffer.[39] Previous religious involvement, personal histories, and family dynamics are moved well beyond the frame of a picture that is painted in stark black and white. Little room is afforded for nuanced understandings of the particular series of decisions and accidents that might lead a person toward affiliation with a new religious movement. What brought one person into a cult is the same as what brought another person into a different cult. Members are seen as pawns in the dangerous games of power-mad cult leaders. The American Family Foundation sums up that perspective with the terse assertion that "conversion to cults is not truly a matter of choice."[40] But critics of that position, who are often labeled "cult apologists" by anticultists,[41] have raised serious questions about the descriptive, analytical, and interpretative adequacy of that representation of how people become members of new religious movements. They have produced a rich literature of alternative understandings of the process of conversion.[42] For now, it suffices to note that the way in which the American Family Foundation, Hassan, Ross, Singer, and their allies render the process by which individuals become members of new religious movements is not always accepted as the neutral, bias-free description that they claim it to be.

Despite Hassan's arguments to the contrary, it can also be asked whether what many anticult workers describe as "mental health" leaves any room at all for deep religious conviction. At least some indictments of cults raise the question of whether personal submission to the will of a deity, either directly or as mediated by a human leader, must necessarily be taken as an indication of pathology. Freud, for example, famously argued in *The Future of an Illusion* that religious ideas are merely wish-fulfillments that should be left behind as the individual achieves a progressively more accurate and mature grasp of reality.[43] Since religions frequently include traffic with supernatural entities whose existence cannot be scientifically confirmed, they are all vulnerable to criticisms that they intentionally mislead their followers. Since any lasting religious group features some kind of leadership, they also could be open to the criticisms that they fail to provide full disclosure to prospective members, act in their own self-interest, and devote their energies to keeping members enmeshed in a wholly fictional world. It is possible, then, to conceive of many anticult activists as either implicit or explicit proponents of a contemporary secular worldview that is fundamentally at odds with any religious claims, whether they come from established or new religious movements.

Contemporary cult opponents' claims to be selfless servants of objective truth are embedded in a particular view of the world as much as are the Raëlians' belief in a race of space creatures known as Elohim or The Family's expectation of the imminent end of the world. As a result, the conflict between new religious movements and their adversaries is more complicated than it may superficially appear. Both sides are deeply committed to specific views of the world, history, human nature, and the goals of life. Each side accepts a certain set of fundamental conceptions as rock-bottom givens. In many ways the worldviews of the secular antagonists are as incompatible with those of new religious movements as are the worldviews of their Christian or Jewish foes. At bottom, the different groups espouse fundamentally different values. For example, in the eyes of many religious people the drive for individual self-determination will eventually come into conflict with the necessity of obedience to the will of God. More specifically, for observant Jews obedience to the whole Torah of Moses militates against acknowledging Jesus of Nazareth as the Messiah, and the Church of Jesus Christ of Latter-day Saints' acceptance of the *Book of Mormon* as "another testament of Jesus Christ" strikes many Christians as heretical. Consequently, the assertion that one worldview is obviously more correct, true, or somehow simply better than another demands a complex and detailed supporting argument; the truth of the assertion is never self-evident. In most cases, however, cultural opponents of cults have been much better at describing what they are against than what they are for.

The adversaries of cults often try to minimize the role that worldviews play in the ongoing cultural conflict by emphasizing that they deal with observable behavior rather than theological ideas.[44] But behavior is not unmotivated, and many theological ideas are specifically intended to inspire distinctive types of behavior. The expectation of the imminent end of the world, for example, is a theological idea, but in the cases of both the Branch Davidians and the Children of God/The Family it motivated communal living arrangements, sustained missionary activity, and promoted the acceptance of the paramount authority of David Koresh and Moses David Berg, respectively. Scholars of religion have long noted the mutual reinforcement of ideas and actions. One of the founding fathers of the sociology of religion, Emile Durkheim, defined religion as a set of beliefs and practices that unites all who adhere to them into a single moral community.[45] Similarly, Clifford Geertz proposed that religions form both moods and motivations, both states of mind and feeling and tendencies to act.[46] Thus, when anticultists sever thought from action they destroy the coherence of religious systems. Actions only become meaningful within a coherent intellectual framework or worldview. The act of touching one's head to the ground, for example, could be viewed as either appropriate respect or craven cowardice, depending on the context of interpretation provided by a particular worldview. What cult foes do by ignoring the theological motivation or rationale for certain actions is simply to substitute a motivation that the cult members themselves would not recognize or countenance for one that the members would acknowledge and endorse. In the end, the anticultists' argument boils down to the confident assertion that they know better than any cult members what their behavior really means.

Cult opponents also adopt an unwavering focus on the leader. In Margaret Singer's words, "a cult is a mirror of what is inside the cult leader."[47] When Singer looks at cults she sees the monstrous pathology of Jim Jones played out over and over again. In her view "all cults are variations on a single theme."[48] If that is indeed the case, the pathological aspects of one case can be expected to reappear in another. Rather than making a statistical survey of however many cult movements she might identify in the contemporary United States, Singer instead chooses to advance a few dramatic cases, most notably Jonestown and Waco, as accurate models of all others. What is true about one is implicitly avowed to be true about all others. The leader, who in anticult rhetoric is inherently deranged, unstable, manipulative, and corrupt, is the pivot around which the entire anticult movement turns. It is remarkable, then, that in anticult literature there is little serious engagement with either classic or contemporary analyses of leadership. Although the term *charisma* is frequently mentioned, there appears to be little understanding of how and in what context sociologist Max Weber developed the term for the analysis of leadership nor of the subsequent academic discussions of how charismatic leadership is claimed, recognized, denied, challenged, and adapted in specific social contexts.[49] Steven Hassan, for example, observes that "charismatic cult leaders often make extreme claims of divine or 'otherworldly' power to exercise influence over their members."[50] Hassan does not disclose, however, what makes a claim extreme as opposed to average, the bases on which power is asserted to be divine or otherworldly, the criteria against which an audience measures such claims to see whether they are persuasive, the specific channels through which such claims become influential, the degree to which they exercise influence on different members of an audience, or the duration of their purported influence. In the stereotype promulgated by cult adversaries the characteristics of the cult leader are unvarying, influence flows only from the leader to the followers, and the same exploitative relationship is repeated over and over again. The anticultists see little if any dynamism in the interactions of leaders and followers; followers are simply acted upon and leaders retain unshakeable command and control. In their view, the situation is the same in Heaven's Gate as it was in the Peoples Temple and as it was at the origins of the Mormon church. If a group is defined as a cult, everything else necessarily follows. Historians, sociologists, and scholars of religion, however, have developed rather different understandings of leadership, as the following pages will show.

Choosing a Descriptive and Analytical Vocabulary

As the brief review of contemporary cult controversies shows, there is substantial variation and instability in fundamental descriptive terms. Members of both the anticult and countercult movements have wrenched the term *cult* from its previously stable academic meanings and turned it into a polemical weapon. Sociologists and historians of religion have tried to establish the terms *new religious movement, alternative religion, emergent religion,* or even *first-generation religion* as relatively neutral descriptions of sectarian and other innovative groups, only to be accused of being cult apologists when they fail to view the objects of their study with sufficient alarm. Similarly, cult opponents believe that intentionally neutral terms like *conversion* are pallid substitutes that thoroughly misread the power dynamics in what they see as coercive persuasion, mind control, or brainwashing. Inevitably, to choose a descriptive vocabulary is to take a stand in the cult wars that show few signs of abating. This book will adopt the standard practice of the academic study of religion as it is pursued in several disciplines, including history, sociology, and religious studies. This book will employ the general descriptive term *new religious movement,* with the implicit conviction that it *does not* constitute an endorsement of any particular group or class of groups. It simply follows the important analytical distinction between description and explanation. With specific reference to the topic of religious experience, Wayne Proudfoot has argued that a student of religion's first responsibility is to render the experience as clearly as possible in terms that the subject of the experience can acknowledge as substantially accurate. As Proudfoot writes, "where it is the subject's experience which is the object of study, that experience must be identified under a description that can plausibly be attributed to him."[51] That description, however, does not commit the observer to the explanation of that experience that the subject himself or herself would hold. Again, in Proudfoot's terms, "the explanation the analyst offers of that same experience is another matter altogether. It need not be couched in terms familiar or acceptable to the subject. It must be an explanation of the experience as identified under the subject's description, but the subject's approval of the explanation is not required."[52]

Description and interpretation or explanation of religious experience are two separate, if overlapping, intellectual processes. The same holds true for new religious movements. Religious groups that their opponents see as heresies or as destructive cults see themselves as religions, and new groups often emphasize their innovative nature. It is thus descriptively accurate to describe a group like the Church Universal and Triumphant (CUT), the Unification Church, the Rastafarians, or the International Society for Krishna Consciousness as both new and religious, insofar as that accords with their self-understanding. That does not, however, also entail accepting assertions that CUT has accurately recovered the lost teachings of Jesus, that the Unificationists have identified the Lord of the Second Advent, that smoking marijuana (*ganja*) is a sacrament, or that the Bhagavad-Gita should become the sole scripture for all humanity. Each new religious group has both explicit and implicit claims for its own significance that make ultimate sense within its own view of the world. Outside observers, however, as Proudfoot emphasizes, need not accept any religion's claims about itself and may certainly choose to offer other analytical and interpretative contexts for the data they use. The adoption of the term *new religious movement* in this book does not, therefore, represent a substantial ideological claim about the ideas and practices of any specific group or about new religious movements in general. But that choice of a descriptive term does express the critical opinion that new religious movements can be studied in the same ways and for the same purposes that any other religious phenomena are studied, because that study can yield interesting, significant, and even helpful insight into how human beings construct meaningful lives. As such, the general orientation of this book does represent a commitment to the standards of argument and evidence that typify the academic study of religion, particularly as it is practiced in North American colleges and universities. Anyone who enters the discussion of cults or new religious movements—students, teachers, reporters and commentators in the media, interested persons in the general public, members or partisans of particular groups, or their dedicated antagonists—unavoidably stakes a claim by the choice of a descriptive vocabulary and the implicit endorsement of the interpretive framework that it is founded on. In a contentious atmosphere, one can only hope to express one's position with clarity and precision, but one cannot control how others perceive it. It is in the best interests of everyone if those claims are clearly articulated, explicitly supported with accessible evidence, and directly related to their fundamental authorizing assumptions.

What's New about New Religious Movements— and What's Not

The description of a religious movement as *new* only begs further questions. Novelty can be in the eye of the beholder, or in the mind of someone claiming to be innovative, in both or in only one. That is to say that religious movements are judged to be new only in particular contexts and by certain audiences. They may claim, for example, to retrieve and correctly represent proper past practice, which has somehow been neglected or forgotten. But their opponents might view the same claims as dangerous and deviant inventions. New religions themselves often manifest a pronounced ambivalence about their own novelty. The visions that inaugurated the prophetic career of Joseph Smith in 1820, for example, assured him that none of the Christian sects that were contending for members in what came to be known as the "burned-over district" in Upper New York State possessed the true message of Jesus Christ. Smith alone had been chosen to bring to the world the newest and clearest version of that gospel in the *Book of Mormon*. But that book was itself an account of events in ancient Israel and on the American continent that set the stage for the Mormon church. Even as it claimed to be an innovation, the movement Smith led anchored itself firmly in an authoritative past. As Jan Shipps incisively observed about the Church of Jesus Christ of Latter-day Saints, "the past is of fundamental importance to new religious movements. The assertions on which they rest inevitably alter the prevailing understanding of what has gone before, creating situations in which past and future must both be made new."[53] In that comment, Shipps identifies a fundamental dynamic in new religious movements: they strive to present themselves as both new and old, as both unprecedented and familiar. From their perspective, a new revelation necessitates the reconceptualization of all of history. Claude Vorilhon's proclamation that human life had actually been created by an incredibly advanced race of extraterrestrials fundamentally changes the Raëlians' understanding of who they really are and their place in the cosmos.[54] Similarly, "Yacub's history," which traced the creation of white people to the efforts of an early mad scientist, forever altered the self-understandings of Elijah Muhammad's early followers in the Nation of Islam.[55] The novelty of new religions cuts both ways; it can just as easily excite the interest of potential adherents as it can strain their credulity. As they spread their messages to those whose interest, approval, and even acceptance they hope to secure, new religious movements proclaim both their challenging novelty and their comforting familiarity.

In their sectarian forms, new religious movements attempt to recapture the lost purity of an idealized past. Sects typically have prior ties to a religious organization from which they have intentionally broken off. They aim to return to the pristine origins of the tradition and reestablish its foundations. Sectarian forms of Christianity frequently exhort their partisans to get "back to the Bible"; contemporary Islamic sects yearn for the purity of the times of the prophet Muhammad. Sects thus define themselves both with relation to the broader world and with relation to their specific tradition, both of which are perceived to threaten their purity of belief and practice.

In their typology of responses to secularization, Rodney Stark and William Sims Bainbridge contrast cults to sects. Even though their attempt to rescue the term *cult* as a precise, neutral descriptive term may not be able to counterbalance its popular, polemical use, their position merits attention. Eschewing the polemical definition of cults spawned by their cultural opponents, they define them as independent religious traditions. They may be imports from another culture, such as the International Society for Krishna Consciousness or the Holy Spirit Association for the Unification of World Christianity in the United States, or independent products of the society in which they develop, such as the Church of Scientology or various forms of the New Age Movement. Like sects, cults will often find themselves in tension or conflict with the broader society, simply by virtue of being new and different. Because they, too, want to locate themselves in relation to an authoritative past, the groups Stark and Bainbridge describe as cults also lay some claim to previous tradition. The Unificationist Movement of Sun Myung Moon retells the salvation history of the Christian

Bible; New Age thought often claims to revive ancient wisdom; the Hare Krishnas of the International Society for Krishna Consciousness present the ancient Indian Bhagavad-Gita "as it is." What separates cults from sects in their relation to previous traditions is that cults typically do not have a history of institutional conflict and eventual separation. Cults are marked from their beginnings as new entities. When the first Unification-ist missionaries came to the United States in the early 1960s, for example, their message was immediately marked as something new. Similarly, in the case of those who profess to channel ancient entities such as Ramtha or Lazaris, there is a yawning gap between the ancient religions and their contemporary revival. Both sects and cults, then, in terms of Stark and Bainbridge's typology, simultaneously declare their novelty and sink their roots in the past.

If individual new religious movements try to make for themselves a meaningful past, new religions in the United States also have a collective history. Despite alarmist assertions that cults constitute a peculiarly contemporary problem,[56] new religious movements have always been part of American life. In a recent survey, Phillip Jenkins stated that "there is no period, including colonial times, in which we cannot find numerous groups more or less indistinguishable from the most controversial modern movements."[57] Also, for as long as new religious movements have been part of American history, so has strenuous public opposition to them. Jenkins, for example, charts an historical cycle of cult and anticult reactions, and proposes that the term first acquired its negative connotations around 1900 in relation to non-Western religions.[58]

Some examples of the vigorous polemic against the Shakers in the late eighteenth century were cited earlier in this chapter. That a group now known primarily for its dwindling numbers, sober way of life, and the simple elegance of its furniture could arouse such determined hostility in its early days suggests that the relations between a new religious movement and the society in which it locates itself are likely to be tumultuous at least some time in the group's history. It also indicates that external perceptions can be altered as a new group persists from one generation to another and succeeds in incorporating itself to some degree into the social fabric. Thus, some attention to the history of individual groups and the history of their relations with their social environments can offer an antidote to the cult essentialism that from the outset denies "destructive cults" any legitimacy and simply cannot foresee that either the groups in question or outsiders' reactions to them can change.

Vigorous and sometimes bloody opposition to new religious movements can be traced throughout the nineteenth century. From their inception, the Mormons drew particular ire. The relentless pressure on the Mormon church gradually pushed it across the country, until Smith's followers were able to organize a stable community in Utah in the mid-nineteenth century. In the meantime Smith had been assassinated in Carthage, Illinois, in 1844. The later part of the nineteenth century also featured vigorous activities against several groups. Anti-Mormon tracts, often offering lurid exposés of life in polygamous households, appeared from the 1870s on, and agitation increased against other religious groups, like John Humphrey Noyes' Oneida community, whose alternative sexual practices aroused public ire. Helena Petrovna Blavatsky, a founder and central figure in the Theosophical Society, was accused of fraud almost as soon as she began to make claims about receiving messages from distant spiritual masters. One of the two Fox sisters who had been at the center of the Spiritualist movement of the mid-nineteenth century published a memoir after she had joined the Roman Catholic Church in which she admitted to practicing deception as a Spiritualist. Other examples of purportedly bizarre belief and behavior fed the news media's appetite for sensational stories.[59]

Two incidents involving alternative religious groups stand out in the years leading up to World War II. Acting on their religion's understanding of the prohibition in Exodus 20:3–5 against the worship of graven images, schoolchildren who were Jehovah's Witnesses refused to salute the flag, as was required by law in at least thirty states. In multiple legal cases in the early 1940s, the Witnesses' claim to be exercising their religious freedom was rejected and many of their children were expelled from school. The Witnesses' steadfastness provoked what one recent observer has called the greatest outbreak of religious intolerance in twentieth-century America.[60] Only with the 1943 Supreme Court decision in *West Virginia State Board of Education v. Barnette* was the Witnesses' right not to salute the flag acknowledged. In that instance, the Court acted to preserve the distinctiveness of an alternative religious movement and to allow its members to continue their practices, no matter how much they may have antagonized their neighbors.

The second case involved one of the prominent precursors of the contemporary New Age Movement. In 1940 the government began prosecution of Edna Ballard, leader of the "I AM" Movement started by her husband Guy, for mail fraud. In a striking departure from the principle of immunity for religious beliefs articulated in the Supreme Court decision in

1879 against polygamy, Ballard was tried specifically because her religious beliefs were asserted to be untrue and therefore her dissemination of religious materials through the mail constituted fraud. Ballard's conviction on seven counts at the original trial was a crippling blow against the "I AM" Movement and served as an ominous threat to other newly formed religious groups. Only in 1954 was the Post Office's fraud order revoked, but by then Ballard's movement could not recover its former vigor.

The history of new religious movements in the United States is by no means limited to their interactions with hostile outsiders; members of new groups continued to contemplate and develop interpretations of their special messages, to enact their distinctive rituals, and to shape their lives to fit their particular ethical demands. But a brief overview shows clearly that the contemporary controversies are not unprecedented. Wherever and whenever they have arisen, new religious movements have provoked intense reactions. As Kenelm Burridge remarked in a different context, "a prophet cannot identify himself in terms of the community as it is: he identifies himself in an image of what might or should be."[61] To the extent that they give voice to a vision of what might or should be, new religious movements necessarily trouble the status quo. A plea for change is rarely welcomed by all who hear it. Change unsettles established authority; threatens the social order; promises to reorder power, prestige, and authority; exacts costs from some unwilling to bear them; and bestows benefits on those who had no previous access to them. Change shakes things up. People who have something to lose in the process of change may well oppose agents of change. So it is with new religious movements, which often explicitly intend to produce personal, religious, and social change.

The fundamental dynamics of the encounter between insurgent religious movements and the established order are similar, no matter what the cultural context or historical period. The history of new religious movements in the United States, in particular the history of their conflict with entrenched opponents, reveals another dimension of the polemical arsenal of contemporary cult foes. The declaration that destructive cults constitute an urgent and unprecedented problem for contemporary American society is simply a modern twist on an ancient tale, designed to heighten anxiety and move people to action. But that call to arms has been sounded many times before. During the first centuries of the Common Era, for example, representatives of traditional Roman culture and religion bemoaned the influx of "oriental" cults. They lambasted all forms of superstition and traced many of what they saw as fraudulent claims to divine power to the practice of magic. The followers of a crucified carpenter from the eastern end of the Mediterranean basin were not spared from the blanket condemnation of new religious movements.[62] Although the vocabulary of invective employed in the first centuries of the Common Era differed from that employed in the opening years of the twenty-first century, it was used to identify perennial concerns. For example, in one broadside against the new religion of Christianity, published late in the second century, the author expressed his opinion that Jesus' entire life story was a blatant fabrication, that during his mission Jesus was able only to convince the gullible, that Jesus had accomplished nothing noteworthy in his life, that anything he did accomplish should be traced to magic rather than divine power, and that he was generally a laughable candidate for the status his followers had ascribed to him.[63] Similar examples of suspicious reactions to new religious movements can be adduced from other historical periods and other cultural areas. In many ways, the very newness of a new religious movement is sufficient in itself to touch off conflict. Novelty, especially when it makes serious claims about fundamental issues, inspires controversy.

What's Religious about New Religious Movements— and What's Not

Much of the preceding discussion has implied a rough equivalence between what anticult activists call destructive cults and what most scholars call new, alternative, emergent, or first-generation religious movements. As the anticult argument has developed, however, it has come to include more than religious groups under its umbrella category. Steven Hassan, for example, asserts that "in addition to religious cults, there are psychotherapy cults, political cults and commercial cults. There are also personality cults, particularly if one person absolutely controls another (or a small group of people, such as in a family)."[64] Rick Ross and Margaret Singer cast similarly wide nets.[65] But the focus of the contemporary anticult movement, as well as the Christian and Jewish countercult movements, remains on groups that identify themselves as religious, even if their opponents are very skeptical about those claims.

In order to describe accurately that self-presentation some sense of what religion entails will be helpful. The enterprise of defining religion, however, has failed to produce substantial agreement among scholars and remains itself a contentious field. Scholars differ, for example on whether religion is primarily something private and personal or public and social, or some combination of the two. They wrangle over whether religion refers to an actual ontological reality, often termed the "holy" or the "sacred," or constitutes a projection of human wishes and desires onto wholly fictitious entities that humans then internalize while remaining ignorant of their origins. They argue over whether religion's origins might be found in sexual guilt, violent scape-goating, or an inbred intuitive capacity. The disputes about the definition of religion will not be settled here, but some relatively practical guidance is in order. Neither the etymology or the history of the use of the term *religion* offers much help.[66] Throughout history, "religion" has been defined in myriad ways, but one of its uses is particularly revealing here. As Jonathan Z. Smith has observed, "the most common form of classifying religions, found in both native categories and in scholarly literature, is dualistic and can be reduced, regardless of what differentium is employed, to 'theirs' and 'ours.'"[67] In that sense the attempts to label certain religious groups as destructive cults simply continues an age-old endeavor to separate true religion from false religion, and "ours" from "theirs." But, as Smith stresses, "'religion' is not a native term; it is a term created by scholars for their intellectual purposes and therefore is theirs to define. It is a second-order, generic concept that plays the same role in establishing a disciplinary horizon that 'language' plays in linguistics and 'culture' plays in anthropology."[68] Any definition of religion, therefore, represents a choice, a deliberate decision to focus on some, but not other, elements of the data at hand in order to advance discussion of some, rather than other, topics. Since there is no universally accepted definition of religion; any definition is a tool for investigation, not a statement of unvarying truth.

In this book religion will be understood as a set of processes through which human beings build for themselves distinctive worlds of meaning that they then inhabit. As Peter Berger put it, "religion is the human enterprise by which a sacred cosmos is established."[69] William Paden has developed that notion of cosmos or world, stating that "a world is one's environment—the unity of existence and place. Human cultures construct an enormous variety of environments through language, technology, and institutions. We are born and die in these systems of symbols and imagination. Among these forms, religion in particular is a great definer and generator of worlds and alternative worlds."[70] Particularly important for the study of new religious movements is Paden's observation that religions can attempt to generate *alternative* worlds, ones that offer a choice and consequently exist in some tension with other worlds of meaning.

Religious worlds, however, are not simply matters of symbols and imagination, because, as Paden succinctly puts it, "religion is something people *do*."[71] As part of their religious lives, people eat or fast, have sexual relations or refrain from them, sing, shout, dance, work or pause in their labors, and even kill or die, among many other actions. Despite attempts to reduce them to belief alone, religions involve actions, as least as much as thought.[72] In some cases the performance of religious actions can precede sustained reflection on the meaning of those actions. The importance of actions is neatly summed up in an incident from the life of Malcolm X. While he was in prison after being convicted of burglary, Malcolm was introduced to the Nation of Islam by his brothers Philbert and Reginald. Though he was initially resistant to any form of religion, Malcolm was intrigued by what his brothers described as "the natural religion of the black man" and also by the promise that if he stopped smoking cigarettes and eating pork that he would get out of prison.[73] Soon after hearing about Islam, somewhat to his own surprise, Malcolm acted:

> I wasn't even thinking about pork when I took my seat at the long table. Sit-grab-gobble-stand-file out was the Emily Post in prison eating. When the meat platter was passed to me, I didn't even know what the meat was; usually you couldn't tell, anyway—but it was suddenly as though *don't eat any more pork* was flashed on a screen before me.
>
> I hesitated, with the platter in mid-air; then I passed it along to the inmate waiting next to me. He began serving himself; abruptly he stopped. I remember him turning, looking surprised at me.
>
> I said to him, "I don't eat pork."[74]

By refusing the pork, Malcolm took a tentative step toward membership in a new religious world. When he began to learn about the teachings of Elijah Muhammad and the Nation of Islam that action would be situated within a coherent world of meaning, but at the outset the action stood on its own as a still dimly understood token of commitment. Not all religious actions are so divorced from the context of belief that gives them meaning, but the example of Malcolm X serves to emphasize the importance of action within a religious world. Actions shape belief as much as beliefs shape actions. Religions summon people to think, feel, and act in ways that mutually reinforce each other. Paden emphasizes that "each religious community acts within the premises of its universe, its own logic, its own answers to its own questions."[75] That is no less true of new religions than it is of established ones. In fact, the innovative premises, logic, questions, and answers of a new religious movement stand out, open to challenge, precisely because they are new and therefore different from the taken-for-granted premises of the established order of society.

As systems of thought and action religions help their members chart a path for their lives, find meaning in their daily experience, and respond to life's major challenges. As Clifford Geertz puts it, religions help people address "the problem of meaning."[76] Geertz identifies three different dimensions to the problem of meaning. In its cognitive form, the problem is bafflement, which stems from the limits of humans' analytical capacities. Topics such as the origin of humanity and the earth come under this heading. Religions frequently respond with creation stories or interpretations of traditional stories. The Raëlians, for example, thoroughly revise the import of the creation story in the biblical book of Genesis. They claim that "Elohim" is not simply one of the names of God, but rather refers to "those who came from the sky," the advanced race of extraterrestrials who actually created life on earth.[77] Also, throughout history humans have devoutly desired to know how both their own lives and humanity as a whole will end. Many millennialist groups, often keying their attention to the biblical book of Revelation, have produced elaborate apocalyptic scenarios of the end of the world as we know it. The nineteenth-century Millerites, as well as the groups that grew out of them, including the Seventh-Day Adventists and Jehovah's Witnesses, are prominent examples. So, in a rather different way, is the loose contemporary New Age Movement, with its generally sunny expectations of human advancement.

The second dimension of Geertz's problem of meaning is suffering, which poses a threat to human powers of endurance. Religions frequently address the apparent ubiquity of suffering. Among contemporary new religious movements one of the most sustained and complex considerations of the origins, causes, and potential amelioration of human suffering is contained in the *Divine Principle* of the Unificationist Movement. The *Divine Principle*'s analysis of the Fall sets the stage for the mission of Rev. Moon, who in the last days brings a revelation that offers humankind the chance to return to an Edenic state. The account in the *Divine Principle* offers Unificationists a comprehensive context for understanding human suffering.

The third dimension of the problem of meaning, the presence of evil, is often closely related to the second. Evil challenges people's abilities to exercise moral insight. In many sectarian movements, the world as a whole is portrayed as the bastion of threatening evils. In response, such groups encourage their members to remove themselves in thought and practice from worldly influences. The Family, for example, stresses that "our homes, possibly more than any other place or institution in society today, are free from all forms of 'substance abuse,' legal or illegal. Our children are born absolutely free of the effects of alcohol, caffeine, nicotine, cocaine, or any other damaging drugs."[78] In *Science and Health with Key to the Scriptures,* Mary Baker Eddy simply denied the existence of evil, contending that "If God, or good, is real, then evil, the unlikeness of God, is unreal."[79] By providing distinctive answers to their own questions, by offering a picture "of the way things in sheer actuality are,"[80] by extending comfort and counsel to those in need, and by recommending specific courses of action, religions strive to equip their members to struggle effectively with the multiple dimensions of the problem of meaning. In doing that, new religious movements are no different than older ones, except that they explicitly claim to offer newer and better equipment that will get the job done more effectively.

Those who endorse the worldview of a particular religion and attempt to put into practice the way of life that it advocates typically form a social group, though groups can have various degrees of cohesion and can exert more or less influence over their members. The tightest form of group is the communal congregation. Communal groups themselves have a long history in the United States and their formation has often been motivated by religion.[81] At one time or another communal living has been practiced by the Mormons, the Peoples Temple, The Family, the Branch Davidians, the Church Universal and Triumphant, the International Society for Krishna Consciousness, and the Heaven's Gate group, among many others. In some instances communal living is required, but in others it is simply an elective option. In the Church of Scientology, for example, the most committed members will live communally while those who have lesser commitments will not. In any case, the formation of clearly identifiable social groups that maintain distinct boundaries between themselves and the rest of the world is often an important factor in conflicts between new religious movements and their opponents. As Stark and Bainbridge remark, "the more a cult mobilizes its membership, the greater the opposition it engenders" and "the more total the movement, the more total the opposition to it."[82]

As Paden has stressed, religions are not the only cultural systems that provide meaningful worlds for their adherents. Other systems strive to provide compelling views of the world that make cognitive sense, sketch out appropriate responses to all dimensions of the problem of meaning, and mobilize individuals into social groups that can enact their vision of a better human society. From some angles and to some observers, new religious movements may appear rather to be forms of therapy or political groups. For example, in part because of its origins in L. Ron Hubbard's *Dianetics: The Modern Science of Mental Health* and in part because it still relies on Hubbard's "technology" for achieving personal autonomy and "total freedom," the religious nature of the Church of Scientology has often been questioned, even after its official recognition by the U.S. Internal Revenue Service (IRS). The church, as is its common practice, has responded vigorously to any doubters and reasserted its fundamentally religious character.[83] Similarly, groups on the contemporary far right, such as Christian Identity churches, have been accused of using religion as a smokescreen for their radical political programs.[84] While remaining aware that some groups may straddle the boundaries between politics and religion or religion and therapy, this book will err in the direction of inclusiveness. Following the canons of description articulated earlier, it will take seriously the self-description of any group, at least as a starting point. If a group presents itself as religious, it will first be understood on those terms rather than being dismissed out of hand because it does not fit a preestablished image of what a religion should look like. That descriptive openness will produce the fullest range of examples.

What's American about New Religious Movements— and What's Not

The example of the Shakers has served as a paradigm for many facets of the careers of new religious movements in the United States. But the United Society of Believers in Christ's Second Appearing was transplanted from somewhere else. Throughout history, religions have rarely been limited to specific national boundaries. Ancient Roman religion, for example, was practiced throughout the empire, not only in its capital. Even Judaism, with its definitive connections to the land of Israel, has been practiced beyond its borders at least from the period of the Babylonian exile (586–538 B.C.E.) to the present. In the history of the United States, as the example of the Shakers suggests, new religious movements have not been constrained by national boundaries. Movements founded in the United

States, like the Mormons, the Theosophical Society, the Jehovah's Witnesses, and the Branch Davidians, have spread abroad. Groups founded elsewhere, like the Unificationist Movement, the Rastafarians, the Raëlians, and the Baha'i Church, have found hospitable receptions among some people in the United States. Thus, the subject of new religious movements in America is a moving target. Not only do new groups arise and either develop or fade away in the context of American society, but groups born elsewhere are adopted by people in the United States and naturalized by them. Again, this book will take a fairly inclusive approach. It will include groups that have had a notable presence in American life at some point in history. In some cases, it may be a judgment call, but the judgment will err in favor of inclusion, rather than exclusion. Attention will be fixed on the most prominent groups, whether their notoriety is due to large numbers of adherents, public scrutiny and controversy, or spectacular events.

Sorting Them Out: Typologies of New Religious Movements

The rich variety of new religious movements needs to be ordered in some way, and there have been many attempts at sorting them out. Anticult authors' simple separation of destructive cults, which warrant everyone's urgent attention, and other groups, which merit no further discussion, can swiftly be dismissed as not up to the task of classification. The data, however, are too abundant and diverse to be lumped into a single category. Beyond that, however, no single taxonomic scheme has dominated the study of new religious movements. A review of some of the more prominent proposals will pave the way for a rough system of classification that will be used in the book.

In a 1988 survey of typologies of new religious movements Thomas Robbins stressed that classification systems are formed and used in order to further analysis and interpretation and that "particular typologies are vindicated by their theoretical purposes."[85] His observation remains helpful. There is no necessary system of classification for new religious movements that reproduces their inherent characteristics; taxonomies are helpful to the extent that they meet particular analytical and interpretive goals. Observers may endeavor to separate groups according to their relative age, provenance, or specific analytical categories. In his widely used *Encyclopedic Handbook of Cults in America,* for example, J. Gordon Melton differentiates what he calls "the established cults," which include

Christian Science, the Church of Jesus Christ of Latter-day Saints, Spiritualism, Theosophy, and other groups that had their beginnings in the nineteenth or earlier twentieth centuries, from both the "New Age movement" and "the newer cults," which includes the Church of Scientology, the International Society for Krishna Consciousness, the Unification Church, and Neo-Paganism, among others. Melton's classification promises no great theoretical insights and simply represents an effort to sort groups on the basis of relative longevity.

Irving Hexham and Karla Poewe have offered a similarly rudimentary taxonomy on the basis of provenance. Arguing that "all religions fall into the categories of two major traditions," they separate new religious movements into those derived from the Yogic tradition, which originated in India, and those in the Abramic tradition, which began in the Ancient Near East.[86] Hexham and Poewe assert that virtually all new religions can be related to one or the other of those two great traditions, although they do not pursue the classification of the acknowledged anomalies.[87] Addressing the question of novelty, Hexham and Poewe propose that "the thing that is 'new' in new religions is the content of their mythological idioms and their conscious use of images, practices, and theories from anywhere in the world."[88] While Hexham and Poewe do offer some guidelines for making both distinctions and connections, in *New Religions as Global Cultures* they do not apply them to any sustained case studies.

In *America's Alternative Religions*, which he edited, Timothy Miller tackles the question of classification head-on. Echoing Robbins' admonition that typologies should serve theoretical purposes, he acknowledges that "there are many possible bases for categorization: geography (grouping religions by places of origin), major world religions (from which major tradition did an alternative religion derive?), theology, leadership and structure, and others."[89] Eventually, in conversation with his contributors, Miller decided on a more complex version of Hexham and Poewe's classification by provenance. Recalling Melton's use of "established cults," Miller starts with "established Christian alternatives," going back as far as the Anabaptists and including the Adventist tradition, Christian Science, Mormons and their offshoots, Quakers, Swedenborgianism, and Unitarian Universalism. He follows that first group with contemporary Christian and Jewish movements, movements derived from Asia and the Near East, African American movements, the New Age and other groups that represent ancient wisdom, and finally and forthrightly, a miscellaneous category that includes the Church of Scientology, UFO groups, and Satanism, among others.[90] Miller deals directly with the permeability of those categorical distinctions, the movement of some groups across categories during their life spans, and the possible polemical weight of classifying a group along with Satanism, for example.[91] He helpfully emphasizes that the process of categorization should be a preliminary guide rather than a fatal trap.[92] Typologies of the sort Miller uses can facilitate comparison; in his scheme the basic comparative question concerns "where religious bodies stand in relation to other bodies."[93] His classification scheme is therefore designed to highlight in just what ways a group may be considered new in relation to a parent or predecessor; used effectively, it can highlight both lines of continuity and elements of innovation.

Other typologies can serve other descriptive and theoretical ends. In an effort to comprehend how new religious movements see themselves in relation to the broader world, for example, Roy Wallis adapted Max Weber's analysis of religious attitudes to the world to distinguish world-rejecting, world-affirming, and world-accommodating groups.[94] That schema puts into the foreground certain characteristics of new religions and implicitly deems other dimensions less interesting. Similar attempts have focused on the types of communities represented among new religious movements and types of participants in new religions.[95] Whatever typology of new religious movements is employed, the comparisons it promotes are only the beginning, rather than the end, of analysis. As Jonathan Z. Smith has persuasively argued, "there is nothing 'given' or 'natural' in those elements selected for comparison" and "the 'end' of comparison cannot be the act of comparison itself."[96] Instead, Smith proposes that in general "the aim of . . . comparison is the redescription of the exempla (each in light of the other) and a rectification of the academic categories in relation to which they have been imagined."[97] In this book, the examples to be examined are the various groups that come under the umbrella category of "new religious movement" and they will be examined so as to shed fresh light on the groups themselves and on academic categories such as cult, conversion, myth, ritual, and many others.

The Plan of This Book

In categorizing the groups it discusses, this book follows a scheme most similar to Miller's. The classification is designed to highlight a group's relation to a precursor tradition or traditions, in relation to which it can arguably be described as new. Since there is some accuracy to Hexham and Poewe's contention that a distinguishing mark of many contemporary new religious movements is that they draw on a wide variety of sources,[98] it should not be surprising if a particular group could be argued to belong in one category rather than another. For example, I include Vodou, Santeria, and the Rastafarians in a chapter devoted to groups that root themselves in African traditions, even though they could also be put into the chapter on groups influenced by the broad biblical tradition. My argument is that those groups share more in common with each other than they do with, for example, the Branch Davidians or the Millerites. The categorization of groups in this book is more a loose, preliminary sorting that should facilitate comparison rather than a declaration of their fundamental identity.

In addition to locating successive "families" of groups in relation to significant sources and precursors, each chapter endeavors to give some sense of the history of new religious movements in American history. Discussion is not limited to the most notorious contemporary groups, nor does it exclude them. But it also attempts to add depth to the understanding of the current cult wars by examining the rise and reception of new religious movements in earlier periods of American history. To return to the opening example of this chapter, this book argues that understanding an episode like the arrival of Ann Lee and the other Shakers in North America in the late 1700s provides an interesting and potentially illuminating comparative context for comprehending the careers of new religious movements in the early twenty-first century. For the initial purposes of comparison, specific differences between the Shakers and any contemporary group are less important than the general similarities in the dynamics of the origins, growth, and eventual "success" or "failure" of new religious movements.

Within the discussion of each group and family of groups, this book relies on the arguments of many different scholars of religion, as it has in this introduction. This book is specifically interested in new *religious* movements, even when their religiousness is a matter of controversy either because of cultural opposition or because of ambiguities in their relation to other cultural domains, such as therapy or politics. More specifically, this book often has recourse to the theoretical formulations of Stark and Bainbridge's *The Future of Religion: Secularization, Revival, and Cult*

Formation. They argue from the empirical evidence of the persistence of religion, despite frequent predictions of its imminent demise over the last century or so, that the phenomenon of secularization, rather than being an inexorable process, is self-limiting.[99] As their title indicates, they identify two primary forms of religious innovation that occur in response to secularization: revival or sectarianism and cult formation. In their estimation, "the sources of religion are shifting constantly in societies but . . . the amount of religion remains relatively constant."[100] New religious movements, then, in either sectarian or cultic form,[101] are part of a complex religious economy in which the distribution of forms of religious groups is perpetually in flux. This book limits its attention to sectarian groups that represent substantial enough innovations to be rejected by their parent bodies and be recognized by other audiences as distinctive, new bodies. The Mormon church is a good example. Despite its explicit claims to be part of the Christian tradition, the practices and doctrines of the Church of Jesus Christ of Latter-day Saints are sufficiently distinctive to warrant it being classified as a new religious movement. Admittedly, there are some borderline cases, which will be dealt with in turn. Sects can continue their innovations to the extent that they become stand-alone movements, but they can also bank the fires of independence and return toward, if not to, their parent bodies. More of this book's attention is devoted to the groups Stark and Bainbridge define as cults, groups that either through transplantation from another culture or through sheer invention have appeared on the American scene as thoroughgoing innovations.

The distinctions that Stark and Bainbridge make between various kinds of cults are also useful. They identify three types. "Audience cults" make few if any demands on their adherents. They do not require conversion to a specific movement and they allow great flexibility on the part of their adherents. Those who are part of audience cults are nibblers, taking one idea from one source, a certain practice from another, but the individual, not the group, remains the ultimate arbiter of the belief system. Stark and Bainbridge have in mind a relatively undifferentiated group of people who send away for pamphlets and tapes, attend lectures and workshops, try out therapies, and attend courses in a continuously shifting pattern of associations. This is the most difficult segment of cultic practitioners to pin down.[102] Other researchers have referred to the "occult underground" or to a generalized "cultic milieu."[103] Religions in Stark and Bainbridge's second category, "client cults," are more organized than audience cults. They are primarily concerned with providing or selling some service, principally forms of therapy. They provide numerous examples of the privatization of religion that Peter Berger has discussed as an effect of secularization.[104] Clients may stay with the cult only until specific transactions are completed, although the cults may attempt to develop a system of transactions that necessitates continued participation. Scientology, as it is practiced by those who are not dedicated members of its "Sea Org," is a primary example of a client cult. Clients go through a process of "auditing" in order to remove from their minds the negative effects of past experiences; the goal of auditing is to get "clear." Becoming clear appears to the novice client to be a fairly simple operation, but once enmeshed in the process the client is informed of greater levels of complexity. Client cults do not generally have a high degree of social organization, but they may become the primary social group for an elite. In contrast, Stark and Bainbridge define cults that have become the primary social group for their adherents as "cult movements." Cult movements are full-fledged organizations. They require conversion and do not tolerate dual membership. Cult movements have attracted the attention of the broader public, especially when they have become total institutions, providing lodging, work, and spiritual nourishment in a communal setting. The commitments that cult movements demand of their participants can be arranged along a continuum moving from forms of partial or intermittent allegiance to total commitment. Especially when cult movements demand activities of their adherents that depart from social norms, they arouse the ire and opposition of that broader society.

The consideration of individual groups will thus be marked by three pronounced orientations. First, because new religious movements typically express some ambivalence about their own novelty, particular attention will be devoted to how each group claims, reconstructs, and/or invents for itself an authoritative past. That focus will highlight the creative and interpretive dimensions of new religious movements, the ways in which they originate, articulate, and extend compelling worldviews, both in conversation with their members and in conflict with their opponents. Although creativity is not limited to the early stages of a new religious movement, it is often particularly evident in the founding generation. Second, because new religious movements do not exist in a vacuum, attention will also be devoted to the history of innovative religious groups in the United States. That focus will provide a critical context for contemporary claims that the current cult problem is unprecedented. It will help to chart the ebbs and flows of the religious economy of the United States over the past three centuries. Appreciation of the history of new religious movements in the United States will also contribute to removing them from the realm of the incomprehensible exotic and locating them among the many, familiar examples of human religious expression. In his study of Jonestown David Chidester suggested that "any religion is an irreducible experiment in being human."[105] New religious movements are, perhaps, more obviously experimental than their more long-lived counterparts, but they are part of a long history of religious experimentation both within the mainstream and at the margins of society. A sense of the contours of that history will set the stage for informed comparisons and the conclusions about charged topics such as the purported novelty, danger, or pathology of a given group or of new religions in general. A third focus of this book will be on the appropriate and effective use of theoretical ideas about religion in general, its typical forms of expression and practice, and religious leadership, among other topics, in the description, analysis, and interpretation of new religious movements. Much of the significance of new religious movements in American history lies in their ability to offer to their adherents a view of the world, a way of life, and the experience of community that they have not been able to find elsewhere. On the surface, at least, that is no more pathological in new religious movements than it is in other, older ones. For the people who join them, the religious function of new religious movements is primary, no matter what the cultural opponents of new religions might claim. Accordingly, those claims will be taken seriously as this book attempts to illuminate the attractions of different groups.

The heart of this book is six chapters on different families of religious groups. They are organized on the basis of their provenance or inspiration, including groups in the broad biblical tradition, the New Age and other groups re-presenting ancient wisdom, groups inspired by Eastern texts or teachers, groups that develop Middle Eastern or African traditions, those re-creating and creating pagan traditions, and new foundations. Those chapters are followed by one that addresses significant issues in the lives of new religious movements such as the nature of leadership and the relations between leaders and followers, the processes by which individuals enter (and exit) groups, the possible connections between new religious movements and violence, and the roles of women and children in new religious movements. A selective, annotated guide to resources for the study of new religious movements and a glossary offer guidance for further study.

Notes

1. See Valentine Rathbun, *An Account of the Matter, Form, and Manner of a New and Strange Religion, Taught and Propagated by a Number of Europeans, Living in a Place Called Nisqueunia, in the State of New-York* (Providence, RI: Bennett Wheeler, 1781).

2. Ibid., p. 19. For a thorough history of the Shakers, see Stephen J. Stein, *The Shaker Experience in America* (New Haven: Yale University Press, 1992).

3. Rathbun, *An Account*, p. 22.

4. Ibid., p. 17.

5. Stein, *Shaker Experience*, p. 30.

6. Ibid., pp. 30–31.

7. On the Church of Scientology, see chapter 7.

8. Rathbun, *An Account*, p. 22.

9. Ibid., p. 19.

10. Ibid., p. 7.

11. See, for example, Steven Kent, *From Slogans to Mantras: Social Protest and Religious Conversion in the Late Vietnam War Era* (Syracuse: Syracuse University Press, 2001).

12. On the International Society for Krishna Consciousness and Transcendental Meditation, see chapter 4.

13. See J. Gordon Melton, "The Modern Anti-Cult Movement in Historical Perspective," in Jeffrey Kaplan and Helene Lööw, eds., *The Cultic Milieu: Oppositional Subcultures in an Age of Globalization* (Walnut Creek, CA: AltaMira, 2002), pp. 265–89, esp. pp. 265–66.

14. On the Children of God, now known as The Family, see William Sims Bainbridge, *The Endtime Family: Children of God* (Albany: State University of New York Press, 2002); James D. Chancellor, *Life in the Family: An Oral History of the Children of God* (Syracuse: Syracuse University Press, 2000); James R. Lewis and J. Gordon Melton, eds., *Sex Slander and Salvation: Investigating The Family/Children of God* (Stanford: Center for Academic Publication, 1994); David E. Van Zandt, *Living in the Children of God* (Princeton: Princeton University Press, 1991); and Miriam Williams, *Heaven's Harlots: My Fifteen Years as a Sacred Prostitute in the Children of God Cult* (New York: William Morrow, 1998).

15. Melton, "The Modern Anti-Cult Movement," p. 268.

16. For Patrick's account of his own career, see Ted Patrick and Tom Dulack, *Let Our Children Go!* (New York: Dutton, 1976).

17. Robert Lifton's *Thought Reform and the Psychology of Totalism* (New York: Norton, 1961) played then and has continued to play a crucial role in the formulation of anticult arguments about brainwashing.

18. On the controversies about deprogramming and brainwashing, see David Bromley and James T. Richardson, eds., *The Brainwashing/Deprogramming Controversy* (New York: Edwin Mellen, 1983) and Benjamin Zablocki and Thomas Robbins, eds., *Misunderstanding Cults: Searching for Objectivity in a Controversial Field* (Toronto: University of Toronto Press, 2001). For an example of a contemporary approach to removing individuals from cults by a prominent anticult activist, see Steven Hassan, *Releasing the Bonds: Empowering People to Think for Themselves* (Somerville, MA: Freedom of Mind, 2000). Hassan maintains an extensive Web site at

www.freedomofmind.com. For an interview with Hassan, see www.religioscope.info/
article_48.shtml. On exit counseling, see Carol Giambalvo, *Exit Counseling: A Family Intervention: How to Respond to Cult-Affected Loved Ones,* 2nd ed. (Bonita
Springs, FL: American Family Foundation, 1992). An influential anticult group, the
American Family Foundation's Web site is www.csj.org.

19. See Melton, "The Modern Anti-Cult Movement," p. 269.

20. On the term *cult,* see James T. Richardson, "Definitions of Cult: From Socio-
logical-Technical to Popular-Negative," in Lorne L. Dawson, ed., *Cults in Context:
Readings in the Study of New Religious Movements* (New Brunswick, NJ: Transaction, 1998), pp. 29–38.

21. As quoted in Marcia R. Rudin, "The Cult Phenomenon: Fad or Fact," in Gary
D. Eisenberg, ed., *Smashing the Idols: A Jewish Inquiry into the Cult Phenomenon*
(Northvale, NJ: Jason Aronson, 1988), p. 26.

22. See Margaret Singer, with Janja Lalich, *Cults in Our Midst: The Hidden Men-
ace in Our Everyday Lives* (San Francisco: Jossey-Bass, 1995). For a subtle and thor-
ough academic treatment of the connection between cults and violence, see Catherine
Wessinger, *How the Millennium Comes Violently* (New York: Seven Bridges, 2000);
see also John R. Hall, with Philip D. Schuyler and Sylvaine Trinh, *Apocalypse
Observed: Religious Movements and Violence in North America, Europe, and Japan*
(New York: Routledge, 2000) and David G. Bromley and J. Gordon Melton, eds.,
Cults, Religion, and Violence (Cambridge: Cambridge University Press, 2002).

23. See, for example, the lists of groups compiled by Steven Hassan at www.
freedomofmind.com/resourcecenter/groups/ and Rick Ross at www.rickross.com/
sg_alpha. html. In *Cults in Our Midst* Singer puts the number at three thousand to five
thousand (p. 5).

24. See Hall et al., *Apocalypse Observed,* pp. 70, 188, for example.

25. John Ankerberg and John Weldon, *Encyclopedia of Cults and New Religions*
(Eugene, OR: Harvest House, 1999), p. viii. On the Christian countercult in general,
see Douglas E. Cowan, *Bearing False Witness? An Introduction to the Christian Countercult* (Westport, CT: Praeger, 2003).

26. Statement of purpose from the Christian Research Institute welcome page at
www.equip.org.

27. Gary Eisenberg, "Introduction," in Eisenberg, *Smashing the Idols,* p. xvi.

28. Mission statement on the welcome page of Jews for Judaism at www.jewsfor-
judaism.org/web/mainpages/missionary_cult_challenge.html.

29. For Socrates' classic *apologia,* see Plato, *Apology* in any contemporary translation; for Paul's *apologia,* see Acts 22.

30. See www.freedomofmind.com/resourcecenter/faq/#8.

31. See www.freedomofmind.com/resourcecenter/faq/#7.

32. See www.rickross.com/coping.html.

33. See ibid.

34. See www.rickross.com/prep_faq.html.

35. See Singer, *Cults in Our Midst,* pp. xx, 3, 5, 28, 79, 83, among others.

36. Ibid., p. 17.

37. Ibid., p. 210.

38. Ibid., p. 247.

39. For examples of definitions of destructive cults, see www.rickross.com/faq.
html and www.freedomofmind.com/resourcecenter/faq/#2.

40. See www.csj.org/studyindex/studycult/cultqa4.htm.

41. See, for example, Singer, *Cults in Our Midst*, pp. 23–25, 221–23.

42. See, for example, Eileen Barker, *The Making of a Moonie: Brainwashing or Choice* (London: Blackwell's, 1984).

43. See Sigmund Freud, *The Future of an Illusion*, ed. and trans. James Strachey (New York: Norton, 1989).

44. See, for example, www.rickross.com/prep_faq.html.

45. Emile Durkheim, *The Elementary Forms of the Religious Life*, trans. Karen E. Fields (New York: The Free Press, 1995), p. 44.

46. See Clifford Geertz, "Religion as a Cultural System," in idem, *The Interpretation of Cultures* (New York: Basic, 1973), pp. 87–125.

47. Singer, *Cults in Our Midst*, p. 258.

48. Ibid., p. 15.

49. For a recent treatment of charismatic leadership, see Lorne L. Dawson, *Comprehending Cults: The Sociology of New Religious Movements* (Oxford: Oxford University Press, 1998), pp. 139–48; see also Charles Lindholm, *Charisma* (Oxford: Basil Blackwell, 1990). For the classic statement, see Ephraim Fischoff, trans. Max Weber, *The Sociology of Religion* (Boston: Beacon, 1993) and S. N. Eisenstadt, ed., *Max Weber on Charisma and Institution Building* (Chicago: University of Chicago Press, 1968).

50. Hassan, *Releasing the Bonds*, p. 4.

51. Wayne Proudfoot, *Religious Experience* (Berkeley: University of California Press, 1985), p. 194.

52. Ibid.

53. Jan Shipps, *Mormonism: The Story of a New Religious Tradition* (Urbana: University of Illinois Press, 1985), p. 53.

54. See, for example, Claude Vorilhon (Raël), *The Message Given to Me by Extra-Terrestrials*, pp. 2–30.

55. See Malcolm X, with Alex Haley, *The Autobiography of Malcolm X* (New York: Ballantine, 1973), pp. 164–67.

56. See, for example, Singer, *Cults in Our Midst*, pp. xxii, 3, 5.

57. Phillip Jenkins, *Mystics and Messiahs: Cults and New Religions in American History* (Oxford: Oxford University Press, 2000), p. 4.

58. See ibid., pp. 13, 21, 48.

59. For a brisk and vivid account of the period, see ibid., pp. 25–45, with a helpful table on p. 35.

60. See John Noonan, *The Lustre of Our Country: The American Experience of Religious Freedom* (Berkeley: University of California Press, 1998), p. 243.

61. Kenelm Burridge, *New Heaven New Earth: A Study of Millenarian Activities* (New York: Schocken, 1969), p. 14.

62. On critiques of Christianity in the Greco-Roman world, see Robert L. Wilken, *The Christians as the Romans Saw Them* (New Haven: Yale University Press, 1984).

63. The critique of Christianity written by the philosopher Celsus is preserved in the Christian theologian Origen's response to Celsus. See Henry Chadwick, trans., *Origen, Contra Celsum* (Cambridge: Cambridge University Press, 1965). For the specific topics mentioned, see I.28, II.1, I.67, I.68, and VII.53, respectively. On the argument about Jesus, see Eugene V. Gallagher, *Divine Man or Magician? Origen and Celsus on Jesus* (Chico, CA: Scholars, 1982).

64. See www.freedomofmind.com/resourcecenter/faq/#3.

65. See www.rickross.com/faq.html and Singer, *Cults in Our Midst*, pp. 3–5.

66. See Jonathan Z. Smith, "Religion, Religions, Religious," in Mark C. Taylor, ed. *Critical Terms for Religious Studies* (Chicago: University of Chicago Press, 1998).

67. Ibid., p. 276.

68. Ibid., pp. 281–82.

69. Peter Berger, *The Sacred Canopy: Elements of a Sociological Theory of Religion* (Garden City, NY: Doubleday, 1967), p. 24.

70. William Paden, *Religious Worlds: The Comparative Study of Religion* (Boston: Beacon Press, 1994), pp. 52–53.

71. Ibid., p. 10; his emphasis.

72. On the reduction of religion to faith, see Smith, "Religion, Religions, Religious," p. 271.

73. See *The Autobiography of Malcolm X*, pp. 155, 156.

74. Ibid., p. 156.

75. Paden, *Religious Worlds*, p. 7.

76. See Geertz, "Religion as a Cultural System," pp. 100–108.

77. Raël, *The Message Given to Me by Extra-Terrestrials*, p. 15.

78. See www.thefamily.org/dossier/statements/heritage.htm.

79. Mary Baker Eddy, *Science and Health with Key to the Scriptures* (1875; rpt. Boston: First Church of Christ Scientist, 1994), p. 470.

80. See Geertz, "Religion as a Cultural System," p. 89.

81. See Timothy Miller, *The Quest for Utopia in Twentieth Century America: 1900–1960* (Syracuse: Syracuse University Press, 1998); idem, *The Sixties Communes: Hippies and Beyond* (Syracuse: Syracuse University Press, 2000).

82. Stark and Bainbridge, *The Future of Religion*, pp. 35, 36, respectively.

83. See Church of Scientology, *Scientology: The Theory and Practice of a Contemporary Religion* (Los Angeles: Bridge, 1998), also available at www.theology.scientology.org/eng/pdf/Scientology-bonafide.pdf.

84. On the Christian Identity Movement, see Michael Barkun, *Religion and the Racist Right: The Origins of the Christian Identity Movement* (Chapel Hill: University of North Carolina Press, 1994) and Jeffrey Kaplan, *Radical Religion in America: Millenarian Movements from the Far Right to the Children of Noah* (Syracuse: Syracuse University Press, 1997), esp. chapter 2.

85. Thomas Robbins, *Cults, Converts, and Charisma: The Sociology of New Religious Movements* (Beverly Hills, CA: Sage, 1988), p. 159.

86. See Irving Hexham and Karla Poewe, *New Religions as Global Cultures: Making the Human Sacred* (Boulder, CO: Westview, 1997), pp. 99–100.

87. See ibid., p. 116.

88. Ibid., p. 162.

89. Timothy Miller, ed., *America's Alternative Religions* (Albany: State University of New York Press, 1995), p. 8.

90. See ibid., pp. vii–ix.

91. See ibid., p. 8.

92. In a recent survey written for a popular audience in the United Kingdom, David B. Barrett makes much the same point. After proposing his own five major categories of groups with origins in Christianity—those that originate in other "religions of the book," groups of Eastern origin, esoteric and neo-pagan religions, and personal development groups—he admits that "any categorization of this type is arbitrary" (p. 17). See David B. Barrett, *The New Believers: Sects, "Cults," and Alternative Religions* (London: Cassell, 2001).

93. Miller, *America's Alternative Religions*, p. 8.

94. See Roy Wallis, "Three Types of New Religious Movements," reprinted in Lorne Dawson, ed., *Cults in Context: Readings in the Study of New Religious Movements* (New Brunswick, NJ: Transaction, 1998), pp. 39–71.

95. See the summary in Robbins, *Cults, Converts, and Charisma*, pp. 134–60 for these and other examples.

96. See Jonathan Z. Smith, "The 'End' of Comparison: Redescription and Rectification," in Kimberley C. Patton and Benjamin C. Ray, eds., *A Magic Still Dwells: Comparative Religion in the Postmodern Age* (Berkeley: University of California Press, 2000), pp. 237–41, passage quoted from p. 239.

97. Ibid.

98. I would argue, however, that synthesizing diverse influences has long been a characteristic of new religious movements. The early Christian adoption of Greek philosophical categories to express Christian faith and the early Islamic absorption of both Jewish and Christian stories, themes, and figures into the Qur'an are prominent examples.

99. Stark and Bainbridge, *The Future of Religion*, p. 2.

100. Ibid., p. 3.

101. See ibid., p. 19.

102. See ibid., pp. 27–28.

103. The term *cultic milieu* was coined by the British sociologist Colin Campbell. See his essay and other related papers in Kaplan and Lööw, *The Cultic Milieu*.

104. See Berger, *The Sacred Canopy*, pp. 133, 147. Berger offers the pithy formulation that in the contemporary world, "cosmology becomes psychology" and "history becomes biography" (p. 167).

105. David Chidester, *Salvation and Suicide: An Interpretation of Jim Jones, the Peoples Temple, and Jonestown* (Bloomington: Indiana University Press, 1988), p. 1.

Chapter 2

Groups within the Biblical Tradition

On February 28, 1993, a heavily armed force of agents from the U.S. Bureau of Alcohol, Tobacco, and Firearms (BATF) attempted a "dynamic entry" at the Mount Carmel Center outside of Waco, Texas. The BATF agents intended to serve a search and arrest warrant at the Center, suspecting that some residents were illegally converting semi-automatic weapons to fully automatic machine guns. The Mount Carmel Center was the home and church of a group of Bible students known as the Branch Davidians, who had come from all over the world to study the meaning of the book of Revelation with David Koresh, a high school dropout with a flair for preaching the Bible's apocalyptic message. Quickly after the heavily armed BATF agents exited the cattle trailers they had arrived in, the agents and those inside the Center exchanged gunfire. The ensuing firefight lasted around three hours. Shortly after the gunfire began, the Branch Davidians placed a call to their local 911 emergency number, demanding that the attack be stopped. In the midst of a conversation with Lt. Larry Lynch of the Waco Sheriff's Department, Koresh tried to interject his preaching about the imminent end of the world. Part of the exchange went like this:

> KORESH: It's in your Bible, there are Seven Seals. Now there—
> LYNCH: Yes, sir.
> KORESH: —are some things in that Bible that have been held as mysteries of Christ.
> LYNCH: Yes, sir.
> KORESH: Now, in the prophecies it says—
> LYNCH: Let me—can I interrupt you for a minute?
> KORESH: Sure.
> LYNCH: All right. We can talk theology, but right now—

KORESH: Look, this is life, this is life and death.
LYNCH: Okay.
KORESH: —theology really is life and death.[1]

On April 19, 1993, the tragic ending of the fifty-one-day siege at the Mount Carmel Center proved Koresh's words to be frighteningly true.

During the prolonged standoff at the Mount Carmel Center and in the postmortems that immediately followed the lethal fire, the previously obscure group of Bible students became an internationally notorious example of a cult. Koresh himself was widely excoriated as a mentally unstable con man; his sexual encounters with under-aged girls were luridly detailed as examples of the harm that a cult leader can perpetrate, and his fondness for guns was seen to be a harbinger of the group's violent end. When any attention was directed to them at all, the Branch Davidians themselves were portrayed as unfortunate dupes of a cunning manipulator.[2] In all of that discussion very little serious attention was paid to the group's beliefs and practices. The FBI's conclusion that Koresh was simply spouting "Bible babble" apparently sufficed in the public eye as a description of the group's religious convictions.[3] The public perceptions of the Branch Davidians, which were largely shaped by an investigative report from the *Waco Tribune-Herald,* both repeated and reinforced the already popular image of cults purveyed by anticult activists.[4] But there was more to the Branch Davidians than sex, guns, and David Koresh's rock 'n' roll.

Although they had several distinctive beliefs and practices, the Branch Davidians were part of a history of Christian sectarianism that goes back to the first century of the Common Era. The Bible itself preserves multiple paradigms of divinely sanctioned innovation by prophetic figures, from Jesus' "you have heard that it was said to the men of old . . . but I say to you" in the Sermon on the Mount (Matt. 5:21–22), to Paul's claimed ascent into the heavens in 2 Corinthians 12, to the divine commissionings of Hebrew prophets like Isaiah (Isaiah 6). That fact has certainly not been lost on the founders of many sectarian movements who have appealed to biblical justifications for innovation. As early as the second century, in the backwaters of Phrygia, the prophet Montanus and the prophetesses Prisca and Maximilla proclaimed under the inspiration of the Holy Spirit that the heavenly New Jerusalem, described in the final two chapters of the book of Revelation, was soon to descend upon the small village of Pepuza. The prophets enjoined asceticism on their followers as a way of preparing for the imminent transformation of the world. As the movement spread

The Koresh family, 1987. © Elizabeth
Baranyai/CORBIS SYGMA.

through Asia Minor to North Africa it continued to gain adherents,
including the prominent theologian Tertullian, and opponents. The Montanist Movement was condemned by a series of synods but maintained
flickers of life into the sixth century.[5] The history of Montanism suggests
that the potential for sectarian innovation in the Christian tradition was
actualized early and subsequent Christian history shows that it was realized often.

It is no surprise, then, that sectarian groups have played an important
role in U.S. religious history. While the roles of some sectarian groups like
the Puritans and Quakers are a familiar part of American history,[6] the
focus in this chapter will be on groups that either through their own determined innovation or through the reaction of others have been located at
or beyond the boundaries of mainstream Christianity.[7] That is, some
groups, despite their declared intentions to return to the purity and clarity
of the origins of the religious traditions with which they identify themselves, appear to others to be so thoroughly innovative that they constitute
new, independent religious bodies rather than renovations of existing

ones. In the analytical typology of Stark and Bainbridge that was described in chapter 1, they are perceived more as cults than as sects. The students who gathered around David Koresh provide a good example. Although the great majority of them saw themselves as firmly rooted within the Seventh-Day Adventist tradition and thus within Christianity, both the surrounding society and the Seventh-Day Adventist church saw them as a radically, and dangerously, innovative group whose new practices and beliefs definitively separated them from the mainstream.[8] The difference between the way Koresh and his students saw themselves—as faithful adherents of the Christian tradition who were diligently pursuing its true meaning—and the way that most outside observers saw them—as radical innovators who could lay no legitimate claims to being Christian—highlights some of the difficulties in identifying any group as a sect or a cult. Despite the efforts of sociologists like Stark and Bainbridge to establish the categories as neutral descriptive and analytical terms, they are most frequently used with a polemical edge. Most often, to describe a group as a cult is inherently to question its legitimacy, its good faith, and its motivations. In some usages "sect" carries similar values, particularly when one contender for legitimacy, authority, and power within a tradition uses the term to describe a rival. In addition, over time groups may migrate from one category toward another; radical innovations can accommodate themselves to the requirements of a more mainstream tradition or moderate renovations of a tradition can become progressively more radical until they are perceived to reach and pass over the boundaries of a tradition. Consequently, when a specific group lays claim to an authoritative interpretation of the biblical tradition, as David Koresh and his students did, its status as a sect or a cult will frequently be contested on both descriptive and theological bases.

All of the groups discussed in this chapter have been drawn into the contemporary controversy over cults in one way or another. Even when their members have vigorously contended that they are simply unveiling the true meaning of the Bible, restoring the original practices of the primitive Christian church, recovering the original meaning of Jesus' teaching, or responding to a fresh revelation from the God of the Bible, outsiders have seen their practices and beliefs as such dramatic departures from the mainstream tradition that they merit equally vigorous opposition, correction, condemnation, or even extirpation. Thus, depending on the perspective from which they are viewed, the groups discussed in this chapter appear unequivocally to be part of the sectarian history of Christianity or

Judaism, or, with equal certainty, to be so different from their parent religions as to constitute new kinds of religion altogether. The definitions of cult that have been employed in the contemporary controversy have been sufficiently various and malleable to admit a wide variety of groups into the discussion, even when their inclusion might strike some observers as wholly unwarranted. The broad biblical tradition has always been an incredibly fertile breeding ground for new religious movements and many of them have been drawn into the recent arguments about cults.

The groups in this chapter, then, represent a selection of those movements that have grown out of the biblical tradition in U.S. history and have been perceived by at least some external observers to be such thorough and perhaps pernicious departures that they have merited pejorative description as cults. Some of them, such as the Branch Davidians, are parts of relatively long and complex sectarian histories; others, such as the Church of Jesus Christ of Latter-day Saints, have themselves spawned a variety of sectarian splinter groups. Others, such as the Unificationist Movement of the Rev. Sun Myung Moon, have been imported to the U.S. from elsewhere and thus fit one of Stark and Bainbridge's descriptions of a cult. But the practices of Moon's movement also aroused such intense social opposition that it also was branded a cult in the negative sense. Some, such as the various Christian Identity churches, have managed to secure only a small number of adherents, but others, such as the Mormons, have become dynamic religious movements with a worldwide presence. All of them have provoked strenuous opposition and thus offer glimpses into the complex dynamics of how new religious movements attempt to establish legitimacy and attract adherents in an often hostile social and religious environment.

From William Miller to David Koresh: Adventist Groups

Groups in the Adventist strand of the Christian tradition share a common origin and common orientation to human history. The Millerite Movement of the mid-nineteenth century, which itself was part of a broader upsurge of millennial expectations, provided a crucial context for the development of American millennialism.[9] After prolonged and careful study of the Bible, William Miller, a New York farmer and Baptist layman, came to the conclusion that the second coming of Jesus Christ would occur sometime between March 21, 1843, and March 21, 1844. He subsequently recalculated the date to October 22, 1844, on which the "Great Disappointment" was experienced, when the hoped-for end failed to materialize. The seriousness with which his supporters considered Miller's efforts is indicated in the testimony of one of the converts. Henry B. Bear wrote of the impact of Miller's writing on him in 1843: "I read the lectures carefully at first, and later prayerfully. Miller's manner of reasoning; his explanation of the prophecies, and the starting point he gave to them, appeared to me so correct that they caused convictions to grow up in my mind that he was correct in his views."[10] As Bear's testimony indicates, the development of American millennialism in the mid-nineteenth century depended upon a broad diffusion of the Bible in the pre–Civil War United States and a tendency in the early part of the nineteenth century for individuals to develop their own interpretations of the Bible, independent of ecclesiastical influence.[11] As they read their Bibles, many devotedly searched for indications of the imminent end of the world. They tried to align the prophecies in the books of Daniel and Revelation with the signs of the times in order to construct confident predictions of when the end would actually come. Often, they declared that it would come in the near future. Some groups, like the Millerites and the Jehovah's Witnesses, confidently set dates for the return of Jesus Christ, and when their fondest hopes were unfailingly betrayed by events they had to cope with a disappointment that threatened the foundations of their religious identities. Other groups retreated from setting specific dates while maintaining that the advent of the Lord could be expected in an indefinite, but still immediate, future.[12] All of the groups in the Adventist tradition have devoted themselves to substantial missionary efforts and many of them now count more members outside of the United States than within.

Beyond generally exhorting their members to be prepared for the coming end, different groups have drawn different practical conclusions from the anticipated dawning of the millennium. Although they both developed out of the post-1844 disintegration of the Millerite movement, the Jehovah's Witnesses, for example, differed from the Seventh-Day Adventists in maintaining that only through membership in their group could one be saved.[13] Among the Witnesses' other beliefs and activities that separated them from their immediate social environment were their practice of holding the Lord's Supper only once a year on what they take to be the traditional date of the Jewish Passover, refusal to serve in the military, refusal to pledge allegiance to the flag on the basis of the prohibition against graven images in Exodus 20:3–5, and refusal to accept blood transfusions, based on texts such as Genesis 9:5–6, Leviticus 17:10, and Acts 15:20, 28, 29, which has been officially maintained since 1945.[14] They have erected and maintained strong boundaries between their group and what they continue to see as a sinful and damned outside world. In contrast, especially in the years after its founding generation, the Seventh-Day Adventist church has accommodated itself much more to the world.[15] It is particularly noteworthy today for maintaining a large number of educational and health care facilities.

For all of the groups in the Adventist tradition, dedicated reading and interpretation of the Bible has always been a central practice. Authoritative interpreters of the text, like Miller, Ellen G. White, Charles Taze Russell, and David Koresh, have played central roles in their respective groups, and the relationship between the authority of the interpreter and the authority of the text is a topic of substantial discussion and debate. On the one hand, interpreters can claim that the message of the Bible is clear and accessible to all; on the other hand, they can emphasize that it is only through their superior insight into the text that its true meaning can be grasped. The tension between those two assertions is nicely captured in a statement by the founder of the Jehovah's Witnesses. Charles Taze Russell claimed of his own six volumes of *Studies in the Scriptures* that they "were practically the Bible topically arranged."[16] The gap between "literally" and "practically" and the process of arrangement of the scriptures would open up substantial opportunity for Russell to shape the interpretation of the text.

The shifting balance between virtually universal access to the text of the Bible and the necessity of seeing the Bible through the eyes of an inspired interpreter has also contributed to the initiation of dissident movements within all of the Adventist groups. In the wake of the "Great Disappointment" of October 22, 1844, for example, three distinct groups developed out of Miller's followers. Despite his manifest error, Miller and other leaders of the movement continued to hold out hope for the imminent end; a small Adventist church that still exists today traces its origins to that group. Others contended that the end had in fact occurred on October 22, but in a spiritual sense, but many of them soon migrated to other groups such as the Shakers. Also, by the end of 1845, a small group of New Hampshire Millerites had begun to coalesce around Joseph Bates, James White, and Ellen G. Harmon, who would marry White in 1846. The group argued that October 22, 1844, had in fact been a crucial date for human salvation, because Jesus Christ had entered the heavenly Temple on that day in preparation for the final judgment. His return would happen at an unspecified time in the future. Bates and the Whites laid the foundation for the Seventh-Day Adventists. In their subsequent histories, both the Seventh-Day Adventists and the Jehovah's Witnesses have experienced schisms. One set of fissures within the Seventh-Day Adventists eventually produced the Branch Davidians.

The group of dedicated Bible students that gathered at Mount Carmel had a long history in the Waco area and an even longer history before that. With only a few exceptions, Koresh's disciples had religious roots in the Seventh-Day Adventist tradition. They continued the practice of painstaking study of the scriptures under the guidance of their teacher David Koresh. During negotiations with the FBI during the 1993 siege at the Mount Carmel Center, one of the Branch Davidians, Steven Schnieder, showed how seriously he and his fellow students took the study of the Bible by attesting that "all [we] are and what [we] want to be revolves around what [we] see him [Koresh] showing from that book."[17]

These statements signal several important dimensions of Millerite and subsequent Adventist millennialism. Most important, it is focused on the biblical text; it is a highly intellectual enterprise that seeks patterns, correlations, and correspondences. The Bible is treated as a coherent whole, with a single, unified message. As David Koresh put it, "every book of the Bible meets and ends in the book of Revelation."[18] Consequently, any individual's status as an authoritative interpreter was always subject to an outside check, the text of the Bible itself. As Henry Bear measured Miller's "explanation of the prophecies" against the letter of the text, so would others who encountered Miller's "midnight cry." Similarly, David Thibodeau, who survived the Mount Carmel fire, told negotiators that "it's just opening the book for myself, seeing what it says and saying, wow, is this guy [Koresh] found in the book, you know, and all the Psalms, you, you, really got to sit down and listen to him talk, I mean with the book open."[19] Adventist groups have always expended considerable effort in encouraging members and potential members to devote serious, sustained attention to the study of the Bible. From their headquarters in Brooklyn, New York, for example, leaders of the Jehovah's Witnesses direct a vast missionary effort designed to lead people to and through careful study of the Bible. The official Web site of the Witnesses promises that "the Bible shows where we came from, why we are here, and where we are going," and offers to arrange an individual study session for anyone who is interested.[20] The Jehovah's Witnesses have also produced their own translation of the Bible that highlights their distinctive ideas.

In any millennial movement focused on the Bible an apocalyptic message is generated through the triangular interrelationships of text, interpreter, and context. While the text remains fixed, both the interpreter and the context are open to change. One such change for the Millerites was the recalculation of the date of the end to October 22, 1844. When Jesus failed to reappear on that second date, it only diffused rather than decreased the general Adventist fervor.

More than the Millerites before them, the Seventh-Day Adventists came to constitute a distinctive religious community rather than an interpretive approach to the Bible. As their name implies, they observed the seventh day, Saturday, as the religiously enjoined day of rest in explicit opposition to what they saw as the misguided "pagan" and Roman Catholic hallowing of Sunday.[21] To their observance of the seventh-day Sabbath, Bates and the Whites added another distinctive theological tenet. They believed that God's will is revealed progressively and that each new generation could expect to receive its "present truth" or "new light." That doctrine introduced a dynamism into the Seventh-Day Adventist tradition that would contribute to the schisms that eventually produced Koresh's group of Branch Davidians. In her small group of disappointed yet still hopeful millennialists Ellen White was the recipient of that new light; her visions provided the basis for her extensive writings. The contemporary Seventh-Day Adventist church describes the balance between White's authority and that of the Bible in this formal statement: "her writings are a continuing and authoritative source of truth which provide for the church comfort, guidance, instruction, and correction. They also make clear that the Bible is the standard by which all teaching and experience must be tested."[22]

In addition to their sabbath practices, the Seventh-Day Adventists also accepted the dietary laws of the Hebrew Bible. Like the Jehovah's Witnesses, they expressed a sectarian concern for recovering the original practices of Jesus and his followers. A 1980 formal declaration of the church describes the seventh-day Sabbath as part of "God's unchangeable law."[23] A similar incorporation of traditional Jewish rituals into Branch Davidian practice complicated the 1993 negotiations when outsiders failed to understand that the Branch Davidians' observation of Passover would last eight days. Features like the sabbatarianism of the mainstream Seventh-Day Adventists, and other distinctive ritual practices in related groups, continue to be a source of tension between them and the mainstream.

None of the groups in the Adventist tradition has ever presented itself as a deviant innovation. Leaders like Miller, White, Russell, and Koresh saw themselves as finally uncovering and revealing the true message of the Bible. Nevertheless, what they found in the Bible frequently set them at odds with the neighbors. Among other examples, Miller was accused of promoting insanity; Russell was accused of adultery, theft, and perjury; and David Koresh was derisively known as the "Wacko from Waco."[24] Contemporary Christian countercult writers frequently include the Jehovah's Witnesses among religious cults. Ankerberg and Weldon, for example, devote more space to unmasking their doctrinal errors than they do to any other of their fifty-seven examples.[25] Rick Ross offers a substantial dossier of information about the Witnesses but appends a disclaimer that the inclusion of the group does not necessarily mean that is a "destructive cult."[26] Steven Hassan includes information about the group on his Web site and explicitly notes that his information has been derived from former members.[27]

Seventh-Day Adventists have received a more mixed reception from opponents of cults. David Koresh's group of Branch Davidians has been universally condemned by both anti- and countercult writers, and the mainstream Seventh-Day Adventists have been criticized for their doctrinal errors by the Watchman Fellowship and included in its index of "cults and religions."[28] But Walter Martin, one of the most influential Christian countercult writers, rendered a different judgment. He argued that "one cannot be a true Jehovah's Witness, Mormon, Christian Scientist, etc., and be a Christian in the biblical sense of the term; but it is perfectly possible to be a Seventh-day Adventist and be a true follower of Jesus Christ despite certain heterodox concepts."[29] The diversity of the contemporary countercult movements' estimations of the Seventh-Day Adventists shows how they continue to press against what many see as the boundaries of Christian orthodoxy. In some cases, as with Koresh's Branch Davidians, there is broad agreement that the boundary has been crossed and that a new religious movement has been formed; in others, the judgment is more difficult to determine. But in any case, the Adventism that originated in William Miller's attempts to determine the date of the second coming of Jesus has continued to be a dynamic factor in American religious life.

The Church of Jesus Christ of Latter-day Saints and the Church of Christ, Scientist

Millerism was certainly not the only source of religious innovation in the nineteenth century. Beginning in 1820 a young teenage boy in upper New York State experienced a series of visions that led to the establishment of a new religious movement. Troubled by the different interpretations of the Bible advanced by various sects in a local revival, Joseph Smith sought God's guidance. He was rewarded with a vision that informed him that none of them was right.[30] Although his claims quickly provoked considerable scorn from local preachers and other religious people, Smith accepted the divine guidance and did not join any of the established sects. Then, in 1823, he encountered the angel Moroni, who told Smith "that God had a work for [him] to do,"[31] which would involve the discovery and eventual translation of a hidden book inscribed on golden tablets. The angel linked Smith's new mission to the biblical prophecies of the coming day of the Lord. Translated, the hidden book became the *Book of Mormon*, the foundational text of a new millennial movement.[32] Smith found his first converts within his immediate family and slowly began to draw others to acceptance of the new Bible.

The specific goal of Smith's movement was to restore, on the basis of fresh revelation and as closely as possible, the Christian community described in the New Testament book of Acts. Superimposed on that image of the church was a prophetic leadership, first embodied in Smith himself, that was modeled on the Hebrew Bible.[33] As Smith put it in the "Articles of Faith" that he crafted for the Mormon church: "We believe in the same organization that existed in the Primitive Church . . ." and "We believe in the literal gathering of Israel and in the restoration of the Ten Tribes; that Zion (the New Jerusalem) will be built upon the American continent; that Christ will reign personally upon the earth; and, that the earth will be renewed and receive its paradisiacal glory."[34]

Establishing that kingdom was not an easy task for Smith's early followers. The opposition that attended Smith's initial claim to visionary communication with the divine only intensified during the early years of Mormon history. Outright violence against Mormons climaxed with the assassination of Smith in 1844 in Carthage, Illinois. In the meantime the center of Mormon activity had moved progressively westward, as it would until the "Saints" finally settled in Utah after the "Great Trek" of 1846–47 under Brigham Young. That movement to Utah also marked a cleavage in the Latter-day Saint tradition. In the succession crisis that followed the

Angel Moroni delivering book to Joseph Smith. © Bettmann/CORBIS.

prophet's murder, parties who believed that leadership should be inherited by a member of Smith's family clashed with those who followed a charismatic figure, James J. Strang, and those who invested authority in the established ruling group of Brigham Young and the "Quorum of the Twelve." In addition to the departure of Young's group for Utah, that conflict also sparked the founding of the Reorganized Church of Jesus Christ of Latter-day Saints (RLDS), under the leadership of Joseph Smith III. The RLDS church was eventually headquartered in Independence, Missouri, which the prophet Joseph Smith had earlier identified as the place where Zion would be built.[35] Those who moved to the Great Salt Lake basin would also impose a biblical template on the local geography.

In addition to their different conceptions of leadership, one of the issues that separated the LDS and RLDS wings of the movement was the practice of polygamy. Introduced by Joseph Smith to an inner circle of church officials in Kirtland, Ohio, in 1841, the practice of "plural marriage" not only divided the Latter-day Saint community, but it attracted the ridicule and animosity of outsiders and eventually led to government action against the Utah community. In 1857, for example, President Buchanan authorized a military expedition designed in part to wipe out the practice of polygamy. At the same time, legislative actions culminated in the Supreme Court's 1879 decision that "bigamy" was unconstitutional. In its decision the Court distinguished between religious beliefs and religious practices and claimed the right to regulate only the latter. Finally, in his 1890 manifesto, Wilford Woodruff, then president of the church, declared his intention to abide by the laws of the nation and his pronouncement was accepted as authoritative by the general conference of the church. Soon after, in 1896, Utah achieved statehood. Small dissident Mormon groups who reject the 1890 decision, however, continue to practice polygamy and to get embroiled in legal actions today.[36]

As the resolution to the polygamy controversy lessened the tension between the Utah community and outsiders, it also reinforced the need for Mormons to demonstrate their distinctive status through other means. "Plural marriage" was part of Smith's efforts literally to restore the practices of both the early Christian church and the patriarchs of Israel. He wanted his followers actually to live in a perpetual biblical present, undertaking the same religious actions performed by their biblical predecessors. In the absence of polygamy, Mormons relied on other ways of distinguishing themselves. Mormons today are well known for their sober way of life that includes abstention from alcohol, caffeine, and tobacco; their extensive missionary endeavors; their focus on family life; and their practice of tithing, among other things. Also, although services at Mormon churches are open, the group retains its private Temple ceremonies, which include baptism on behalf of the dead, initiations into its Aaronic and Melchizedek priesthoods for all males, weddings, and baptisms, among other services. Mormon theology also remains distinctive, with, for example, its doctrines of the premortal existence of the soul as a spiritual being, the transit of the soul after death to the spirit world where it is judged for its qualifications to enter one of the "three degrees of glory," and the *Book of Mormon*'s unique accounts of ancient Israel and the mission of Jesus to the American continent.

Although there is still disagreement about whether the Mormons should be considered a Christian sect, a new religion, a people, or some other entity, there is no doubt that their growth has been remarkable. In terms of sheer numbers, they are the most successful new religious movement to have been born in the United States. Despite decisions that have reduced their tension with mainstream American society, the Mormons continue to be described as cultic by evangelical Christian countercult writers.[37] But the historian Jan Shipps has made a persuasive case that the Mormons have so transformed their biblical heritage that they should be considered an independent new religious movement, with its own scriptures, beliefs, and practices.[38] Their history, consequently, gives some indications of how new religious movements succeed.

Rodney Stark has argued that in order to achieve success a new religious movement would need to (1) retain cultural continuity, (2) maintain a medium level of tension with its environment, (3) effectively mobilize its members, (4) attract a normal age and sex representation among its members, (5) exist within a favorable social ecology, (6) maintain a dense network of internal relations, (7) resist secularization, and (8) socialize the young into the world of the group.[39] The connections between the *Book of Mormon* and the Christian Bible substantially satisfied the first criterion and the abandonment of polygamy mitigated tension between the Mormons and American society. Missionary efforts, the practice of tithing, and the emphasis on lay leadership helped to accomplish the third task, and the focus on family life helped to meet the fourth and sixth. In contrast to the strong opposition experienced in New York, Ohio, Missouri, and Illinois, the Utah territory provided a hospitable context for the development of a Mormon community with relatively little outside interference. And the development of a comprehensive social structure, including religion, social and political life, education, and commerce, addressed the final three criteria. The path along which the Mormon church has moved in integrating itself into American life has never been straight and smooth, but in many ways the church stands poised to assume a more mainstream status as a fourth major monotheistic tradition, alongside of Christianity, Judaism, and Islam.

The late nineteenth century also saw the development of new religious movements rooted in the biblical tradition. Although it also expressed the desire to "reinstate primitive Christianity,"[40] the Church of Christ, Scientist, founded by Mary Baker Eddy, expressed a markedly different view of the world than the Mormons. Where Joseph Smith, in support of his desire literally to restore the practices of the early church and the Hebrew patriarchs, had declared in 1843 that "all spirit is matter," Eddy, on the basis of her own experience of spiritual healing of physical infirmities in 1866 concluded that "matter is mortal error."[41] Eddy saw her discovery that only "spirit is the real and eternal"[42] as the beginning of a process of revelation that continued throughout her life. Even after she completed the first edition of *Science and Health with Key to the Scriptures* in 1875, Eddy continued to study her own book and to revise it as she achieved fuller understanding of its message.[43] Still today, study of Eddy's text along with the Bible remains a central practice in Christian Science.

Because of her unwavering focus on the reality of Spirit and consequent unreality of matter, Eddy also had no interest in the kind of millennialism that was at the core of the Adventist tradition and the Mormon church. She nonetheless rooted her movement directly in the biblical tradition. A summary of the tenets of Christian Science affirms that "as adherents of Truth, we take the inspired Word of the Bible as our sufficient guide to eternal Life."[44] Eddy portrayed Christian Science itself as the fulfillment of the promise in the gospel according to John 14:26 that after the departure of Jesus God would send the Paraclete or Comforter. Eddy asserted that "this Comforter I understand to be Divine Science."[45] As with the Adventist groups and the Mormons, however, Eddy's own perceptions, as expressed in *Science and Health* and her other extensive writings, offered the only reliable key to understanding the scriptures. Eddy's religious system offered its adherents the assurance that sin, evil, and disease could indeed be overcome and that Jesus provides the clear example of how that can be accomplished.[46] Eddy's reading of the Lord's Prayer, which she inserts between the lines of the standard Christian prayer, succinctly indicates her position. Where the prayer asks, "and lead us not into temptation, but deliver us from evil," Eddy understands it to mean that "God leadeth us not into temptation, but delivereth us from sin, disease, and death."[47]

Initially, Eddy's new religious system attracted a few adherents from the factory town of Lynn, Massachusetts, and nearby areas. But she faced substantial opposition from prominent Protestant ministers in Boston. In 1885 she gave a brief address in response to criticisms of Christian Science made by the Rev. Joseph Cook, a popular Protestant minister.[48] In the ten

Mary Baker Eddy in her study, c. 1903. Courtesy of the Mary Baker Eddy Collection.

minutes Eddy was allotted, she affirmed her belief in God, denied that Christian Science healing was done by "one mind acting on another mind," and vigorously distanced her movement from Spiritualism.[49] She proclaimed that "Christian Science is not a remedy of faith alone, but combines faith with understanding, through which we may touch the hem of his garment; and know that omnipotence has all power."[50] Eddy's efforts at attracting believers in her message eventually bore substantial fruit and by the time of her death in 1910 Christian Science was a vigorous organization and its message was spreading throughout this country and overseas. In order to maintain control over the expansion of her church, Eddy paid particular attention to its structure and governance. *The Manual of the Mother Church,* published in 1895, lays out in extraordinary detail how the affairs of the church, including its Sunday services, should be conducted. Partly in reaction to that attempt at control, Christian Science, like the other groups considered in this chapter, has seen a number of other groups split off from the parent body. Early on, in 1885, for example, Emma Hopkins split with Eddy and her Massachusetts Metaphysical College to form the Hopkins College of Metaphysical Science. Through some of her students Hopkins became an important influence on the New

Thought Movement, which combines ideas from Eddy and the prominent faith-healer Phineas Quimby. Out of the New Thought Movement developed the Unity School of Christianity, founded by Charles and Myrtle Fillmore in 1903, and the Church of Religious Science, founded by Ernest Holmes in 1948. Also, in the succession crisis that followed Eddy's death, one of the board of directors, John Dittemore, joined with Annie Bill to form the Christian Science Parent Church. As recently as 1975, the United Christian Scientists broke away from the Mother Church in reaction to the strong control exercised by the church officials.[51]

Readers of *Science and Health* today laud its effects on those suffering from various kinds of maladies,[52] but the practice of spiritual healing continues to be a point of contention between Christian Scientists and nonmembers. Just as the journal and official Web site of the Christian Science Mother Church in Boston maintain an extensive inventory of testimonies about spiritual healings, so also, for example, does the anticult Web site of Rick Ross maintain an archive of stories of the intense suffering experienced by Christian Science practitioners who relied, to no effect, on spiritual healing to address their illnesses.[53] In the last few decades several high-profile court cases have involved Christian Science parents withholding medical care from their minor children, and disaffected former members have published exposés and formed advocacy groups to prevent the denial of medical care to children.[54]

Although Christian Science presents a vibrant face to the world through its many publications, including the respected *Christian Science Monitor,* and a recent $50 million renovation of its library in Boston, most outside observers agree that its total membership has been in decline for some time.[55] Unlike the continued upward trend in Mormon membership, the total number of Christian Scientists seems to have peaked and fallen. While church leaders and individual members remain deeply committed to Eddy's religious system, skirmishes with medical and legal authorities over the treatment of illness have taken their toll. In Stark's terms the church has found it difficult to retain cultural continuity and with the ever-extending reach of contemporary medicine does not exist in a particularly favorable social context. In addition it seems not to have developed as successful a way of socializing young people into its world as has, for example, the Mormon church. In contrast to other groups, like the Branch Davidians, the Church of Church, Scientist nonetheless retained a substantial following of somewhere near 100,000 members in 2003. Despite a fluctuating membership it is an example of a new religious movement in the United States that has survived the generation of its founder, consolidated its members into a lasting organization, and spread itself throughout the world. If it does not show signs of becoming a major world religion in terms of sheer numbers, neither does it seem ready to fade quickly away.

The Unification Church and the Peoples Temple

The Unification Church of the Rev. Sun Myung Moon and the Peoples Temple of the Rev. Jim Jones were certainly among the handful of the most notorious new religious movements of the 1970s. Like the other groups considered in this chapter they both grew out of the Christian tradition, one rather suddenly and one gradually.

The Unification Church had its origins in an event similar to Joseph Smith's call by God. On Easter morning, 1936, in Korea, the sixteen-year-old Sun Myung Moon experienced a vision of Jesus that led him to undertake a thoroughgoing revision of salvation history. As a church pamphlet tells the story: "it was at sunrise on Easter morning while he was in deep prayer that a great vision came to him. Jesus appeared to him and told him that he was chosen to complete the mission Jesus had begun 2,000 years ago."[56] To provide a context for Moon's mission, the *Divine Principle*, the central scriptural text of the Unificationist Movement, develops an extended interpretation of biblical history from the creation and fall of humankind through the career of Jesus to the imminent arrival of a new Messiah who will gather humanity into a single loving family in accordance with God's original wishes. According to the Unificationists, all previous human interpretations of the Bible have failed to grasp its meaning, and what is needed now "is not another human interpretation of the Bible, but God's interpretation."[57] Although it is rooted firmly in the biblical tradition, the *Divine Principle* emphatically stresses its novelty, declaring that "today's religions have failed to lead the present generation out of the dark valley of death into the radiance of life, so there must now come a new truth that can shed a new light."[58]

Moon's new truth focused on the failures of Adam and Eve and of Jesus. Originally, Adam and Eve were to live happily, peacefully, and undisturbed in the garden, fulfilling the commandments to be fruitful, multiply, and have dominion over the earth (Gen. 1:28). Eve, however, entered into a sexual relationship with Satan, precipitating the Fall and estranging human beings from God. Jesus, in the *Divine Principle*'s understanding,

Supporters at a rally for Rev. Sun Myung Moon, October 27, 1981. © Bettmann/
CORBIS.

was supposed to rectify the effects of the Fall and restore humanity to its original state by forming a perfect loving family on earth, united with each other and with God. Tragically, he also failed. Humanity now waits for a "third Adam" or "Lord of the Second Advent" who will complete that mission of restoration. In the eyes of many Unificationists, the Rev. Moon is that messianic figure.

Although Moon began to preach publicly in 1946, the Unification Church did not arrive in the United States until the early 1960s, when it was introduced by Young Oon Kim in California, David S. C. Kim in Oregon, and Bo Hi Pak in Washington, D.C.[59] Even though they tried to make several clarifications of the movement's message in order to make it more attractive to potential converts, the early missionaries met with little success. Only with the arrival of a new group of Unificationists from Korea and Japan in San Francisco in 1966 did the movement begin to develop a successful strategy for recruitment. By late 1971, when Moon himself moved to the United States to oversee operations, the movement was ready to enter its most significant period of growth. During the early 1970s members of the Unification Church became infamous for their dedicated missionary efforts, often including marathon bouts of witnessing to strangers on the streets and fund-raising through the sale of flowers, attempts to recruit college-age youths, and intensive educational efforts in workshops often held in remote locales. As the new focus on recruiting began to bear some fruit, the Unification Church attracted the suspicions of families and friends of those who became members. Their attention, as it often does with cultural opponents of new religious movements, focused on the process of conversion, which some of them characterized as brainwashing. When the anticult activists turned their attention to the Unification Church, their suspicions were confirmed by a flood of memoirs with titles like *Crazy for God* and *Hostage to Heaven*.[60] The Unification Church thus became the first major battleground where a public understanding of the process of conversion was determined. The vivid morality plays of former members' memoirs proved much more attractive to a general audience than did more careful and detailed academic treatments of conversion and they consequently helped to cement in the public's mind the image of the brainwashing cult.[61]

The formal name of the Unification Church during its heyday in the 1970s was the Holy Spirit Association for the Unification of World Christianity. Two specific practices enacted that goal of unification. The first, which was particularly attractive for unattached young people, was communal living. In the recollection of one former member, "I found a group of people, mostly my age, living in such a close way I couldn't believe it. . . . There was a lot of talk in old-fashioned terms about love and duty to the collective goals."[62] The exhilarating experience of idealism in group homes fueled the missionary work of many of the young members. For those entering another phase of their lives, the church offered another opportunity to demonstrate their commitment to unifying races, cultures, and religions and to form the type of perfect, sinless family that God had originally intended for them. Following Rev. Moon's own 1960 marriage, Unification thought holds that it is now possible to form the ideal family of "true children" into which all of humanity can be incorporated through the marriage ceremony of "the Blessing."[63] As the church explains it, "through the Blessing we renounce the false love which has polluted the human family throughout history, and commit together with God to building a world of true love."[64] The Blessing ceremony remains one of the primary ways in which the Unificationist Movement strives to build a world community and between June 1998 and February 1999, for example, the church claims to have performed the Blessing ceremony for 240 million couples.[65]

Always malleable in its theological emphases, organizational form, and missionary focus, the Unificationist Movement has continued to change in the past decade. After the fortieth anniversary of the original Holy Spirit Association for the Unification of World Christianity in 1994, the Rev. Moon announced a new "era of the family" and incorporated all of the organizations he had created into the Family Federation for World Peace and Unification. Around the same time the focus of the church's work moved to South America, where the movement purchased millions of acres near the Pantanal wetlands of Brazil for the New Hope East Garden. As it has throughout its existence, however, the church has continued to be buffeted by social opposition. In 1998, Nansook Hong, the former wife of Moon's son Hyo Jin, published a tell-all book that detailed her husband's many moral failings and, more important, accused Rev. Moon himself of hypocrisy and sexual misconduct.[66] In addition the movement has had several clashes with the government of Brazil over its extensive landholdings.[67] Additional changes are likely for Unificationism with the Rev. Moon having turned eighty in 2000, but it seems likely that it will maintain its focus on the proclamation of a second advent through Moon's messianic mission, continue to focus on the *Divine Principle* particularly as viewed through Moon's own speeches and sermons, and still strive to bring together people of diverse religious, cultural, and racial backgrounds in pursuit of a unified family.

The Peoples Temple of Rev. Jim Jones also had a tumultuous organizational career. Its origins go back to the 1950s in Indianapolis, Indiana, where Jones first worked as an associate pastor and then formed his own congregation, initially named the Community Unity Church, then Wings of Deliverance, and finally, in 1955, the Peoples Temple Full Gospel Church. In 1960 the Peoples Temple was accepted as a congregation by the Christian Church, Disciples of Christ and in 1964 Jones was ordained a minister. Throughout his ministry Jones had two abiding concerns, racial integration and socialist politics. During the 1960s he became more concerned with the possibility of nuclear war. In response, he eventually moved his congregation to northern California, which he saw as one of the places that might be safe from nuclear destruction. Jones' congregation prospered and by 1970 it was also active in San Francisco. By that time, however, Jones' preaching was moving well beyond the bounds of Protestant orthodoxy.

Jones had developed a fascination with Father Divine, the founder of the Peace Mission, as early as the 1950s.[68] As Jones assimilated Father Divine's identity as a messianic living God into his own persona, his movement left its moorings in the Christian tradition and became something new and independent. One person who spent six years in Jones' group was deeply impressed by what appeared to be its successful integration of black and white families. She wrote that "I had never before witnessed the warmth and love I was seeing in this totally integrated group."[69] But she was also put off by Jones' theatrically staged healings, the congregation's apparent worship of Jones, and his denigration of the King James Version of the Bible.[70] She struggled with the contradictions she saw but eventually joined the Peoples Temple with her husband. Although the Peoples Temple won considerable support for its social activism, it also became the target for investigative reports focused on Jones' aspirations to divine status and other aspects of the church. In September 1972, the *San Francisco Examiner* began to print a series of critical articles by Rev. Lester Kinsolving that was halted halfway through, perhaps because of the influence of the Peoples Temple. In 1973 eight leaders left the group, increasing Jones' sense of vulnerability. Despite those setbacks, Jones continued to receive accolades for his political activism and his social service work. But Jones perceived further defections and a 1977 exposé in *New West* magazine created an intolerable situation for the Peoples Temple. By mid-July of

Rev. Jim Jones. © Bettmann/CORBIS.

1977 Jones himself relocated to the Peoples Temple Agricultural Mission in Jonestown, Guyana, which had been started in 1975. By September 1977, nearly a thousand people had left California to join him.

During his time in Guyana, Jones completed his transition from a liberal Christian pastor to the leader of a new religious movement. As his religious thinking developed throughout the 1970s, he left the trappings of Christianity far behind and came to see the Bible, particularly in its King James translation, as the source of social ills such as racism, sexism, ageism, and other forms of oppression rather than their antidote.[71] Jones also ridiculed the creation story of Genesis as involving a limited and self-absorbed "Sky God"; in its place he wove a story of cosmic redemption that included his own prior existence on another planet, his messianic role, and the promise of true redemption through the construction of a socialist utopia in the Guyanese jungle.[72] With the near total abandonment of a Christian frame of reference, Jones portrayed himself as the embodiment of the goal of the Peoples Temple, "apostolic socialism."[73]

From its inception, however, Jones' heaven on earth was plagued by serious problems. Carving a new world out of the jungle was no easy task, particularly since many of the older members were able to contribute very little labor. Through illness and indulgence Jones himself disintegrated into drug addiction and his behavior became progressively more erratic. Jones' desire to exercise strict control over the lives of members placed further strain on the fragile community. Complaints by former members continued to assail the group and eventually provoked a fateful visit to Jonestown in November 1978 by Rep. Leo Ryan (R-California).

The "Jonestown" that has become such a powerful symbol in American public discourse was created on November 18, 1978. As 914 people died, Jones' conversation with others on that fatal "White Night" was caught on audiotape. It reveals at least some of the rationale behind the community's extraordinary actions. It is clear from the tape that Jones had already made up his mind that the community should commit "revolutionary suicide." Referring to defections of influential members and the efforts of a group of "concerned relatives" to remove their loved ones from Jonestown, he asserts that "a handful of our people, with their lies, have made our lives impossible" in "the betrayal of the century."[74] In his comments Jones maximizes his authority as he tries to minimize the experience of death. In response to one member's objections he claims that "without me, life has no meaning" and "I am a prophet."[75] Adopting consciously biblical imagery he contends that "I made my manifestation and the world was not ready for me" and explicitly compares himself to the apostle Paul as being "a man born out of due season."[76] Jones insists that "it's just not worth living like this," referring to being besieged from without by a coalition of the media, concerned relatives, and politicians and betrayed from within by defectors from the cause. Consequently, he urged his followers to "step over to another plane" by committing revolutionary suicide.[77] In his final comments Jones interpreted the mass murder/suicide as a symbolic memorial of the cause of the Peoples Temple, arguing that "we didn't commit suicide, we committed an act of revolutionary suicide protesting the conditions of an inhumane world."[78]

In the aftermath of Jonestown, Jones' attempt to invest the deaths with symbolic meaning was quickly eclipsed by other interpretations. He became the paradigm of the unhinged cult leader who would stop at nothing to exercise his power over his followers and Jonestown became the primary cautionary tale about the dangers of cults. The symbolic power of Jonestown was thereafter frequently summoned by anticult activists to stigmatize other groups, as in Margaret Singer's comment that "Waco was a replay of Jonestown."[79] It is clear, however, that although they both drew sustenance from the biblical tradition the Peoples Temple and the Branch Davidians had very different worldviews, religious practices, ways of life, and interactions with their social environments. Only by discounting those differences can the two groups be asserted in any way to be the same. Since new religious movements themselves are highly malleable and since their relations with others are constantly shifting, the causes of the violent ends of the Peoples Temple and the Branch Davidians need to be sought in much more complex religious, social, and historical contexts. The issue of new religious movements and violence will be taken up again in chapter 8.

Christian Identity and Jews for Jesus

The biblical tradition has inspired the formation of so many sectarian and cultic groups in American history that they cannot all be discussed within the confines of this chapter. The Adventist and Latter-day Saint traditions, however, have been two of the most energetic and influential religious strands in American history and the Unification Church and the Peoples Temple have also done much to shape the contemporary perceptions of new religious movements. Discussion of two other groups will round out this chapter.

The May 31, 2003, capture of Eric Rudolph, who had been sought for the Centennial Olympic Park bombing in Atlanta as well as the bombing of a gay night club in Atlanta and a health clinic in Birmingham, Alabama, again brought the Christian Identity Movement into the public eye. Although Rudolph does not seem to have been a member of any Christian Identity church, his views and actions have pronounced similarities to the shared worldview that animates a loose conglomeration of groups and individuals on the contemporary radical right.[80] Christian Identity has its roots in the earlier and relatively benign ideology of British-Israelism, which held that white Europeans were the descendants of the lost tribes of ancient Israel. From the late 1930s on, British-Israelism attracted the attention of racist ideologues in the United States who transformed it into virulently racist and anti-Semitic religious ideology. Although there is no central organization, authority, or doctrine for the movement, it typically holds that whites are the true Israel, that Jews are literally children of Satan, that various colored "mud people" will have no share in the coming kingdom, and that the world is on the verge of an imminent transformation.[81] The statement of beliefs provided by Kingdom Identity Ministries on its Web site clearly weaves together the prominent themes of Christian Identity:

> WE BELIEVE the White, Anglo-Saxon, Germanic and kindred people to be God's true, literal children of Israel. Only this race fulfills every detail of Biblical Prophecy and World History concerning Israel and continues in these latter days to be heirs and possessors of the Covenants, Prophecies, Promises and Blessings YHVH God made to Israel. This chosen seed-line making up the "Christian Nations" (Gen. 35:11; Isa. 62:2; Acts 11:26) of the earth stands far superior to all other peoples in their call as God's servant race (Isa. 41:8, 44:21; Luke 1:54). Only these descendants of the 12 tribes of Israel scattered abroad (James 1:1; Deut. 4:27; Jer. 31:10; John 11:52) have carried God's word, the Bible, throughout the world (Gen. 28:14; Isa. 43:10–12, 59:21), have used His Laws in the establishment of their civil governments and are the "Christians" opposed by the Satanic Anti-christ forces of this world who do not recognize the true and living God (John 5:23, 8:19, 16:2–3).[82]

As the frequent recourse to biblical references in this passage shows, Christian Identity thinkers are as devoted in their own ways to searching the scriptures to support of their beliefs as any of the other groups discussed in this chapter. They devote particular ingenuity to their interpretation of Genesis. For example, Dan Gayman, leader of the Schell City, Missouri, Church of Israel has developed an influential "two seedline" theory out of his reading of Genesis 3:15, where God tells the serpent, "I will put enmity between you and the woman and between your seed and her seed." In an interpretation that recalls the treatment of the Fall in the *Divine Principle,* Gayman argues that Eve's sin was having sexual relations with Satan. From that union came Cain and then the Jews, who are literally the children of Satan. From Eve's intercourse with Adam came Abel, Abraham, and eventually the white race, the children of Adam who are made in the image of God.[83] Christian Identity adherents, therefore, see it as their religious duty to promote the survival and expansion of the white race. As Ben Klassen puts it in the sixteen commandments of *The White Man's Bible,* "it is our sacred goal to populate the lands of this earth with White people exclusively."[84]

Christian Identity adherents see a variety of forces arrayed against them. They vitriolically condemn the Jews for perpetrating a worldwide conspiracy; they see the U.S. government as being under the influence of that conspiracy; and, sometimes eagerly, they anticipate an imminent showdown with the forces of the Zionist Occupation Government.[85] Their millennial hopes are no less fervent than those of the Millerites or the early Mormon church, though they take a different form. They often advocate the violent destruction of the current world order, but only rarely have they acted on their desires. One exception was The Order, founded in 1983 by Robert Matthews. In a career that demonstrates the overlapping subcultures of the contemporary radical right, Matthews had been involved with the tax protestors' movement and the neo-Nazi National Alliance as well as the Christian Identity movement. In its brief existence before Matthews died in a gunfight with FBI agents on December 9, 1984, on Whidby Island, off the coast of Washington state, The Order was responsible for the murder of Denver talk-show host Alan Berg and a series of thefts including two armored car robberies. In a letter published after his death, Matthews asserted that "there is a small, cohesive alien group within this nation working day and night" to dilute its white population and that "thus I have no choice. I must stand up like a White man and do battle." Anticipating his own martyrdom, Matthews wrote that "the worst the enemy can do to me is shorten my tour of duty in this world. I will leave knowing that I have made the ultimate sacrifice to ensure the future of my children."[86] Despite heated discussions in the movement about the appropriate uses of violence, Christian Identity still inspires periodic outbreaks of violence and some under its umbrella see violent actors as heroes. As a posting on the Aryan Nations Web site stated after the capture of Eric Rudolph, "let His enemies gloat for their days are numbered. There will always be another to fill the shoes of a fallen hero. The enemy has not won and will never win for our victory is preordained by our Father YHVH!"[87] The passion of that statement suggests that as long as the local, national, and international conditions against which they protest remain, it seems likely that the loosely organized and thinly populated subculture of Christian Identity believers and churches will continue to attract adherents.

Many of the movements discussed in this chapter have been explicitly interested in restoring to the present a state of affairs that they imagine to have obtained in the past. So do contemporary Jews who have accepted Jesus as their Messiah. As the Messianic Jewish Alliance of America states, "Yeshua was and still is the foundation of Messianic Judaism."[88] Perhaps the most visible among the Messianic Jewish groups is the Jews for Jesus, officially founded in 1973 by Moishe Rosen, himself a Jewish convert to evangelical Christianity. The group conducts a vigorous missionary outreach, including direct personal contacts, a full Web site, a toll-free number, and an extensive publishing venture. The group currently maintains two separate Web sites, one for "believers" and one for "seekers."[89] The message of the group is simple. As their "statement of faith" asserts, "we believe that Jesus the Messiah died for our sins, according to the Scriptures."[90] The Web site for seekers includes an extensive inventory of life stories that testify to the transformative effect on individual Jews of accepting Jesus as their Messiah.[91] The site even includes several longer e-books that can be downloaded. In one of them, *Loss to Life: A Jewish Woman's Journey to Messiah,* Susan Perlman describes how a chance encounter with a Christian singer led her to a reexamination of the Bible and the eventual conclusion that Jesus was the Messiah. She summarizes her life up to that point, by writing that "I was not looking for God—but apparently God was looking for me."[92] Concerned for a while that she was the only Jew who had taken such a step, she eventually found others of her kind and concluded that "it was like 'coming home.'"[93]

As might be expected, Jews' acceptance of Jesus as the Messiah has provoked sharp reactions from within Judaism. One rabbinic opponent lumped them in with Hare Krishnas and Moonies as "one of several aberrant religious or pseudoreligious cults flourishing today on the American scene."[94] Similarly, the organization Jews for Judaism devotes itself to countering missionary efforts to convert Jews to other religions. Echoing the rhetoric of other countercult groups, it inveighs against deceptive practices adopted by missionaries and cult groups to seduce Jews away from their religion. Like Jews for Jesus, Jews for Judaism also provides a selection of vivid personal testimonials on its Web site.[95] Contemporary forms of messianic Judaism, then, are caught up in the same crossfire of claims, accusations, and responses that shapes the context for other new religious movements in the United States. Jews who embrace Jesus risk being misunderstood or worse by their families, opposed by their former coreligionists, and labeled as bizarre and deviant cultists. In responding to their critics they appeal to transformative personal experiences, purportedly transparent evidence in the scriptures, and the transcendent blessing of

God's love. Like the other new religious movements that have developed out of the biblical tradition, the messianic Jews are wrestling for control of the biblical heritage. They strive to understand both their present and future in terms of the past that through their interpretive efforts they are making new.

Conclusions

In their own ways, each of the groups discussed in this chapter would endorse David Koresh's statement that "theology really is life and death." The Adventist groups who devoutly tried to determine whether the prophesied signs of the end were indeed coming true in their own times, the Mormons who have embraced the distinctive teachings of Joseph Smith's "gold Bible," the Unificationists who have tried to unite cultures in their own married lives while anticipating a second advent, the members of the Peoples Temple who gave their lives in the cause of "divine socialism," the members of Christian Identity churches who anxiously look forward to the revolutionary reestablishment of the white race in its proper ascendancy, and the messianic Jews who have accepted Jesus as their messiah have all given evidence of a passionate commitment to theological ideas. As they have developed and promulgated their religious visions, they have all attracted other, like-minded people—enough to form distinctive religious movements, and, in many cases stable, long-lasting religious organizations. They have also, however, consistently evoked the animosity of both the religious traditions to which they have laid claim and the broader societies in which they have made their way. What has made them new and attractive to some, has made them suspicious and deviant to others. Interaction with foes of various sorts, whether the Protestant ministers who ridiculed the teachings of Mary Baker Eddy or the aggrieved family members who inspired Leo Ryan's investigation of the Peoples Temple in Guyana, became a necessary part of each group's self-definition.

Notes

1. See James D. Tabor and Eugene V. Gallagher, *Why Waco? Cults and the Battle for Religious Freedom in America* (Berkeley: University of California Press, 1995), p. 99. For other treatments of the "Waco" siege, David Koresh, and the Branch Davidi-

ans, see Dick J. Reavis, *The Ashes of Waco: An Investigation* (New York: Simon and Schuster, 1995); Stuart A. Wright, ed., *Armageddon in Waco: Critical Perspectives on the Branch Davidian Conflict* (Chicago: University of Chicago Press, 1995); and David Thibodeau and Leon Whiteson, *A Place Called Waco: A Survivor's Story* (New York: Public Affairs, 1999).

2. See, for example, some of the first wave of popular books, including Brad Bailey and Bob Darden, *Mad Man in Waco: The Complete Story of the Davidian Cult, David Koresh and the Waco Massacre* (Waco, TX: WRS, 1993); Tim Madigan, *See No Evil: Blind Devotion and Bloodshed in David Koresh's Holy War* (Fort Worth: The Summit Group, 1993); and Clifford Linedecker, *Massacre at Waco, Texas: The Shocking True Story of Cult Leader David Koresh and the Branch Davidians* (New York: St. Martin's, 1993); especially important in the public understanding of the Waco incident was former member Marc Breault's book, written with Martin King, *Inside the Cult: A Member's Chilling, Exclusive Account of Madness and Depravity in David Koresh's Compound* (New York: Signet, 1993).

3. See Tabor and Gallagher, *Why Waco?* pp. 52, 108–10, for example, and the sources cited there.

4. The *Waco Tribune-Herald*'s report was entitled "The Sinful Messiah" and its first installment was published February 27, 1993. It was quickly picked up and either reprinted verbatim or used as the primary source for coverage in the *San Francisco Chronicle*, the *New York Times*, the *Fort Worth Star Telegram*, the *Washington Post*, and the *Chicago Tribune*, among other newspapers. See Tabor and Gallagher, *Why Waco?* pp. 117–20.

5. On Montanism, see Christine Trevett, *Montanism: Gender, Authority and the New Prophecy* (Cambridge: Cambridge University Press, 1996) and Ronald E. Heine, *The Montanist Oracles and Testimonia* (Macon, GA: Mercer University Press, 1989).

6. See, for example, the thorough account in Sidney Ahlstrom, *A Religious History of the American People* (New Haven: Yale University Press, 1972); see also Catherine Albanese, *America: Religions and Religion*, 2nd ed. (Belmont, CA: Wadsworth, 1992).

7. See Miller, *America's Alternative Religions*, pp. 2–3, for a brief but thoughtful discussion of defining the mainstream.

8. On the Seventh-Day Adventists' perceptions of Koresh and his students, see Ronald Lawson, "Seventh-Day Adventist Responses to Branch Davidian Notoriety: Patterns of Diversity within a Sect Reducing Tension with Society," *Journal for the Scientific Study of Religion* 34 (1995): 323–41.

9. See Whitney R. Cross, *The Burned-over District: The Social and Intellectual History of Enthusiastic Religion in Western New York, 1800–1850* (New York: Harper's, 1965); Michael Barkun, *Crucible of the Millennium: The Burned-Over District of New York in the 1840s* (Syracuse: Syracuse University Press, 1986).

10. Henry B. Bear, *Henry B. Bear's Advent Experience* (Whitewater, Ohio, n.d.), as reproduced in Ronald L. Numbers and Jonathan M. Butler, eds., *The Disappointed: Millerism and Millenarianism in the Nineteenth Century* (Knoxville: University of Tennessee Press, 1993), pp. 217–26, passage quoted from p. 217.

11. See Philip L. Barlow, *Mormons and the Bible: The Place of the Latter-day Saints in American Religion* (Oxford: Oxford University Press, 1991), pp. 3–10.

12. On the consequences of the failure of millennial prophecies, see Jon R. Stone, ed., *Expecting Armageddon: Essential Readings in Failed Prophecy* (New York: Routledge, 2000).

13. See the statement on their official Web site at www.watchtower.org/ library/ rq/article_13.htm.

14. In general, see M. James Penton, *Apocalypse Delayed: the Story of Jehovah's Witnesses,* 2nd ed. (Toronto: University of Toronto Press, 1997), pp. 127–56, 191–93; for an account of growing up in the Jehovah's Witnesses, see Barbara Grizutti Harrison, *Visions of Glory: A History and Memory of Jehovah's Witnesses* (New York: Touchstone, 1978).

15. On the tension between maintaining millennialist commitment and accommodating to the world in the Seventh-Day Adventist Church, see Kenneth Newport, "The Heavenly Millennium of Seventh-Day Adventists," in Stephen Hunt, ed., *Christian Millennialism: From the Early Church to Waco* (Bloomington: Indiana University Press, 2001), pp. 131–48, esp. pp. 132, 142, 143, 146; and Ronald Lawson, "The Persistence of Apocalypticism within a Denominationalizing Sect," in Thomas Robbins and Susan J. Palmer, eds., *Millennialism, Messiahs, and Mayhem: Contemporary Apocalyptic Movements* (New York: Routledge, 1997), pp. 207–28.

16. As quoted in Penton, *Apocalypse Delayed,* p. 32.

17. FBI transcript of negotiation Tape 130, March 16, 1993, p. 20. Taped conversations between FBI negotiators and the Branch Davidians are available in transcript form at the FBI reading room at the Bureau's Hoover Building headquarters in Washington, D.C. Tapes will be referred to by number, date, and page of the transcript.

18. Koresh, "The Seven Seals of the Book of Revelation," in Tabor and Gallagher, *Why Waco?* p. 197.

19. Negotiation Tape 87, March 7, 1993, p. 26.

20. See www.watchtower.org/library/w/2001/7/1/article_01.htm.

21. For a detailed account of the Seventh-Day Adventist understanding of the sabbath, see www.adventist.org/beliefs/other_doc6.html.

22. See www.adventist.org/beliefs/index.html; statement #17.

23. See ibid., statement #19.

24. See the references in Barkun, *Crucible of the Millennium,* p. 41; Penton, *Apocalypse Delayed,* p. 43; and Tabor and Gallagher, *Why Waco?* pp. 117–30.

25. See Ankerberg and Weldon, *Encyclopedia of Cults and New Religions,* pp. 127–209. Similarly, Walter Martin's *The Kingdom of the Cults* (Minneapolis: Bethany House, 1997) devotes more space to the Witnesses than to any other example.

26. See www.rickross.com/groups/witness.html.

27. See www.freedomofmind.com/resourcecenter/groups/j/jehovah/.

28. See www.watchman.org/profile/sdapro.htm.

29. Walter Martin, "The Puzzle of Seventh-day Adventism," in idem, *The Kingdom of the Cults,* pp. 517–608, passage quoted from p. 517.

30. "Joseph Smith—History," pp. 19–20, available at www.scriptures.lds.org/js_h/1.

31. Ibid., p. 33.

32. On Mormon millennialism, see Grant Underwood, *The Millenarian World of Early Mormonism* (Urbana: University of Illinois Press, 1993).

33. See Shipps, *Mormonism,* pp. 67–85.

34. See www.scriptures.lds.org/a_of_f/1.

35. For a brief account and analysis, see Shipps, *Mormonism,* pp. 104–6. For this period in the broader context of Mormon history, see Leonard J. Arrington and Davis Bitton, *The Mormon Experience: A History of the Latter-day Saints,* 2nd ed. (Urbana: University of Illinois Press, 1992).

36. On contemporary Mormon polygamous groups, see Irwin Altman and Joseph Ginat, *Polygamous Families in Contemporary Society* (Cambridge: Cambridge University Press, 1996).

37. See, for example, Ankerberg and Weldon, *Encyclopedia of Cults and New Religions,* pp. 274–338.

38. See Shipps, *Mormonism.*

39. See Rodney Stark, "How New Religions Succeed: A Theoretical Model," in David G. Bromley and Phillip E. Hammond, eds., *The Future of New Religious Movements* (Macon, GA: Mercer University Press, 1987), pp. 11–29, esp. p. 13.

40. From Mary Baker Eddy, *The Manual of the Mother Church,* p. 17; electronic version available at www.mebinstitute.org/Prose_Works/Manual.doc.

41. Mary Baker Eddy, *Science and Health with Key to the Scriptures* (1875; rpt. Boston: The First Church of Christ, Scientist, 1994), p. 468.

42. Ibid.

43. See Stephen Gottschalk, *The Emergence of Christian Science in American Religious Life* (Berkeley: University of California Press, 1973), p. 36.

44. Ibid., p. 497.

45. Ibid., p. 55.

46. See ibid., p. 4.

47. Ibid., p. 17.

48. For a full treatment of this incident, see Gottschalk, *The Emergence of Christian Science,* pp. xv–xxix.

49. For the text of the address, see www.mbeinstitute.org/Prose_Works/MiscWriting_PartTwo.html.

50. Ibid.

51. On the early history of splintering, see Gottschalk, *The Emergence of Christian Science,* pp. 114–24, 254, 284–85. On New Thought today, see www.newthoughthome.com/. For the Unity School today, see www.unityworldhq.org/. For Religious Science today, see www.religiousscience.org/. See also the brief summary of fragmentation in Barrett, *The New Believers,* pp. 179–80.

52. See, for example, the brief testimonies at www.tfccs.com/gv/SH/SHHealing.jhtml.

53. See www.rickross.com/groups/cscience.html.

54. On the court cases, see Caroline Fraser, "Suffering Children and the Christian Science Church," *The Atlantic Monthly,* April 1995, available at www.theatlantic.com/unbound/flashbks/xsci/suffer.htm; see also Fraser's full-length critique of the church, *God's Perfect Child: Living and Dying in the Christian Science Church* (New York: Metropolitan, 1999); see also the Web site of CHILD, Inc., an organization founded by former Christian Scientists, www.childrenshealthcare.org/.

55. See, for example, www.pbs.org/wnet/religionandethics/week624/cover.html. The church does not make membership figures public.

56. "Sun Myung Moon," in Michael Mickler, ed., *The Unification Church II: Inner Life* (New York: Garland, 1990), p. 108.

57. Ibid., p. 3.

58. Anonymous, *Divine Principle* (New York: The Holy Spirit Association for the Unification of World Christianity, 1973), p. 10; on the authorship of the *Divine Principle,* see George D. Chryssides, *The Advent of Sun Myung Moon: The Beliefs and Practices of the Unification Church* (London: Macmillan, 1991), pp. 23–24.

59. See David G. Bromley and Anson D. Shupe Jr., *"Moonies" in America: Cult, Church, and Crusade* (Beverly Hills, CA: Sage, 1979), p. 65.

60. See Christopher Edwards, *Crazy for God* (Englewood Cliffs, NJ: Prentice-Hall, 1979) and Barbara and Betty Underwood, *Hostage to Heaven* (New York: Clarkson N. Potter, 1979). For an analysis of these two books and the issue of conversion to the Unification Church, see Gallagher, *Expectation and Experience*, pp. 63–86.

61. For a sociological theory of conversion based on early fieldwork with members of the Unification Church, see John Lofland and Rodney Stark, "Becoming a World-Saver: A Theory of Conversion to a Deviant Perspective," *American Sociological Review* 30 (1965): 862–74 and John Lofland, "Becoming a World-Saver Revisited," in James T. Richardson, ed., *Conversion Careers: In and Out of the New Religions* (Beverly Hills: Sage, 1978), pp. 10–23. For the fullest treatment of conversion to the Unification Church, see Eileen Barker, *The Making of a Moonie: Choice or Brainwashing* (Oxford: Basil Blackwell, 1984).

62. Underwood, *Hostage to Heaven*, p. 44.

63. See Chryssides, *The Advent of Sun Myung Moon*, pp. 131–48.

64. See www.unification.org/intro_blessing.html.

65. For a report on recent Blessings, see Massimo Introvigne, "From the Unification Church to the Unification Movement, 1994–1999: Five Years of Dramatic Changes," at www.cesnur.org/testi/moon_1199.htm.

66. See Nansook Hong, *In the Shadow of the Moons: My Life in Reverend Sun Myung Moon's Family* (Boston: Little, Brown, 1998).

67. See the news articles archived at www.rickross.com/groups/moonie.html.

68. See, for example, David Chidester, *Salvation and Suicide: An Interpretation of Jim Jones, the Peoples Temple, and Jonestown* (Bloomington: University of Indiana Press, 1988), p. 7; John R. Hall, *Gone from the Promised Land: Jonestown in American Cultural History* (New Brunswick, NJ: Transaction, 1987), pp. 50–52, 72–73. On Father Divine, see Jill Watts, *God, Harlem U.S.A.: The Father Divine Story* (Berkeley: University of California Press, 1992).

69. Jeannie Mills, *Six Years with God, Life Inside Rev. Jim Jones's Peoples Temple* (New York: A & W, 1979), p. 117.

70. See ibid., pp. 118–21.

71. See Chidester, *Salvation and Suicide*, pp. 64–67.

72. See ibid., pp. 82–85, 107–9.

73. See Mary McCormick Maaga, *Hearing the Voices of Jonestown: Putting a Human Face on an American Tragedy* (Syracuse: Syracuse University Press, 1998), p. 8, for example.

74. I follow the transcript in ibid., pp. 147–64, quotation from p. 147. For several versions of the transcript and a wealth of other materials, see the site maintained by Rebecca Moore at www.jonestown.sdsu.edu/.

75. Maaga, *Hearing the Voices of Jonestown*, p. 151.

76. Ibid., p. 154.

77. Ibid., pp. 162, 161.

78. Ibid., p. 164.

79. Singer, *Cults in Our Midst*, p. 28.

80. On Rudolph, see www.abcnews.go.com/sections/us/WorldNewsTonight/rudolph_beliefs030531.html.

81. For summaries and analyses of Christian Identity ideas, see Barkun, *Religion and the Racist Right* and Kaplan, *Radical Religion in America*.

82. See www.kingidentity.com/doctrine.htm.

83. For an analysis of Gayman's exegesis, see Scott R. Stroud, "Tales of Hate and *Differance*: A Narrative Analysis of Gayman's 'The Book of Adam,'" *Speaker and Gavel* 39 (2002): 23–35; also available at www.members.aol.com/stroud76/ gman.htm.

84. Ben Klassen, *The White Man's Bible* (Billings, MT: Creativity Book Store, 1981), p. 436.

85. See Jeffrey Kaplan, "Real Paranoids Have Real Enemies: The Genesis of the ZOG Discourse in the American National Socialist Subculture," in Catherine Wessinger, ed., *Millennialism, Violence, and Persecution: Historical Cases* (Syracuse: Syracuse University Press, 2000), pp. 299–322.

86. As quoted in Kaplan, *Radical Religion in America,* p. 63.

87. Original text preserved at www.publiceye.org/rightist/rudolph.html. I retain the idiosyncratic capitalization of the original.

88. See www.jmaa.org/resources/revival/standard.html.

89. See www.jews-for-jesus.com.

90. www.jfjonline.org/about/statementoffaith.htm.

91. See, for example, www.jewsforjesus.org/stories/index.htm.

92. See www.jewsforjesus.org/library/ebooks.htm, p. 12.

93. Ibid., p. 18.

94. Roland B. Gittelsohn, "Jews for Jesus: Are they Real?" in Eisenberg, ed., *Smashing the Idols,* pp. 164–73, passage quoted from p. 171.

95. See www.jewsforjudaism.org/web/mainpages/stories.html.

Chapter 3

The New Age and Its Antecedents

One evening in the early 1980s a young man rang the doorbell of a beach house in Malibu, California. He had been referred to the owner by a mutual acquaintance. By the time Kevin Ryerson met Shirley MacLaine, she had become deeply enmeshed in what she described as her "quest for my self."[1] MacLaine's thirst for spiritual enlightenment had taken her all over the world and introduced her to wide array of spiritual practitioners. Ryerson himself had earned a substantial reputation as a "very well-respected trance medium."[2] Primed by an earlier visit to a Swedish channeler and months of reading, MacLaine was eager to explore what Ryerson could offer her. Before getting to the actual channeling session, Ryerson described how he began to serve as a channel between this world and another one. He admitted that "I didn't know what was happening to me either when this all first started. . . . Spirit came through during one of my meditations. I didn't even know it. But someone ran and got a tape recorder and got the whole thing."[3] In statements that echoed the claims of Joseph Smith and the Rev. Sun Myung Moon, Ryerson emphasized that he had not sought his function as a bridge between two worlds but that he was completely convinced that spiritual guides were speaking through him. Whatever an audience did with the channeled messages, he assured MacLaine, was up to them. In Ryerson's view of the world, receiving spiritual guidance from another realm was virtually a commonplace. When asked whether spiritual guides are available to everyone, Ryerson replied, "Why sure, that's what the soul does after it passes out of the body. Souls that have died, so to speak, help those who are still in the body. Why, that's what spiritual understanding is all about."[4]

In the religious world described in Shirley MacLaine's best-selling memoir, *Out on a Limb,* moments of communication between disembodied spiritual entities and people in this world are thrilling but, in some ways, unexceptional. MacLaine recounts her travels through the contemporary landscape of New Age spirituality with the same matter-of-fact tone that she uses to detail her various love affairs and her professional life as an actress and dancer. In the 1980s perhaps no other person did as much as Shirley MacLaine to popularize a variety of practices and beliefs usually grouped under the umbrella category of the New Age. In particular, she embedded in the public consciousness the notion that there was a host of entities in a spiritual realm who were eager to converse with persons in this world in order to promote their spiritual development.

That idea, like the New Age worldview of which it is a part, was not as new as some of its proponents thought. In fact, the New Age Movement itself is part of a long history of alternative religion in Western civilization that goes back to at least the first centuries of the Common Era.[5] The contemporary New Age Movement also has prominent predecessors in American history. MacLaine was not the first person to seek help from spirits of the deceased, nor was Kevin Ryerson the first to offer it. Ryerson's notion that "souls that have died . . . help those who are still in the body" expresses a widespread theme in religious life and responds to what William James identified as "the core of the religious problem: Help! Help!"[6] As one contemporary group soothingly puts it, "the masters are here to help you in every area of life."[7] Many Americans have sought such help from those who have left this material world. They have developed and participated in a variety of ritual practices for establishing such communication, such as the channeling session in which MacLaine and Ryerson took part. They have also identified legions of disembodied spirits who offer everything from simple reassurances to extensive discourses on human and divine nature. The claimed ability to establish communication with another world has empowered thousands of Americans, a notable number of women among them, to become religious leaders and their claims have also attracted the suspicion, scrutiny and, often, ridicule of unbelieving audiences.

Although figures like Jesus do make occasional appearances, the groups in this chapter typically locate themselves well outside the biblical tradition, either by tapping other primary sources of inspiration or by offering such idiosyncratic interpretations of biblical themes and figures that they persuade very few of their orthodoxy. Also, while groups in the previous chapter often focused their energies on forming ideal human communities, often in anticipation of the imminent transformation of the world as we know it, groups in this chapter focus on the transformation of the individual self and often downplay the importance of community. Along with that focus on the cultivation of the self comes a relative indifference to the founding and maintenance of stable organizations. As MacLaine's movement in and out of brief relationships with providers of spiritual services suggests, many of the figures and groups discussed in this chapter grew out of a fertile cultic milieu in the United States over the past 150 years. As the example of nineteenth-century Spiritualism will show, there seems to have been a very broad audience that was interested in communication with the spirits of the dead. But, due largely to Spiritualism's insistence that the individual was "the ultimate vehicle of truth,"[8] it proved very difficult to form and maintain any significant Spiritualist organizations. As MacLaine's encounter with Kevin Ryerson also suggests, the focus on the cultivation of the spiritual self fosters interactions in which the individual, as a client, seeks specific, limited benefits from a series of religious providers. The emphasis is more on what the individual can gain than on the bonding together of individuals into a lasting community.

Despite their distinctive differences in leadership, doctrine, practices, and organizational form, the groups in this chapter share with those in chapter 2 a concern to legitimize their practices and beliefs with reference to some superior authority. In many instances they also root themselves in a past already conceded to have broad legitimacy. For example, the Church Universal and Triumphant of Mark and Elizabeth Clare Prophet asserts that it is "sponsored by the ascended masters Jesus Christ and Gautama Buddha."[9] Others range much farther afield. Ramtha, the entity channeled by JZ Knight, claims to be 35,000 years old and to have lived in Lemuria, at the northern end of the lost continent of Atlantis.[10] But in the mid-nineteenth century Spiritualism largely eschewed appeals to history and mythology in favor of claiming a scientific basis for its communication with spirits of the dead. Clearly, the ways in which an individual or group appeals to a legitimizing authority also determines the audiences most likely to respond positively, and negatively, to its message. Although even a persisting client relationship may not be strong enough and complete enough to warrant being called a conversion, the groups in this chapter have attracted, and continue to engage, their own partisans. As with other new or alternative religious movements, their slightest success has been met with social opposition of various sorts. Thus, the groups in this chapter find themselves entangled in the same thicket of claims and counterclaims that has ensnared other groups identified as cults. That social opposition has shaped both the self-understanding of groups and their adherents and the ways that they have presented themselves to an often curious but wary populace.

Spiritualism

The same region of Upper New York State that gave birth to the Church of Jesus Christ of Latter-day Saints in the 1820s and the Millerite Movement in the 1840s was also the cradle of modern Spiritualism. On March 31, 1848, in Hydesville, near Rochester, two young sisters, Margaret and Kate Fox, declared that they had discovered the source behind a series of curious "rappings" that they had been hearing for several months in their home. Initially, the sisters claimed to be in contact with a former resident of the house who had been murdered. As word of their extraordinary abilities spread, however, they added a roster of other spirits to their list of interlocutors. The spirits initially communicated in rudimentary fashion, answering simple questions with one rap for a "yes" and two for a "no" or by spelling out words by making sounds when appropriate letters of the alphabet were recited. By 1850 a positive notice in Horace Greeley's *New York Tribune* and a summer stay in New York City had turned the Fox sisters into public celebrities and spurred the appearance of other Spiritualist mediums throughout the northeastern United States.

One of the prominent things that Spiritualist mediums offered was consolation to those who had lost loved ones. For example, a message to a mother informed her that "your little seraph boy is not *dead,* but *liveth*. In his uncontaminated love, find comfort for the ills of life."[11] That message put the facts of the matter in a radically different light. What appeared to be death was really life; the existence of another, better realm was confirmed, and since living communication was possible between seraphs and mortals, the trials of this life were ameliorated. As Clifford Geertz has argued, the contribution of religion to the problem of human suffering is not to obliterate suffering, because that would be impossible, but to make suffering meaningful, bearable, and acceptable.[12] Spiritualist communication with spirits of the dead did that by repairing the breach between this world and the world of the spirits and restoring relationships that had been sundered by death.

As practiced by the Fox sisters and the hundreds of spirit mediums who appeared in their wake, Spiritualism was more an ad hoc ritual procedure designed to promote communication than it was the expression of a fully developed religious system. It implied a theology but did not grow out of a fully articulated one. Spiritualism found a congenial metaphysical system, however, in the "Harmonial Philosophy" of Andrew Jackson Davis, originally developed a few years before the Hydesville "rappings." Davis claimed to have been inspired to compose his own comprehensive work, *The Principles of Nature, Her Divine Revelations, and a Voice to Mankind* by experiencing a vision of the Swedish mystic and philosopher Emmanuel Swedenborg. Swedenborg himself had followed a successful career as a scientist with an extended period of visionary encounters with God, Jesus, and other spiritual entities. Davis believed that Swedenborg had now appeared to him and promised that further communications from the spirit world would soon be forthcoming. Davis's new revelation made little headway until he linked it with the spiritual manifestations that began with the Fox sisters.[13] Although it was the vividness and immediacy of the work of Spiritualist mediums that made them popular, Davis's system set Spiritualist phenomena into a coherent worldview for anyone with the inclination to investigate it.

As the example of the Fox sisters shows, Spiritualism also offered many women the possibility of exercising religious leadership that they could not claim in other settings. Spiritualism both contributed members to the burgeoning women's rights movement and other reform efforts and attracted some of those movements' most prominent members.[14] Its emphasis on individualism, absence of dogma, and rejection of organizational control over members promoted the participation of individuals in progressive social causes. An openness to women's religious leadership has remained one of the defining characteristics of movements that focus on the reception and transmission of messages from disembodied spirits, from nineteenth-century Spiritualism to the contemporary New Age. In the case of Spiritualism, women were able to turn perceived weaknesses of their gender, such as their purported passivity, into the bases of a special receptivity to communication from the world of spirits.[15] Variations on that theme can be found in contemporary groups as well.

As the Spiritualist movement grew, mediums branched out into other forms of demonstrating their intimacy with the spirit world. Trance mediums gave public lectures, and more spectacular attempts to have the spirits make visual or auditory manifestations captured the public imagination.

Musical instrument levitates at séance. © Hulton-Deutsch Collection/CORBIS.

Ann Braude has observed that "trance speakers were the missionaries of Spiritualism, and their far-reaching itinerancy aided the rapid spread of the movement."[16] But with its rising popularity, Spiritualism also acquired substantial opposition. In 1857, after Harvard University had expelled a divinity student for fraudulently posing as a medium, the *Boston Courier* challenged proponents of Spiritualism to demonstrate their claims before a panel of Harvard scientists, with a $500 reward as an incentive. All who attended agreed that the spirit manifestations were very weak, and the panel concluded that any involvement with Spiritualism "corrupts the morals and degrades the intellect."[17] Despite its similarity to Transcendentalism's conception of nature as filled with divinity, Spiritualism also received scathing comments from Ralph Waldo Emerson.[18] But it was Spiritualism's challenge to the entrenched Biblicism of the Christian churches that earned the strongest opposition. One critic warned that "spiritualism is fraught with great evil to those who are foolish enough to welcome it as a new religion, and a substitute for Christianity."[19]

Despite its efforts to portray itself as based on empirical observation, Spiritualism continually suffered from exposure of the chicanery practiced by many mediums. The constant tension between Spiritualism and its cultural opponents, along with its strict reliance on individual freedom in investigating spiritual matters and concomitant disinterest in developing stable organizations, contributed to the marked decline in public support for Spiritualism in the period after the Civil War. The conflict between individualists and those who favored forming an organizational body for Spiritualism was played out in successive national conventions. One of the most popular mediums of her time, Cora Hatch, told the Second National Convention in 1865, "I am *bitterly* opposed to religious organizations of any kind—to anything that fetters or binds the human mind."[20] But the delegates to the convention voted against the impassioned pleas of Hatch and other mediums and established the American Association of Spiritualists. That organization, however, was to have a brief and stormy life, and it wasn't until 1893, well past the peak in Spiritualism's popularity, that an organization was founded, the National Association of Spiritualists, that still exists.

Since its incorporation, the National Association of Spiritualists, now known as the National Spiritualist Association of Churches (NSAC), has been recognized as the primary legal entity that represents Spiritualist churches. Its stated goals are

- to teach the truths and principles expressed in the Declaration of Principles and in the Definitions of "Spiritualism," "Spiritualist," "Medium," and "Spiritualist Healer" as adopted by the National Spiritualist Association of Churches of the United States of America
- to teach and proclaim the Science, Philosophy, and Religion of Modern Spiritualism
- to encourage lectures on all subjects pertaining to the spiritual and secular welfare of humanity
- to protest against every attempt to compel humanity to worship God in any particular or prescribed manner

- to advocate and promote spiritual healing and to protect and encourage Spiritualist teachers and mediums in all laudable efforts in giving evidence to humanity of a continued communication between the living and the so-called dead
- to encourage every person to hold his or her beliefs always open to examination as growing thought and investigation reveal new understanding of truths thereby leaving every individual free to follow the dictates of reason and conscience in spiritual as well as secular affairs[21]

As these statements show, the NSAC has incorporated into its declaration of objectives the same tensions that complicated its founding. On the one hand, it rejects any attempts to impose a certain kind of worship on anybody, but on the other, it strives to organize Spiritualist churches and to articulate substantial areas of agreement among practitioners. Prominent among those common ideas are the beliefs that "the personal identity of the individual continue[s] after the change called death" and that "communication with the so-called dead is a fact, scientifically proven by the phenomena of Spiritualism."[22]

But efforts to describe, let alone implement, a Spiritualist orthodoxy have always been undermined by the unfettered exercise of individuality that has marked modern Spiritualism since its beginnings in 1848. The First Spiritual Temple of Brookline, Massachusetts, provides an example of the diversity of contemporary Spiritualism. It was founded by Marcellus Seth Ayer on June 28, 1883, and its teaching encompasses a wide range of influences. It explicitly acknowledges its eclecticism, noting that "the scope of our teaching ministry ranges from more traditional Christian theology, to modern and ancient Spiritualism, to parapsychology, to metaphysics and what is known as the Ancient Wisdom."[23] The First Spiritual Temple explicitly disagrees with the NSAC on the question of reincarnation, for example, and argues that on such issues "much of the contradiction seems to come from within the more traditional Spiritualist movement."[24] The eclecticism of the First Spiritual Temple indicates that within contemporary Spiritualism, as throughout its history, it is much easier to identify similarities of practice and belief from a distance than it is to establish them as binding on any individuals or groups. The primacy of the individual investigator in Spiritualism virtually guarantees the continual appearance and reappearance of authoritative groups and teachers as they rise up from and return into the fertile cultic milieu that seeks and receives communications from the spirit world.

Theosophy

The religious ferment produced by the spread of Spiritualism in the 1870s also facilitated a fateful meeting that would quickly produce another new religious development. When a New York City lawyer, Col. Henry Steel Olcott, heard of extraordinary happenings at the Eddy homestead in Chittenden, Vermont, he decided to investigate in person. The Eddy children were renowned for their "materializations," which made visible to those in attendance everything from musical instruments to deceased family members. Olcott reported his observations in the *New York Sun* and was soon engaged by another newspaper, the *Daily Graphic*, to return for a longer period during the summer and fall of 1874 and issue twice-weekly reports.[25] Olcott's dispatches caught the eye of a mysterious Russian emigre, Helena Petrovna Blavatsky, or "HPB," who decided to go to Vermont to see for herself what the spirits were up to and to see if she could garner publicity from Olcott for her own efforts as a spirit medium. Her fondest hopes were quickly rewarded. As Col. Olcott recalls their first meeting, "I found she had been a great traveler and seen many occult things and adepts in occult science, but at first she did not give me any hint as to the existence of the Himalayan Sages or of her own powers. She spoke of the materialistic tendency of American spiritualism, which was a sort of debauch of phenomena accompanied by comparative indifferences to philosophy."[26] The nucleus of the Theosophical Society that Olcott and Blavatsky would start in 1875 was contained in that statement. It unites HPB's shadowy biography, her focus on Eastern wisdom derived from the Tibetan Masters Morya and Koot Hoomi, her exalted sense of self, and a critique of inadequacies of Spiritualism. Blavatsky's deliberately cultivated air of mystery would be a prominent feature of her religious leadership throughout her career.

The theosophy, or "divine wisdom," that HPB taught was centered on the communications that she received from the group of Mahatmas, Masters, or Adepts.[27] They revealed to her a coherent system of ancient teaching that predated any of the world's religions. As she put it in *Isis Unveiled,* "the secret doctrines of the Magi, of the pre-Vedic Buddhists, of the hierophants of the Egyptian Thoth or Hermes, and of the adepts of whatever age and nationality, including the Chaldean kabalists and the Jewish *nazars,* were *identical* from the beginning."[28] In HPB's conception all wisdom flows from a single source; through her writings she is recovering and representing an original oneness of spiritual insight that has been lost through the historical vicissitudes of individual religious traditions. Though very different in its details, Blavatsky's project of reviving ancient wisdom has structural similarities to the Mormon quest to restore the situation of the early Christian church, for example.

Echoing the claims of her Spiritualist predecessors and her New Age successors, Blavatsky denied that she was, in fact, the author of her teachings. She was, instead, simply the conduit through which they flowed. As she described her experience in a letter to her sister Vera,

> something miraculous is happening to me. You cannot imagine in what a charmed world of pictures and visions I live. I am writing *Isis;* not writing, rather copying out and drawing that which She personally shows to me. Upon my word, sometimes it seems to me that the ancient Goddess of Beauty in person leads me through all the countries of past centuries which I have to describe. I sit with my eyes open and to all appearances see and hear everything real and actual around me, and yet at the same time I see and hear that which I write. I feel short of breath; I am afraid to make the slightest movement for fear the spell might be broken. Slowly century after century, image after image, float out of the distance and pass before me as if in a magic panorama; and meanwhile I put them together in my mind, fitting in epochs and dates, and know *for sure* that there can be *no mistake.*[29]

Blavatsky's spirit contacts differed substantially from those typical in Spiritualism. She had no time for facilitating comforting family reunions between the living and dead. She concentrated instead on contacting the most authoritative sources of religious wisdom. She had little interest, for example, in "either the exoteric Buddhism instituted by the followers of Gautama-Buddha, nor the modern Buddhistic religion"; her focus was on "the secret philosophy of Sakyamuni, which in its essence is certainly identical with the ancient wisdom-religion of the sanctuary, the pre-Vedic brahmanism."[30]

As HPB explained in *The Secret Doctrine,* the unified ancient wisdom consists of three foundational propositions. First, it posits the existence of an omnipresent, eternal, boundless, and immutable principle that is the one Absolute Reality. Second, it asserts that in the boundless plane of the

Helena Blavatsky

eternal universe there is an absolute universality of the "law of periodicity, of flux and reflux, ebb and flow." Finally, it affirms the fundamental identity between individual souls and the universal "over-soul," or between the individual and the universe. HPB asserts that "the pivotal doctrine of the Esoteric philosophy admits no privileges or special gifts in man, save those won by his own Ego through personal effort and merit throughout a long series of metempsychoses and reincarnations."[31] Within the abstract worldview sketched out by those propositions, human nature has two aspects. Humans are seen as sparks of the divine essence temporarily incarnated in matter. Their task, in each of their incarnations, is to evolve toward their higher, immortal being. As Blavatsky put it in *The Secret Doctrine*, "it is the Spiritual evolution of the *inner,* immortal man that forms the fundamental tenet in the Occult Sciences."[32] That evolution can be furthered by dedicated application to the study of the teachings of the Mahatmas, particularly as mediated through HPB herself.

The convoluted esoteric teachings of HPB and the Theosophical Society lacked the drama and immediacy of Spiritualist seances. Blavatsky's contact with the Mahatmas did not yield heart-warming epigrams but ponderous tomes of metaphysical speculation. Accordingly, the Theosophical Society never experienced the popular approval that Spiritualism had in its heyday. It attracted largely middle- and upper-class individuals, alienated to an extent from conventional society and possessing the leisure and means to pursue their occult interests. In Bruce Campbell's formulation, Theosophy appealed to individuals who saw themselves as "solitary cosmic pilgrims."[33]

Although the Theosophical Society appealed more narrowly than Spiritualism to seekers after occult wisdom who were willing to do the requisite "lots of plain, hard thinking,"[34] its limited audience did not help it avoid criticism. From the start, Madame Blavatsky was branded a plagiarist and charlatan. HPB's initially cordial relations with Spiritualists, beginning with her experiences at the Eddy homestead in Vermont, had quickly turned sour after the formation of the Theosophical Society in 1875. By March 1876, HPB offered a scathing denunciation of Spiritualism in a letter. Casting herself as a martyr because of the opposition to her teaching, HPB exclaimed, "indeed happy am I if, in losing my reputation, I save millions who are lost now in the illusion that all spirits who communicate with them are angels of purity, disembodied spirits. . . . remember that my worst enemies, they who do not stop at any baseness, any infamy, are the spiritualists and the mediums."[35] In the same letter HPB contrasts the vitriolic opposition to the Theosophical Society to the sober efforts of its members, asking,

> and why this hate which nothing can soften, this constant malign frenzied persecution which in itself would transform a criminal, a thief, and a mother of harlots into a martyr? All this because our Society is composed at this time of seventy-nine members, and all instructed people, and almost all, although skeptics, ardently desirous of being convinced of the grand truth of immortality, of spirit intercourse working to separate the good seed from the heap of manure, in order to assure and to prove to others there is a world of spirits discarnate, composed of liberated souls labouring to progress and be purified in order to mount higher in approaching the grand divine Source, God, the great Principle, pure and invisible.[36]

Much of the critical attention directed to HPB focused on the claims that she merely received, rather than composed, the messages from the Masters. In the early 1880s, for example, Emma Coulomb, who was then working at the Indian headquarters of the Theosophical Society in Adyar, published a series of letters from HPB that detailed how HPB produced "apparitions" through the manipulation of dummies and dolls. In 1884, the recently formed Society for Psychical Research published a report based on firsthand research that branded HPB "one of the most accomplished, ingenious, and interesting imposters in history."[37] In addition, one Spiritualist investigator of *Isis Unveiled* claimed to find nearly two thousand plagiarized passages in it.[38] Despite her efforts to fend them off, HPB continued to be hounded by accusations of plagiarism and general fakery until her death in 1891.

While HPB and her followers were coping with external attacks, the Theosophical Society itself was undergoing significant organizational transformations. By the end of 1878 HPB and Col. Olcott had moved to India, settling first in Bombay and then establishing a headquarters for the Theosophical Society in Adyar, Madras, which remains today an important center for Theosophy. For a time, HPB moved back and forth between India and Europe, settling eventually in London, where she established the European headquarters of the Theosophical Society in 1890, a year before her death. Despite her rigorous travels, HPB kept up a vigorous writing schedule that eventually produced *The Secret Doctrine* in 1888 and *The Key to Theosophy* and *The Voice of Silence* in the following year.

In the last years of her life HPB's relations with Col. Olcott became strained. When she went off to Europe, he stayed behind in Adyar. She wanted more power over the Theosophical Society for herself and he resisted. Among other things the conflict between the two founders of the Theosophical Society centered on different visions of leadership, with HPB favoring the continuance of her charismatic authority and Olcott attending to the maintenance of an organizational structure.[39] After a very complex set of interactions among various claimants to authority in the movement, three prominent theosophical organizations emerged in the years following the death of HPB. Following Olcott, Annie Besant assumed the leadership of the Theosophical Society based in Adyar, India. Through her energetic efforts at spreading the message, the Society saw an upsurge in membership. The leadership of the American section of the Society, which had declared its independence under the influence of William Q. Judge in 1895, fell to Katherine Tingley. Most notable among her projects was the establishment of an utopian community at Point Loma, California. Finally, in the early twentieth century Robert Crosbie founded the United Lodge of Theosophists, dedicated to the propagation and study of the writings of HPB.[40]

Among other things, Besant was instrumental in proclaiming a young Indian, Jiddu Krishnamurti, the heralded World Teacher, a mission from which he eventually withdrew in 1929. Although he abandoned the Theosophical Society and denied any interest in attracting followers or in founding an alternative organization, Krishnamurti kept up an active career as a spiritual teacher until his death in 1986.[41] Alice Bailey also helped spread theosophical ideas in the early decades of the twentieth century. After some conflicts with Besant, she founded the Arcane School in New York in 1923. Bailey claimed to compose her work under the direction of the Tibetan Master Djwal Kul. The school continues to offer correspondence courses "to help the student grow spiritually toward acceptance of discipleship responsibility and to serve the Plan by serving humanity."[42]

The "I AM" Religious Activity and the Church Universal and Triumphant

The fragmentation of the Theosophical Society after the death of HPB helped to diffuse ideas about traditions of esoteric wisdom throughout American culture. Despite HPB's best efforts, she was never able to impose an orthodoxy on Theosophists and other spiritual explorers. Individuals like Alice Bailey felt free to receive and promulgate their own communications from the Masters and to offer guidance to those who wanted to realize their full human potential. In the work of others, HPB's concept of the Masters as highly evolved human beings who have voluntarily incarnated in order to facilitate communication between humans and the members of the "Great White Brotherhood" was adapted to new circumstances and experiences. Different religious visionaries formed relationships with different members of the Brotherhood, making some Masters much more prominent in some groups than others. The Masters shared, however, an astonishing volubility; they continued to go far beyond the simple "yes" or "no" answers and laboriously spelled out responses that characterized early Spiritualist contacts with the beyond. When the Masters have contacted someone on earth, they have apparently always had a lot to say.

In 1930, an "Ascended Master" from outside the circle of Theosophical familiars contacted Guy Ballard at Mount Shasta in California. Apparently to facilitate his understanding, he handed Ballard a cup filled with liquid "directly from the Universal Supply, pure and vivifying as Life Itself; in fact it is Life—Omnipresent Life."[43] The being who appeared to him confirmed Ballard's special status, saying that "I see within you a certain Inner Understanding of the Great Law,"[44] and then launched into a long discourse concerning the processes through which human beings could realize their true, divine nature. Ballard quickly realized that he was in the presence of the Ascended Master Saint Germain, who revealed that he had been subtly guiding Ballard since his birth.[45] Ballard's story of his initial encounter with Saint Germain puts him in the company of figures like Joseph Smith and Sun Myung Moon, who were also recruited by supernatural figures to serve as their messengers. His commissioning to preach a new message also fits a common pattern in the lives of prophetic figures throughout history.[46] In time, Saint Germain also designated Ballard's wife, Edna, and son, Donald, as messengers.

Although the messages that Ballard continued to receive were quite elaborate, at their core was a positive and uplifting assertion. As Ballard said of his own book, "those who accept the Truth herein recorded will find a new and powerful 'Force' entering their lives. Each copy carries with it this Mighty Presence, Its Radiation and Sustaining Power. All who study these pages honestly, deeply, sincerely, and persistently, will know and make contact with the Reality of that Presence and Power."[47] Saint Germain wanted Ballard to assure human beings that "every individual has the Divine Flame of Life within, and That God Self of him has Dominion wherever he moves in the universe."[48] That "God Self" or "Christ Self" quickly became identified with the fundamental nature of God as the "Mighty I AM Presence," a designation with its roots in God's self-disclosure to Moses in Exodus 3:14 and in the many "I am" sayings of Jesus in the gospel according to John.[49] That focus on the "Mighty I AM Presence" gave Ballard's movement its name.

The instructions that Saint Germain gave to Guy Ballard also had specific social and historical dimensions. Just as Saint Germain had recognized the distinctive receptivity of Ballard, he also revealed that the United States would play a pivotal role in the spiritual transformation of the planet. He told Ballard that "in your beloved America in the not-so-far-distant future will come forth a similar recognition of the Real Inner Self, and this her people will express in high attainment. She is a Land of Light, and her Light shall blaze forth brilliant as the sun at noonday among the nations of the earth."[50] The strongly nationalist elements of Saint Germain's communications led the Ballards to express conservative opposition to many of the New Deal policies of Franklin Delano Roosevelt and reflected the Ballards' interactions with William Dudley Pelley's neo-Nazi Silver Legion, from which they recruited several students.[51]

In addition to embracing the diligent study of Saint Germain's teachings, those who accepted Ballard's message were urged to engage in making positive decrees or affirmations, practices with some similarities in both the affirmations of Christian Scientists and the New Thought Movement.[52] One collection of affirmations, communicated by the Master Chanera, includes these two short examples: "'I Am'! The Eternal Ceaseless Flow of the Blazing Light from my 'I AM Presence' through my mind and body"; "Because 'I AM' Thee and Thou are me, 'I AM' Protected, Illumined, Supplied and Free!"[53] In addition to reasserting fundamental aspects of the "I AM" worldview, such as the nature of the divine and the nature of human beings, affirmations can be used to reinforce social relations within the group. Fellow students of Saint Germain's teachings, for example, are directed to say to each other, "'I AM' the 'Presence' that loves you into your perfect Ascended Master Activity. 'I AM' the 'Presence' that loves you into your conscious ability to do this."[54] In addition, affirmations could be directed to specific physical, social, and moral situations or conditions. The decrees are designed to accomplish in short statements what the teachings of Saint Germain do in much greater detail; they provide students with a comprehensive response to the intellectual, moral, and physical dimensions of what Geertz called the problem of meaning. Both the teachings and the affirmations create and maintain a world of meaning for Ballard's students that answers fundamental questions about the nature of the divine and the universe, the place of human beings within the cosmic scheme, and the best course of action that they can take in order to realize their fullest potential. If, as William James claimed, the core of the religious problem is a cry for help, the Ascended Masters who communicated with the Ballards were ready to respond to that plea.

Ballard continued to receive messages from the Masters throughout the 1930s and he recorded them in a lengthy series of books. But the movement he founded suffered severe setbacks in the decade after his death in December 1939. In 1940 Gerald Bryan published a series of attacks on the "I AM" Movement in the provocatively titled *Psychic Dictatorship in America,* with its implicit and timely comparisons of Ballard to Hitler and Mussolini. Employing tactics that would be taken up again by the contemporary anticult movement, Bryan orchestrated media opposition to the Ballards and encouraged some former students to file lawsuits against the publisher of Ballard's books.[55] The lawsuit, which accused the Ballards of mail fraud because their books contained some eighteen "false representations," dragged on until from 1940 to 1946 and its aftereffects were still felt as late as 1957.[56] One respected legal scholar has observed that "not before, nor since, has the federal government indicted a religious leader for propagating the beliefs of her religion."[57] Although the Saint Germain Press continues to publish the Ballards' books, their movement has never regained the vigor that it displayed in the 1930s. A few splinter groups have formed, including the Bridge to Freedom in which Geraldine Innocente received messages from the Masters and a group devoted to the teachings of A.D.K. Luk.[58] But the most prominent contemporary influence of the Ballards has been on the Church Universal and Triumphant.

In the early 1950s, a former member of the Bridge to Freedom movement, Francis Ekey, started another religious enterprise in the "I AM" tradition. His Lighthouse of Freedom's newsletter featured more messages from Ascended Masters, communicated through an anonymous recipient. The anonymous messenger was in fact Mark L. Prophet, who had been contacted by the messenger El Morya early in his life. By 1958, at El Morya's urging, Prophet had split from Ekey to form the Summit Lighthouse in Washington, D.C.[59] Perhaps most fateful for the future of Prophet's teaching was his meeting with Elizabeth Clare Wulf Ytreberg in 1963. They soon left their previous spouses to marry each other and Mark tutored Elizabeth in the teachings of El Morya and Saint Germain through the early to mid-1960s. In the late 1960s and early 1970s Elizabeth settled into a role as a co-messenger with Mark, and after his sudden death in 1973 she established herself as the unquestioned leader of the group, which in 1974 was renamed the Church Universal and Triumphant (CUT).

Soon after his death in 1940, Edna Ballard had declared that Guy had been elevated to the status of an Ascended Master himself, assuming the name of Godfre Ray King. She effusively proclaimed that "he is now our Beloved Ascended Master of Light who can give Limitless Help to all who will accept and apply the Ascended Masters' Instruction of the 'I AM' which He gave, under the Direction of our Beloved Ascended Master, Saint Germain. He is glorious, beyond words to describe! His Love and Light are Limitless and He pours them to all for the Freedom of America and all mankind."[60] Edna Ballard's elevation of her husband to exalted status represented, among other things, an effort to retain within the Ballard family control over the "I AM" teachings. Elizabeth Clare Prophet made a similar assertion after Mark's death, announcing that he had achieved

Elizabeth Clare Prophet of the Church Universal and Triumphant. © Akhtar Hussein/
CORBIS SYGMA.

Ascended Master status as "Lanello."[61] Elizabeth, however, went well
beyond Edna Ballard in creating for herself a sustained independent career
as a messenger of the Great White Brotherhood.

In a lecture given in 1975 at a conference on spiritual freedom at
Mount Shasta, Elizabeth explicitly linked her teaching mission to the Ballards, claiming that "I was ordained by the master Saint Germain to represent him and to complete the mission of the beloved Godfre Ray King
(Guy Ballard)."[62] Ballard himself attended the conference, indirectly,
through a dictation given by Godfre only twenty minutes after Elizabeth's
lecture.[63] It is clear that Elizabeth saw herself as continuing a tradition that
included the Ballards but was by no means limited to them. Saint Germain
remains an important source of the Church Universal and Triumphant's
teachings, along with El Morya, Jesus, whose lost teachings the church
claims to have recovered, and Buddha, among many others.

Like the "I AM" Movement, the Church Universal and Triumphant
offered its students the chance to progress toward the divine. In his 1975
instruction, Godfre offered this summary, "behold the message to the new
student and to the student of long standing that it is the teaching of the I
AM Presence and the chart of the I AM Presence that is the *key* to your
immortality! It is the *key* to your ascension! Take that as the law and let it
be the legacy which you give to mankind."[64] That goal of ascension into

higher, nonmaterial realms was consistent with the teachings of the Ballards. From its inception in the early teachings of Mark Prophet, however, that message about individual transformation was embedded in a broader apocalyptic scenario. As early as 1965 Mark Prophet had warned that evil extraterrestrials had long been endeavoring to impede the path to spiritual perfection. When Elizabeth assumed the leadership of the movement, she added her own twist to things. Although it was not the only focus of her teachings, she repeatedly warned about the possibility of a nuclear conflict. As it did in the Peoples Temple at around the same time, that fear contributed to important organizational transformations. Eventually, it also led to a severe diminishment of CUT's membership.

As Mark Prophet gained more students, he moved the center of his operations from Washington, D.C., to Colorado Springs, Colorado. After his death, when his movement outgrew those headquarters, it purchased in 1977 for its new site a former college campus in the Santa Monica mountains near Malibu, California. Elizabeth's attempt to isolate the campus that she called "Camelot" from the surrounding society caught the attention of anticult activists in the area and of investigative journalists. In the aftermath of the Jonestown tragedy of late 1978, relations between alternative religious movements and their critics became much more hostile. In addition, several former members filed lawsuits against the church in which they claimed, among other things, to have been subjected to involuntary servitude.[65] Those experiences only strengthened Elizabeth's convictions that hostile forces were arrayed against the church and that she had to maintain clear boundaries between her group and the rest of society. By the beginning of the 1980s the church began to purchase parcels of land in an isolated area of Montana adjacent to Yellowstone National Park with the intention of moving the church's headquarters and all of its most committed members there.

The move took place gradually from 1981 to 1986 as the church acquired more land and established a largely self-sufficient community in the wilderness. In late 1985 Saint Germain, through Elizabeth, confirmed the importance of the new location as a spiritual center, proclaiming that "the company of priests and priestesses of the sacred life who tend the flame of the altar of the Inner Retreat are indeed tending the flame of the Royal Teton Ranch Retreat and our abode in the Grand Tetons."[66] The following Thanksgiving another message from Saint Germain increased the group's apocalyptic anticipation. In that message Saint Germain directed the members of the Church Universal and Triumphant to prepare for a coming nuclear war by building underground fallout shelters.[67] After some indecision about the date of the impending catastrophe, the church eventually determined that it could be expected on March 15, 1990. CUT's apocalyptic expectations drew substantial attention from the local and national press, as did the evident failure of their prophecy when the stipulated date passed and March turned into April.

In the aftermath of the failed prophecy, the church lost thousands of members, many of whom had made substantial sacrifices in order to move to the ranch in preparation for the end. Despite its efforts to rationalize the unexpected turn of events by claiming that the members' piety had averted the catastrophe, the church suffered from heightened public ridicule and defections by disillusioned members. CUT never really recovered from the failure of the predicted apocalypse to occur. In the 1990s the church went through several transformations. For a time Elizabeth tried to integrate herself into the general New Age Movement, but she eventually tired of what she saw as its "anything goes" mentality. Moderately successful recruitment drives were made in Latin America as well. But the most jarring event was Elizabeth's own withdrawal as the result of Alzheimer's disease from the movement she had led for more than twenty years. Her declining health forced on the movement the necessity of developing an organizational structure and teaching function that could persist in the absence of the messenger. Since none of Elizabeth's adult children remains associated with the church, it is not yet clear whether and how the Church Universal and Triumphant will perpetuate itself after Elizabeth's departure from this world. In 1996, however, a splinter group, the Temple of the Presence, was formed by former members Monroe and Carolyn Shearer, who claim to be co-messengers of the Ascended Masters.[68] They claim "ongoing current contact with the Ascended Masters through Live Dictations in order to receive their Radiation, Wisdom and Guidance."[69]

The New Age: Channeling

The proliferation of contacts between human beings and disincarnate entities from another realm reached its greatest expansion to date with the practice of channeling in the contemporary New Age Movement. Although several of its predecessors also heralded the arrival of such a significant transformation of human life that it would amount to a New Age, the contemporary New Age Movement has its roots in England in the 1960s, when a variety of groups influenced by Theosophy and its various offshoots began to study prophecies about imminent spiritual revolution.[70] It migrated to the United States soon after. The New Age has always been much less an organized and highly structured social movement than a loose alliance of individuals and groups with overlapping and complementary interests. It has been variously identified as a "large-scale decentralized religious subculture," a "religious discourse community," and a "contemporary manifestation of a western alternative spirituality tradition going back at least to the Greco-Roman world."[71] Participants in New Age practices and beliefs represent the type of "audience cult" that was described in chapter 1, following the analysis of Stark and Bainbridge. New Age practitioners typically pledge allegiance to no single organization but rather pick and choose among various religious options as it suits them. They are spiritual nibblers. At times they may engage in specific provider-client relationships, as when they participate in workshops or training sessions, but with a few exceptions they are not joiners. Shirley MacLaine's attitude toward various spiritual practitioners provides a good example of New Age eclecticism.

Although beliefs and practices in the contemporary New Age Movement are extraordinarily diverse, at least one observer has argued that "channeling is possibly the single most important and definitive aspect of the New Age."[72] A multitude of spiritual entities has spoken and continues to speak through a wide range of vehicles, and they have produced an expansive body of literature. The practice of channeling clearly has its roots in nineteenth-century Spiritualism, but its contemporary practice has also been influenced by Theosophy, New Thought, and other groups as well. As one observer puts it, "the common goal of all channels is to *link up*, to make an emotionally satisfying connection to higher powers and to their own divine essence."[73] The entities who speak through human channels emphasize their desire to help. For example, Lazaris, who speaks through Jach Pursel, states that "we want very much to have the opportunity to share with you as specifically as we can our observations of your reality, as you have created it, offering you perhaps insights and suggestions of how you might alter your perspective, change your approach, such as to create a reality more to your own liking."[74] Those statements highlight three prominent aspects of the channeling experience and also its similarities to messages from the Ascended Masters received in the Church Universal and Triumphant and the "I AM" Activity. First, the entities who communicate from beyond this world are benevolent; they want to provide the help that religious seekers desire. Lazaris, for example, emphasizes that he is neither a guru nor a master but simply a friend, ready to aid those in need.[75] Similarly, Ramtha claims, "I am not a sage. I am not a fortuneteller, I am not a priest. I am but a teacher, servant, brother unto you."[76] Second, the communication stresses that humans have extraordinary powers, that they can truly "create their own reality." Consequently, they have the ability to transform both their own situations and themselves. Third, the ultimate goal of that transformation is to ascend from this earth, into higher spheres of spiritual existence. As Jach Pursel himself says about Lazaris, "He is taking us home."[77]

The focus of channeling is radically individualistic. In Michael Brown's analysis, it posits an "absolute denial of the social nature of human existence," and it offers a "dream of community without society."[78] The explicit goal of many channeled communications is to awaken in individuals a sense of their true identity. As Lazaris says in his characteristically polite and tentative fashion, "we would suggest that you are also a spark of consciousness,"[79] that is, a part of the single divine consciousness. The only difference between spiritual entities like Lazaris and most human beings, he indicates, is that "we know it. You don't . . . yet."[80] From that perspective, the primary goal of human life becomes abundantly clear; individuals should devote themselves to acquiring the knowledge that will lead them to the discovery and cultivation of their true selves, which, in turn, will enable them to liberate themselves from this earthly realm and achieve a higher, better identity. As Ramtha, the 35,000-year-old entity channeled by JZ Knight, succinctly reveals, "you are God."[81]

The careers of human channels are often marked by dramatic moments when they realize that they have been chosen to be vehicles of spiritual messages. Jach Pursel, for example, thought that he had simply fallen asleep while trying to meditate, but his wife Peny told him otherwise: "two hours later, Peny didn't hear my sheepish apology for having dozed off. She was excitedly tumbling over words trying to tell me that an entity had spoken through me."[82] JZ Knight's introduction to Ramtha was the culmination of a series of predictions, premonitions, and practices. Early on, she had been told by a fortune teller that she would meet "The One." After a weekend of experimenting with "pyramid power," she suddenly saw a large being in her kitchen, glowing with purple light. The following exchange then took place:

You are so beautiful. Who are you?

I am Ramtha, the Enlightened One. I have come to help you over the ditch.[83]

Although both the experience and Ramtha's statement were initially puzzling, Knight marked that Sunday in February 1977 as the beginning of her relationship with Ramtha. She received important confirmation of her experience from a subsequent visit to a Spiritualist church, where she learned about the phenomenon of spirit mediumship and had her own status as a channel acknowledged. Knight began her first public teaching sessions with Ramtha in November 1978 and quickly developed a substantial following.

While Ramtha's teachings echo many common themes on contemporary channeled material, Knight has also developed a distinctive structure to aid individuals in their spiritual quests. Ramtha's School of Enlightenment, located in Yelm, Washington, has been structured both to foster access to Ramtha's teachings and to encourage individuals to adopt spiritual practices that will enhance their spiritual progress. The ultimate goal is extraordinary. Ramtha claims that "it is possible to never die. It is possible to ascend this body."[84] Moreover, "it is possible in one lifetime to do it all."[85] What Edna Ballard claimed for her husband Guy and Elizabeth Clare Prophet claimed for her husband Mark—ascent into the company of the Masters—is potentially available to every human being. To facilitate the accomplishment of that goal, Ramtha's School trains students in Consciousness and Energy exercises that will help them hold certain ideas in their minds and eventually to manifest them, thus creating their own reality. Students also engage in "Fieldwork" that is also designed to unfetter their powers of perception.

Like other new religious movements, JZ Knight's activities as a channel and Ramtha's School for Enlightenment have not escaped serious opposition. For a time there were serious tensions between the population of Yelm and Ramtha's School. In 1987, the TV news show "20/20" aired a highly critical investigative report. At least one Christian evangelical countercult writer suspected that Ramtha might well be a demon and Knight a victim of possession. The outsider's attacks, however, left Ramtha's School shaken but not shattered. Ramtha continues to pursue an energetic teaching ministry.[86]

The specific, prescribed spiritual discipline that is accepted by the students at Ramtha's School imposes a strong organizational framework on a spiritual quest that is usually much more loosely organized and personally driven in the contemporary New Age Movement. In forming the Ramtha School of Enlightenment, Ramtha, in his own way, is attempting to provide order and continuity for his revelations, just as HPB, Edna Ballard, and Elizabeth Clare Prophet also attempted to contain the torrents of revelations from the spirit world within the banks of orthodoxy. They are joined in those efforts by Lazaris, who asserts that "we are the only one, as we have suggested, from our levels of awareness who has ever or who will ever communicate with your planet. And the only one we shall ever come through is the Channel."[87] But since Spiritualism widened the portals through which communication with the spirit world could occur and increased the traffic through them, subsequent attempts to narrow the gates and control access have all been failures. The desire to receive authoritative messages from other places and other times is one of the most vital features of the contemporary religious scene. At times those messages come from traditionally sanctioned beings and flow through established channels in mainstream organizations, but at others they come from unexpected visitors to our contemporary world, such as Ramtha, Lazaris, El Morya, Saint Germain, and other members of the Great White Brotherhood. The appearance of such unanticipated help from beyond only supports William James' observation that a crucial part of the human religious consciousness is a plea for help.

Conclusions

In addition to providing loving help to religious seekers, the religious systems in this chapter share some other similarities. In different ways and to different degrees, they attempt to make public previously secret sources of wisdom. Robert Ellwood has argued persuasively that they continue a long tradition of alternative wisdom in Western civilization.[88] The claim to be in possession of special, secret wisdom was a hallmark of several "gnostic" groups in the early centuries of the Common Era. Their particular "gnosis," or knowledge, addressed fundamental questions, including as a famous formulation from the second century had it, "who were we, what we have become, where were we, whither have we been cast, whither do we hasten, from what have we been set free?"[89] Lazaris's contention that he knew the true nature of humanity, but that his audience didn't, expresses the same type of crucial knowingness. The notions that human beings are more than they appear to be, that in their essentials they are divine, and that they can recapture the exalted status that they have unfortunately left behind by attending to the teachings of superior entities from beyond this world all express a fundamentally gnostic vision of human life. Like the ancient gnostics, Ramtha, for example, sees this life as something that is to be left behind. Life on this earth is not something to cling to. As Ramtha describes it, invoking the theory of reincarnation,

> life upon life, existence upon existence, you became so immersed in the illusions of this plane that you forgot the wonderful fire that flows through you. In ten and one-half million years you have come from being sovereign and all-powerful entities, to where you are utterly lost in matter; enslaved by your own creations of dogma, law, fashion, and tradition; separated by country, creed, sex, and race; immersed in jealousy, bitterness, guilt, and fear. You so identified yourselves with your bodies that you entrapped yourselves in survival and forgot the unseen essence that you truly are.[90]

As Lazaris put it, the function of the channeled teachings is to lead humans out of their entrapment in this material world to their true spiritual home.

Ancient gnostic systems frequently featured a redeemer figure, who exposed humans to the teachings of the light and showed them the way to liberate themselves from darkness of their material existence. In some ways, figures like Saint Germain, Lazaris, and Ramtha and the other Masters perform the same function. In the later phases of the Peoples Temple, Rev. Jim Jones also cast himself as a gnostic redeemer figure. Gnostic teachers also resemble the shamans of tribal societies who travel into the spirit world often in order to effect healings for their clients in this world. Like those tribal shamans the entities who communicate through channels aim to produce positive benefits for their clients. Ramtha, for example, claims that "truth is only truth when it is relevant to personal growth."[91] It is not accidental, then, that some New Age participants have also taken up shamanism, not simply as a topic for study, but as a personal practice.[92]

The quest for self that has animated Shirley MacLaine's spiritual odyssey has motivated many other spiritual seekers. The self of which she wrote has often been formed in conversation with compassionate figures who exist beyond this material world. In the case of early Spiritualism those figures were able to quiet the fears of troubled family members who were afraid that death sundered all bonds. In Theosophy the Adepts proved to be sure and generous guides to the complicated nature of the evolving universe and the place of humans within it. In the "I AM" Movement and the Church Universal and Triumphant, the Ascended Masters offered the keys to unlocking the human potential to ascend from this world into a fully spiritual existence. Contemporary New Age channels similarly provide aid to persons who strive to create their own reality and transcend their material limitations. The movements or groups discussed in this chapter have all attempted to respond to the cognitive needs of their partisans by sketching out full, and sometimes very complex, worldviews. Though they have not been blind to the problem of human suffering, they have tended to describe it merely as a transitory phase, and they have rarely addressed directly widespread social ills, preferring to see them as subsidiary to the project of individual transformation.[93] In the characterization of William James, they are religions of "healthy-mindedness."[94] As a result, they have developed only rudimentary moral systems, again centered on the individual. Nonetheless, they have attracted both a great number of casual participants and a smaller, but still significant, group of dedicated practitioners. The search for wisdom from diverse sources in the world beyond has been and remains a significant element in new religious movements in the United States.

Notes

1. Shirley MacLaine, *Out on a Limb* (New York: Ballantine, 1983), p. 5; her lightly fictionalized memoir does not, unfortunately, provide a very precise chronology.

2. Ibid., p. 176. For Ryerson's current activities, see www.kevinryerson.com/.

3. MacLaine, *Out on a Limb,* p. 179.

4. Ibid., p. 183.

5. See Robert Ellwood, "How New is the New Age?" in James R. Lewis and J. Gordon Melton, eds., *Perspectives on the New Age* (Albany: State University of New York Press, 1992), pp. 59–67; see also idem, *Alternative Altars: Unconventional and Eastern Spirituality in America* (Chicago: University of Chicago Press, 1979).

6. William James, *The Varieties of Religious Experience* (New York: New American Library, 1958), p. 137.

7. From the welcome page of The Summit Lighthouse, "the official source for teachings of the ascended masters from world-renowned authors, Mark and Elizabeth Prophet and their students" at www.tsl.org/.

8. Ann Braude, *Radical Spirits: Spiritualism and Women's Rights in Nineteenth-Century America* (Boston: Beacon, 1989), p. 6.

9. See www.tsl.org./AboutUs/TheMysticalPath.asp.

10. See J. Gordon Melton, *Finding Enlightenment: Ramtha's School of Ancient Wisdom* (Hillsboro, OR: Beyond Words, 1988), pp. 17ff.

11. As quoted in Braude, *Radical Spirits*, p. 41.

12. See Geertz, "Religion as a Cultural System," p. 104.

13. See Braude, *Radical Spirits*, pp. 34–36; R. Laurence Moore, *In Search of White Crows: Spiritualism, Parapsychology, and American Culture* (New York: Oxford University Press, 1977), pp. 9–12; Ellwood, *Alternative Altars*, pp. 95–97. For a brief introduction to Swedenborg, see Eugene Taylor, "Swedenborgianism," in Miller, ed., *America's Alternative Religions*, pp. 77–85.

14. See Braude, *Radical Spirits*, passim.

15. See, for example, ibid., p. 23. See also Ann Braude, "The Perils of Passivity: Women's Leadership in Spiritualism and Christian Science," in Catherine Wessinger, ed., *Women's Leadership in Marginal Religions: Explorations Outside the Mainstream* (Urbana: University of Illinois Press, 1993), pp. 55–67.

16. Braude, *Radical Spirits*, p. 88.

17. As quoted in Moore, *In Search of White Crows*, p. 34.

18. See Braude, *Radical Spirits*, p. 44f.

19. As quoted in Moore, *In Search of White Crows*, p. 50.

20. As quoted in Braude, *Radical Spirits*, p. 165. Hatch's emphasis.

21. www.nsac.org/objects/index.htm.

22. www.nsac.org/spiritualism/index.htm.

23. www.fst.org/sp_teachings.htm.

24. www.fst.org/sptwld1.htm.

25. See Braude, *Radical Spirits*, pp. 176–79; Bruce F. Campbell, *Ancient Wisdom Revived: A History of the Theosophical Movement* (Berkeley: University of California Press, 1977), pp. 20–21; Peter Washington, *Madame Blavatsky's Baboon: A History of the Mystics, Mediums, and Misfits Who Brought Spiritualism to America* (New York: Schocken, 1993), pp. 27–29.

26. Henry Olcott Steel, *Old Diary Leaves: The True Story of the Theosophical Society, First Series, 1874–1878,* vol. I, pp. 3–6, as quoted in Sylvia Cranston, *HPB: The Extraordinary Life and Influence of Helena Blavatsky, Founder of the Modern Theosophical Movement* (New York: G. P. Putnam, 1993), p. 126.

27. For an historian's attempt to recover the identities of the Masters, see K. Paul Johnson, *The Masters Revealed: Madame Blavatsky and the Myth of the Great White Lodge* (Albany: State University of New York Press, 1994).

28. Helena Petrovna Blavatsky, *Isis Unveiled*, vol. II, p. 142, available at www.theosociety.org/pasadena/isis/iu2–03.htm; her emphasis.

29. www.blavatskyarchives.com/blavlet2.htm; her emphasis.

30. Blavatsky, *Isis Unveiled*, vol. II, p. 142, available at www.theosociety.org/pasadena/isis/iu2–03.htm.

31. See www.theosociety.org/pasadena/ivit-sd/invss-2.htm#threefundprop. See also www.theosophy.org/tlodocs/ThreeFun.htm. For a full exposition of Theosophical ideas, see Robert Ellwood, *Theosophy: A Modern Expression of the Wisdom of the Ages* (Wheaton, IL: Quest, 1986).

32. www.theosociety.org/pasadena/sd/sd1-3-16.htm.

33. Campbell, *Ancient Wisdom Revived*, p. 45.

34. See "Study of Theosophy" at www.theosophy.org/tlodocs/StudyOfTheosophy.htm.

35. See www.theosociety.org/pasadena/corson/cors-lt2.htm for the full text of the letter.

36. Ibid.

37. On the Coulomb affair, see Campbell, *Ancient Wisdom Revived*, pp. 88–90; for the SPR report, see pp. 91–93, quotation from p. 93.

38. See ibid., pp. 32–35. But see the defense of HPB in Cranston, *HPB*, pp. 379–87.

39. On the general question of the exercise of authority in Theosophy, see Catherine Wessinger, "Democracy vs. Hierarchy: The Evolution of Authority in the Theosophical Society," in Timothy Miller, ed., *When Prophets Die: The Postcharismatic Fate of New Religious Movements* (Albany: State University of New York Press, 1991), pp. 93–106.

40. Campbell, *Ancient Wisdom Revived*, provides a helpful chart of the offspring of the Theosophical Society on p. 205.

41. For a basic guide to Krishnamurti's life and teachings, see www.kinfonet.org/.

42. www.lucistrust.org/arcane/about.php.

43. Godfre Ray King, *Unveiled Mysteries*, Saint Germain Series, vol. I (Schaumberg, IL: Saint Germain, 1934), p. 3. In quotations from King I retain his distinctive capitalizations.

44. Ibid., p. 4.

45. See ibid., p. 15.

46. See, for example, Isaiah's commissioning in Isaiah 6, Jeremiah's call in Jeremiah 1, and the account of Jesus' baptism in Mark 1.

47. King, *Unveiled Mysteries*, p. xv.

48. Ibid., p. 17.

49. See J. Gordon Melton, "The Church Universal and Triumphant: Its Heritage and Thoughtworld," in James R. Lewis and J. Gordon Melton, eds., *Church Universal and Triumphant in Scholarly Perspective* (Stanford, CA: Center for Academic Publication, 1994), pp. 1–20, esp. p. 6. For a critique of the study of which Melton's article is a part, see Robert W. Balch and Stephan Langdon, "How the Problem of Malfeasance Gets Overlooked in Studies of New Religious Movements: An Examination of the AWARE Study of the Church Universal and Triumphant," in Anson Shupe, ed., *Wolves Within the Fold: Religious Leadership and the Abuses of Power* (New Brunswick, NJ: Rutgers University Press, 1998), pp. 191–211.

50. King, *Unveiled Mysteries*, pp. 42–43.

51. See Bradley C. Whitsel, *The Church Universal and Triumphant: Elizabeth Clare Prophet's Apocalyptic Movement* (Syracuse: Syracuse University Press, 2003), p. 24.

52. See ibid., p. 25.

53. Chanera, *"I AM" Adorations and Affirmations*, Saint Germain Series, vol. 5, pt. 1 (Schaumberg, IL: Saint Germain, 1937), pp. 49, 57, respectively.

54. Ibid., pp. 69–70.

55. For a brief account, see Melton, "The Church Universal and Triumphant," pp. 12–13; see also Kenneth and Talita Paolini, *400 Years of Imaginary Friends: A Journey into the World of Adepts, Masters, Ascended Masters, and their Messengers* (Livingston, MT: Paolini International LLC, 2000), pp. 221–27. The Paolinis have also reprinted Bryan's book. Contemporary opposition to "I AM" can be found on the Web at www.home.gil.com.au/~perovich/Ballards/.

56. For a full treatment, see John T. Noonan, *The Lustre of Our Country: The American Experience of Religious Freedom* (Berkeley: University of California Press, 1998), pp. 141–76.

57. Ibid., p. 143.

58. The Ascended Masters Teaching Foundation keeps alive the teachings of Innocente; see www.ascendedmaster.org/. For Luk, see www.lawoflife.com/.

59. See Whitsel, *The Church Universal and Triumphant,* pp. 27–28.

60. As quoted in Paolini and Paolini, *400 Years of Imaginary Friends,* p. 233.

61. See Whitsel, *The Church Universal and Triumphant,* p. 37.

62. Elizabeth Clare Prophet, *The Great White Brotherhood in the Culture, History, and Religion of America* (Livingston, MT: Summit University Press, 1976), p. 61.

63. Godfre, "Freedom through Obedience to the Law of Being," in Prophet, *The Great White Brotherhood,* pp. 73–80.

64. Ibid., p. 76. For stories of ex-members, see www.lifeincut.com.

65. See Whitsel, *The Church Universal and Triumphant,* pp. 53–58.

66. As quoted in ibid., p. 81.

67. See ibid., p. 87.

68. See ibid., pp. 155–56. See also www.templeofthepresence.org.

69. www.templeofthepresence.org/reason.htm.

70. See J. Gordon Melton, "New Thought and the New Age," in James R. Lewis and J. Gordon Melton, eds., *Perspectives on the New Age* (Albany: State University of New York Press, 1992), pp. 15–29, esp. p. 20. For more background on the New Age, see Paul Heelas, *The New Age Movement* (Oxford: Basil Blackwell, 1996).

71. Lewis and Melton, "Introduction," Catherine L. Albanese, "The Magical Staff: Quantam Healing in the New Age," and Robert Ellwood, "How New is the New Age," all in Lewis and Melton, *Perspectives on the New Age,* pp. ix, 73, 59, respectively.

72. Melton, "New Thought and New Age," in ibid., p. 21; on channeling, see also Wouter J. Hanegraaff, *New Age Religion and Western Culture: Esotericism in the Mirror of Secular Thought* (Albany: State University of New York Press, 1998), pp. 23–41.

73. Michael Brown, *The Channeling Zone: American Spirituality in an Anxious Age* (Cambridge, MA: Harvard University Press, 1997), p. 37.

74. www.chat.lazaris.com/publibrary/pubexplains.cfm.

75. Ibid.

76. As quoted in Melton, *Finding Enlightenment,* p. 58.

77. www.chat.lazaris.com/publibrary/pubjach.cfm.

78. Brown, *The Channeling Zone,* pp. 68, 184, respectively.

79. www.chat.lazaris.com/publibrary/pubexplains.cfm.

80. Ibid.

81. Ramtha, *The Plane of Bliss: On Earth as it is in Heaven* (Yelm, WA: JZK, 1997), p. 43.

82. www.chat.lazaris.com/publibrary/pubjach.cfm.

83. As quoted in Melton, *Finding Enlightenment,* p. 15.

84. Ramtha, *The Plane of Bliss,* p. 90.

85. Ibid., p. 54.

86. See the material at www.ramtha.com; www.jzkpublishing.com; and www.beyondtheordinary.net, a Web-based radio program featuring teachers from Ramtha's School of Enlightenment.

87. www.chat.lazaris.com/publibrary/pubexplains.cfm.

88. See Ellwood, *Alternative Altars,* for example.

89. Clement of Alexandria, *Stromateis, Excerpta ex Theodota,* 78.2. For an English translation and brief discussion of the passage in the context of gnostic speculations about the origins of the world, see Kurt Rudolph, *Gnosis,* trans. Robert McLachlan Wilson (San Francisco: Harper and Row, 1983), p. 71.

90. As quoted in Melton, *Finding Enlightenment,* p. 74.

91. As quoted in ibid., p. 73.

92. See, for example, www.shamanworld.com/. See also Michael Harner, *The Way of the Shaman,* 10th ed. (San Francisco: Harper, 1990) and the related Web site of the Foundation for Shamanic Studies www.shamanicstudies.com/.

93. Shirley MacLaine records an interesting exchange with the late activist and U.S. Representative Bella Abzug (D-New York) in which MacLaine argues that "*inner reform must precede social reform.*" *Out on a Limb,* p. 353; her emphasis.

94. See James, *The Varieties of Religious Experience,* p. 83, for example.

Chapter 4

Eastern Groups and Gurus

On March 7, 2002, actor Richard Gere made a presentation to the Committee on International Relations of the U.S. House of Representatives. Speaking as the chairman of the International Campaign for Tibet, Gere described his own travels "as a religious pilgrim" to receive an initiation from the Dalai Lama, continuing Chinese efforts to destroy monasteries and other Buddhist religious institutions within Tibet, and the plights of a Buddhist monk and nun who had to flee their homeland for exile in India.[1] Gere's efforts to enlist the U.S. government on behalf of the Tibetan community was an expression of both his ongoing religious explorations and his political activism. In interviews Gere has explained how his first encounter with the Dalai Lama galvanized his interest in Tibetan Buddhism. He recalled, for example, that a

> real Tibet dream comes when you meet his Holiness because then—it's actualized. And that's what happened to me. I saw the Dalai Lama but he's also this extraordinary man, extraordinary professor, extraordinary father, extraordinary friend—all of that. It really shows you that there's a way of making this work, of using his system, a religious psychological system that can really transform everything. The dream becomes kind of wonderful because it's possible to actualize it.[2]

Gere was hardly the first American to have a dream of transformation awakened by a religious teacher from the East. In the last decade alone many other entertainers have espoused the cause of Tibetan freedom. Like Gere, the Beastie Boys, inspired by member Adam Yauch's embrace of Tibetan Buddhism, established a charitable foundation, the Milarepa Fund.[3] Beginning in 1996, the Beastie Boys also put together a series of benefit Tibetan Freedom Concerts, featuring a variety of popular musical performers, that raised millions of dollars for the Tibetan cause. The Beastie Boys' 1994 CD, *Licensed to Ill,* included both an instrumental titled "Shambala," after the Buddhist paradise, and the vocal "Bodhisattva Vow," which includes its own version of the dream of transformation that Gere described:

> As I develop the awakening mind
> I praise the Buddhas as they shine
> I bow before you as I travel my path
> To join your ranks, I make full the task
> For the sake of all beings I seek
> The enlightened mind I know I'll reap
> Respect to Shantideva and all the others
> Who brought down the dharma for sisters and brothers.[4]

With their acceptances of the Dalai Lama as a religious teacher, Adam Yauch and Richard Gere continue a tradition of American fascination with Eastern religious wisdom that goes back at least 150 years.

The New England Transcendentalists were the first group of American intellectuals to acknowledge formally the wisdom of the East. In an 1850 essay on Plato, for example, Ralph Waldo Emerson observed admiringly of the conception that all things are fundamentally unified that "this tendency finds its highest expression in the religious writings of the East, and chiefly in the Indian Scriptures, in the Vedas, the Bhagavat Geeta, and the Vishnu Purana. Those writings contain little else than this idea, and they rise to pure and sublime strains in celebrating it."[5] Similarly, Henry David Thoreau testified that "the reader is nowhere raised into and sustained in a higher, purer, or *rarer* region of thought than in the Bhagvat-Geeta" and asserted that "it is unquestionably one of the noblest and most sacred scriptures that have come down to us."[6] A century later writers from the Beat generation displayed a similar passion for Zen Buddhism. Jack Kerouac's autobiographical novel, *The Dharma Bums,* portrays Japhy Ryder as a paragon of Zen. The model for Ryder was, in fact, the poet Gary Snyder, who had studied Chinese and Japanese at the University of California, Berkeley and had learned about Zen from the influential teacher D. T. Suzuki.[7] Snyder was also a friend of Alan Watts, who was one of the most influential popularizers of Zen from the late 1950s on. Kerouac, Snyder, and their associates were prominent members of a diffuse American audience for Zen teachings and themselves became influential proponents of Zen. In terms of Stark and Bainbridge's analysis they could be described as both members of an audience cult and significant practitioners within it. They were, however, too individualistic and changeable to constitute a well-defined social movement. But the Beats' engagement with Zen, like the Transcendentalists' fascination with Eastern scriptures and the late nineteenth-century Theosophists' dedication to the teachings of Himalayan Mahatmas, helped to spread awareness of the teachings and practices of various Eastern religious traditions into at least some segments of American culture, even when it did not result in the formation of lasting movements or communities.

In the examples already mentioned, individual practitioners have adopted, and inevitably adapted, long-standing religious traditions. Although their practices appear to be new in the American context, they are often rather faithful reproductions of traditional ways. Richard Gere's pilgrimage to India to receive an initiation from the Dalai Lama and Gary Snyder's travels to Zen temples in Japan are good examples of how many Americans who incorporate themselves into Eastern religious traditions attempt to maintain orthodoxy. Although their religious commitments may prompt raised eyebrows, quizzical looks, and outright criticisms from their peers and families, individual practitioners have largely avoided the vitriolic attacks that are frequently leveled against cults. The diffuse nature of the individual practitioners' engagement with Eastern religious traditions and the paucity of any organized opposition to them demonstrates the converse of Stark and Bainbridge's observation that "the more total the movement, the more total the opposition to it."[8]

A second way in which Eastern religions have become part of American society is through immigration, particularly after the 1965 repeal of the Asian Exclusion Act. Immigrants to the United States have always brought their religions with them and from the beginnings of American history have contributed to the diversity of American society and religious life. As with the case of individual practitioners, the religions of immigrants may indeed seem new to certain onlookers, but most often they have deep roots in their home countries. Religions practiced by immigrant communities, with a few exceptions to be discussed in the following chapter, have generally not been drawn into contemporary controversies about cults and fall outside of the scope of this book. But their very presence in the United States has spread awareness of religious alternatives to more familiar Jewish and Christian groups.

A third way in which Eastern religions have come to the United States is through dedicated missionary activity, which began in earnest in the late nineteenth century. The 1893 Parliament of the World's Religions in Chicago gave a forum to several representatives of Eastern religions. Swami Vivekananda, for example, followed his appearance at the Parliament with an extended speaking tour in the Midwest, East, and England. Vivekananda himself was a disciple of Ramakrishna Paramahansa, a Bengali brahmin who was a priest of the goddess Kali. Ramakrishna was thought by his disciples to have achieved such deep consciousness of unity with the divine, or *samadhi,* that he himself was eventually recognized as an *avatar,* or incarnation, of God.[9] After overcoming initial skepticism through a transformative encounter with Ramakrishna, the man who would become known as Swami Vivekananda eventually became part of Ramakrishna's circle of students. After a period of monastic wandering in India, he decided to attend the 1893 Parliament in order to raise funds to help ameliorate Indian poverty and to bring Hindu teaching to America. Vivekananda called his teaching "Vedanta," the end or culmination of the Vedas, the ancient sacred scriptures of India. More specifically, Vivekananda preached *advaita,* or nondualist, Vedanta, a system initially formulated by the philosopher Shankara in the ninth century C.E. Among its basic tenets are that truth is one, that humans are divine in their essential nature, that the goal of life is to realize that divinity, and that there are several spiritual disciplines, or *yogas,* through which that goal can be achieved. Vivekananda advanced his teaching mission by founding the first Vedanta Society in New York in 1896. After his death in 1902 other direct disciples of Ramakrishna took up the teaching mission, most notably Swami Nikhilananda, who attracted several prominent disciples. Outposts of the Vedanta society continue to thrive in the United States and to maintain a presence on the World Wide Web.[10]

Beginning in 1920, another Indian guru, Swami Yogananda, began a speaking tour in the United States. Both his speeches and his *Autobiography of a Yogi* attracted adherents to his teachings, and in 1935 he established his own organization, the Self-Realization Fellowship.[11] The Fellowship continues to publicize Yogananda's teachings about yoga in order "to disseminate among the nations a knowledge of definite scientific techniques for attaining direct personal experience of God."[12] The Self-Realization Fellowship preaches a universalism that is also characteristic of other Hindu movements in the United States. It aims, for example, "to reveal the complete harmony and basic oneness of original Christianity as taught by Jesus Christ and original Yoga as taught by Bhagavan Krishna; and to show that these principles of truth are the common scientific foundation of all true religions."[13]

Beginning in the 1960s, several other gurus attracted extensive public attention. For example, Maharishi Mahesh Yogi's teaching about Transcendental Meditation (TM) captivated members of the Beatles and other high-profile entertainers. Although its meditative principles were clearly derived from Hindu practice, its practitioners prefer to describe TM as a science rather than a religious discipline. As the Maharishi described it,

> Transcendental Meditation is a simple, natural program for the mind, a spontaneous, effortless march of the mind to its own unbounded essence. Through Transcendental Meditation, the mind unfolds its potential for unlimited awareness, transcendental awareness, Unity Consciousness— a lively field of all potential, where every possibility is naturally available to the conscious mind. The conscious mind becomes aware of its own unbounded dignity, its unbounded essence, its infinite potential.[14]

Despite the claims that it is not religious, TM's promises to unleash the full powers of the human mind and to promote realization of the essential unity between individuals and the cosmos have evident similarities to the teachings of other groups in this chapter. Both the centrality of the guru, or religious teacher, and the quest to transform individual consciousness are continuing themes in the groups discussed in this chapter. The following sections will examine in more detail four groups that have been perceived as new religious movements in the United States, even though each claims significant continuities with religious traditions that go back hundreds or even thousands of years.

International Society for Krishna Consciousness

For a time in the late 1960s and 1970s the saffron-robed devotees of the Indian deity Krishna were so ubiquitous in American public spaces that the 1980 film *Airplane* could easily spoof their insistent entreaties that passers-by make a donation or buy a book.[15] The dedicated missionary work of Hare Krishnas in airports and on street corners and their colorful public worship punctuated with singing and dancing were part of a mission to spread Krishna consciousness throughout the United States and the rest of the world. That mission was begun by A. C. Bhaktivedanta Swami Prabhupada in 1965. When he was twenty-six Prabhupada had been given the charge to spread the worship of Krishna beyond India during a chance encounter with the guru Bhaktisiddhanta Sarasvati.[16] The beginning of his missionary activity, however, was substantially delayed as Abhay Charan De, who only later would become known as Swami Prabhupada, pursued a career in business. During that time, Prabhupada generously supported the publication of books about Krishna and in 1944 founded an English-language magazine, *Back to Godhead*. Only in 1959, in his early sixties, did Prabhupada formally renounce worldly activity and become a *sannyasa*, "one who casts off." Six years later, at age sixty-nine, he began his mission in America.

Prabhupada repeatedly emphasized that he was part of a "disciplic succession" that went back not only to his own guru but to Krishna himself.[17] Prabhupada wrote that he "was born in the darkest ignorance, and [his] spiritual master opened [his] eyes with the torch of knowledge."[18] Prabhupada's guru did for him what his predecessors in the succession had previously done and what Prabhupada, through the International Society for Krishna Consciousness, offered to do for others. One of the most important figures in that succession of teachers was the sixteenth-century Bengali mystic Sri Caitanya, who deemphasized the importance of elaborate rituals and caste distinctions and stressed the immediate devotion to God, through joyful worship, or *bhatki*. Prabhupada asserted, for example, that "this movement of Krsna consciousness was introduced by Lord Caitanya five hundred years ago in Bengal."[19] Like many other bearers of innovative messages, Prabhupada denied that he was saying anything new. He claimed to present only the clear, unvarnished message of the Bhagavad-Gita. In his understanding, any interpretation was the enemy of the transcendent clarity of the text. He asserted that "Vedic knowledge is not a question of research. Our research work is imperfect because we are researching things with imperfect senses. We have to accept perfect knowledge which comes down, as it stated in the Bhagavad-gita, by the *parampara* (disciplic succession). . . . We must accept the Bhagavad-gita without interpretation, without deletion and without our own whimsical participation in the matter."[20] In fact, Prabhupada contended that people needed to read *only* the Bhagavad-Gita, because it is spoken by Krishna himself. It should become, he believed, the "one common scripture for the whole world."[21]

In Prabhupada's formulation, the goal of encountering Krishna is to uncover one's true human identity. He wrote that "the purpose of this Krsna consciousness movement is to awaken man's original consciousness. . . . We are all part and parcel of God; that is our real identity."[22] As he described it, however, the quest to retrieve that lost identity was both

Hare Krishna festival at Venice Beach, ca. 1990. © Catherine Karnow/CORBIS.

simple and arduous. Especially in the current age, when humans have almost completely lost sight of their true nature, Prabhupada recommended that the chanting of a simple mantra could reawaken their consciousness of God. The mantra that repeats the praises of God, "Hare Krishna, Hare Krishna, Krishna Krishna, Hare Hare / Hare Rama, Hare Rama, Rama, Rama, Hare Hare," as one devotee put it, "is the biggest connection we have to Krishna. All other things are based on it."[23] Another devotee reported that "when you chant Hare Krishna you become purified. Your awareness is acutely intensified. Your awareness of everything: your spiritual awareness, your physical awareness, your awareness of everything around you."[24] But even after several years of dutifully reciting the mantra, the same devotee acknowledged that the effects of chanting were not immediate. With firm resolve, she reported: "I want to learn to perfect the chanting of the Hare Krishna mantra. That's a main goal. I want to learn to chant Hare Krishna and actually become pure. I've been making spiritual advancement, so I want to make more progress. I want to actually realize that Krishna is God and that everyone won't be happy until they are situated back into the practice of serving God, serving Krishna."[25] Prabhupada taught that the discipline necessary to chant with full consciousness the necessary sixteen daily rounds of the mantra on a 108-bead rosary could only be developed in the context of a guru-disciple relationship. He asserted that "one who is serious about understanding spiritual life requires a guru."[26] Because he saw the guru's task as ensuring that no human being suffers in the material world and because suffering stems from ignorance, Prabhupada insisted that "the guru's first business is to rescue his disciple from ignorance."[27] The guru does that by leading the ignorant sufferer to the Bhagavad-Gita and to the greatest mantra, "Hare Krishna." Being acutely aware of the competition among many who would claim to be gurus, Prabhupada assured his audiences that the only trustworthy gurus would be found within a specific tradition of teachers, or disciplic succession, that could trace itself back through Prabhupada's own guru to Caitanya and eventually to Krishna himself.

The surrender to Krishna through the guru that was a central characteristic of the new identity that Hare Krishnas adopted was accompanied by significant changes in outward appearance and behavior, including shaved heads for males, Indian styles of dress, new Sanskrit names, a vegetarian diet, acceptance of a hierarchical system of authority, a new worldview, and, in many cases, communal living. In many ways acceptance of Prabhupada's message of Krishna consciousness increased the distance, and often the tension, between his American devotees and the surrounding society. In a gentle conversation with his daughter, the father of one devotee put the situation bluntly, "nobody in America knows from Hindu. Over here you just look like a bunch of kooks."[28] Although Prabhupada and many of his disciples continually stressed that theirs was by no means a new religion, the International Society for Krishna Consciousness (ISKCON) nevertheless became assimilated to the popular image of the suspicious cult.[29] In 1976, for example, a former devotee, Robin George, and her mother filed a multimillion-dollar lawsuit charging that the devotee had been kidnapped, brainwashed, and falsely imprisoned. The initial award to the plaintiffs of $32 million was contested by ISKCON, with the support of several mainstream religions, and after extensive litigation was reduced first to less than $10 million and eventually to less than $500,000. George and ISKCON reached a confidential settlement in 1993 after seventeen years of legal wrangling.[30] After the Jonestown tragedy in November 1978, ISKCON became cemented into the popular image of dangerous cults, where it generally has remained despite various efforts by devotees to portray a different image of the group.[31]

Prabhupada's death in November 1977 introduced substantial instability into the organization. Like many other charismatic leaders he had not provided precise instructions about who would lead the organization when he "left his body." He had established the Governing Body Commission in 1970 to help oversee the administration of ISKCON, but in the summer of 1977 he had also empowered a group of his disciples to perform initiations for devotees. Soon after his death several of the initiating gurus began to see themselves as the successors to Prabhupada in the disciplic succession and to claim the honor, and even worship, that they believed was due to them. Some of them, however, led lives at odds with the exalted religious status that they claimed. In the four years after Prabhupada's death, ISKCON was rocked by a series of "guru controversies" that threatened to fracture the movement, drive out faithful devotees, and endanger the entire project of spreading Krishna consciousness in the West. The controversies put the bureaucratic authority of the GBC in conflict with the claimed charismatic authority of the gurus who had been chosen by Prabhupada to perform initiations in his absence. Some of the gurus also competed among themselves for preeminence. The contention for authority within the movement shook the commitment of some of the devotees. One reported that "with Srila Prabhupada's disappearance, my commitment fluctuates, depending on how strictly Prabhupada's orders are being carried out by ISKCON."[32] In 1982 a splinter group broke off from ISKCON and affiliated with Maharaja Swami in India, a former associate of Prabhupada. But in the wake of those defections, the GBC consolidated its power and the remaining gurus acknowledged its primacy in directing the Krishna consciousness Movement.

In the following decades ISKCON assumed a relatively lower profile, as it strove to heal the wounds of the bitter conflicts that followed Prabhupada's death. But at the turn of the century it was once again thrust into the news because of shocking accusations of child abuse at its boarding schools in the United States and India during the 1970s and 1980s. A federal lawsuit, *Children of ISKCON v. ISKCON,* was filed in Dallas in 2000 by former members who claimed that they had been abused in the *gurukula* schools by representatives of the organization.[33] In October 1998, leaders of the movement had acknowledged that numerous children had suffered abuse in the movement's schools, but many critics were not fully satisfied by that statement or by the actions that followed it. In the summer of 2003 Hare Krishna temples in the United States were filing for chapter 11 bankruptcy protection and one of their leaders called the decision an attempt to protect ISKCON from a lawsuit that "threatens to shut down an entire religion."[34] Whether ISKCON would indeed be destroyed by the lawsuit remained to be seen in 2004, but the continuing troubles of the movement suggest that it will not be able soon, if ever, to return the prominence in American religious life that it experienced in the 1970s.

The abuses of power and people that marked the post-Prabhupada years of ISKCON lent additional support to the anticult movement's generic characterization of cult leaders as exploitative con men, but it is important to note that it was not the founder of ISKCON but rather the first generation of his would-be successors to whom the abuses can be traced. It is possible that the potential for abuse is at least as inherent in certain types of situations, such as the control that the successor gurus exercised over their devotees, as it is in certain types of people. In his analysis of the interrelationships between the leader of the Japanese new religion Aum Shinrikyo, Shoko Asahara, and his disciples, Robert Jay Lifton cautioned that "guru, disciple, and the bond between them are all more complex than usually described."[35] As the lawsuit against ISKCON and its consequences unfold, Lifton's warning should lead observers away from simplistic analyses to more nuanced views of the relations between gurus and those who submit to their authority, as it should in general whenever the interactions between leaders and followers are under examination.

Bhagwan Shree Rajneesh/Osho

One of the most colorful and flamboyant Indian spiritual teachers ever to work in the United States arrived in 1981 to set up a utopian community in the hostile desert environment of eastern Oregon. He already carried with him more than a whiff of notoriety, occasioned by the radical therapies that had once been practiced at his Indian ashram and for his outspoken views on sex, politics, and religion. By the time he arrived he had already attracted thousands of religious seekers from all over the world to his ashram in Poona and considerable opposition from the Indian government and others for his unorthodox views. The teacher, then known as Bhagawan ("the enlightened or awakened one") Shree ("master") Rajneesh (his family name), claimed to have experienced enlightenment in 1953, at the age of twenty-one. In the late 1950s through the mid-1960s he completed his studies, earning a master's degree in philosophy, and began to teach at the University of Jabalpur. He gave up his academic post in 1966, after a series of clashes with other academics and with various Indian political figures, to devote himself to the study and teaching of meditation. He began by sponsoring "meditation camps" at a variety of locales and eventually opened his ashram in Poona in 1974.

From the beginning Rajneesh's teaching had been eclectic and focused on meditative practice. Like Swami Prabhupada, his ideas had their roots in the Hindu Advaita Vedanta tradition, with its emphasis on the denial of all dualities such as those between the material and spiritual and between man and God, and included the common Hindu and Buddhist notions that life in the world inhibited one's search for self-realization and that attachments to this world and to the individual ego needed to be abandoned in order to approach enlightenment.[36] But Rajneesh was often fiercely critical of religion in general and of specific religious traditions, including Hinduism, Buddhism, and Christianity. He had no interest in developing an alternative religious or philosophical system. He explicitly rejected the notion of ideological consistency in favor of a flexible concept of "atomistic truth," in which what was true in one moment would not necessarily be so in the next.[37] In his estimation, commitment to an unvarying system of beliefs could easily prevent his students from being in the "herenow," a fundamental prerequisite for the successful practice of meditation.[38]

Some of the flavor of Rajneesh's teaching about the goals and practice of meditation can be gleaned from his retrospective account of his own experience of enlightenment. He recalls that "for many lives I had been

Bhagwan Shree Rajneesh, July 20, 1985. © Bettmann/CORBIS.

working—working on myself, struggling, doing whatsoever can be done— and nothing was happening."[39] It was the striving for enlightenment itself that was holding him back. Rajneesh writes that, seeing his efforts as futile, he simply gave up trying to achieve enlightenment. Then, to his surprise, "the day I was not expecting something to happen, it started happening. A new energy arose—out of nowhere."[40] From that he realized the crucial lesson of detachment—from his striving, from his self, from his history, from his autobiography, and from anything else that asserted his separation from the rest of the universe. His perceptions were further confirmed by a visionary experience in which he awoke to feel "a great presence around me in the room. It was a very small room. I felt a throbbing life around me, a great vibration—almost like a hurricane, a great storm of light, joy, ecstasy. I was drowning in it."[41] His experience confirmed for him what he had learned from Buddha and the great Indian philosopher Shankara, that this world is *maya,* a mirage or illusion. But on the other hand, "another dimension became available. Suddenly it was there, the other reality, the separate reality, the really real, or whatsoever you want to call it—call it god, call it truth, call it dhamma, call it tao, or whatsoever you will. It was nameless."[42] Rajneesh summed up his experience with a classic image of nondualism, claiming that "for the first time I was not alone, for the first time I was no more an individual, for the first time the drop has come and fallen into the ocean."[43] Rajneesh's goal was to facilitate such experiences among his students.

His most distinctive personal contribution toward that end was the practice known as dynamic meditation. As he explained it to one of his students, "when you are doing the Dynamic, this is not really meditation. First you have to throw out all the junk, speediness, impatience, hurry, repressions that prevent you from going into silence. You have woken yourself up by jumping, dancing, breathing, shouting. These are all devices to make you more alert. Then—waiting. *Waiting with full awareness is meditation.*"[44] The clearing away of obstacles to being in the "herenow" is a consistent theme in both Rajneesh's statements about meditation and those of his students. For example, Rajneesh told a story of his encounter with a Sufi mystic who had for thirty years been diligently following a particular method of meditation, but, in Rajneesh's view, he had become more dependent on the method than the goal it was supposed to help him achieve.[45] Similarly, he told a student that she had effectively achieved outer silence, but that inside her head there was still far too much chattering going on.[46] Rajneesh taught that the need to abandon attachments extended to him as well. One student remembers being told "You're not to follow me—I don't have followers—I have lovers, I have friends. You are not to imitate me, all I want is for you to become yourself. Be like you!"[47] The same student attested that "a good part of discipleship is getting over my own barriers to becoming myself."[48]

Rajneesh's willingness to shock people in order to awaken them, whether through physical exertions or outrageous statements, contributed to his welcoming a variety of therapists from the Human Potential Movement, most notably associated with the Esalen Institute in California, to the Poona ashram. Beginning in 1975 Rajneesh began to incorporate a variety of therapies into the practices of the ashram. Freed from the regulatory and professional constraints in their countries of origin, some of the therapists undertook radical experiments, including the use of violence and sexual encounters for ostensibly therapeutic goals. But when one of the founders of Esalen, Richard Price, denounced the practices at the ashram and others opened the unconventional practices to public scrutiny, Rajneesh terminated the experiments in therapy after about five years. But the lingering aftertaste of that exposure, along with the continued bad blood produced by Rajneesh's vitriolic criticisms of an Indian politician, led Rajneesh to consider moving his base of operations.[49] After failing to secure acceptable sites in India, Rajneesh set his sights on the United States.

Although he initially settled in New Jersey, Rajneesh soon moved to eastern Oregon, where some of his students had purchased 64,000 acres of land constituting the former Big Muddy Ranch and leased another adjacent 17,000 acres, near the tiny town of Antelope. Rajneesh's goal was to create a "Buddhafield," which one student described as "a place where individual seekers can gather with other individual seekers in the voyage of self-discovery" and where "distinctions are dissolved. Identities and conditioning slip away. Religion and race, nationality and caste, gender and status, color and creed disappear in the oneness of meditation and inner exploration."[50] Many of the programs of the Poona ashram were continued in Oregon at Rajneeshpuram, but for many residents self-discovery often took a back seat to the intense physical labor needed to create a new city in an inhospitable environment. Life at the ranch soon became complicated by both internal and external factors. One of Rajneesh's students, an Indian woman known as Sheela, had played an instrumental role in purchasing the Oregon property. Her position of influence within Rajneeshpuram was not unrelated to the money that she had contributed to the movement, derived from successive marriages to wealthy Americans. But where Rajneesh rejected consistency, cherished spontaneity, and focused on the "herenow," Sheela had both a talent and a thirst for organization and power. From the time of its purchase until her abrupt departure in September 1985, as a result of accusations of multiple illegal acts, Sheela exerted extraordinary control over Rajneeshpuram. Her attempts to regiment life within the commune, restrict access to Rajneesh, and even codify the teachings of the avowed opponent of systematization created severe and persistent tensions within the group. Her attempts to extend the control of Rajneeshpuram over the neighboring town of Antelope sharply exacerbated the tensions between the group and the local population. The aggressive attempts to take control of the entire area prompted the formation of a diverse coalition of local ranchers and other property owners, environmentalists concerned about potential negative effects of expansion, conservative Christians, and others whose suspicions about strange, new religions had been sharpened by the Jonestown tragedy in 1978.[51] The opponents succeeded in attracting the attention of the U.S. government, which for some time had been embroiled in controversies concerning Rajneesh's immigration status. Eventually, Rajneesh was deported in 1985 on a series of immigration charges.

Rajneesh's restless reinvention of himself continued when he eventually resettled in India after his expulsion from the United States and his unsuccessful attempts to gain entry and establish a base in several other countries. In 1988 he experimented with a number of self-designations, including "Zorba the Buddha" to emphasize freedom, spontaneity, and enjoyment in the search for enlightenment, but in 1989 he settled on the name "Osho," whose meaning has been variously interpreted.[52] Osho passed from this world in January 1990, although a memorial notes that he was "never born" and "never died."[53] His passing, however, has had little effect on at least some of his devotees. In a doctrinal statement that at least unconsciously echoes the Christian understanding of the Holy Spirit, one devotee reports that "his leaving the body has had little effect on his living presence. Whether in the Osho Commune International in Pune, at other communes and meditation centers around the world or wherever his *sannyasins* and lovers gather in his name, hear him, read him, or talk about him, Osho is tangibly present."[54] The ashram in India, which describes itself as a "commune [that] belongs to individuals who have joined hands with each other because they are going on an inner journey where they will be alone," maintains a full schedule of events and Osho's own discourses, along with many other texts, are available on the Internet in text, audio, and video formats.[55] One longtime follower of Osho reports only partly in jest that "sanyassins joke that the new information highway will soon double as a transformation highway."[56] Osho's teachings and even his presence remain only a mouse click away, almost instantly available to those who seek his help in their quests for personal transformation.

Adidam

Swami Prabhupada and Bhagwan Shree Rajneesh/Osho both helped to create and conformed to a widespread stereotype of the Exotic eastern guru who came to the United States to accumulate followers for his strange new religion. But the pattern of interchange between the United States and the East has always been more complicated, as the frequent pilgrimages of

Western devotees to temples, ashrams, monasteries, and other sites in the East already suggest. Those complications are vividly expressed in the career of the religious teacher currently known as Ruchira Avatar Adi Da Samraj. Born Franklin Albert Jones on Long Island in 1939, the guru who would later be known by a succession of honorific names including Bubba Free John, Da Free John, Da Love-Ananda, and Da Avabhasa recalls that virtually from birth he was aware of his special status. He reports that

> from my earliest experience of life I have Enjoyed a Condition that, as a child, I called the "Bright." . . . Even as a baby, I remember only crawling around inquisitively with a boundless Feeling of Joy, Light, and Freedom in the middle of my head that was bathed in Energy moving unobstructed in a Circle. . . . It was an Expanding Sphere of Joy from the heart. And I was a Radiant Form, the Source of Energy, Love-Bliss, and Light. . . . I was the Power of Reality, a direct Enjoyment and Communication of the One Reality.[57]

Despite that early experience, Jones had to follow a difficult path before he could begin his teaching ministry as an adult. He reports that his initial consciousness of the "Bright" quickly faded into unconsciousness and only flickered to light intermittently, even though he assiduously applied himself to spiritual practices under the direction of his guru Rudrananda in New York City and "Rudi's" own masters, Swami Muktananda and Swami Nityananda, in India.[58] Franklin Jones only permanently reawakened to his true identity in 1970 while meditating in a Hindu temple in southern California. Adi Da describes that event in this way: "There was no meditation. There was no need for meditation. There was not a single element or change that could be added to make my State Complete. I sat with my eyes open. I was not having an experience of any kind. Then, suddenly, I understood most perfectly. I Realized that I had Realized. The 'Thing' about the 'Bright' became Obvious. I *Am* Complete. I *Am* the One Who *Is* Complete."[59] That experience began Jones' formal teaching career, but a later experience of "yogic death" in 1986 altered the direction of his teaching. As the official Web site of the Adidam organization describes the consequences of that experience,

> until now, the Avatar Adi Da Samraj Himself had not been aware that His Avataric Descent was still partial. From the age of two, He had Sympathetically participated in the conditions of human life. But now there was further Revelation. By virtue of those decades of utter Submission to the

human state, the Divine Yoga of His Descent had truly become complete. He Knew, and His devotees could observe without a doubt, that the Spirit-Force of the "Bright" had now Come all the way Down. By this fullest Descent into His own human Body, the Divine Avatar was, thereby, embracing to the root the plight of all human beings.[60]

That experience was followed by a similar "yogic event" in 2000 in which Adi Da experienced "direct Entry into the "Bright" Itself (the "Midnight Sun"), which is infinitely beyond the body and the spheres of colored lights that make up the Cosmic Mandala."[61]

Adi Da's complete realization of his identity as an avatar of the divine gave his teaching a focus that it has since retained. In Adidam, the disciple's relationship with the guru is of the utmost importance. Adi Da himself has written that "Satsang with Me is (Itself) the only sadhana, the only true Spiritual practice. Living, working, sitting with Me is sadhana. It is meditation. It is Realization."[62] He sums up the practice of Adidam as "Your turning to Me and My Transmission of My own Spiritual Presence—My 'Bright' Spiritual Transmission in response to you—these two together, that is Adidam."[63] Accordingly, residence at one of the sanctuaries of Adidam, in Fiji, Hawaii, and northern California, among which Adi Da himself circulates, is highly desirable for the members.[64] Those who cannot interact with the guru directly are instructed to perform their acts of worship (puja) before a photograph of him. The devotee's discipline of devotion to Adi Da through meditation and study is also complemented by a recommended vegetarian diet and yogic regulation of sexuality.[65]

Despite Jones' early association with a series of gurus and the evident similarities between the practices of Adidam and a variety of traditional yogic disciplines, Adi Da asserts that he has brought a unique revelation to a world in crisis.[66] He has proclaimed about his message that "I did not get anything from books. I got it from no one. I Did it all, I 'Ate' it all, and I Transcended it all. That is how the Great Way of Adidam came into being."[67] Demonstrating an awareness of how gurus and their new religions are subject to widespread suspicion and a recognition of how the intensity of the guru-disciple relationship in Adidam could be open to such questioning, Adi Da has also declared that "I am not here to be the center of a cult."[68] Thus, like other new religious movements, Adidam presents itself as a strikingly novel religious message and also as one that is sufficiently familiar to religious seekers that it may attract their attention.

The testimony of his followers indicates that both through his writings, which have scriptural status within the group, and through direct encounters, Adi Da has wrought profound changes in his disciples. One religious seeker recounts that he had an initial skepticism when he went to India to seek a spiritual master and was told about Adi Da. He reports, "I knew very little about Avatar Adi Da. I had a good feeling and intuition about Him, but He was an American, so I did not give him much attention, for it seemed obvious that America could not produce One of Great Realization."[69] After reading one of the guru's books, however, the seeker experienced a momentous transformation: "my heart was broken by the unbelievable Love of Avatar Adi Da. It was the first time in my life that I truly felt loved without any limitation whatsoever, loved *to* and *from* infinity. I felt like God in Person was loving me and tacitly I knew that Avatar Adi Da was my Master and had been my Master before all time."[70] Other devotees report similarly intense experiences upon encountering Adi Da in person. One female follower recalls that

> I had never had a Spiritual experience in my life, never seen anything except the ordinary material reality. But the minute He sat down, His eyes held me and His face began to "melt." Another Reality was unveiled. . . . I was undone with a force of recognition. My heart said, "You are God"—the Divine Light in Human form. And I loved Him—I felt that I had always loved Him, had always known Him, and yet not until now. I wept with an aching ecstasy in every cell of my being.[71]

Such followers constitute the backbone of the Adidam organization, whether they take up residence at one of the group's sanctuaries or exercise their devotion to Adi Da while still involved in their secular pursuits. They believe that through his teaching and his person Adi Da has shown them the way to true and perfect happiness by the abandoning of the ego and embracing the unity of the universe.

Like ISKCON and the Rajneesh/Osho organization Adidam has also been shaken by accusations of financial and sexual malfeasance. In 1985, the *San Francisco Chronicle* ran a series of articles that detailed charges made by former members that their guru had engaged in sexual exploitation, abuse of the guru-disciple relationship, and fraudulent appropriation of funds.[72] Representatives of the group acknowledged that there was evidence to support some of the charges, but also retaliated with a lawsuit of their own against a group of ex-members.[73] Although the group weathered the 1985 crisis intact when the lawsuits were dropped, it continues to receive criticism from former members. One wrote in 2000 about his growing disillusionment with both the guru's conduct and what he perceived as the failure of the communal living situation in Fiji. He observed that "the whole focus had shifted to an increasingly incomprehensible literature that was far removed from any but the most academic analysis. And the Fiji experiment seemed to have reverted to a kind of jungle rot, like a second-rate movie scenario of an idealistic cult gone to seed around an increasingly mad charismatic leader who had become out of touch with the fundamental tenets of his own original teaching."[74]

Suspicions about its practices and accusations that the group is a cult continue to be voiced. When the group purchased a home in northern California in 1999, it tried to deal directly with the neighbors' concerns. A group representative reported that

> they had various concerns including: Are we a cult? And, what are we doing there? ... We aired everything and we said to the neighbors, "Look, your complaints about traffic are completely right. There's been way too much traffic and that will change." And it has. Because we were just disorganized. There was quite a bit of traffic and it was annoying to the neighbors. And quite properly. ... So we discussed everything with them and subsequently we heard from many of them, almost all of them, saying that they understand our situation and they've kind of relaxed about it now that they know where we're at and where we're coming from. We want to be good neighbors.[75]

In Adidam, as in other new religious movements, actions and beliefs that promote dissonance with the rest of society often coexist with gestures designed to reduce any tension; extraordinary claims made by the leader and devoted followers are vigorously disputed by disillusioned former members, their families, and those who sympathize with them. The Adidam organization remains as changeable as its central figure and will likely continue to transform itself for the rest of his lifetime and as it confronts the transition to a second generation with the inevitable passing of its guru.

Soka Gakkai

As the involvement of the Beats with Zen suggests, India was not the only source of Eastern religious movements that became popular in the United States. In the 1950s a distinctive form of Buddhism was brought to the United States by the Japanese wives of servicemen returning from the Korean War. It ultimately had its origins in the career of Nichiren Daishonin in the thirteenth century. Born as the son of a fisherman, Zenshobo Rencho had a religious experience at the age of thirty-two that convinced him that the *Lotus Sutra* was the supreme expression of the Buddha's teachings and that its essence was contained in its title, *Myo-renge-kyo*.[76] After he took the name Nichiren, or "Sun-Lotus," he began to proselytize vigorously for his new vision of Buddhist truth, to advocate for a democratic Buddhism of the people rather than one controlled by elites, and to deny that any other Buddhists or practitioners of any other religions could be in possession of the truth. Nichiren came to identify himself as the "True Buddha" of the final stage of Buddhism and he recommended the chanting of "*Nam Myoho-renge-kyo*," now translated by English-speaking Nichiren Buddhists as "devotion to the Mystic Law of the Lotus Sutra," as the central practice for his followers.[77] Nichiren's aggressive defense of his own teaching as the only true Buddhism earned him substantial opposition, and even a death sentence, in his own time, but the movement that he founded, though fractured into dozens of sects, has continued to the present time.

The contemporary history of the Soka Gakkai Nichiren Buddhist organization begins in Japan in the 1920s with educator Tsunesaburo Makiguchi. With his protégée Josei Toda, Makiguchi converted to Nichiren Buddhism in 1928 and in 1930 they formed the group known as the Soka Kyoiku Gakkai, or Educational Society for the Creation of Value, which was critical of Japanese educational practices. Gradually the focus of the group came to center more on the practice of Buddhism than on educational reform. The Soka Gakkai group opposed both the Japanese state religion and World War II. Makiguchi and Toda were imprisoned for their views and Mikiguchi died in prison in 1944. While reading the Lotus Sutra during his incarceration, Toda experienced enlightenment. Daisaku Ikeda, the third president of Soka Gakkai International, recalls that incident as a turning point for the movement. He asserted that "very simply, Mr. Toda's enlightenment should be remembered as the moment that clearly revealed the Soka Gakkai as the true heir to the Daishonin's Buddhism. That was the starting point of all our propagation activities and our development today, and I firmly believe it was an epoch-making event in the history of Buddhism."[78] After his release, Toda renamed their group the Soka Gakkai, "Value-Creating Society," in 1946. Soon after, it was imported to the United States by Japanese women who had married U.S. military men. Phillip Hammond and David Machacek have observed that the career of Soka Gakkai in the United States has been a story of "low-key perseverance."[79] Eschewing the high-pressure tactics that had marked Nichiren's own career and that some Nichiren Buddhists still favor, Soka Gakkai has spread in the United States largely through preexisting social networks of religious seekers.[80] For example, one convert affirmed that "my responsibility is to prove the power of Buddhism in daily life, so that people want to ask about it."[81]

Like many of the other groups, Soka Gakkai offers a deceptively simple but powerful promise of self-transformation, based on the message of the Lotus Sutra. A recent book published by Soka Gakkai International puts it this way: "This book has the power to change your life. Although it is not, strictly speaking, a self-help book, it includes the most time-honored and effective self-help secrets ever formulated—the all-embracing system of thought that is Buddhism. It is titled *The Buddha in Your Mirror* because of its most fundamental insight: the Buddha is *you*. That is, each and every human being contains the inherent capacity to be a *Buddha*."[82] In Soka Gakkai, the path to achieving Buddahood is the same one that Nichiren sketched out more than seven hundred years ago. It includes chanting "*Nam Myoho-renge-kyo*" and chanting before one's personal copy of an elaborate mandala known as the Gohonzon, which reproduces the law of the Lotus Sutra and the life of Nichiren, among other things.[83] Soka Gakkai practice also involves study of the Nichiren Buddhist approach to life and the spreading of the message of Nichiren Buddhism throughout the world. President Ikeda stresses both the centrality of the message of the Lotus Sutra and its immense power of transformation. He proclaims that "the Lotus Sutra teaches of the great hidden treasure of the heart, as vast as the universe itself, which dispels any feelings of powerlessness. It teaches a dynamic way of living in which we breathe the immense life of the universe itself. It teaches the true great adventure of self-reformation."[84]

Members of Soka Gakkai attest to having attained extraordinary benefits from their practice. Jazz musician Herbie Hancock, for example, observed that by applying the teachings of Daisaku Ikeda "on how to harness the power of Nam-myoho-renge-kyo—the mystic principle that drives the universe—I have knocked down wall after wall of obstacles in my life and seen the fulfillment of so many of my goals and dreams. I am solid in my conviction that I can handle whatever life throws at me."[85] In her autobiography, Tina Turner recounts how her adoption of Soka Gakkai chanting practice reinforced her resolve to leave her abusive relationship with her husband Ike and strike out on her own. She attested that "the chant brings you into harmony with the hum of the universe, that kind of subtle buzz at the center of all being."[86] Another practitioner linked ritual practices to self-cultivation, claiming that "the essence of my religion is myself, that is to say my 'Buddha nature.' It is a treasure and it is in yourself. The Gohonzon and the chanting are the means that allow it to come out. They are efficient tools."[87] Members of Soka Gakkai have no qualms about chanting for practical benefits, but they typically emphasize that such tangible accomplishments are only preludes to more profound changes in the individual and, eventually, society itself. One British member described the connection this way: "[we] are encouraged to set specific goals when we practise . . . and although they can often be quite self-centered when we start chanting, they mark an important initial step in proving to ourselves that the practice works. Once we have gained this proof, so our practice tends increasingly to turn outwards, towards practising for the happiness of other people or overcoming our own weaknesses or failings."[88] In that view transformation can easily proceed from the material to the spiritual and from the individual to the social. The more people who take up chanting, the more likely is the transformation of the world.

Although the guru-disciple relationship is not as central in Soka Gakkai as it is in ISKCON, the Osho Movement, and Adidam, practitioners nonetheless acknowledge the importance of leadership. For example, one member reports that "when you practise Buddhism, you bring out your negativity; you therefore need encouragement and guides who can show you how to surmount that. If you don't have that, the practice can make you negative. Without good leadership, you can go wrong."[89] A significant factor in diffusing authority throughout the movement was the acrimonious split between the lay organization of Soka Gakkai and the Nichiren priesthood in 1991. Up until that time Nichiren priests had held all ritual authority in Soka Gakkai. They were responsible for providing copies of the Gohonzon for all new believers, officiating at weddings and funerals, and maintaining the central temple in Japan, a place of pilgrimage for believers. But there was a built-in tension between the authority exercised by the priests and that claimed by the lay leadership of Soka Gakkai, each group understanding itself to be the true successors of Nichiren. The split had substantial implications for both sides. The priests lost the patronage and financial support of millions of laypersons worldwide, even though they have established their own lay organization. Nichiren Shoshu issued strong criticisms of Soka Gakkai, claiming, for instance, that "though their religion may seem the same as ours, they lack the single unbroken line of heritage of the Law received directly from Nichiren Daishonin. If one's faith is not based on this line of inheritance, it is worthless to embrace the Gohonzon, for no benefit will be forthcoming."[90] The 1991 split between the priests and lay organization shows again how crucial it is for new religions to settle issues of authority if they are going to build stable and long-lasting organizations. Soka Gakkai was able to withstand the blow of having its members excommunicated by the Nichiren priesthood by forming relationships with priests who had themselves left the Nichiren organization and by developing both a governance system and forms of ritual oversight that fit the group's ethos, particularly in the United States.

In their study of Soka Gakkai in the United States Hammond and Machacek emphasize that the movement consistently puts a higher priority on legitimacy than on growth. They argue that one consequence is that "Soka Gakkai simply never experienced the kind of public conflict that plagued other new religions entering the field at about the same time. It went quietly about the business of organizational development, while many of its competitors . . . were publicly attacked, found bursts of growth short-lived, and now struggle to survive in the USA."[91] Although it is very risky to predict the future of any new religious movement in the United States, Soka Gakkai clearly offers a paradigm for achieving success different than such aggressively proselytizing movements as the Mormons, Jehovah's Witnesses, Unificationists, and Hare Krishnas. Specifically by emphasizing that chanting could be done to achieve material benefits, Soka Gakkai addresses several of Stark's criteria for achieving success. In particular, it retains cultural continuity between the practices of its members and dominant U.S. cultural values, which in turn reduces the level of tension between Soka Gakkai and its immediate social environment.[92] Similarly the movement's emphasis on both self-cultivation and promoting world peace strengthens its appeal to potential members.[93] Those factors suggest that Soka Gakkai may continue to attract members through "low-key perseverance."[94]

Conclusions

The groups in this chapter focus on self-transformation through religious discipline. Among other things, that discipline can involve intensive study of religious texts and ritual practices such as chanting or specific forms of meditation. In many instances, it also involves submitting to the religious authority of a guru. The guru-disciple relationship has often been viewed warily by outsiders as an example of unhealthy abandonment of personal autonomy and such perceptions have contributed to the caricatures of both the stereotypical cult leader and cult follower that are often marketed by the contemporary anticult movement and purveyed by members of the news media who depend on anticultists as their primary sources. But the dynamic interactions between religious leaders and their followers are much more complex than the oversimplifications of the cunningly manipulative leader and the overly submissive follower would suggest.

The topic of leaders and followers in new religious movements will be taken up again in the final chapter, but it is appropriate to note here that it brings to the fore another, more indirect, way in which religions from Asia have had an impact on the United States. As mentioned in the first chapter, Robert Jay Lifton's work has long played an important role in the polemics of the anticult movement. His study of the Japanese new religion, Aum Shinrikyo, has augmented that influence. In *Destroying the World to Save It: Aum Shinrikyo, Apocalyptic Violence and the New Global Terrorism* Lifton develops an analysis of what he calls "guruism" and especially what he sees as its more pathological forms of "totalistic guruism" and "attack guruism." Lifton's work is important not only for its careful examination of Aum and its leader Shoko Asahara, but also because he extends his analysis to include figures like Jim Jones of the Peoples Temple, David Koresh, and Marshall Applewhite, one of the leaders of the Heaven's Gate group. Lifton's analysis shows that the study of new religious movements, like the spread of the movements themselves, is not confined by national boundaries. New religious movements in the United States must be studied in a global, rather than only a national, context. Individual groups, like ISKCON, the Mormons, or Unificationism, have spread throughout the world, and even if they are headquartered in the United States their interaction with other cultures shapes both their self-understanding and self-presentation. Furthermore, controversies about new religious movements in specific local settings also cross-pollinate; the 2003 conference of the American Family Foundation, for example, featured reports on cults in Canada, Spain, and China, in addition to the United States.[95] In addition, because at least some of the academic work on new religious movements gets incorporated into cult controversies on the more popular level, studies of new religious movements outside the boundaries of the United States, such as Japan's Aum Shinrikyo or China's Falun Gong, can help shape the environment for new religious movements within the United States as well. Both Aum Shinrikyo and Falun Gong were covered extensively by the U.S. press and although neither had significant numbers of members in the United States that coverage nonetheless both expressed and shaped the ways in which many people saw them as cults or new religious movements.[96] A new religious group, therefore, need not have a physical presence in the United States to influence the ways in which new religious movements are perceived and treated.

Notes

1. For his testimony, see www.savetibet.org/news/NewsPrint.cfm?ID=1055 &c+66. On Tibetan Buddhism in the United States, see Amy Lavine, "Tibetan Buddhism in America: The Development of American Vajrayana," in Charles S. Prebish and Kenneth K. Tanaka, eds., *The Faces of Buddhism in America* (Berkeley: University of California Press, 1998), pp. 99–115.

2. www.pbs.org/wgbh/pages/frontline/shows/tibet/interviews/gere.html.

3. See, respectively, www.gerefoundation.org and www.milarepa.org.

4. Beastie Boys, "Bodhisattva Vow," from *Ill Communication* (1994), as reprinted in Thomas A. Tweed and Stephen Prothero, eds., *Asian Religions in America: A Documentary History* (Oxford: Oxford University Press, 1999), p. 350.

5. As quoted in ibid., p. 94. For the full text, see www.emersoncentral.com/plato1.htm.

6. As quoted in Tweed and Prothero, *Asian Religions in America*, p. 96. For the full text, see www.walden.org/thoreau/default.asp?MFRAME=/thoreau/writings/week/Default.asp.

7. For a clear and detailed account of the Beats and Zen, see Ellwood, *Alternative Altars*, pp. 139–58.

8. Stark and Bainbridge, *The Future of Religion*, p. 36.

9. For a brief, official biography of Ramakrishna, see www.ramakrishna.org.

10. See, for example, www.vedanta-new york.org.

11. For an online version of *Autobiography of a Yogi*, see www.crystalclarity.com/yogananda/index.html.

12. www.yogananda-srf.org/aboutsrf/aims_ideals.html.

13. Ibid.

14. www.tm.org/news/science_mind.html. For further information, see also www.maharishi.org and www.mum.edu. For a now dated archive of anti-TM materials, see http://minet.org/.

15. On the Hare Krishnas' public activities, see E. Burke Rochford Jr., *Hare Krishna in America* (New Brunswick: Rutgers University Press, 1985), pp. 171–89.

16. See Larry Shinn, *The Dark Lord: Cult Images and the Hare Krishnas in America* (Philadelphia: Westminster, 1987), pp. 34–39.

17. See A. C. Bhaktivedanta Swami Prabhupada, *Bhagavad-Gita as It Is* (Los Angeles: Bhaktivedanta Book Trust, 1983), p. 34, for the full list of the disciplic succession.

18. Ibid., p. 1.

19. A. C. Bhaktivedanta Swami Prabhupada, *The Science of Self Realization* (Los Angeles: Bhaktivedanta Book Trust, 1968), p. 163.

20. Prabhupada, *Bhagavad Gita as It Is,* p. 15.

21. Ibid., p. 33.

22. Prabhupada, *The Science of Self Realization,* p. 72.

23. As quoted in Shinn, *The Dark Lord,* p. 108. For the text and an audio file of Prabhupada's explanation of the "maha mantra," see www.introduction.krishna. org/Articles/2000/09/00124.html.

24. As quoted in Rochford, *Hare Krishna,* p. 100.

25. As quoted in ibid., p. 122.

26. Prabhupada, *The Science of Self Realization,* p. 63.

27. Ibid., p. 61.

28. As quoted in Nori Muster, *Betrayal of the Spirit: My Life Behind the Headlines of the Hare Krishna Movement* (Urbana: University of Illinois Press, 1997), p. 49.

29. For Prabhupada's insistence on the antiquity of the Krishna Consciousness Movement, see Shinn, *The Dark Lord,* p. 84; Prabhupada, *The Science of Self Realization,* p. 83.

30. For a brief summary of the case, see www.hinduismtoday.com/archives/1993/8/1993-8-15.shtml.

31. See, for example, Nori Muster's account of her own efforts as part of the ISKCON public relations staff to counteract damaging portrayals in *Betrayal of the Spirit,* pp. 47–60.

32. As quoted in Rochford, *Hare Krishna,* p. 238.

33. See the materials collected at www.surrealist.org/gurukula/lawsuit.html.

34. As quoted in Julia Lieblich, "Abuse Victims Say Religion Trying to Reduce Payments," *Chicago Tribune,* February 7, 2002, archived along with related news stories at www.rickross.com/reference/krishna. For material on the bankruptcy declaration, see www.surrealist.org/gurukula/bankruptcy1.html.

35. Robert Jay Lifton, *Destroying the World in Order to Save It: Aum Shinrikyo, Apocalyptic Violence, and the New Global Terrorism* (New York: Henry Holt, 1999), p. 114.

36. See Lewis F. Carter, *Charisma and Control in Rajneeshpuram: The Role of Shared Values in the Creation of Community* (Cambridge: Cambridge University Press, 1990), p. 3.

37. See ibid., pp. 35–36.

38. On being in the "herenow" as a prerequisite for meditation, see Bhagwan Shree Rajneesh, *The Book of Wisdom,* vol. I: *Discourses on Atisha's Seven Points of Mind Training* (Rajmeeshpuran, OR: Rajneesh Foundation International, 1983), pp. 7, 8.

39. For the autobiographical account of Rajneesh's enlightenment, composed in 1972, see www.sannyas.org/quotes/19530321.htm. Students have put together a 1,500-page biography formed from a mosaic of his own statements; see www.oshoworld.com/biography/biography.asp.

40. Ibid.

41. Ibid.

42. Ibid.

43. Ibid.

44. Rosemary Hamilton, *Hellbent for Enlightenment: Unmasking Sex, Power, and Death with a Notorious Master* (Ashland, OR: White Cloud, 1998), p. 20; see Carter, *Charisma and Control,* pp. 45–46. For a current presentation of the meaning of dynamic meditation, see www.oshoworld.com/onlinemag/dec_issue/htm/meditation.asp.

45. See Rajneesh, *The Book of Wisdom*, pp. 13–14.

46. See Hamilton, *Hellbent for Enlightenment*, p. 37.

47. Swami Veet Atito in Susan J. Palmer, "The Meaning of Discipleship: Interview with a Rajneesh Therapist, Swami Veet Atito (Dr. Jack Rains)," in Susan J. Palmer and Arvind Sharma, eds., *The Rajneesh Papers: Studies in a New Religious Movement* (Delhi: Motilal Banarsidass, 1993), pp. 85–101, quotation from p. 100.

48. Ibid.

49. On these conflicts, see Carter, *Charisma and Control*, pp. 61–70.

50. Amit Jayaram, "The Story of Osho—Master, Mystic, Madman," available at www.lifepositive.com/spirit.masters/osho/osho-master.asp.

51. See, for example, Hamilton, *Hellbent for Enlightenment*, pp. 115–18, for a personal account; Carter, *Charisma and Control*, pp. 158–240, for a detailed analysis of the conflicts between the commune and its opponents; Sue Appleton, *Bhagwan Shree Rajneesh: The Most Dangerous Man Since Jesus Christ* (no city, West Germany: Rebel, 1987), pp. 44–45 for a hagiographic defense of Rajneesh.

52. See Palmer and Sharma, eds., *The Rajneesh Papers*, pp. 54, 138.

53. See www.sannyas.org/osho02.htm.

54. Amit Jayaram, "The Story of Osho—Master, Mystic, Madman," available at www.lifepositive.com/spirit/masters/osho/osho-master.asp. See Matthew 18:20 for a parallel assertion.

55. For an entry into the extensive collection of material, see www.oshoworld.com.

56. Hamilton, *Hellbent for Enlightenment*, p. 205.

57. The Ruchira Sanyassin Order of Adidam Ruchiradam, *Adi Da: The Promised God-Man is Here* (Middletown, CA: Dawn Horse, 2003), pp. 3–4. I retain the idiosyncratic punctuation of the original in all citations of Adi Da's writings.

58. See www.adidam.org/adi_da/learning_human/index.html. The Ruchira Sanyassin Order of Adidam Ruchiradam, *The Way of Adidam: Five Steps to an Ecstatic Life of Communion with Real God* (Middletown, CA: The Dawn Horse Press, 2002), pp. 17, 112.

59. Ibid., p. 19.

60. www.adidam.org/adi_da/yogic_events/january_1986.html.

61. www.adidam.org/adi_da/yogic_events/april_2000.html.

62. Ruchira Sanyassin Order, *The Way of Adidam*, p. 107.

63. www.adidam.org/adi_da/bright_thumbs/incarnate_divine.html.

64. For brief descriptions of the sanctuaries, see Ruchira Sanyassin Order, *Adi Da*, p. 342.

65. See Ruchira Sanyassin Order, *The Way of Adidam*, pp. 59–69.

66. On the present dire state of the world, see ibid., pp. 23, 73, 74, 81, 85.

67. Ibid., p. 87.

68. Ibid., p. 88.

69. Ibid., p. 90.

70. Ibid., pp. 90–91.

71. Ibid., pp. 9–10.

72. For a selective archive of articles, see www.rickross.com/groups/adida.html; for a fuller collection, see www.lightmind.com/library/daismfiles/. For the text of Beverly Jacobs O'Mahony's complaint, depositions in her case, and other legal materials, see www.lightmind.com/library/daismfiles/omahony.html.

73. The interactions between the group and its accusers are chronicled in the articles collected at www.lightmind.com/library/daismfiles.

74. www.lightmind.com/library/daismfiles/former.html.

75. www.northcoastjournal.com/011499/cover0114.html.

76. For a searchable English translation of the text, see www.sgi-usa.org/buddhism/library/Buddhism/LotusSutra/index.html.

77. For a summary of Nichiren's teachings, see Jane Hurst, "Nichiren Shoshu and Soka Gakkai in America: The Pioneer Spirit," in Prebish and Tanaka, eds., *The Faces of Buddhism in America*, pp. 79–97, esp. pp. 82–85. See also www.sgi-usa.org/buddhism/bofnd.html. On Soka Gakkai in general, see Karel Dobbelaere, *Soka Gakkai: From Lay Movement to Religion* (Salt Lake City: Signature, 2001, ET).

78. Daisaku Ikeda et al., *The Wisdom of the Lotus Sutra: A Discussion,* vol. I (Santa Monica, CA: World Tribune, 2000), p. 21.

79. Phillip Hammond and David Machacek, *Soka Gakkai in America: Accommodation and Conversion* (Oxford: Oxford University Press, 1999), p. 4.

80. See ibid., pp. 139–41, 149.

81. As quoted in Dobbelaere, *Soka Gakkai*, p. 41.

82. Woody Hochswender, Greg Martin, and Ted Morino, *The Buddha in Your Mirror: Practical Buddhism and the Search for Self* (Santa Monica: Middleway, 2001), pp. 6–7.

83. On the meaning and layout of the Gohonzon, see www.sgi-usa.org/buddhism/bofnd.html#gohonzon and www.sgi-usa.org/buddhism/library/Nichiren/Gohonzon/.

84. Ikeda et al., *The Wisdom of the Lotus Sutra,* p. 14.

85. Hochswender, Martin, and Morino, *The Buddha in Your Mirror,* p. xiii.

86. Tina Turner, with Kurt Loder, *I, Tina: My Life Story* (New York: Avon, 1986), p. 194.

87. As quoted in Dobbelaere, *Soka Gakkai*, p. 48.

88. As quoted in ibid., p. 42.

89. As quoted in ibid., p. 54.

90. As quoted in Hurst, "Nichiren Shoshu and Soka Gakkai in America," p. 92.

91. Hammond and Machacek, *Soka Gakkai in America,* pp. 102–3.

92. See Stark, "How New Religions Succeed," p. 13, and Hammond and Machacek, *Soka Gakkai in America,* pp. 108, 122.

93. See Hammond and Machacek, *Soka Gakkai in America,* pp. 123, 126.

94. Ibid., p. 4.

95. For the program, see www.cultinfobooks.com/infoserv_events/2003/aff_conference_2003_1oct_events.htm.

96. On both groups, see the articles archived at www.cesnur.org.

Chapter 5

Groups of Middle Eastern and African Origins

In 1948, while he was in prison in Concord, Massachusetts, after being convicted on multiple counts of burglary, Malcolm Little received a letter from his brother Philbert. In it, Philbert told his brother that he had found the "natural religion for the black man."[1] Had he heard that message from anyone else, it is likely that Malcolm Little would have rejected it. Although his *Autobiography* recounts in gripping detail his conversion first to the idiosyncratic teachings of the Nation of Islam and then to Muslim orthodoxy as a consequence of his pilgrimage to Mecca, Malcolm had long been set against religion. Malcolm's father had been a Baptist preacher, but his son remembered him much more for his espousal of Marcus Garvey's black nationalism. Recalling a visit to church as a child, he wrote that "even at that young age, I just couldn't believe in the Christian concept of Jesus as someone divine. And no religious person, until I was a man in my twenties—and then in prison—could tell me anything. I had very little respect for most people who represented religion."[2] Philbert's letter, however, addressed another topic that had long agitated Malcolm: his experience of racism.

Philbert's letter promised to restore to Malcolm a true identity of which he wasn't even aware. Philbert told his brother that

> you don't even know who you are. . . . You don't even know, the white devil has hidden it from you, that you are of a race of people of ancient civilizations, and riches in gold and kings. You don't even know your true family name, you wouldn't recognize your true language if you heard it. You've been cut off from the devil white man from all true knowledge of your own kind. You have been a victim of the evil of the devil white man ever since he murdered and raped and stole you from your native land in the seeds of your forefathers.[3]

Although Malcolm didn't immediately respond to the letter, he remembered that it struck a positive chord. In fact, Philbert's letter, based on the teachings of the Nation of Islam and its leader Elijah Muhammad, offered Malcolm a comprehensive explanation of his own experience. It offered a view of the world that addressed the cognitive, moral, and even physical dimensions of the problem of meaning. It set the experience of slavery and its aftermath in a sharply dualistic context that attributed evil intent to an entire class of people, the "white man." It held out the promise of a new, and true, identity for all people of African descent, which would link them to a glorious past and recover for them a history and lineage that would ennoble, rather than degrade, them. At the core of the religious ideology was the assurance that Malcolm, like his many African brothers and sisters, would have the opportunity to discover who he really was, to fashion his own identity rather than one that had been impressed upon him. The offer quickly turned out to be one that Malcolm Little could not refuse. At first gradually and then very quickly he immersed himself in the teachings of Elijah Muhammad, who claimed to have been entrusted by Allah himself with a special message to the black people who constituted "the Lost-Found Nation of Islam here in the wilderness of North America."[4] Soon he would become widely known in American society by the new name that signaled his conversion to the Nation of Islam, Malcolm X.

The Nation of Islam will be discussed at greater length later in this chapter, but Malcolm's initial encounter with the movement articulates themes that will be addressed by several of the groups in this chapter. The dream of personal transformation that has been pursued by devotees of Krishna, Rajneesh/Osho, Adidam, and Nichiren (as discussed in the previous chapter), and devotees of New Age teachings (covered in chapter 3) centered on finding one's true identity. In ISKCON, the Rajneeshis, Adidam, and Soka Gakkai, among many other groups focused on Eastern gurus, the material world itself was perceived as an impediment to discovering that identity. In this chapter, the role of specific historical experiences, such as the forcible deportation of Africans to the New World as slaves, in creating false identities will be more prominent. In an effort to get out from under identities and cultural practices that have been foisted upon them and to establish personal autonomy, many Americans, especially African Americans, have turned to religious movements that have promised to reconnect them with their historical roots. Although that has certainly not been the only appeal exerted by religions of Middle Eastern or African origin for people in the United States, it has nonetheless been a prominent one.

On the other hand, there are new religious movements from the same cultural areas, such as the Baha'i faith, that attempt to break down, rather than reassert, cultural distinctiveness. They emphasize what human beings have in common rather than what sets them apart. Finally, there are, as always, individual practitioners who engage with new religious movements on their own terms, feeling free to adopt and adapt whatever attracts them in a given religious system, regardless of whether their participation would be welcomed by other members of the movement or group. In so doing, they demonstrate what Peter Berger has identified as one of the hallmarks of the contemporary religious scene. In his classic treatment of the sociology of religion, *The Sacred Canopy,* Berger argued that in the contemporary world the practice of religion has become increasingly individualized and privatized. As a result, the individual, rather than the community, an institution, or a specific leader, wields the authority to determine religious practices and beliefs. Such is the case for those who participate in what Stark and Bainbridge called an "audience cult" or what Colin Campbell identified as the "cultic milieu."[5] Although there are still many participants in new religious movements who willingly accept external authorities, those who do not often create their own religious worldviews and practices from an eclectic range of sources. That will be true of some figures in this chapter who imaginatively borrow elements from religious traditions, like Vodou or Santeria, that originally had strong ties to particular ethnic groups. Motives for participating in new religious movements and ways of appropriating them never fit a single pattern; they are as diverse as the individuals who engage new teachings. That general guideline holds true for the groups in this chapter.

The Moorish Science Temple

Although it is clear that West African Muslims who were shipped to the New World as slaves attempted to maintain their religious practices, it is possible to gain only brief glimpses of how they conducted their religious lives under the oppressive regime of slavery. For example, in his account of a visit to a plantation in North Carolina at the middle of the nineteenth century, Charles Ball, an ex-slave himself, observed that "there was one man on this plantation, who prayed five times every day always turning his face to the East, when in the performance of his devotions."[6] The extraordinary deprivations of systematic slavery, however, made it difficult for individuals to preserve their religious commitments and to exercise them publically. It does not seem, however, that organized fusions of Muslim slaves' native religion with the Christianity of the slaveholders developed into full-blown movements, as they did with Vodou in Haiti, Santeria in Cuba, or Candomble in Brazil. The Islam that slaves brought with them from West Africa seems largely to have died with them.

In the early twentieth century, however, the former Timothy Drew succeeded in creating an Islamic movement that attracted substantial numbers of African Americans, the Moorish Science Temple. Drew produced his own sacred text, *The Holy Koran of the Moorish Science Temple,* claimed to be a prophet, and gave himself a new name, Noble Drew Ali, to signify his religious status. His message suggested that a great transformation was about to occur. He wrote that "the last Prophet in these days is Noble Drew Ali, who was prepared divinely in due time by Allah to redeem men from their sinful ways; and to warn them of the great wrath which is sure to come upon the earth."[7] Anticipating the teaching of the Nation of Islam about the true nature of African-Americans, Drew Ali warned that "the fallen sons and daughters of the Asiatic Nation of North America need to learn to love instead of hate; and to know their higher self and lower self. This is the uniting of the Holy Koran of Mecca, for teaching and instructing all Moorish Americans."[8] One of Drew Ali's primary goals in his *Holy Koran,* which bears virtually no substantive resemblance to the Qur'an of orthodox Islam, was to establish a lineage for African Americans. He asserted that "the inhabitants of Africa are the descendants of the ancient Canaanites from the land of Canaan" and in Africa "many of their brethren from Asia and the Holy Lands joined them."[9] Consequently, he offered his followers a new, exalted identity: "what your ancient forefathers were, you are today without doubt and contradiction."[10]

Apparently unsatisfied with linking his African American audience with the holy lands of Canaan, Africa, and Arabia, Drew Ali devoted much of his text to describing how a recovery of the true "genealogy of Jesus with eighteen years of the events, life works, and teachings in India, Europe, and Africa" contributed to his religious system.[11] In fact, his *Holy Koran* is a highly eclectic combination of a retelling of the life of Jesus that emphasizes the so-called lost years, detailed "moral directives" for proper conduct of members of the Temple, and assertions about the glorious past of African Americans. Throughout the text, Drew Ali's aim is to encourage his readers to "know thyself and thy father God Allah" and to live out the consequences of that knowledge with pride, dignity, and purpose.

In 1913 Noble Drew Ali founded his first community in Newark, New Jersey. The movement grew steadily over the next decade and temples were established in Detroit, Philadelphia, Cleveland, Pittsburgh, Chicago, and other cities in the East and Midwest. By 1923 Drew Ali had moved headquarters to Chicago and in 1928, he settled on the name of Moorish Science Temple for his own community. He composed the *Holy Koran* in 1927. Drew Ali exhorted his followers to a sober morality. In language that recalled the King James Version of the Bible, he reminded them that "Ye are the children of one father, provided for by his care; and the breast of one mother hath given you suck. Let the bonds of affection, therefore, unite thee with thy brothers, that peace and happiness may dwell in thy father's house. And when ye separate in the world, remember the relation that bindeth you to love and unity; and prefer not a stranger before thy own blood."[12] Drew Ali's moral exhortations make up about half of his *Holy Koran* and they are founded on an explicitly stated view of human nature. He tells his readers that "thou art, from the womb of thy mother, various and wavering, from the loins of thy father inheriteth thou instability."[13] Help is available, however, in the teachings of Allah, as proclaimed by his prophet Noble Drew Ali.

Noble Drew Ali's teaching reflected the Pan-Africanism of his time. He cast his net widely to include Moors, Egyptians, "Hindoos," and Central and South Americans under the banner of the "Asiatic Nations" whose true and natural religion was Islam. He drew Jesus into the orbit of Islam both by detailing his sojourns in India and Africa and by having him testify that Allah was the one, true God.[14] Perhaps influenced by his familiarity with esoteric sources such as *The Aquarian Gospel of Jesus the Christ,* Drew Ali reported that in a sermon given in Benares, India, Jesus claimed that

> the nations of the earth see Allah from different points of view, and so he does not seem the same to every one. Man names the part of Allah he sees, and this to him is all of Allah; and every nation sees a part of Allah, and every nation has a name for Allah. You Brahmans call him Parabraham; in Egypt he is Thoth; and Zeus is his name in Greece; Jehovah is his Hebrew name; but everywhere he is the causeless Cause, the rootless Root from which all things have grown.[15]

Drew Ali thus attempted both to homogenize and to transform his audience's sense of history. In his exposition, Africa became the root source of human civilization and Allah became the object of all human religions. An awareness of history, he believed, would lead inexorably to African Americans recognizing who they really were and how they should live their lives in accordance with that knowledge. To signify their new identities, Drew

Ali gave converts to his movement new names to indicate their African heritage and identification cards that expressed their allegiance to "all the divine prophets, Jesus, Mohammad, Buddha, and Confucius."[16]

Although it met with some success, the Moorish Science Temple was plagued by divisions virtually from the beginning. In a shocking development, Drew Ali was arrested in 1929 and charged with the shooting death of one of his rivals. He died soon after he was released from jail on bond to await his trial. The movement then fragmented into factions as several of Drew Ali's original disciples contended for leadership positions. Despite ongoing investigations by the FBI, on suspicion of having expressed seditious pro-Japanese sentiments during the Second World War among other things, the Moorish Science Temple, in various forms has continued to attract members up to the present.[17] In the 1990s one of the movement's newspapers made a familiar plea to college students: "while you are working toward your undergraduate and graduate degrees, you should also work toward an understanding of who you are, what is your name and nationality."[18]

Among the groups that claim to continue the tradition of Noble Drew Ali is the Sid-Jul Mosque, which seems to have its primary manifestation in cyberspace. It claims to represent the "Renewed Moorish Movement" that simultaneously continues and alters Drew Ali's teachings. In some matters it seems inclined more toward Muslim orthodoxy. For example, as its Web site explains, "The Moorish American Sid-Jul Mosque does not observe the *Moorish American Prayer* of the MSTA. Under the leadership of the Caliph of Prophet Noble Drew Ali, the SJM recognizes al-Hamd (al-Faatihah) as the Du'aa of the Upright Ummah and Moorish America."[19] That is, it replaces a prayer apparently composed by Noble Drew Ali with the recitation of the opening Sura, or chapter, of the Qur'an, the Fatihah. Similarly, the Sid-Jul Mosque does not observe a holiday on the birthday of Noble Drew Ali, as the Moorish Science Temple had.[20]

Another group that traces its origins to the work of Noble Drew Ali is the Moorish Orthodox Church of America. Despite its claim to Orthodoxy, the group, which was started by a handful of white poets and jazz musicians in the 1950s in Washington, D.C., developed a thoroughly eclectic theology. The group's own description of its history gives the flavor of its various influences. The church's Web site reports that in the 1960s it

more or less abandoned all "Orthodoxy" (though not the name) and found its true spirit in Sufism. What interested us most was Sufism of various unorthodox varieties, including Ismailism (the teachings of the

Assassins). But many other strains were woven into the M.O.C. in the 60's, including Advaita Vedanta, Tantra, Neo-American-style psychedelic mysticism, Native American Symbolism, and insurrectionist activism.[21]

The Moorish Orthodox Church sees its connection with Noble Drew Ali primarily in Drew Ali's fascination with esoteric lore as evidenced in some of the more obscure statements in the *Holy Koran,* such as "Allah and man are one."[22] In emphasizing that dimension of Drew Ali's teaching, the Moorish Orthodox Church has simultaneously played down the importance of Drew Ali's central assertion that African Americans need to recover a sense of their true identity and their extraordinary history. It is an open question whether Drew Ali would recognize his teaching in the group that claims to continue his legacy.

Even at its peak in the 1920s Moorish Science appears to have attracted no more than forty thousand adherents. But, in all of its various forms, it served as a vehicle to spread ideas like the Asiatic origins of African Americans, the notion that they had forgotten their true identities and history, and the claim that there was a natural affinity between people of African descent and the religion of Islam. All of those ideas would receive a much broader currency in a religious movement that began in the 1930s.

The Nation of Islam and Its Offshoots

At the beginnings of the Nation of Islam stands the enigmatic figure of W. D. Fard, who was also known by several other names. When he appeared in Detroit in the summer of 1930 as a peddler of Asian and African goods, he also had another mission. He told one of his earliest followers, "I have come from the Holy City of Mecca. More about myself I will not tell you yet, for the time has not yet come. I am your brother. You have not seen me in my royal robes."[23] In itself that statement hints at a similar blend of ideas that marked the teaching of Noble Drew Ali in the previous two decades, including proselytization for Islam, focus on the true identity and history of African Americans, racial solidarity, and impending dramatic transformations. Like Drew Ali, Fard found a ready audience in the African American community. Another early convert reported that "up to that day I always went to the Baptist church. After I heard the sermon from the prophet, I was turned around completely."[24] Like Noble Drew Ali, Fard used Christianity as a platform for his innovative teaching. Although he claimed to be a prophet of Allah, he also portrayed himself as someone who would "displace the old Christ that Christianity gave black people."[25] Also like Drew Ali, Fard also claimed to be able to reveal the true identity of Africans in America. But unlike Drew Ali, he declared them to be "members of the lost tribe of Shabazz, stolen by traders from the Holy City of Mecca 379 years ago."[26] Echoing Drew Ali, but with a somewhat tighter focus, Fard asserted that "the original people must regain their religion, which is Islam, their language, which is Arabic, and their culture, which is autonomy and higher mathematics, especially calculus."[27] His references to higher mathematics indicated that Fard, too, was interested in esoteric wisdom.

Among those who were galvanized into action by Fard's preaching was Elijah Poole. Born in Georgia as the son of a Baptist preacher, Poole was part of the great migration of southern blacks to northern cities in the early part of the twentieth century. He would find his true calling as an acolyte of W. D. Fard and as the founder of the Nation of Islam. In a move that guaranteed not only the centrality of Fard to the movement but also ensured his own supreme authority within the Nation of Islam, Poole, who soon took the name Elijah Muhammad, proclaimed not only that Fard was a prophet of Allah but that he was Allah himself. Elijah Muhammad pulled no punches in his characterization of Fard. He wrote that "Allah came to us from the Holy City Mecca, Arabia, in 1930. . . . He came alone. He began teaching us the knowledge of ourselves, or God and the devil, of the measurement of the earth, of other planets, and of the civilization of some of the planets other than earth."[28] In that view, Fard's wisdom moved well beyond the identity and history of Africans to much more esoteric topics.

During his long career as head of the Nation of Islam, Elijah Muhammad would often appeal to his closeness to Fard, who in 1934 vanished as mysteriously as he had appeared in 1930, in order to reassert his own authority.[29] In 1960 Elijah Muhammad told a large group of his followers, "I am the man, I am the Messenger. . . . I came directly from God. I am guided by God. I am in communication with God, and I know God. If God is not with me . . . protecting me, how can I come and say things no other man has said and get away with it?"[30] Elijah Muhammad's teaching about the true history and identity of African Americans and, importantly, the true nature and history of their white oppressors quickly spread beyond the black neighborhood in Detroit where Fard had first appeared. But the spread of the movement was also frustrated by several factors. After Fard's disappearance, Elijah Muhammad had moved the headquarters of the movement to Chicago and attempted to consolidate his power by identifying Fard as Allah and himself as a prophet of Allah. Several of the early followers, including Elijah Muhammad's brother Kallat, took issue with these proclamations and some of them set up their own organizations. Reacting to death threats, Elijah Muhammad spent some seven years roaming the East Coast, preaching wherever he could. The onset of the Second World War created further difficulties for the fledgling movement. The Nation of Islam's interactions with several pro-Japanese organizations attracted the attention of the FBI. In 1942 Elijah Muhammad and his son Emmanuel were convicted of failing to register for the draft and they spend the period from 1942 to 1946 in prison. While in prison, however, they continued an active ministry, and prisons have remained a fertile recruiting ground for black nationalist groups like the Nation of Islam up to the present day. When he was released from prison in 1946 Elijah was the uncontested leader of the Nation and his subsequent efforts produced a substantial increase in membership throughout the 1950s.[31]

Certainly the most influential convert from that period was the petty criminal, Malcolm Little. When Malcolm himself was released from prison in 1952, through the intercession of his family he had already committed to the Nation of Islam and conducted a lengthy correspondence with Elijah Muhammad. While in prison Malcolm had honed his considerable intellectual skills through extensive reading and had already turned them to the service of the Nation of Islam. He was especially vigorous in debates with his fellow inmates. One of them recalled that "they would be debating different things on race, religion, and Malcolm would back 'em to the wall with his questions and answers."[32] One of his fellow Muslims explained Malcolm's readiness to take up the cause of Islam in this way:

> When Malcolm came out, he was full o' fire. . . . He got out at the right time and the right place, so he could expound. He came to Detroit, and he was surprised to find that there were so few people in this powerful teaching. He got on the podium, and he told them, "I'm ashamed. I'm surprised that you are sitting here, and so many empty seats." He said, "Every time you come here, this place should be full." And that excited the Honorable Elijah Muhammad, it excited the believers who had any energy. And we brought in people, just hundreds of them.[33]

Malcolm quickly became the foremost exponent of the Nation of Islam, with his public recognition soon surpassing that of Elijah Muhammad.

Elijah Muhammad seated with Martin Luther King Jr., February 23, 1966. ©
Bettmann/CORBIS.

Malcolm accepted one of the central myths of the Nation of Islam as an
explanation of the current situations of both black and white people.
"Yacub's history" teaches that the original humans were black people
and that they founded the city of Mecca. Among them was a group of
twenty-four scientists, one of whom created the "especially strong black
tribe of Shabazz," the ancestors of contemporary African Americans. Some
time later, however, a dissident preacher and scientist, Mr. Yacub, began a
series of eugenics experiments that would eventually produce a race of
"blond, pale-skinned, cold-blue-eyed devils." In his *Autobiography,* Malcolm reported that "Mr. Elijah Muhammad teaches his followers that
within six months time, through telling lies that set the black men fighting
among each other, this devil race had turned what had been a peaceful
heaven on earth into a hell torn by quarreling and fighting." Things only
got worse from there. Allah, according to the myth, sent Moses to civilize
the white race and it was prophesied that they would rule the earth for six
thousand years, up until the present time. It was also prophesied that at
the end of that period, "the black original race would give birth to one
whose wisdom, knowledge, and power would be infinite." That person

was W. D. Fard, whose messenger was Elijah Muhammad.[34] "Yacub's history" set the experience of slavery and continuing white racism in a broader mythological and historical context; it provided a promise of the reversal of the current degraded situation of the "original men" that would restore their dignity as individuals and reconnect them with their own culture. It is in that context that Malcolm understood the adoption of "X" as a last name. As he put it, "for me, my 'X' replaced the white slave-master name of 'Little' which some blue-eyed devil named Little has imposed on my paternal forebears."[35] The transformation of identity that was symbolized by the adoption of a new surname was mirrored on a larger scale by an anticipated transformation of society. Elijah Muhammad affirmed that "in these days of Allah, the righteous (the Muslims) are now gaining power over the wicked and will soon rule the earth again as they did before the creation of the white race."[36] Elijah Muhammad and Malcolm X anticipated the "fall of America" and the establishment of a new kingdom for the tribe of Shabazz under the guidance of Allah.[37]

Because of increasing tensions with Elijah Muhammad over his role as a spokesman for the movement, his dawning awareness of Elijah's substantial ethical lapses, and a growing interest in orthodox Islam, Malcolm X severed his ties with the Nation of Islam in March 1964. At the same time he established a new organization, the Muslim Mosque, Inc. The next month Malcolm performed the ritual pilgrimage to Mecca, one of the five pillars of Islam, and he followed it with visits to several African countries. On his return to the United States at the end of June, Malcolm established a separate political group, the Organization of Afro-American Unity. Neither of those new organizations got to develop fully, however, because on February 21, 1965, Malcolm X was gunned down, probably by members or former members of the Nation of Islam, under circumstances that remain debated to this day.[38] Almost exactly ten years later Elijah Muhammad died.

In the aftermath of those deaths the movement developed in two divergent ways. Wallace Dean Muhammad immediately succeeded his father as the head of the Nation of Islam in 1975. But he guided the Nation toward a substantial reconciliation with mainstream Islam. He gave the movement a series of new names that emphasized its continuity with orthodoxy, finally settling on the Muslim American Community in the 1990s and then the American Society of Muslims. He also changed his own name to Warith Deen Muhammad because "Warith Deen" means "inheritor of the faith" in Arabic. During his period of leadership, he has introduced a series of changes to the fundamental doctrines of his father's movement. Instead of identifying white people as devils, he castigated a "Caucasian mentality" that could distort the perceptions of people of any race; he undid the deification of people of African descent and the myth of the original black man; in 1976 he began to refer to both his father and W. D. Fard as Masters or teachers, rather than prophets or deities; he returned to the more mainstream Islamic concept of a transcendent rather than an anthropomorphic God; and he transformed the notion of an apocalyptic "fall of America" into an expectation of psychological and philosophical transformation. Warith Deen Muhammad used the various publishing organs of the Nation of Islam to promulgate these changes and to acquaint his audience with the ritual demands of the five pillars of Islam.[39] Although many members of the Nation of Islam accepted Warith Deen Muhammad's move toward orthodoxy, some criticized him for abandoning his father's distinctive teachings. In 1978 Louis Farrakhan, also known as Minister Louis X, left the group, intending to reestablish the original emphases of the Nation of Islam, including the acceptance of W. D. Fard as the embodiment of Allah, the stress on black self-sufficiency, and the anticipation of the imminent "fall of America."

In the years after his split with Warith Deen Mohammad, Farrakhan has maintained a much higher public profile. Known like Malcolm X for his fiery speeches, Farrakhan has been controversial for his remarks on Judaism, his ties to Libya, and his outspoken advocacy of the original tenets of the Nation of Islam.[40] Farrakhan stressed his continuity with the Nation of Islam by claiming to be the spiritual son of Elijah Muhammad and asserting that "I know of no other father but him. . . . He fathered me in wisdom, knowledge and understanding."[41] Farrakhan also maintained the movement's interest in esoteric knowledge. In 1985, he reported, he was taken by a spaceship to the Mother Ship or Mother Wheel, a small man-made planet that figures prominently in the eschatological vision of the Nation of Islam. Elijah Muhammad claimed that "The present wheel-shaped plane known as the Mother of Planes, is one-half mile by a half mile and is the largest mechanical man-made object in the sky. It is a small human planet made for destroying the present world of the enemies of Allah. . . . This is only one of the things in store for the white man's evil world. Believe it or believe it not! This is to warn our people to fly to our own God and people."[42] On his trip to the Mother Plane, Farrakhan learned that Elijah Muhammad was still alive and was authorized by him to lead black people in the last days.[43] Among the other teachings of Elijah

Muhammad that Farrakhan also reaffirmed were the account of the origin of white people in "Yacub's history" and the belief that humans were supposed to develop into gods.

Farrakhan's maintenance of many of the idiosyncratic beliefs of the Nation of Islam meant that the movement under his leadership would remain in tension with more mainstream Islam. Although he promoted a degree of orthopraxy by informing his followers about the proper conduct of daily Muslim prayers, for example, Farrakhan insisted that Elijah Muhammad "never intended for us to follow completely what is called orthodox Islam."[44] Most important, Farrakhan reasserted the conviction that W. D. Fard was Allah and that Elijah Muhammad was the Messiah and claimed that the Nation of Islam thus received superior guidance that distinguished it from the rest of the Islamic world.[45] Not surprisingly, then, Farrakhan has received ample criticism. A Web site maintained by the Muslim Students Association, for example, compares statements by the Nation of Islam to statements in the Qur'an and finds that the Nation deviates from Muslim orthodoxy.[46] From another angle, the Anti-Defamation League characterizes Farrakhan as an anti-Semitic and antiwhite extremist and provides a frequently updated digest of his own statements to support its view.[47] Both Rick Ross and Steve Hassan include the Nation of Islam on their Web sites dedicated to fighting dangerous cults and provide links to news stories and other resources that cast the Nation in an unflattering light.[48] Despite his capacity for generating controversy and opposition, however, Farrakhan has continued to attract the interest of many African Americans, particularly in large urban areas, and the Nation of Islam remains a vibrant part of African American culture.

Although the split between Warith Deen Muhammad and Louis Farrakhan was the major development after the death of Elijah Muhammad in 1975, there were other, smaller groups that developed largely within the orbit of the Nation of Islam. In 1977, for example, a member of the Nation of Islam, Silis Muhammad, declared "spiritual war" against the reconciliation between the Nation and mainstream Islam and challenged Warith Deen Muhammad to return to the teachings of his father. Silis wrote to Warith Deen that "your undoing of your father's work has resulted in a complete death of the Lost-Found Nation of Islam, rather than its rebirth. This has destroyed the one ounce of hope Blacks in America ever had of being respected as a people of worth."[49] Silis questioned the inevitability of the transmission of traditionally sanctioned authority from father to son and offered an alternative genealogy of authority that resembled Farakhan's claim to be the "spiritual son" of Elijah Muhammad. He asserted that "I will fight against the holy family, if necessary, to give to the Muslims all that is theirs according to the laws of truth. I beg all Muslims to pray to Allah that there be no fighting whatever among Muslims. This can be accomplished by seeking the truth, and by questioning the lie until it dies. I have been ordained by your father to be your spiritual brother, and I am his spiritual son."[50] Although Silis Muhammad's movement has never attained the public recognition of Farrakhan's Nation of Islam, it does maintain more than a dozen mosques throughout the country. Silis Muhammad has actively advocated for reparations for African Americans whose ancestors were enslaved and to stress the need for separateness and independence for descendants of Africans.[51]

Before Silis Muhammad and Louis Farrakhan assumed leadership of their respective groups another schism within the Nation of Islam produced a splinter group that continues to attract a substantial audience, particularly in urban centers on the East Coast. In 1963 Clarence 13 X left the Nation of Islam's Temple #7 in Harlem, which was then under the direction of Malcolm X, to found his own group. He rejected the teaching that W. D. Fard was divine and asserted instead that all persons of African descent should collectively be identified as Allah.[52] Although the new group was initially known as the Five Percent Nation of Islam to indicate that only 5 percent of those of African descent would originally appreciate the truth, while 85 percent of their comrades would remain ignorant and another 10 percent would collaborate with the whites in the exploitation of their own people. As the group developed, it changed its name to the Nation of Gods and Earths, identifying males as Gods and females as Earths, and continued to move away from any substantial connections with mainstream Islam. In a recent essay, one member of the group, I Majestic Allah, claimed that "to place the NGE in an Islamic scope does a disservice to both groups."[53] The author argues that it had always been the founder's intent to separate his group both from mainstream Islam and from the Nation of Islam. It seems, therefore, that what the Nation of Gods and Earths retains from the Nation of Islam is a symbolic language whose primary assertion is that "Allah is the Blackman, who after gaining an acute awareness of his positive qualities, history, and the world around him, actualizes these positive qualities in order to be the creator of his own destiny and a positive enriching influence in his family and community."[54] In that context, the Nations of Gods and Earths' identification of its leader as "Allah" stresses that he has achieved an identity toward which other members should strive. As I Majestic Allah acknowledges, Islam simply gives the Nation of Gods and Earths a set of metaphors for describing a value system, a view of history (including Yacub's history), and a focus on positive African identity that has as much in common with other religious movements as it does with mainstream Islam.

Whatever its sources, the eclectic black nationalist ideology of the Nation of Gods and Earths has had a strong influence on contemporary African America urban culture. One of its primary channels of influence has been rap music and the hip-hop culture that it spawned. References and allusions to the teachings of the Nation of Gods and Earths appear on the album covers and in the lyrics of both mainstream artists, like Erykah Badu, Ice Cube, and the Wu-Tang Clan, and more underground artists.[55] Ice Cube, for example, rapped "I met Farrakhan and had dinner / And you ask if I'm a five-percenter, well, No, / but I go where the brothers go / down with Compton Mosque, Number 54."[56] Followers and sympathizers of the Nation of Gods and Earths also circulate a wide range of magazines, books, and other artistic creations, all of which help diffuse the group's distinctive worldview.[57] Like the Nation of Islam, the Nation of Gods and Earths has also maintained active communications with African Americans in prisons. Relations between the two groups have been cordial, but the Nation of Gods and Earths has received the same criticism of its lack of orthodoxy, and from many of the same sources, that the Nation of Islam has.

Although the beliefs and practices of the Nation of Islam and its various offshoots often moved well beyond the borders of mainstream Islam, their idiosyncracies were far surpassed by a group that was founded in the mid-1960s by a man then known as Dwight York. Since then the group has gone through a number of significant transformations, all of them mirrored in both the teachings and the self-designations of its leader. At its foundation the group offered a form of Sufi Islam for African Americans, perhaps as an explicit alternative to the Nation of Islam. By 1969 the Ansar Pure Sufi movement became known as the Nubian Islaamic Hebrews, stressing the African origins of African Americans and their ties through Islam to the religion of Abraham. York himself claimed to have been born in Nubia and to have been descended from the nineteenth-century Sudanese Mahdi, the leader of a millennialist movement against colonial rule. He styled himself as Sayyid Isa Al Haadi Al Mahdi to reflect those origins.[58] Like the Nation of Gods and Earths, the Nubian Islaamic Hebrews offered a radical reinterpretation of what it meant to be a Muslim. In 1995 York

wrote that "we are only Islamic in the sense that we are in a state of peace
. . . when practicing our cultural observances passed down to us by Abraham, which makes us true Hebrews."[59] In recent years, however, the esoteric interests that also marked the Nation of Islam and its spinoffs seem
to have eclipsed many of the other dimensions of York's group. In the early
years of this decade York presented himself as "Our Own Pharoah
NETER A'aferti Atum-Re," the leader and chief mystagogue of "The
Ancient Egiptian Order."[60] On some 500 acres in Eatonville, Georgia, he
has constructed an "Egiptian" city, Tama-Re, or the "Egypt of the West,"
complete with pyramids, ankh symbols, and many other "Egiptian" arti-
facts. Moving beyond Farrakhan's encounter with the Mother Ship, York
emphasizes his extraterrestrial identity, claiming

> I am a being from the 19th galaxy called Illyuwn. We have been coming
> to this planet before it had your life form on it. I manifest into this body
> to speak through this body. I am an Entity an Etheric being. . . . I traveled
> by one of the smaller passenger crafts called SHAM out of a motherplane
> called MERKABAH or NIBIRU. Then in 1970 A.D., was my time to come
> in the flesh to start my work of breaking the spell of sleep called the SPELL
> OF LEVITHAN or KINGU, the moon spell or lunatic state of mind with the
> power as the "Sun of Righteousness" (Malachi 4:2).[61]

In effect, York has developed a complex gnostic redeemer myth, in which
he himself plays the crucial role. He is the bearer of secret saving knowledge (gnosis) that originates beyond this world; his task is to awaken sleep-
ing human beings to their true identity and glorious history, in his case the
"inner wisdom of the Egiptians" and the origins of the present-day
Moors.[62] Throughout his movement's many literal and figurative changes
of costume, York has never wavered from the conviction that he could
deliver to his audience the truth about both their individual identities and
their ties to a glorious past.

Given the highly distinctive nature of his teaching, it is not surprising
that York has accumulated detractors. Some have tried to reveal the
sources on which his purportedly unique esoteric wisdom rests, others
have sought to bring internal contradictions to light.[63] York's community
has also had several run-ins with its Georgia neighbors. But the most damaging blow to York's leadership of the group was his 2002 arrest on
charges of child molestation. York was convicted of child molestation in
January 2004 and in April was sentenced to 135 years in prison.[64] York's
followers, however, continue to assert his innocence and promise an

appeal.[65] Although York's personal future has been dramatically curtailed, his movement has persisted for nearly forty years, and it is likely that his copious teachings, in some 460 books, will survive him and potentially nourish some sort of successor movement.

Black Jews, Black Hebrews, and Black Israelites

York's claim that "Judaism is part of our culture by way of Abraham, son of Terakh and Nuwna. Abraham was of the dark brown race, and was said to be the father of all nations (Gen 17:4)"[66] raised the issue of connections between African Americans and Jews. Assertions of such a connection have taken two primary forms. One is the more well-known metaphorical use of materials from the Hebrew Bible to describe the experience of African Americans. Moses and the Exodus, for example, were often put to powerful symbolic use in the interpretation of another group's experience of slavery. But beginning around the turn of the twentieth century several groups began to assert a different connection between African Americans and Jews; they were not *like* Jews, they actually *were* Jews. Those groups addressed the same topics of personal identity and communal history that many of the Islamic groups discussed in the previous sections also took up.

One of the first groups, the Church of the Living God, the Pillar Ground Truth for All Nations, was founded in Tennessee in 1886 by F. S. Cherry and soon thereafter moved its headquarters to Philadelphia. Ten years later, William S. Crowdy founded the Church of God and Saints of Christ in Lawrence, Kansas.[67] His church, now based at Temple Beth El in Suffolk, Virginia, is led by the prophet Crowdy's great-grandson Jehu A. Crowdy and has congregations in several locations in the United States as well as in Jamaica and southern Africa.[68] The group endorses the ideas that the original Israelites were of African origin and that Jesus was not God but rather a strict adherent of Judaism.[69] A dissident group, claiming to represent the true Church of God and to continue the original teachings of the founder, has been formed by the prophet Cornelius Owens and is under the direction of Bishop Robert D. Grant.[70] The group acknowledges Crowdy as a prophet, but accepts Jesus as its "Lord and Savior" and also differs with its parent group on some ritual observances.[71]

Two more contemporary groups are worth mention. In May 1967 three leaders of the Abeta Hebrew Israel Cultural Center in Chicago flew

A teacher instructs her class in a Black Hebrew compound in Israel, 1993. © Ricki Rosen/CORBIS SABA.

to Liberia and eventually secured 300 acres of land on which they could establish a settlement in the land of their ancestors. Metaphorically, they were fleeing "Babylon" (the United States) to establish a black Zion in which they could reconnect with their history and cultivate their new, true identities. During the exodus to Liberia one of the members of the group, known by the Hebrew name Ben Ammi, emerged as its leader. After the initial exultation of their return to Africa, however, the members of the group were faced with the hard daily chores of carving a community out of the forest and providing for their basic needs. As the fascination with Liberia waned, they began to focus on another homeland, Israel. In late 1969 Ben Ammi led the vanguard of a new settlement to the promised land. Although the group had formally appealed to Israel's "right of return" policy in order to resettle in "our land and the land of our fore-fathers,"[72] the Israeli government rejected their requests and set into motion a long period of tension between the Black Hebrew Israelites and the government. Relations were complicated by the group's self-under-standing. In an argument that had logical similarities to the ones made by Farrakhan and others about the relationships of their movements to main-stream Islam, Ben Ammi claimed that "our customs are different from yours. We believe only in the Torah, not what was added later. What man has the right to add anything to the Torah?"[73] Members believed that by following the guidance of the Hebrew scriptures they could "establish the Kingdom of God."[74]

While in Israel Ben Ammi consolidated and extended his authority over the group. He claimed that

> my anointing did not come until after we had arrived in Israel. The Father sent a prophet to anoint me and to let me know the further off or great portion of my mission. . . . At the time he anointed me . . . I received the name Nasi Hashalom [The Prince of Peace]. . . . Later on this same prophet came again to tell me according to the word of God that at a later date someone would be sent to anoint me to sit on the throne of David in the spirit and to fulfill the prophecies of he that was to sit on the throne of David.[75]

The characterization of Ben Ammi on his group's Web site, which places him in a line of prophets going back to Moses and Jeremiah, only supports Ben Ammi's own testimony about his significance.[76]

Although Ben Ammi's group, now known as the African Hebrew Israelites of Jerusalem, has long been headquartered in Israel, specifically in the southern Negev town of Dimona, he has frequently traveled back and forth between Israel and the United States in order to spread his message. His statement that "I'm an Israelite. I'm an African. Israelites are, were, and always will be African as far as the continent"[77] effectively captures his conflation of black nationalism and resurrected Israelite religion. His emphasis on improving the situation of African Americans has even earned him the respect of Louis Farrakhan, although Ben Ammi remains wary of too close an association with any groups that could be considered enemies of Israel.

Other contemporary groups are also built on perceived connections between African Americans and Israel. Founded in 1997, for example, "the LawKeepers, Co, is a TORAH based organization of Hebrew Yisraelites (not Jewish) of so-called African Decent (Black) scattered throughout the diaspora."[78] In the group's August 2003 newsletter, its president repeated that "ultimately our goal is to return to Canaan and establish a TORAH only Hebrew Community."[79] In addition to trying to reestablish the link between African Americans and their Israelite heritage, the LawKeepers also explicitly support the call of Silis Muhammad of the Lost-Found Nation of Islam for reparations to the descendants of slaves.[80] Other groups made the connection to Israel in other ways. For example, the Commandment

Keepers Congregation of Harlem, founded in 1919 by Wentworth Arthur Matthews, identified itself with the black Jews of Ethiopia and saw them as the ancestors of contemporary African Americans. On the other hand, Beth Elohim, also in New York City and founded in 1983, is a congregation of black Hebrews that rejects the racialization of terms like "Israelite."[81]

Probably the most controversial group of contemporary black Hebrews is the Nation of Yahweh, led by Yahweh ben Yahweh, the former Hulon Mitchell. Founded in 1979 and based in Miami, Florida, the Nation of Yahweh embraces the goal of returning African Americans to the land of Israel. The Nation, however, departs from the mainstream of either Judaism or Christianity by exalting Yahweh ben Yahweh as the son of God. The group's Web site effusively states that he "is the Grand Master of the Celestial Lodge, Architect of the Universe, and the Blessed and only Potentate. He is here to set the captives free and to cause them that are bound to stand perpendicular on the square of righteousness. For behold, one greater than Solomon is here!"[82] The Nation sets the activity of Yahweh ben Yahweh within both an historical frame designed to bring to descendants of Africans their true history that has long been suppressed and a cosmic frame that identifies the enemies of the Nation as forces of evil. Like the Nation of Islam, the Nation of Yahweh sees itself as living in the last days of an apocalyptic scenario, and it melds its focus on the identity of African Americans as Israelites with a millennial vision that derives largely from Christian sources. An article in the Nation's September–October 2002 newsletter, for example, vividly expressed the millennialist hope of the group. Depicting the mission of Yahweh ben Yahweh as a turning point in history it argued that before his arrival "the great mysteries of the Bible were shocking, disturbing, frightening, and distressing. However, today, because of His teachings, His disciples are not only able to read, comprehend, and consider the prophecies of the Last Days, but are also able to 'reveal' them with astonishing accuracy."[83] As with the Nation of Islam, the imminent transformation of the world that the Nation of Yahweh envisions will restore African Americans to their previous glory, reestablish their true identities, and reconnect them with their proper history.

The Nation of Yahweh has been enveloped in controversy, however, for most of its history. As Yahweh ben Yahweh began both to elevate his own status and to exert tighter control over his group in the early 1980s, he began to resort to violence both to control defectors and to lash out at white society. Although the Nation of Yahweh's official Web site offers an extensive defense of the leader's innocence under the heading "The Crucifixion," in 1992 he was convicted for his part in fourteen murders in the Miami area and was sentenced to prison.[84] Yahweh ben Yahweh was released in 2001. Despite its leader's conviction and the extensive negative publicity it generated, the group managed to maintain itself during Yahweh ben Yahweh's incarceration. One participant in the group's 2001 conference, held just after Yahweh ben Yahweh's release from prison, reported that he had tried to visit Miami in 1993 "to see the Kingdom, firsthand" but that he had found the Temple closed down. But he wrote to Yahweh ben Yahweh in prison and received an uplifting message, "telling me to keep studying and believing in him, and the Kingdom would some day be restored." His final remark was that "I believe that day has finally come."[85] That believer's testimony indicates not only the resiliency of the Nation of Yahweh but of new religious movements in general. Despite ample evidence of the leader's malfeasance and betrayal of the movement's principles, at least some members have managed to view the government's interaction with him and the group as persecution rather than justified prosecution. Although the example of the Nation of Yahweh may be extreme, it suggests that the Nation, like many of the other groups in this chapter, was able to address serious interests and issues among some African Americans and that the attraction of the message, for some, was sufficient to persuade them to reject or radically reinterpret the case against Yahweh by the U.S. government. Simply dismissing the group as a black racist cult or a hate group risks misunderstanding the force of the attraction that its teachings exert.

Rastafari, Santeria, and Vodou

The groups in this section developed as new religious movements in the Caribbean before they entered the United States and were part of a general religious ferment in the Caribbean basin during the slavery and post-slavery periods. Both Santeria in Cuba and Vodou in Haiti grew out of interactions of slave communities with the Catholic Christianity of slaveholders; Rastafari emerged in the 1930s in Jamaica, after the official abolishment of slavery but with the deprivations of slavery's aftermath as a primary concern. All three religions connect their participants with their African heritage. In Santeria and Vodou, although the *orishas* and the *lwa,* respectively, serve as "faces of the gods," the African origins of the spiritual beings are frequently very evident.[86] Connections to Africa are made in multiple practices and beliefs, and those who are perceived to have particularly strong ties to Africa reap substantial prestige.[87]

Like many religions of Asian origin, religions from the Caribbean have been brought to the United States primarily by immigrants. The practice of these religions in immigrant communities has sometimes created serious tension with their neighbors. Perhaps the most striking instance of such conflict is the case of the Church of the Lukumi Babalu Aye in Hialeah, Florida. In the early 1990s the City of Hialeah attempted to prevent the church from carrying out the animal sacrifices that had always been part of Santeria; the church sued to protect its ability to perform its rituals and in 1993 the Supreme Court eventually ruled in favor of the church.[88] The Hialeah Santeria church was not the only one to experience tension with society because of its practice of animal sacrifice, and Rastafarians have also attracted negative public attention for their ritual practice of smoking marijuana, or *ganja*.[89]

Gradually, the practice of several Caribbean religions has spilled beyond the boundaries of immigrant communities and attracted new adherents in the United States. Although there has not yet been extensive scholarly study of those for whom participation in a Caribbean religion in the United States seems to be more of a conversion experience than a continuation of a traditional religious practice in a new locale, a few examples can be cited. For some practitioners, the adoption of new religious practices helps them reconnect with their heritage, in much the same ways as advocated by many of the Islamic and Jewish groups previously discussed in this chapter. Ava Kay Jones in New Orleans, for example, told an interviewer that she went to Haiti to be initiated and took up the practice of Vodou because "I've always been interested in my West African heritage" and "I don't want to turn my back on my heritage."[90] She said of her conversion to Vodou, "I had a calling. Some of the calling was cultural, but most of it was based on my early experiences in the positive occult. I now see my role in life as working with the spirits. There are many spirits of course, and they are not far off. Well my work is to help balance out the spirits."[91] The attraction of Vodou has sometimes crossed racial lines as well, particularly for those who favor an eclectic set of religious practices and beliefs. For example, arguing that "it is time for people to move into a new understanding of creative spirituality"[92] and that the individual is the supreme authority in spiritual matters, Sallie Ann Glassman describes her incorporation of Vodou into her personal religious life in this way: "in

1976, I was drawn to New Orleans to study Vodou, having heard in songs, movies, and books that New Orleans was the Vodou capital of the United States. It was Spirit calling. I have been studying and practicing Vodou ever since. Spirit called out again in 1989 that I begin work on a tarot deck based on the Vodou lwa and the Santeria orishas, consistent with the traditional, Qabalistic framework of the mystical tarot."[93]

In Glassman's appropriation questions of racial identity and heritage are minimized as Vodou is assimilated to Santeria, the Jewish Kabbalah, and other mystical traditions. Vodou and Santeria are removed from their colonial and postcolonial contexts and their communal dimensions are subjugated to the personal needs of practitioners. As Glassman explains her own practice of Vodou, "it feels right. I like it."[94] Glassman's notion that religion is primarily a personal matter brings her appropriation of Vodou and Santeria directly into contact with the governing assumptions that guide many other participants in the contemporary cultic milieu. It is a position quite similar to that evinced by Caucasian Americans who have become entranced with Rastafarianism through listening to reggae. Even more than rap music has communicated the message of the Nation of Islam and its splinter groups, reggae has been the vehicle through which people all over the world have come into contact with the Rastafari. Again, immigrant communities played an important role, but the Rastafarian message quickly moved beyond their borders through the media of popular culture. Items of clothing using the Rasta colors of red, gold, and green, hair woven into dreadlocks, and the smoking of *ganja* became widely adopted symbols of an Afrocentric identity or at least a superficial identification with the African diaspora on the part of some whites. Like the Nation of Islam, the Rastafari gained a sympathetic hearing among many African American prisoners.[95] Although the movement has crossed racial lines, there have not yet been detailed studies about how the Rastafarian focus on African identity has been transformed by, for example, white American Rastas.[96] As with Vodou and Santeria, however, the lack of a single hierarchical organization for all Rastafari creates a hospitable climate for multiple expressions of the Rastafari worldview.

The Baha'is

The Baha'i faith provides a direct counterpoint to the racial exclusiveness of many of the groups discussed in this chapter. The Baha'is developed out of a predecessor movement in mid-nineteenth-century Persia. In 1844 a merchant, Sayyid 'Ali Muhammad, identified himself as the "Bab" (in Arabic "gate" or "door") and began to preach about the imminent arrival of "One Who Would Make God Manifest."[97] The Babi movement developed out of Shi'ite Islam, in which the expectation of a messianic figure, the Mahdi or the hidden twelfth imam, figures prominently.[98] The Bab attracted enough followers to provoke the animosity of the local religious and political establishments, and he was imprisoned in 1848. But the Bab had already engaged the Iranian nobleman Mirza Husayn 'Ali Nuri as one of his followers. Two years after the execution of the Bab in 1850, his most prominent convert had an experience with far-reaching consequences. Mirza Husayn 'Ali Nuri reported that while he himself was imprisoned in 1852, a heavenly maiden appeared to him and informed him of his extraordinary calling. She said to him, "By God! This is the Best-Beloved of the worlds, and yet ye comprehend not. This is the Beauty of God amongst you, and the power of His sovereignty within you, could ye but understand. This is the Mystery of God and His Treasure, the Cause of God and His glory unto all who are in the kingdoms of Revelation and of creation, if ye be of them that perceive."[99] From then on Mirza Husayn 'Ali Nuri identified himself as Baha'u'llah, "the Glory of God," and in 1863 he began a public mission to build a new movement on the foundation set down by the Bab.

Baha'u'llah viewed human religions as part of an evolutionary process. He wrote that "there can be no doubt whatever that the peoples of the world, of whatever race or religion, derive their inspiration from one heavenly Source, and are the subjects of one God."[100] Accordingly, Baha'u'llah saw himself as the latest in a succession of prophets that included Abraham, Moses, Jesus, Muhammad, Krishna, and Buddha. Religious truth, in his understanding, was not the possession of any one group or lineage, but was the common possession of humankind. Its various expressions had been shaped by the conditions of different times and places, but its core was unchanging. As a summary of the Baha'is basic principles succinctly puts it, "there is only one God. All major religions come from God. All humanity is one family."[101] The purpose of God's manifestations in various prophetic figures is, for the Baha'is, ultimately very simple; it is to enable human beings to know God.[102] To that end Baha'is diligently pursue the study of the extensive sacred "Writings" of the movement, pray daily, and endeavor to spread the message of their religion throughout the world. Although there are a few requirements for proper behavior,

The Baha'i House of Worship in Wilmette, Illinois—the only Baha'i temple in North America. © Royalty-Free/CORBIS.

including observation of the Ten Commandments and abstinence from alcohol, drugs, gambling, and gossip, Baha'i religious life focuses on the individual's cultivation of a deep understanding of Baha'u'llah's teachings and private prayer, fasting, and other practices.[103]

The Baha'i movement came to the United States at the end of the nineteenth century and slowly began to attract followers. Its national headquarters are now in Wilmette, Illinois, and its world headquarters are in Haifa, Israel. The Baha'i community claims to number around 5 million members worldwide. It had its greatest spike in membership in the 1970s and currently has over one hundred thousand declared members in the United States. Only in 1993, however, did English speakers get a complete translation of Baha'u'llah's *Kitab al-Aqdas* ("The Most Holy Book").[104] Many members cite the diversity of Baha'i groups as a source of attraction. Recalling the impression that Jim Jones' integrated congregation had on some observers, one Baha'i remarked after seeing a video of a Baha'i youth conference that "it showed all these people with long hair, and some with short hair, blacks and whites, and American Indians and Hispanics and Orientals. And they were enjoying being with each other, and there were no conflicts between the various groups. It really looked like heaven."[105]

Others emphasize the group's intellectual inclusiveness. One member claimed, for example, that "some people appear not to be bothered by the exclusivity of Christianity, or Islam, or whatever, but I think that most of us who have accepted the Faith, we really have found that bizarre that only those in this [Christian group] are 'saved.'"[106] Baha'is are well aware, however, that they have not fully achieved their goals of racial equality. But one member, a convert from the Nation of Islam, expressed his conviction that it was not because of the substance of the teachings of Baha'u'llah. He acknowledged that "there are racist attitudes that exist in some individuals in the Baha'i community. The divine institutions of the Baha'i Faith are capable of handling it. . . . Because there ain't no racism in the Baha'i Faith, but there is racism in individual Baha'is."[107]

Baha'is in general express a robust confidence in the inerrancy of their leadership. When Baha'u'llah died, he appointed his eldest son Abdu'l Baha ("Servant of the Glory") as his successor and the authoritative interpreter of the Baha'i writings. In addition to contributing his own religious writings to the tradition Abdu'l Baha established a structure for the administration of worldwide community affairs. Abdu'l Baha's eldest grandson, Shogi Effendi, assumed the Guardianship of the Faith and exercised leadership of the Baha'i community from Abdu'l Baha's death in 1921 until his own death in 1957. Abdu'l Baha also established the Universal House of Justice (UHJ) as an administrative body, and, in the absence of a designated successor to Shogi Effendi, the UHJ became the sole ruling body of the Baha'is in 1963. Although there had been periodic challenges to the leadership, including to Baha'u'llah himself and also to Abdu'l Baha, the Baha'is pride themselves on never having experienced any fractures in the unity of their faith. Abdu'l Baha attributed the preservation of unity to divine guidance, claiming that "were it not for the protecting power of the Covenant to guard the impregnable fort of the Cause of God, there would arise among the Baha'is, in one day, a thousand different sects as was the case in former ages."[108] As the vanguard of the new society that will be ushered in by Baha'u'llah's teachings, the Baha'i community in its own composition and character provides an indication of what the world will look like when enough people have finally accepted that "humanity is one single race and that the day has come for its unification in one global society."[109]

Although the Baha'is in Iran have been denounced by the Shi'ite majority as heretics and have suffered violent persecution, the community in the United States has largely managed to stay out of contemporary controversies about cults. It has, however, aroused the ire of Christian countercult activists for a variety of reasons. Fundamentally, they argue that the Baha'is vaunted tolerance is not what it claims to be. John Ankerberg and John Weldon assert, for example, that "each religion it claims to accept is not permitted to speak for itself but is re-interpreted to conform, more or less, to the teachings of the Baha'i faith."[110] Not surprisingly, the Baha'i claims to have received a revelation that renders antiquated the message of Jesus and subsumes it within the Baha'i faith draws vigorous refutations from the Christian apologists.[111] Similarly, the most recent edition of Walter Martin's *The Kingdom of the Cults* asserts that "Baha'ism deliberately undercuts the foundational doctrines of the Christian faith by either denying them outright or by carefully manipulating terminology so as to 'tone down' the doctrinal dogmatism that characterizes orthodox Christianity."[112] Not satisfied simply to allow such criticisms of their religion to stand unchallenged, Baha'i authors have engaged in a vigorous exchange with their Christian critics, which has clarified their respective positions even if it appears to have changed few minds.[113]

Conclusions

Religion can be a powerful force in shaping both individual and communal identity. As groups like the Moorish Science Temple, the Nation of Islam, and the African Hebrew Israelites of Jerusalem indicate, religion can be used as a lever to overturn unwanted identities that are perceived to constrain individuals and constrict the possibilities for their development. Religion can offer to individuals and whole classes of people alternative identities that are viewed as more true, more ennobling, and more empowering. New religious movements are particularly well suited to offering such identities because their primary focus is to offer something novel and out of the ordinary, something better than the preexisting options. New religions can link individuals to those who are "really" their own people, their tribes, their ancestors, their forgotten families. Moreover, new religions can effectively reinforce those alternative identities by situating them within a history of extraordinary cultural and religious richness, to which individuals who were previously denied it by oppressive power structures or their own ignorance can again gain access. As individual participants in new religions rediscover their true selves, they also discover the true God.

Religions that address the particular interests and needs of specific racial groups, like African Americans, thus become powerful tools for asserting individuality and distinctiveness; they help individuals understand who they are, what group they belong to, and what they ought to do about it.

As the Baha'is show, however, religions can take another approach. They can emphasize inclusiveness rather than distinctiveness. Instead of honing the sharp edges of differences between "us" and "them" or black and white, they can soften the boundaries between groups and among individuals by focusing on everyone's common humanity. From that perspective the oneness of God and the oneness of humanity far eclipse in importance any differences, which, however important they may seem, are ultimately temporary and ephemeral. While the strong emphasis on group distinctiveness that occurs in groups like the Nation of Islam risks establishing a perpetual tension between the group and the world outside it, the inclusiveness that marks the Baha'is as well as many of the New Age groups discussed in chapter 3 risks both antagonizing those who believe that there substantial and meaningful differences among religions and fostering a vagueness and lack of definition in the group itself. The shape and substance of an individual's or group's religious convictions always have manifold consequences for their interactions with the world.

Notes

1. Malcolm X, with Alex Haley, *The Autobiography of Malcolm X* (New York: Ballantine, 1964), p. 155.

2. Ibid., p. 5.

3. Ibid., p. 161.

4. Ibid.

5. See the discussion in chapter 1, pp. 30–31.

6. As quoted in Richard Brent Turner, *Islam in the African-American Experience* (Bloomington: University of Indiana Press, 1997), p. 24. See also the accounts in Albert J. Raboteau, *Slave Religion: The "Invisible Institution" in the Antebellum South* (Oxford: Oxford University Press, 1978), pp. 46–47.

7. Noble Drew Ali, *The Holy Koran of the Moorish Science Temple of America,* 48:1; available at www.geocities.com/Athens/Delphi/2705/koran45–48.html and at www.geocities.com/Heartland/Woods/4623/. References are given to the chapter and verse divisions of the text. For a survey of early Islamic communities in the United States, see Aminah Beverly McCloud, *African American Islam* (New York: Routledge, 1995), pp. 9–40.

8. Ibid., 45:1.

9. Ibid., 47:1, 5. I retain the spelling of the original.

10. Ibid., 47:10.

11. Ibid., prologue. On the sources used in the composition of the *Holy Koran,* see Turner, *Islam in the African-American Experience,* p. 93.

12. Noble Drew Ali, *The Holy Koran,* 25:1–3.

13. Ibid., 41:2.

14. See ibid., 4:11–16.

15. Ibid., 4:17–19. On Drew Ali's familiarity with esoteric writings, see Turner, *Islam in the African-American Experience,* pp. 93–95. For the Aquarian Gospel, see Levi Dowling, *The Aquarian Gospel of Jesus the Christ* (rpt. Kempton, IL: Adventures Unlimited, 1996).

16. Turner, *Islam in the African-American Experience,* p. 99.

17. For the FBI documents, see www.foia.fbi.gov/moortemp.htm. For an electronic archive of texts, see "The Moorish Science Reading Room" at www.geocities.com/Heartland/Woods/4623/.

18. As quoted in Turner, *Islam in the African-American Experience,* p. 106.

19. www.members.aol.com/sidjulview/index52298.html.

20. See www.members.aol.com/sidjulview/89714.html: "Sidjuls, as Moors of the Renewed Moorish Movement (RMM), do not celebrate Mawlid an-Nabee or the OMM's Prophet's Birthday because they promote the idolization of Muhammad and Noble Drew Ali respectively."

21. www.deoxy.org/moorish.htm.

22. Ibid.

23. As quoted in Turner, *Islam in the African-American Experience,* p. 148.

24. As quoted in C. Eric Lincoln, *The Black Muslims in America,* 3rd ed. (Grand Rapids: Eerdman's, 1994), p. 12. Lincoln's source is Erdmann D. Benyon, "The Voodoo Cult among Negro Migrants in Detroit," *American Journal of Sociology* 43 (1937): 894–907, which is an essential resource for reconstructing the early history of the Nation of Islam.

25. As quoted in Turner, *Islam in the African-American Experience,* p. 150.

26. As quoted in ibid., p. 151.

27. Ibid.

28. Elijah Muhammad, *Message to the Blackman in America* (Atlanta, GA: Messenger Elijah Muhammad Propagation Society, 1965), pp. 16–17. Also available at www.seventhfam.com/temple/books/black_man/blkindex.htm.

29. On Fard's disappearance, see Turner, *Islam in the African-American Experience,* p. 167.

30. As quoted in Lincoln, *The Black Muslims in America,* p. 182.

31. On the history of the Nation of Islam in this period, see Turner, *Islam in the African-American Experience,* pp. 166–70; see also McCloud, *African American Islam,* pp. 41–94, for a survey of Muslim communities in the United States from the 1960s to the 1990s.

32. As quoted in ibid., p. 185.

33. As quoted in ibid., p. 189.

34. This exposition follows that of Malcolm X, *Autobiography,* pp. 164–67; see also Elijah Muhammad, *Message to the Blackman in America,* pp. 2–3, 6, 9.

35. Malcolm X, *Autobiography X,* p. 199.

36. Elijah Muhammad, *Message to the Blackman in America,* p. 23; see pp. 303, 306.

37. On the millennialism of the Nation of Islam, see Martha F. Lee, *The Nation of Islam: An American Millenarian Movement* (Syracuse: Syracuse University Press, 1996), esp. pp. 36–56.

38. See Turner, *Islam in the African-American Experience,* pp. 219–23.

39. On Warith Deen Muhammad's changes, see Mattias Gardell, *In the Name of Elijah Muhammad: Louis Farrakhan and the Nation of Islam* (Durham, NC: Duke University Press, 1996), pp. 102–8. For basic information on his group, now calling itself the American Society of Muslims, see www.taqwa-an-nur.com/Acquaintance.htm. For the newspaper published by the group, see www.muslimjournal.com.

40. On the controversies, see Gardell, *In the Name of Elijah Muhammad,* pp. 232–84.

41. As quoted in ibid., p. 126.

42. Elijah Muhammad, *Message to the Blackman in America,* p. 291.

43. See Gardell, *In the Name of Elijah Muhammad,* pp. 131–34, 158–60.

44. As quoted in Gardell, *In the Name of Elijah Muhammad,* p. 193.

45. See ibid., p. 195.

46. See www.usc.edu/dept/MSA/notislam/?.

47. See www.adl.org/main_islam.asp.

48. See www.freedomofmind.com/resourcecenter/groups/n/nationofislam/ and www.rickross.com/groups/nationofislam.html.

49. www.members.aol.com/akankem/Declare.htm contains the full text of his declaration of spiritual war.

50. Ibid.

51. See www.members.aol.com/akankem/Signed.htm.

52. For a brief history of Clarence 13 X, in catechetical form, see www.awm-online.com/history/nationhistory.html. See also Gardell, *In the Name of Elijah Muhammad,* pp. 224–25.

53. www.awm-online.com/livingmathematics/muslimcom.html.

54. Ibid.

55. See the sample at www.blackapologetics.com/lyrics.html.

56. Ice Cube, "When Will They Shoot," from *The Predator* (1992).

57. See www.truborn.com for a sample of merchandise available and also for an archive of issues of the free monthly magazine *Black Seven.*

58. On York's confusing background, see Kathleen Malone O'Connor, "The Nubian Islaamic Hebrews, Ansaaru Allah Community," in Yvonne Chireau and Nathaniel Deutsch, eds., *Black Zion: African American Religious Encounters with Judaism* (Oxford: Oxford University Press, 2000), pp. 118–50, esp. p. 120.

59. Ibid., p. 122; see p. 123.

60. See www.egiptianmysteries.com/egiptian_mysteries.htm.

61. www.geocities.com/Area51/Corridor/4978/york.html.

62. See www.egiptianmysteries.com/.

63. See www.illuminopolis.hypermart.net/illiyuwm.html and www.illuminopolis.hypermart.net/IAM.html, for example.

64. See Bill Torpy, "York Convicted in Cult Sex Case," *The Atlanta Journal Constitution,* January 24, 2004, p. D1; idem, "Judge Throws Book at Cultist: 135 Years in Prison Ordered, *The Atlanta Journal Constitution,* April 23,2004, p. D4.

65. See www.unnm.com.

66. O'Connor, "The Nubian Islaamic Hebrews, Ansaaru Allah Community," p. 123.

67. On both groups, see Merrill Singer, "Symbolic Identity Formation in an African American Religious Sect: The Black Hebrew Israelites," in Chireau and Deutsch, *Black Zion,* pp. 57–60.

68. See www.cogasoc.org/.

69. www.cogasoc.org/main.html.

70. See www.aboutthelambsbookoflife.net/pages/375513/index.htm for the writings of the prophet Cornelius, which include criticisms of the Virginia-based Church of God and Saints of Christ and www.churchofgod1896.org/ for the organization he inspired.

71. See www.churchofgod1896.org/beliefs.html.

72. Ibid., p. 66.

73. As quoted in ibid., p. 67.

74. Ibid.

75. As quoted in ibid., p. 69.

76. See www.kingdomofyah.com/Ben%20Ammi.htm.

77. As quoted in Singer, "Symbolic Identity Formation in an African American Religious Sect," p. 83.

78. www.thelawkeepers.org/law2.htm. I retain the spelling and capitalizations of the original.

79. www.thelawkeepers.org.

80. Ibid.

81. See the materials at www.members.aol.com/Blackjews/beth1.html.

82. www.yahwehbenyahweh.com/index02.htm.

83. See www.yahwehbenyahweh.com/the_good_news.htm.

84. www.yahwehbenyahweh.com/crucifixion.htm. For a hostile alternative view from a Christian countercult perspective, see www.apologeticsindex.org/n04.html.

85. "Followers of Yahweh Reemerge in Canada," *Miami Herald,* October 15, 2001, archived at www.rickross.com/reference/yahwehben/yahwehben15.html.

86. The phrase "faces of the gods," is from Leslie Desmangles, *The Faces of the Gods: Vodou and Roman Catholicism in Haiti* (Chapel Hill: University of North Carolina, 1993). On the African character of the saints in Santeria, see Joseph M. Murphy, *Santeria: An African Religion in America* (Boston: Beacon, 1988), pp. 32–33. On the spirits or *lwa* in Haitian Vodou, see Karen McCarthy Brown, *Mama Lola: A Vodou Priestess in Brooklyn* (Berkeley: University of California Press, 1991), pp. 3–4, for example.

87. See, for example, McCarthy Brown, *Mama Lola,* pp. 29–33.

88. For the court case, see 1993 *Church of the Lukumi Babalu Aye, Inc. v. City of Hialeah,* 508 U.S. 520, available at www.supct.law.cornell.edu/supct/html/91–948.ZO.html. For current information on the church, see www.church-of-the-lukumi.org/.

89. On the use of *ganja* by Rastafarians, see Ennis Barrington Edmonds, *Rastafari: From Outcasts to Culture Bearers* (New York: Oxford University Press, 2003), pp. 60–62. For the 2001 report of the Jamaican National Commission on Ganja, see www.home2.netcarrier.com/~aahpat/ganja.htm.

90. Ron Bodin, *Voodoo: Past and Present* (Lafayette: The Center for Louisiana Studies, 1990), p. 80.

91. Ibid.

92. Sallie Ann Glassman, *Vodou Visions: An Encounter with Divine Mystery* (New York: Villard, 2000), p. xv.

93. Ibid., p. xvi.

94. Ibid., p. 3.

95. See Randal L. Hepner, "Chanting Down Babylon in the Belly of the Beast," in Nathaniel Samuel Murrell, William David Spencer, and Adrian Anthony McFarlane, eds., *Chanting Down Babylon: The Rastafari Reader* (Philadelphia: Temple University Press, 1998), pp. 199–216, esp. p. 203 on prisons.

96. See ibid., p. 204. At least some of the discussion about participation in Rastafari by people not of African descent is taking place on electronic bulletin boards and in other similar forums. See, for example, the postings at the "Rastafari Times" and "Rastafari Speaks" Web sites, www.rastafaritimes.com/ and www.rastafarispeaks.com. See also the discussions at www.jahworks.org.

97. For brief summaries of Baha'i history, see Michael McMullen, *The Baha'i: The Religious Construction of a Global Community* (New Brunswick, NJ: Rutgers University Press, 2000), pp. 193–95; Moojan Momen, *The Baha'i Faith: A Short Introduction* (Oxford: Oneworld, 1997), pp. 115–29; see also Juan R. Cole, *Modernity and the Millennium: The Genesis of the Baha'i Faith in the Nineteenth-Century Middle East* (New York: Columbia University Press, 1998).

98. See www.bahai.org/article-1-3-0-1.html.

99. As quoted in Momen, *The Baha'i Faith*, p. 119.

100. As quoted at www.bahai.org/article-1-3-0-7.htm.

101. www.bahai.seeker.net/bf_prin.htm.

102. See www.bahai.org/article-1-3-2-12.html.

103. See McMullen, *The Baha'i*, pp. 76–83.

104. See ibid., p. 63.

105. As quoted in McMullen, *The Baha'i*, p. 23.

106. As quoted in ibid., p. 25.

107. As quoted in ibid., p. 166.

108. www.bahai.org/article-1-3-0-3.html.

109. www.bahai.org/article-1-2-0-1.html.

110. Ankerberg and Weldon, *Encyclopedia of Cults and New Religions*, p. 6.

111. See ibid., pp. 15–29, especially.

112. Martin, *The Kingdom of the Cults*, p. 331.

113. See the interviews and responses in ibid.

Chapter 6

Neo-Paganism

In the summer of 1973 a young American woman went to England to see firsthand the coven run by Alex and Maxine Sanders. Alex had founded the Alexandrian tradition of Wicca, claiming that his grandmother had initiated him at the age of seven. The visitor, Margot Adler, has since written one of the most authoritative and influential accounts of contemporary Neo-Paganism, *Drawing Down the Moon*,[1] but at the time she had only been a practitioner of "the Craft" for two years. When she arrived in London she was invited to join in a ritual "circle" that same night. Things got more interesting from there. When Adler arrived at the private home where the ritual was to be held, Alex Sanders was out of town and Maxine was nowhere to be found. Adler nonetheless began to prepare herself to participate, which, since Alexandrians performed their rituals "skyclad," included removing all of her clothing. She gradually learned that the focus of the evening's ritual was to be the initiation of a young woman. As the ritual was about to begin, Adler reports that this conversation took place:

> "Who's the High Priestess" one of the boys asked the woman in black. At this point I began to feel a sense of unease. Wasn't Maxine Sanders the priestess? And where *was* Maxine, anyway?
>
> In response to the man's question the lady in black turned to him, pointed to me (standing nude in the darkness) and said, "She is."
>
> "What?" I said, not believing her words.
>
> "She is," the woman repeated.
>
> I reacted with absolute amazement. "Wait a minute!" I said. "I've just stepped off the street from another country, from another tradition. I have never been in an Alexandrian circle in my entire life. I have no idea what you even *do!* I just don't think this is right at all, and anyway, I don't know how you conduct your rituals!" I was babbling by this time.

"Oh, it's all right," she replied. "It's all in the book, just follow the book."[2]

While that exchange was taking place, the would-be initiate remained naked and blindfolded outside the ritual circle, waiting for her rite of passage to begin. Eventually, Maxine Sanders arrived, and the evening recovered enough from its rocky start for the ritual to begin.

That incident vividly captures several of the prominent aspects of contemporary Neo-Paganism. First, it is focused on ritual and experience much more than on belief. Sarah Pike, for example, argues that "it is in techniques of the body . . . and ritual action that Neopagans most clearly diverge from other religious communities in North America."[3] Second, contemporary Paganism is improvisational, sometimes highly so. The feminist witch, Zsuzsanna Budapest, for example, wrote "rule number one is to improvise any time you feel as though creative juices are flowing. . . . Spontaneous praying is more powerful than the memorized, out-of-the-book kind. What comes through the soul in the moment is more powerful than what is hammered into the brain."[4] Third, there is no single articulated hierarchical system of authority for contemporary Paganism; individuals read and write books, devise prayers and rituals, and construct and hallow symbols virtually unfettered by any external authority. Margot Adler, for example, reported that in an early survey that she conducted, "many people said that they had become Pagans because they could be themselves and act as they chose, without what they felt were medieval notions of sin and guilt."[5] The confusion about whether Adler would officiate at the ritual in London stemmed directly from the rather loose organization of the coven.

Fourth, contemporary Paganism is very diverse. Although it traces its origins to the work of Gerald Gardner in the 1930s in England and to various practitioners, including Gardnerian Raymond Buckland, in the United States in the 1960s, there are many different pieces of the mosaic of contemporary Paganism. They range from Gardnerians who are convinced that they are reviving an ancient pre-Christian religion that had long been suppressed and had nearly died out, through practitioners who avow that they are recovering their own Norse, Germanic, Celtic, Hungarian, or other roots, to feminists who see in the figure of "The Goddess" a powerful symbol that can help women to recover and reappropriate their true selves and stand fast against patriarchal oppression. Fifth, virtually universally in Neo-Paganism there is the casting of the circle to create a ritual space. Contemporary Pagans are not given to the construction of fixed central shrines or other lasting buildings; they re-create a ritual space each time they engage in sacred actions. One practitioner emphasizes that "sacred space provides the setting and contributes to enhancing the mental set necessary for connection with the deeper spiritual aspects of the human psyche. By deepening these connections, we become able to channel the Spiritual Energy of the Inner Self for healing ourselves, for healing others, and for healing the planet."[6] Sixth, as the comment of Adler's unnamed interlocutor suggests, Neo-Paganism, although it prizes improvisational freedom, also frequently displays respect for traditions that are preserved and displayed in books of Pagan lore. Janet and Stewart Farrar, for example, have produced *The Witches' Bible: The Complete Witches' Handbook,* in order to preserve "the exact form and wording of Gardner's rituals, from his original manuscripts."[7] Zsuzsanna Budapest's *The Holy Book of Women's Mysteries* presents a similar potpourri of spells, rituals, and other practical information. Finally, although Adler's initially baffling experience with the Alexandrian coven in London might suggest otherwise, contemporary Neo-Paganism, including Wicca, the practice of magic (sometimes written "magick"), and a variety of other submovements, is a diverse and vibrant religious activity in the United States as well as in other countries.

Those who practice contemporary forms of Paganism differ about its origins. Although it seems largely to have been abandoned in recent years, in the early days of the Pagan revival a powerful myth of origins was widely endorsed. It portrayed Witchcraft as a religion that dated to paleolithic times and was universally practiced under various guises. Later, despite the apparent triumph of Christianity throughout Europe, the Old Religion was kept alive, particularly in rural areas among simpler folk. Even aggressive persecution of witches by the Christian church failed to exterminate the resilient Pagan religion. In the twentieth century a few pioneers were laboring to keep the old traditions alive and to introduce others to their mysteries.[8] Among the important figures in promulgating the contemporary myth of Wicca were Margaret Murray, who in 1921 argued in *The Witch-Cult in Western Europe* that Witchcraft had been the pre-Christian religion of much of Western Europe,[9] and Gerald Gardner, who claimed to have been initiated into a surviving English coven in 1930. After the repeal of English laws against Witchcraft in 1951 and after first having published a novel, *High Magic's Aid,* Gardner published *Witchcraft Today* and *The Meaning of Witchcraft,* which quickly became the basis for a "revival" of Witchcraft in England and elsewhere.[10]

Although the myth of Wicca was widely accepted for a period, the tide has now turned against it. Aidan Kelly, for example, carefully reviewed Gardner's sources and came to the conclusion that "we have no evidence that the Gardnerian movement is in any way a sort of Stone Age religion that was surviving in England in 1939" and that instead it "was founded ... as a distinct religion in September 1939."[11] More recently, both Ronald Hutton and Philip G. Davis have turned critical eyes on the myth of Wicca.[12] Even Raymond Buckland, nurtured in the Gardnerian tradition, acknowledges that "it would seem, then, that there is no *unbroken* tradition" but still affirms "that Wica was a religion of old is certain, as we have seen in the previous pages and has been detailed by Murray and others. But that there have been covens in the second half of the twentieth century who have an unbroken lineage seems unlikely."[13] Ultimately, Buckland asserts, "if Gardner had made up the whole thing, basic idea and all, from scratch, it would not negate Wica as a viable religion today. Its rapid growth around the world attests to its 'rightness' in terms of people's religious needs."[14] In general, the unmasking of the myth of Wicca as a contemporary fiction seems not to have troubled most contemporary Pagans. Although some try to preserve specific connections to ancient religions,[15] others have easily adopted psychological or other interpretations of the myth of Wicca that minimize the importance of its historical accuracy while preserving its symbolic import. T. M. Luhrmann perceptively observes that, as a result, "magicians have it both ways. They appeal to the past, and claim a distinguished blood-stained lineage with all the emotional depth which that entails. . . . Yet magicians free themselves from the need to prove their historical accuracy and the cultural pertinence of the appropriate mythology by arguing that history can serve the role of personal metaphor or myth."[16] If no longer widely believed to portray the past accurately, the myth of Wicca continues to be an evocative symbolic statement for many involved in Neo-Paganism.

It is difficult to map the various forms of a religious orientation that is explicitly and often fervently "non-authoritarian and non-dogmatic."[17] Neo-Paganism also features a substantial proportion of "solitary practitioners" who do not join with others in ritual or other forms of activity.[18] On the basis of her own survey of contemporary Pagans, Helen Berger observed that "most Witches are solo practitioners for some period of time. The reasons for solo practice vary: some individuals prefer to work alone and never join a coven; others . . . leave groups due to conflicts or the disbandment of the coven; still others are solo practitioners at the beginning of their career as Witches, prior to joining a coven."[19] Covens, though designed to be lasting groups of individuals (ideally six men, six women, and a leader) who convene for magical purposes, have generally proven to be rather unstable, with members dropping in and out, departing to form their own covens, or allowing the group to fade away.[20] Larger organizations, such as the Covenant of the Goddess,[21] function more as clearinghouses for information and coordinators of activities than as religious groups in themselves. In sum, there is a broad audience of individuals in the United States who are interested in Pagan topics and who may also perform recognizably Pagan ritual actions; those individuals may or may not come together with some regularity with a small group of like-minded others for study, conversation, and ritual. They may also participate to some degree in broader local, national, or international organizations or take part in periodic festivals that draw a wide spectrum of practitioners together for brief stretches of intense interactions. Thus, contemporary Paganism has several features of what Stark and Bainbridge identified as an audience cult, a diffuse set of individuals who share interests in certain topics, read some of the same books or periodicals, and occasionally meet each other but who have no lasting ties with each other. Adler's comment about how people get involved with Paganism provides a glimpse of that diffuse audience. She reports that "in most cases, word of mouth, a discussion between friends, a lecture, a book, or an article provides the entry point."[22] Within that broad audience, however, more organized groups may crystallize around particular individuals, taking either the form of covens or more diffuse groups of devotees or clients, but they remain more the exception than the rule and are frequently subject to both splintering and dissolution. Consequently, this chapter will not trace the careers of specific groups, as previous chapters have. It instead first focuses on a few conceptions and practices that are broadly acknowledged within contemporary Paganism, then examines a few prominent strands of Neo-Pagan tradition, and finally considers how Neo-Pagans perceive and manage their interactions with other religious traditions and their social environments.

Cultivating the Self: Experience, Magic, and Ritual

At the heart of contemporary Paganism lies an assertion that dramatically elevates the individual. The affirmation, "Thou art Goddess; Thou art God,"[23] posits a fundamental identity between the individual and the divine, and it stresses that the divine is not something far "out there" but something that is immanent in this world, in nature, and in human beings. It raises the processes of discovery and cultivation of the self to the level of religious practices and situates the self in a web of potentially holy interactions with others and the natural world. In contemporary Paganism ritual plays a prominent role in the cultivation of the self. Helen Berger, for example, reports on a "croning" ritual, designed to mark the passage of a woman into the third phase of her life, moving from maiden to mother to crone. The participants first gathered to hear about the purpose of the ritual from the women who had organized it. They were then encouraged to engage in meditation in order to seek the goddess "within ourselves or without" and to reflect on their own lives. The participants were then led through the woods to a lake into which they briefly immersed themselves. Then, "as each woman emerged, she was greeted by a woman who surrounded her with incense, kissed her on the lips, and said, 'Thou art goddess; know thy power.'"[24] When the individuals returned from the lake they were then asked "to honor our mothers and grandmothers—real and spiritual or emotional."[25] In the explicitly feminist context of that ritual, the declaration, "Thou art goddess," restores to women an identity and power that had been systematically denied to them, in a variation on a theme that was so prominent in the African American Muslim and Jewish groups discussed in the previous chapter. In fact, many have been attracted to contemporary Paganism and goddess-worship precisely because of their capacity to support and maintain positive identities for women.[26] But the cultivation of the self is not restricted to women. Sarah Pike observes that "when they travel to festivals, Neopagans say they are making 'a pilgrimage to self.'"[27] Seizing on the example of the Muslim pilgrimage to Mecca as a parallel, one of Pike's informants told her that "I have come to see my journey across America that summer of 1989 as my own Hajj . . . I was drawn forth on a pilgrimage of my own making, seeking a holy land that, ultimately, I could find only in myself."[28] Implicit in that statement is the notion that one's real, true, Pagan self only fully comes out in the ritual context of a festival or smaller-scale performance; otherwise it is to some degree hidden as Pagans go about their everyday lives in "mundania." Even as they strive to nourish their own sense of divinity, contemporary Pagans have to contend with an array of competing demands, sometimes within their own ritual practices, that push and pull their sense of self in other directions. Consequently, the recognition that one is god or goddess is not a momentary realization but an ongoing project that demands serious attention and assiduous application of the individual's will.[29]

The Neo-Pagan self is embedded in a view of the world that recognizes the existence and accessibility of an array of unseen forces that link all forms of life together in a single whole. Starhawk, a well-known feminist practitioner of the Craft, cites a simple chant that metaphorically expresses that worldview: "we are the flow, we are the ebb, we are the weavers, we are the web."[30] She explicitly avows that "the tangible, visible world is only one aspect of reality. There are other dimensions that are equally real although less solid."[31] Sharon Devlin, a Celtic witch interviewed by Adler, emphasized that along with those interconnections comes responsibility. She claimed that "to be a son or daughter of God means you are equal to God and you have a responsibility to the One to get it together and make your Godhood count for something."[32] Some Neo-Pagans also appeal to the "Gaea hypothesis" that the earth constitutes a single, living organism. Morning Glory and Otter G'Zell, for example, put it this way: "the Moon is her radiant heart, and in the tides beats the pulse of her blood. That protoplasm which coursed through the body of that first primeval ancestral cell is the very protoplasm that now courses through every cell of every living organism, plant or animal, of our planet. And the soul of our Planetary biosphere is she whom we call Goddess."[33] Neo-Pagans thus conduct their religious lives in a context in which any action is expected to have multiple reverberations; even those who practice on their own participate in a web of relationships with nature and other beings.

Through the practice of magic, Neo-Pagans can appeal to unseen forces to help them accomplish their particular goals. In keeping with its individualistic orientation, there is no universal agreement on its practice or consensus definition of magic within contemporary Paganism. Earlier ritual magicians, like Aleister Crowley and William Butler, emphasized the exercise of the human will to cause either internal changes within the practitioner or changes in the external world. After his extensive study of magical traditions Isaac Bonewits, a Druid and prominent Neo-Pagan thinker, settled on a more complex definition. In his view, "magic is a general term for arts, sciences, philosophies and technologies concerned with (a) understanding and using altered states of consciousness within which it is possible to have access to and control over one's psychic talents, and (b) the uses and abuses of those psychic talents to change interior and/or exterior realities."[34] Adler provides a broader definition, arguing that

> magic is a convenient word for a collection of techniques, all of which involve the mind. . . . We might conceive of these techniques as including

the mobilization of confidence, will, and emotion brought about by the recognition of necessity; the use of imaginative faculties, particularly the ability to visualize, in order to begin to understand how other beings function in nature so we can use this knowledge to achieve necessary ends.[35]

In a simpler formulation, one person told Adler that magic "is simply the art of getting results."[36] In the history of Neo-Paganism, there have been many attempts to systematize magical concepts, techniques, and practices. Gerald Gardner, for example, identified eight paths for making magic, including meditation, chanting, the use of incense, drugs or wine, dancing, and the "Great Rite" of sexual intercourse.[37] Bonewits provided a fresh synthesis of the fundamental laws of magic and a classification of different types of magic.[38] Contemporary Pagan ritual practice, however, frequently eludes tidy categorization, and magic, like the myth of the origins of Wicca, easily shades over into a metaphorical description of the workings of those in the Craft.

The primary arena for Neo-Pagan ritual activity is the circle. Casting a circle creates a sacred space within which the ritual can unfold; temporarily it unites the participants into a religious community and focuses their attention on common goals.[39] At least some contemporary Pagans explicitly connect the circle with the practices of the Old Religion. One couple described their work this way: "as the ancient Britons did on the Salisbury Plain, we cast our circles where the Earth Mother interfaces with the Sky Father. We salute the four directions which symbolize the four elements and at the circle's center, where all things meet their opposites, we place our altar."[40] The circle becomes, in another Pagan's words, "a portable temple,"[41] a sanctified site that focuses and frames the participants' attention and energy as it brings them into contact with the forces that animate their world.

Within the ritual circle a wide variety of rituals can take place. A "wiccaning" ceremony, for example, introduces a baby to the parents' ritual community and invokes divine protection for the child, but does not commit the child to follow the religious path of its parents. A "handfasting" ceremony unites Pagans in marriage. Specific ceremonies are also performed on holy days throughout the year, such as the equinoxes, in order to attune participants with the rhythms of nature. While specific symbols, prayers, and actions will vary in accordance with the predominant spirit of improvisation, the circle provides the foundation for ritual activity.[42] In a statement that expresses how rituals can transport the participants to another world, one Neo-Pagan wrote that "the majority of our ritual circles are for the praise and worship and contact of and with the Goddess. The protective spirit of our circles is more to shield us from the 20th century than to protect us from malicious harm. Our circles are a haven from the present that frees us to touch the past and to restore our old attunement with nature."[43] Life outside the ritual circle, and by extension outside the worshiping Pagan community, is disconnected from the meaningful past and deaf to its connections with nature. Inside the circle, contemporary Pagans can see, hear, think, and live in a fashion that they find more in tune with the way the world really is. Temporarily, in their rituals, they participate in the world the way it should, and can, be. As one Pagan priest put it, "if we are not an alternative, we are not living our religion."[44]

Figuring out how to live out the consequences of their alternative vision of the world is as challenging for Neo-Pagans as it is for many other religious people. For Neo-Pagans the process of living out their religious convictions is more complicated than it is for some of the groups discussed in this book that have developed their own support structures through, for example, communal living or other forms of regimentation of daily life. Most Pagans live in "mundania" to a significant degree and struggle to live there *as* Pagans.[45] Largely due to investing individuals with primary responsibility for shaping their lives, contemporary Paganism does not have a widely shared ethical system. Its foremost ethical principle is expressed in a maxim called the Wiccan Rede, "An [if] it harm none, do what thou wilt."[46] One scholarly practitioner of Neo-Paganism cautions, however, that the second clause "is not a license to self-indulgence but a challenge: find out what your destiny is and fulfill it."[47] Pagan actions in the world are also subject to the "Law of Threefold Return," which stipulates that whatever good or evil one does returns in triplicate.[48]

Pagan ethical thought, however, is not as fully developed as Pagan reflection on ritual and symbolism, and it is as diverse as contemporary Paganism itself. Some individuals are, however, reflecting seriously on the ethical dilemmas that they face.[49] T. Thorn Coyle, for example, draws a challenging ethical lesson from her recognition that "Thou art Goddess" applies to everyone. She acknowledges that divinity must also be recognized "in our politicians, rescue workers, police, Muslims, Christians, Jews, Pagans, activists, artists, couch potatoes, peacemakers and those who want war. Remembering this helps me to open to compassion instead of being eaten by disgust."[50] One of the most interesting lines of investigation is Starhawk's attempt to develop an "ethic of interconnection." She proposes that "value is embodied not just in the individual but in the greater earth-body, the complex organism in which all creatures are cells. Immanent value cannot exist out of context, as individuals cannot exist outside the web of beings, elements, and relationships that sustain life. We cannot truly value our selves, our lives, unless we value what supports life."[51] In her writing and actions Starhawk weaves together a way of life that is nourished by worship of the Goddess, politically sophisticated, socially activist, and in tune with nature. Through her writing, lecturing, and activism she provides an example of how Pagan religious convictions can inspire ethical action.

Traditions and Institutions

Although contemporary Paganism can seem like a completely unregulated free-for-all in which anything goes, there is a counterbalancing respect for tradition on the part of many Pagans.[52] As the myth of Wicca suggested, and as the efforts of Black Muslims and Black Jews to connect themselves to Africa, Islam, and the religion of Abraham also indicated, the notion of a continuing tradition that endows individuals with a meaningful past that helps to shape their identities in the present can exert a very powerful attraction. Zsuzsanna Budapest, for example, states that "my mother and I come from a long line, a great circle of witches. I am the last branch of an 800-year-old family tree."[53] Starhawk, however, is somewhat more ambiguous about tradition. She claims that "the Old Religion . . . is both old and newly invented. Its roots go back to the pre-Judeo-Christian tribal religions of the West, and it is akin in spirit, form, and practice to Native American and African religions."[54] As these two brief examples show, the importance of historical tradition is understood in various ways within contemporary Paganism. A closer look at three traditions, the Gardnerian, Dianic, and Asatru, will bear that out.

Gerald Gardner's central role in the rise of modern Paganism stems not only from his being among the first to bring Wiccan practice to a wide public but also from the specific claims that he made. Gardner embedded his own experience in the myth of Wicca. Although Gardner also claimed that an ancestor of his had been burned as a witch in 1640 in Scotland, most significant was his claim to have been initiated into a surviving coven of the Old Religion by a high priestess known as "Old Dorothy." Gardner's claim has provoked substantial disbelief among scholars of Witchcraft both within and outside of the Pagan community, but Doreen Valiente, an early initiate and collaborator of Gardner's, claimed to have discovered substantial proof of the existence and identity of Old Dorothy and to have thus secured the likelihood that she did indeed initiate Gardner into a pre-existing religious tradition.[55] The historical accuracy of the myth of Wicca has remained important to Gardnerians and offshoots of that tradition. Raymond Buckland, who was initiated into the Gardnerian tradition and who founded the first Gardnerian coven in the United States in 1964, praises Gardner for having done "more than anyone to establish a return to the old ways, to allow people to once more make contact with the Old Religion."[56] Buckland also criticizes Alex Sanders, founder of the Alexandrian tradition of contemporary Paganism, for being wholly dependent on the Gardnerian *Book of Shadows,* the compendium of rituals that each initiate copies by hand. Janet and Stewart Farrar, though initiated by Sanders, are themselves very concerned to preserve accurately the Gardnerian tradition. They have isolated three primary manuscript traditions for Gardner's *Book of Shadows,* including a final version that Gardner produced with the help of Doreen Valiente, and have attempted to define "what the Gardner/Valiente Book of Shadows actually said."[57] Buckland's efforts and those of the Farrars clearly manifest a concern to identify and continue a tradition that will provide coherence, meaning, and direction to a community of practitioners, no matter how scattered they might be. The Farrars, in particular, are cognizant of how that goal can come into tension with a vision of Paganism as nondogmatic and open to change, growth, and improvisation. They argue that they "are not setting up the definitive Gardnerian Book of Shadows as Holy Writ" and that they do not believe that "the Gardnerian body of rituals is 'better' than other Wiccan systems," but they nonetheless come close to establishing a functional canon of authoritative texts and practices, even if they see the canon as consisting of suggestions rather than commandments. The goal of continuing an authoritative tradition inevitably clashes with the goal of promoting spontaneity and individual autonomy. The Gardnerians' tension between fidelity to tradition and openness to improvisation is a specific instance of the dilemma that all new religious movements face as they strive to assert both the novelty that is part of their urgent claim on their audience and the continuity with the past that renders their new proclamations accessible and reassures their audiences that a transition to new religious commitments can be easily and successfully accomplished.

The desire to ground contemporary practice in a meaningful past is also expressed in explicitly feminist forms of contemporary Paganism. Zsuzsanna ("Z") Budapest, arguably "the closest thing feminist spirituality has to a founder,"[58] not only claims to be part of a lineage of practitioners of the Old Religion, she has also provided a myth of creation for what she has called "the Dianic tradition." For her, that myth expresses "the True Beginning, before the Judeo-Christian Genesis."[59] It shows, Budapest claims, that the worship of the goddess goes back to the earliest Stone Age and is the predecessor and source of today's major religious traditions.[60] Although the ancient goddess was worshiped by both women and men, Budapest is most interested in the "women's mysteries" that involved only females. She finds in those ancient rites a powerful precedent and example for contemporary women. She observes that "today the Dianic traditions are being revived. Women are becoming more aware of how important it is to develop and share collective energies with each other, and to learn how to transcend personality differences by remembering our unity with the Soul of the Wild. In Dianic witchcraft, Diana and Her earth-daughter, Aradia, still reign supreme."[61] Budapest's treatment of the past is less fastidious than the Farrars' concern to separate the manuscript traditions of Gardner's *Book of Shadows*. Although *The Holy Book of Women's Mysteries* re-presents a substantial array of ancient practices, they are interwoven with invocations, chants, and rituals that have been newly created to meet the needs of women today.

Even more than the Farrars, Budapest strives to avoid having her book be received as *the only* authoritative way to worship the goddess. As she explains it, "in this book, I have described in detail the Sabbath proceedings and given the traditional poetry; you get a lot of guidance there. In almost every chapter I have repeated that this religion is improvisation. There is no one way to contact the Goddess. This religion is not a one-book religion like Christianity, and not a one-mantra religion like the Krishna cult, but a body of knowledge which revels in variety, creativity and joy."[62] Budapest envisages women's Paganism as being much more like jazz than classical music. Imaginative pioneers may create or recover specific musical lines, but they long to play in an ensemble in which the other players add their own inventive variations and in which the tune that results is common property of all. Budapest herself does not shy away from leadership, acknowledging, for example, that "my ministry is my gift and my divine act; it is where I am Goddess" and including recognition of her own birthday on a ritual calendar that she has produced.[63] But she strives to exercise leadership more by example than by command. In the analysis of Starhawk, who herself was introduced to contemporary Paganism by Budapest, Budapest aims to exercise two different kinds of power, neither of which is the "power-over" that commands and compels. Budapest's leadership, like that of many of her sisters in the feminist Craft, is founded on "power-with," "the power of a strong individual in a group of equals, the power not to command, but to suggest and be listened to, to begin something and see it happen." That form of leadership, Starhawk proposes, is both complemented by and arises from "power-from-within," whose source is "our sense of connection, our bonding with other human beings, and with the environment."[64]

There are multiple points of intersection between contemporary Paganism and contemporary feminism. The importance that most Pagan groups give to conceptions of deity in female form, the widespread interest in recovering a pre-Christian and pre-Judaic past, the desire to ennoble and empower the individual, the general absence of a male-dominated hierarchy, and the prominence of women in leadership roles have proven to be a congenial fit with many of the emphases of contemporary feminist thought. The "Dianic" tradition identified by Z Budapest is only one of the forms of "women's mysteries" that have appeared and flourished in Neo-Paganism. It is likely that Pagan traditions in many different forms will continue to attract women who see in them nonauthoritarian and non-dogmatic alternatives to the inherent patriarchy of many more mainstream religions.

Among the many attempts to revive forms of paganism associated with particular ethnic groups are the efforts to reinvigorate Germanic and Norse traditions. Legitimations of contemporary practices frequently follow the familiar format of appealing to a pre-Christian past. In the words of one participant, for example, "Asatru is the modern revitalization of the indigenous religion of Northern Europe. This religion was almost completely displaced by Christianity in the Middle Ages. Although the religion was no longer practiced, many aspects survived in the culture."[65] The revival of the Gods of the Northland has the same type of complicated institutional history as other fledgling religious groups. Although there were individual precursors such as the Australian Alexander Rud Mills and Else Christensen, who formed the Odinist Fellowship in 1971 in Florida, the Asatru Free Assembly, formed by Stephen McNallen in Texas in 1973 was the first significant group in the United States.[66] Originally

A Wiccan ritual in Killeen, Texas, 1999. © Rebecca McEntee/CORBIS SYGMA.

named the Viking Brotherhood, the Asatru Free Assembly promoted the worship of the "old Gods" of the North, the Aesir, Vanir, and various land spirits, until it dissolved in 1987. Among its most prominent successor organizations were the Ring of Troth and the Asatru Alliance.[67] Other groups in the same broad tradition include Hrafnar, based in San Francisco and led by Diana Paxson, and the Asatru Folk Assembly, which maintains an active presence on the Web.[68]

As with other forms of paganism, there is substantial variation in belief and practice in the groups that are reintroducing contemporary versions of Nordic and Germanic Paganism. One of the prominent convictions that they share, however, recalls the claims also made by many Black Muslim and Black Israelite groups; it is a desire "to call the sons and daughters of Europe back to their native spirituality and to the tribes which are their birthright."[69] In the perceptions of some, that mission takes on an apocalyptic urgency. Valgard Murray, for example, writes that "the Asatru Kindred is the foundation for the new Asatru Nation, and as such, is the testing ground for the new tribes of our Folk. In the near future, the Kindred will prove to be the living entity that will survive the onslaught of Ragnarok."[70] After that Nordic Armageddon, Murray suggests, kindreds, extended families, and tribes of worshipers of the old Gods will form the basis of a new social order that is kin-based, is rural rather than urban, and rejects the modern notion of the state and all of its apparatuses of control. That social order will have a strong moral dimension, one that is already being implemented by "Asafolk." As one summary puts it,

> we all share a defining personal loyalty to, or "Troth" with, the gods and goddesses of the Northlands, such as Odin, Thor, Frigga, and many others; a deep respect for our Germanic religious cultural and historical heritage; and a strong determination to practice the moral principles followed by our noble predecessors, including Courage, Truth, Honor, Loyalty, Discipline, Hospitality, Industriousness, Self-reliance, and Steadfastness.[71]

The wholehearted embrace of a Germanic/Nordic cultural heritage has attracted avowed racists to some of the groups practicing Northern Paganism. In prisons, for example, Odinism appeals to some of the same white racial supremacists who are attracted to Christian Identity beliefs.[72] Participants who have a more inclusive view of the worship of the Gods of the Northland have frequently had to negotiate conflicts with advocates of white racial superiority. Although the Ring of Troth, the Asatru Alliance, and the Asatru Folk Assembly, for example, have all explicitly and firmly dissociated themselves from racism and bigotry of any sort, there are other currents of thought in the general world of Northern Paganism. One white racialist, for example, wrote to the Arizona Kindred of the Asatru Alliance that "the Arizona Kindred is promoting the corruption of our folk through bastardization, mongrelization and assimilation, which is not only suicide but genocide; and that our communities must not only distance ourselves from the Alliance but demand a Holy war, so to speak, so that the Alliance will remove the corruptors or discontinue referring itself as Odinist."[73] Like the Nation of Islam, the Northern Pagan groups have had to carefully consider the nature of the racial ties that they claim and their implications for their attitudes toward other ethnic groups. Also like the Nation of Islam, the several different points of view on those matters within Northern Paganism have led to the formation of a variety of groups with different emphases. The attraction of Northern Paganism to white supremacists is likely to continue to be a topic that will provoke substantial tension within groups and between them and their social environments.

In addition to providing vivid characterizations of their Gods and Goddesses and nurturing their beliefs in general, the classical texts of Northern Paganism, such as the Prose and Poetic Eddas, the Heimskringla, and other sagas, also guide contemporary ritual practices. The *blot*, or offering of food or drink, and the *sumbel*, or ritual series of toasts, are used to mark seasonal holidays such as the Yule (beginning December 21 and lasting twelve days or more) and important events in the life cycle, among other things.[74] Officiating at rituals are priests (*gothar*, literally those who speak the godly tongue), who may be either male (*gothi*) or female (*gythia*). The process by which someone becomes a priest varies from group to group, and groups express different opinions on the value of regularizing and bureaucratizing the priesthood. The Asatru Alliance explicitly states that it "does not espouse a priest class" and that "each kindred is free to determine its own spiritual and tribal needs."[75] The Ring of Troth, on the other hand, "conducts a training program for prospective Heathen clergy, incorporating study, training and experience in lore knowledge, theology, ceremonial practice, group organization, and counseling, and leading to certification after an extensive evaluation and final examination."[76] In either case, Valgard Murray's caution that "the work of the Gothar is difficult indeed" holds true.[77]

Priests of Northern Paganism need to reconstruct their religious tradition even as they practice it; they have to expend substantial effort in attracting participants and in keeping their communities alive and functioning. Similar pressures led to the demise of the Asatru Free Assembly. Nonetheless, at least some groups, or kindreds, monitor the processes of conversion and affiliation with care. In addition to regular attendance for virtually a full year, Raven Kindred South in the Washington, D.C. area expects its new members to "profess faith in the form of an open oath to the Gods taken during a ritual" and then to be voted on by the members of the Kindred.[78] The paths taken by converts to Northern Paganism are similar to those followed by other Pagans. Stephen McNallen, for example, the founder of the Asatru Free Assembly, reported that he "made a personal conversion to Norse heathendom after reading the historical novel, *The Viking*, by Edison Marshall, which contrasted the values of Asatru and Christianity."[79] Although it wasn't available to McNallen in the early 1970s, interested parties can now seek out "Asatru-U" for online tutorials in the basic beliefs and practices of Northern Paganism.[80] Other Web browsers can find the extensive compendium, *Our Troth*, which was prepared by the Ring of Troth and is designed "to give true folk a wide range of materials from which each may build his or her own troth."[81] Although participants in Northern Paganism often claim that their numbers are steadily growing, it is difficult to state with any precision how many active individuals there actually are. Nonetheless, Northern Pagans constitute a vital part of the general mix of contemporary Paganism.

While individual traditions propagate the Pagan way through a shifting constellation of institutions, some organizations have evolved to serve as focal points and networks for the exchange of information. Founded in 1975, the Covenant of the Goddess has as its purpose "to increase cooperation among Witches and to secure for Witches and covens the legal protection enjoyed by members of other religions."[82] The Covenant of the Goddess publishes a newsletter, sponsors a festival each summer, and promotes national and local networks. It urges both individuals and covens who become members to subscribe to its code of ethics, which includes the "Wiccan Rede," guidance about participation in groups, support for charging "reasonable fees" for services rendered, respect for the lore and requirements of secrecy in the broad Pagan tradition, and an emphasis on the autonomy of each coven and individual.[83] The organization also issues credentials to both priests and priestesses and to elders, providing that they meet certain criteria. The Covenant of the Goddess thus exerts a gentle influence toward standardization of the practice of contemporary Paganism, even while acknowledging the primacy of individuals and small groups.

Another organization that has played a prominent role in contemporary Paganism in the United States is the Circle Sanctuary, founded by Selena Fox in 1974 and now headquartered in southwestern Wisconsin, where it also has a 200-acre nature preserve. Circle Sanctuary describes itself as "dedicated to research, spiritual healing, counseling, and education."[84] It also sponsors a variety of festivals, workshops, and other gatherings. In addition, Selena Fox herself has been a influential Pagan teacher, both through her writings and through her work as an accredited counselor.[85] Like the Covenant of the Goddess, the Circle Sanctuary is strongly interested in securing religious rights for Pagans. In 1985 Fox founded the Lady Liberty League as an advocacy group for Pagans. Its wide-ranging concerns are reflected in this statement: "LLL members include specialists in a variety of focus areas, including public relations, countering harassment, employment issues, child custody issues, military affairs, law enforcement relations, legal affairs, interfaith relations, scholars support, and others."[86] Like other religious groups, the Lady Liberty League conducts an active prison ministry, focused on defending the religious rights of Pagan prisoners. It also provides support services for Pagan youths and their families, particularly when young persons' expressions of their religious convictions set them in conflict with school authorities. The activities of Circle Sanctuary's Lady Liberty League generally help to equip Pagans to defend their religious commitments in arenas where the anti- and countercult movements have exacerbated suspicions about religions that are outside the mainstream.

Paganism and the Cult Controversy

The efforts of both the Covenant of the Goddess and Circle Sanctuary's Lady Liberty League to protect the religious rights of Pagans suggest that many in contemporary Paganism are well aware that their religious lives are viewed with suspicion and alarm by at least some members of society. Those groups are not alone in their quest to counter what they see as prejudicial stereotypes that inhibit the abilities of contemporary Pagans to practice their religions. The Witches' League for Public Awareness, for example, monitors portrayals of Paganism in the media, provides legal resources, and encourages Pagans to participate in the electoral process to protect their freedoms, among other things.[87] Pagans also have attempted to distance themselves from the cult phenomenon in general. Z Budapest distinguished Paganism from the dogmatism of the "one-mantra Krishna cult"[88] and Margot Adler separated contemporary Paganism from a wide range of other religions. She emphasized that "the Pagan movement does *not* include the Eastern religious groups. It includes neither Satanists nor Christians. Almost every religious group that has received massive exposure in the press, from the Hare Krishna movements to the Unification Church to the Peoples Temple, lies outside the Pagan resurgence."[89] In her efforts to establish the distinctiveness of Paganism, Adler inadvertently endorsed the stereotypes purveyed by anticult activists and applied them to virtually any new religious movement but her own. In particular, she focused on the issue of conversion, and implicitly appealed to the participation of manipulative leaders and deluded followers, as a way of distinguishing contemporary Paganism from the array of "cults" and sects. She asserted that "no one *converts* to Paganism or Wicca. You will find no one handing you Pagan leaflets on the street or shouting at you from a corner."[90] In describing her own affiliation with Paganism, Adler subtly conformed it to the outlines of the myth of Wicca. She wrote, "I never converted in the accepted sense—I never adopted any new beliefs. I simply accepted, reaffirmed, and extended a very old experience. I allowed certain kinds of feelings and ways of being back into my life."[91] Thus, Adler used the general outlines and emphases of the contemporary cult controversy as a foil for establishing the comparatively benign character of her own religious commitment. Implicitly endorsing a view of conversion as inherently coercive suited her own apologetic purposes.[92]

For Pagans, legitimating the distinctiveness of their religion and separating it from socially stigmatized groups is not simply a matter of abstract interest. In particular, suspicions and negative feelings about contemporary Paganism boil to the surface when Pagan practices move from the private toward the public sphere. More than a few times, large festivals held on or near public lands have provoked strong reactions. Sarah Pike, for example, reports that police were dispatched to investigate a festival in southern Indiana because they had been informed that the participants were "devil worshipers" who were performing "satanic rites."[93] In fact, Pike argues that "rumors of satanism are so widespread that they do not simply affect Neopagans' freedom to hold their rituals at state parks or other public places. The explanatory power of satanic conspiracy theories threatens Neopagans' lives on many fronts and impacts child-custody cases, employment, and educational experience."[94] Pagans respond to their being branded as Satanists in a variety of ways. They strive, for example, to separate the two religious orientations on matters of substance. One Pagan thinker stresses that Satanism "is a practice of profaning Christian symbolism and is thus a Christian heresy rather than a Pagan religion. The gods of Wicca are in no way connected to Satanic practice."[95] Such statements are frequently made with the hope that publicizing the truth about contemporary Paganism will diminish the tension between Pagans and their critics. Some other Pagans, however, lash out at their Christian antagonists and attempt to exploit perceived hypocrisies and excesses within Christianity and to establish the virtues of Paganism by contrast. One Pagan told Pike that "it kind of seems to me that all of these wild satanistic stories are a form of misdirection, and the people we need to be really concerned about are the extremist 'Christians.'"[96] Still others, however, worry that "Christian-bashing" might indirectly force upon Paganism a rigidity, orthodoxy, and exclusivism that runs counter to its emphases on individual autonomy, creativity, and freedom.[97]

Because it is so decentralized, contemporary Paganism will continue to produce a variety of responses to the individuals and institutions that criticize it. Umbrella organizations, like the Lady Liberty League, The Covenant of the Goddess, and the Witches' League for Public Awareness, and prominent writers within the Craft, like Margot Adler, Z Budapest, and Starhawk, will continue to argue for the religious rights of their fellow practitioners, but individuals and organizers and participants of public events will have to draw on their own resources to cope with the tensions that arise in specific situations. One interesting recent controversy that has engaged contemporary Pagans was triggered by the enormous popularity of the books and films about the exploits of Harry Potter and his class-mates at Hogwarts School of Witchcraft and Wizardry. Some Christians have condemned the books and films for promoting Witchcraft, and there are many articles, books, and videos that accuse the Harry Potter series of insidiously introducing children to the actual practice of Witchcraft. As one alarmed Christian author puts it, "the Harry Potter Books are pure, unadulterated witchcraft . . . introducing millions of children to the prac-tices and rituals of Wicca. The books, marketed to impressionable chil-dren, pose a long-term threat to Judeo-Christian faith and culture."[98] Many individual pagans have vigorously disputed those charges, defend-ing the books as harmless fantasies and denying that they are either accu-rate portraits of their religion or attempts to spread its message. As one Pagan put it in a dispute about whether the Harry Potter books could be read aloud in a local public library, "I've read these books, since I wanted to see what was in them before I gave them to my kids, and I must say that these books no more promote witchcraft than 'Anne of Green Gables' pro-motes moving to Nova Scotia."[99]

Like other new religious movements in the United States, contempo-rary Paganism, in its various forms, exists in some tension with its social environment. Because it does not have a single dominant organization, Paganism has not mobilized its participants to the extent that the Unifica-tionist Movement or the International Society for Krishna Consciousness has. As a result, Paganism's conflicts with society have been diffused over a number of issues and participants rather than focused on specific indi-viduals, like Jim Jones or David Koresh, or issues, like plural marriage or racial ideology. Nonetheless, contemporary Pagans in the United States are consistently reminded, in trivial and more substantial ways, of how far some of their fellow citizens consider them to have departed from the mainstream. As one twelve-year-old girl described her situation of having grown up in a Neo-Pagan family, "in school it [being a Neo-Pagan] sort of does [affect me] 'cause it's dangerous—you can't say what you are—like if someone asks you your religion then you are in a tight spot."[100]

Conclusions

Like other new religious movements, the contemporary practice of Paganism has had to face changes as it incorporated a second generation of members. Because Paganism has not focused on a single leader, the transition has not been marked by that leader's passing, but rather by the incorporation of a younger generation of those either born to Pagans or attracted to Paganism in their youth. The birth of children to Pagan parents has raised some difficult issues. Some Pagans argue, for example, that children should be free to find their own religious paths. One writer expressed concern about diluting commitment within the Pagan community. He wrote that "by bringing people on to the magickal path, as opposed to them finding the path themselves, we run the risk of finding ourselves dealing with an increasingly apathetic magickal community."[101] Others have worried about the impact on children being raised in a nonmainstream religion.[102] But other Pagans believe that the positive value of their religion outweighs any social drawbacks. One suggests that "nearly everything we do at home can be done with Wicca in mind. From rearranging a room to brushing hair, everything can be a spell. . . . And if we share mundane blessings with our children it will become second nature to them."[103]

Prominent figures in contemporary Paganism have also expressed awareness of a transition to a new generation. Starhawk, for example, wrote in the introduction to the twentieth anniversary edition of *The Spiral Dance*, "now I think about who is going to carry on this work when I'm gone, and what I want to be in my next life."[104] The persistence of the Neo-Pagan movement in the United States and elsewhere in the world has led it to face, in diverse ways, not the routinization of an original leader's charisma but the routinization of the movement itself. By facing such questions as how children should be raised, where a new generation of leaders will come from, and to what degree they should allow themselves to build lasting institutions, contemporary Pagans are coming to grips with their future. As the contemporary Pagan movement moves into its second and later generations and attempts to strike an acceptable balance between fealty to tradition and unfettered innovation, it confronts the dilemmas shared by all new religious movements. Just as Pagans would have it, they are involved in creating their own future.

Notes

1. Margot Adler, *Drawing Down the Moon: Witches, Druids, Goddess-Worshippers and Other Pagans in America Today,* rev. ed. (Boston: Beacon, 1986).

2. Ibid., p. 96.

3. Sarah M. Pike, *Earthly Bodies, Magical Selves: Contemporary Pagans and the Search for Community* (Berkeley: University of California Press, 2001), p. xix.

4. Zsuzsanna Budapest, *The Holy Book of Women's Mysteries* (Berkeley, CA: Wingbow, 1980), p. 21.

5. Adler, *Drawing Down the Moon,* p. 23.

6. As quoted in Pike, *Earthly Bodies, Magical Selves,* p. 23.

7. Janet and Stewart Farrar, *The Witches' Bible: The Complete Witches' Handbook* (rpt. Blaine, WA: Phoenix, 1985), pt. I, p. 32.

8. See Adler, *Drawing Down the Moon,* p. 45; see also James W. Baker, "White Witches: Historic Fact and Romantic Fantasy," in James R. Lewis, ed., *Magical Religion and Modern Witchcraft* (Albany: State University of New York Press, 1996), pp. 171–92. For a full presentation of the mythic origins of Wicca, see Raymond Buckland, *Witchcraft from the Inside: Origins of the Fastest Growing Religious Movement in America,* 3rd ed. (St. Paul, MN: Llwellyn, 1995).

9. For the complete text of Murray's book, see www.sacred-texts.com/pag/wcwe/.

10. See T. M. Luhrmann, *Persuasions of the Witch's Craft: Ritual Magic in Contemporary England* (Cambridge, MA: Harvard University Press, 1989), pp. 43–48, on Gardner's writings and initiation. See also Scire (Gerald B. Gardner), *High Magic's Aid* (rpt. Hinton, WV: Godolphin House, 1996); Gerald B. Gardner, *Witchcraft Today,* with introduction by Raymond Buckland (rpt. Lake Toxaway, NC: Mercurey, n.d.); and Gerald B. Gardner, *The Meaning of Witchcraft* (rpt. Thame, England: I-H-O, 2000).

11. Aidan Kelly, *Crafting the Art of Magic,* Book I: *A History of Modern Witchcraft, 1939–1964* (St. Paul, MN: Llwellyn, 1991), pp. xix, 1, respectively. See also Isaac Bonewits, *Real Magic,* rev. ed. (York Beach, ME: Samuel Weiser, 1989), p. 110, for example.

12. See Ronald Hutton, *The Triumph of the Moon: A History of Modern Pagan Witchcraft* (Oxford: Oxford University Press, 1999); Philip G. Davis, *Goddess Unmasked: The Rise of Neopagan Feminist Spirituality* (Dallas: Spence, 1998).

13. Buckland, *Witchcraft from the Inside,* p. 148. I retain his spelling of "Wica."

14. Ibid.

15. See, for example, Farrar, *The Witches' Bible,* pt. I, p. 14, and the interview with Sharon Devlin, who also claims Celtic roots for her practice in Adler, *Drawing Down the Moon,* pp. 136–52.

16. Luhrmann, *Persuasions of the Witch's Craft,* p. 244.

17. Adler, *Drawing Down the Moon,* p. viii.

18. See, for example, Silver Ravenwolf, *Solitary Witch: The Ultimate Book of Shadows for the New Generation* (St. Paul, MN: Llwellyn, 2003).

19. Helen Berger, *A Community of Witches: Contemporary New-Paganism and Witchcraft in the United States* (Columbia: University of South Carolina Press, 1999), p. 50.

20. For a brief treatment of the coven, see Doreen Valiente, *An ABC of Witchcraft* (Custer, WA: Phoenix, 1973), pp. 69–73.

21. See www.cog.org.

22. Adler, *Drawing Down the Moon*, p. 14.

23. See ibid., p. ix.

24. Berger, *A Community of Witches*, p. 39.

25. Ibid.

26. In general, see Cynthia Eller, *Living in the Lap of the Goddess: The Feminist Spirituality Movement in America* (New York: Crossroad, 1993).

27. Pike, *Earthly Bodies, Magical Selves*, p. xxi.

28. Ibid., pp. 27–28.

29. See Sian Reid, "As I Do Will, So Mote It Be: Magic as Metaphor in Neo-Pagan Witchcraft," in Lewis, ed., *Magical Religion and Modern Witchcraft*, pp. 141–67, esp. pp. 150–53.

30. Starhawk, *Dreaming the Dark: Magic, Sex and Politics* (Boston: Beacon, 1982), p. 225.

31. Starhawk, *Truth or Dare: Encounters with Power, Authority, and Mystery* (New York: Harper and Row, 1987), p. 25.

32. Adler, *Drawing Down the Moon*, p. 140.

33. Morning Glory and Otter G'Zell, "Who on Earth is the Goddess," in Lewis, ed., *Magical Religion and Modern Witchcraft*, pp. 25–33, quotation from p. 28.

34. Bonewits, *Real Magic*, p. 211. For Bonewits' homepage, with a good collection of his writings, see www.neopagan.net. For a review of Neo-Pagan understandings of magic, see Graham Harvey, *Contemporary Paganism: Listening People, Speaking Earth* (New York: New York University Press, 1997), pp. 87–106.

35. Adler, *Drawing Down the Moon*, p. 8.

36. Ibid., p. 7.

37. Farrars, *The Witches' Bible*, pt. II, p. 52.

38. Bonewits, *Real Magic*, pp. 1–17, for example.

39. For examples of the process for casting the circle, see Farrars, *The Witches' Bible*, pt. I, p. 38; Budapest, *The Holy Book of Women's Mysteries*, pp. 18–20.

40. As quoted in Pike, *Earthly Bodies, Magical Selves*, p. 49.

41. As quoted in Adler, *Drawing Down the Moon*, p. 108. See Berger, *A Community of Witches*, p. 47; Pike, *Earthly Bodies, Magical Selves*, p. 190.

42. Janet and Stewart Farrar provide a full account of the Gardnerian tradition's understanding of rituals and holidays in *The Witches' Bible*. Budapest covers both the fairly standard calendrical holidays and a set of specific holidays for women in *The Holy Book of Women's Mysteries*.

43. As quoted in Adler, *Drawing Down the Moon*, p. 124.

44. As quoted in ibid., p. 372.

45. On the Neo-Pagan concept of "mundania," see Pike, *Earthly Bodies, Magical Selves*, p. 13 and passim.

46. See Farrars, *The Witches' Bible*, pt. II, pp. 135–44.

47. Chas S. Clifton, "What has Alexandria to Do with Boston? Some Sources of Modern Pagan Ethics," in Lewis, ed., *Magical Religion and Modern Witchcraft*, pp. 269–75, quotation from p. 271.

48. See ibid., p. 272.

49. For a collection of essays, see Chas S. Clifton, ed., *Living Between Two Worlds: Challenges of the Modern Witch* (St. Paul, MN: Llwellyn, 1996).

50. www.thorncoyle.com/musings/18dec2001.htm.

51. Starhawk, *Truth or Dare*, pp. 136–37.

52. See, for example, the set of short descriptions of various Pagan traditions at www.witchvox.com/xtrads.html.

53. Budapest, *The Holy Book of Women's Mysteries*, p. 270.

54. Starhawk, *Dreaming the Dark*, p. xii.

55. On Gardner's initiation, see Buckland, *Witchcraft from the Inside*, pp. 99–100; for Valiente's claims, see Doreen Valiente, "The Search for Old Dorothy" in Farrars, *The Witches' Bible*, pt. II, pp. 283–93, and www.doreenvaliente.com/main/biography/1980s.htm, where she provides copies of Dorothy Clutterbuck's death certificate and last will and testament. On Gardner himself, see Hutton, *The Triumph of the Moon*, pp. 205–40, and www.geraldgardner.com.

56. Buckland, *Witchcraft from the Inside*, p. 102.

57. Farrars, *The Witches' Bible*, pt. II, p. 2.

58. Eller, *Living in the Lap of the Goddess*, p. 55.

59. Budapest, *The Holy Book of Women's Mysteries*, p. 54.

60. Ibid.

61. Ibid., p. 57.

62. Ibid., p. 227.

63. See Eller, *Living in the Lap of the Goddess*, p. 91.

64. See Starhawk, *Truth or Dare*, pp. 8–10, quotations from p. 9.

65. www.witchvox.com/trads/trad_asatru.html.

66. On the Odinist and Asatru traditions, see Jeffrey Kaplan, "The Reconstruction of the Odinist and Asatru Traditions," in Lewis, ed., *Magical Religion and Modern Witchcraft*, pp. 193–236; see also Kaplan, *Radical Religion in America*, pp. 69–99. For an insider's brief account of the tradition's history, see www.thetroth.org/resources/ourtroth/rebrth.html.

67. See www.thetroth.org and www.alliance.eagleut.com, respectively.

68. See www.hrafnar.org and www.runestone.org.

69. www.runestone.org/flash/home.html.

70. Valgard Murray, "The Asatru Kindred" available at www.alliance.eagleut.com/thekin.htm.

71. www.thetroth.org/ourfaith/intro.html.

72. See Kaplan, "The Reconstruction," p. 208.

73. As quoted in ibid., p. 209.

74. See the summary at www.witchvox.com/trads/trad_asatru.html. On the *blot*, see www.webcom.com/~lstead/blot.htm.

75. www.alliance.eagleut.com/bylaws.htm.

76. www.thetroth.org/ourfaith/intro.html.

77. www.alliance.eagleut.com/gothar.htm.

78. www.webcom.com/~lstead/rksouth.html.

79. As quoted in Kaplan, "The Reconstruction," p. 197.

80. See www.asatru-u.org.

81. www.thetroth.org/resources/ourtroth/whatis.html.

82. www.cog.org/general/pamphlet.html.

83. Ibid.

84. www.circlesanctuary.org/page2.html.

85. For a sample of her work, see www.circlesanctuary.org/learn/.

86. www.circlesanctuary.org/liberty/about.html.

87. See www.celticcrow.com.

88. See note 61.

89. Adler, *Drawing Down the Moon,* pp. xi–xii.

90. Ibid., p. x.

91. Ibid., p. 20.

92. For a fuller treatment of Adler's argument, see Eugene V. Gallagher, "A Religion Without Converts? Becoming a Neo-Pagan," *Journal of the American Academy of Religion* 62 (1994): 851–67.

93. See Pike, *Earthly Bodies, Magical Selves,* pp. 88ff.

94. Ibid., p. 91.

95. As quoted in ibid., p. 114.

96. As quoted in ibid., p. 109.

97. See ibid., p. 111.

98. www.chuckmorse.com/harry_potter_witchcraft.html.

99. www.celticcrow.com/news/potter1026.html.

100. As quoted in Berger, *A Community of Witches,* p. 83.

101. As quoted in ibid., p. 84.

102. See ibid., p. 85.

103. Ibid., pp. 96–97.

104. Starhawk, *The Spiral Dance: A Rebirth of the Ancient Religion of the Great Goddess,* special 20th anniversary ed. (San Francisco: HarperCollins, 1999), p. 2.

Chapter 7

New Foundations

In an influential and widely cited 1992 report that he prepared in his capacity as a Supervisory Special Agent for the FBI's Behavioral Science Unit at Quantico, Virginia, Kenneth V. Lanning observed that in the course of his research on claims of "Satanic ritual abuse" he had found more than thirty different groups referred to as "Satanism."[1] Although one might expect to find the Church of Satan, or its offshoot the Temple of Set, or even Witchcraft and the Occult among those groups, the category was also stretched to include the Ku Klux Klan, the Church of Scientology, the Unification Church, the International Society for Krishna Consciousness, the Rajneeshis, Transcendental Meditation, Buddhism, Hinduism, Islam, Mormonism, and even the Roman Catholic Church. Such a broad usage of the descriptive category Satanism indicates something both about the phenomenon itself and about the people who want to extend it to include well-established religious traditions that have long been part of the mainstream of American life. In fact, a widespread fear of the insidious threat posed by Satanism marked the decade from around 1983 to 1993. Satanism, particularly in the form of allegations about Satanic ritual abuse, in which horrible crimes were committed against defenseless young children, became the primary focus of the anticult movement during that period. In the decade of Satanic panic, fears about cults that had been articulated in the late 1960s and 1970s in terms of brainwashing and coercive persuasion were transposed into a new key and given a new focus. Many groups that had little or no connection with formal Satanist organizations or whose doctrines had little or nothing to do with Satan were nonetheless swept up in the pervasive fears about the nefarious doings of an underground conspiracy of evil Satanists. The charge of Satanism became an omnibus tool for expressing deep-seated worries about the negative forces at work in fundamental social institutions.

Although the severity of the Satanism scare has now diminished, the issue has not gone away. Kenneth Lanning's original call for moderation of Satanic panic has not always been heeded. He argued that "until hard evidence is obtained and corroborated, the public should not be frightened into believing that babies are being bred and eaten, that 50,000 missing children are being murdered in human sacrifices, or that satanists are taking over America's day care centers."[2] But, as the claims mentioned in the previous chapter about what really goes on at some Pagan festivals suggest, the image of the Satanic cult remains a ready vehicle for the expression of powerful suspicions, anxieties, and fears. As David Bromley has argued, "the social construction of satanism reasserts control by naming the problem, giving it human shape, and locating its source outside the matrix of social relations to which the social actors are committed."[3] The Satanic panic of the 1980s has thus indelibly colored the background against which any subsequent discussion of Satanism unfolds.

Constructing Satanism

Contemporary cult controversies found a particular focus in the 1980s when a series of spectacular accusations appeared to reveal an extensive Satanic underground that was responsible for a variety of horrible crimes ranging from systematic child abuse in day care centers to ritual murders. One academic observer, Carl Raschke, claimed that there was "a national epidemic of 'satanist-related' crime" in the United States that was "growing faster than AIDS."[4] That sense of alarm was fueled by a series of lurid exposés that claimed to lay bare a vast Satanic conspiracy that had successfully managed to perpetrate its horrors without being detected. Among the most influential books that presented the dangers of what would become known as Satanic ritual abuse to the general public were Michelle Smith's 1980 memoir of having been given over by her mother to a cult of devil worshipers when she was only five. *Michelle Remembers,* written by Smith and her psychiatrist and eventual husband, Lawrence Pazder, detailed the prolonged and difficult process by which she recovered and then coped with the memories of her childhood abuse.[5] In 1988 Lauren Stratford related a similar story in *Satan's Underground,* with an emphasis on the comfort that her turn to Christianity had brought her.[6]

Allegations against teachers at the McMartin Preschool in suburban Los Angeles in 1984, which were soon followed by allegations against other day care providers, added to a widespread sense that predatory Satanists were feeding off the nation's innocent children.[7] For a decade the discussion about new religious movements in the United States was dominated by responses to the claims of a far-reaching and insidious Satanic conspiracy. Not until the tragic standoff at the Mount Carmel Center outside of Waco in 1993 would the focus of public discussions about cults fully shift.

For those who were persuaded by the sweeping allegations of Satanic ritual abuse, the stakes were extraordinarily high. If Raschke's claims about an epidemic more devastating than AIDS could be accepted, the nation was in serious trouble and massive efforts would be needed to combat the plague. Gradually, however, another perspective began to be publicized. Law enforcement officials who had been enlisted in the search for Satanic abusers and killers began to express their frustrations at the lack of hard evidence that could support prosecutions of the accused. Robert D. Hicks, for example, himself a former police officer and now a law enforcement consultant, wrote in 1990 that "I have found no proof that pernicious satanic phenomena exist on a scale worthy of new criminal laws and specialized police task-forces."[8] Hicks lamented that "few members of the law-enforcement community have taken the time to combat publicly the overstatements, generalizations, clearly false and absurd 'facts,' and excursions into illogic relating to the impact of Satanism and the occult on crime."[9] Lanning sounded a similar note of caution. He argued that "after all the hype and hysteria is put aside, the realization sets in that most satanic or occult activity involves the commission of *no* crimes, and that which does, usually involves the commission of relatively minor crimes such as trespassing, vandalism, cruelty to animals, or petty thievery."[10] Such admonitions, however, did not appease those who see Satanism as a widespread social problem. Raschke, for example, accused Lanning and others of being "cult apologists" who were blind to the evils right in front of them.[11] The shrillness of Raschke's argument, however, ultimately fails to compensate for the paucity of the evidence behind it.

Several scholars have made a persuasive case that the Satanic panic that gripped many in the United States from 1983 to 1993 had its origins in sources other than the actual practices of a worldwide underground Satanic conspiracy. As Philip Jenkins and Daniel Maier-Katkin have observed of those who claim to have suffered Satanic ritual abuse, "the study of survivors can tell us a great deal about mental disorders, about the state of American religious belief, or the therapeutic process. What 'occult survivors' cannot tell us about is the occult."[12] Similarly, Jeffrey Victor has argued that

> the metaphor of a "Satanic cult" combines two powerful symbols: a cult and Satan. . . . when people label a group a "cult," they mean to denote that it is a dangerous, manipulative, secretive, conspiratorial group. Moreover, a cult is seen as a heresy, a threat to decent, traditional cultural values. . . . The hidden meaning conveys the complaint: "The moral order of our society is being threatened by mysterious and powerful evil forces, and we are losing faith in the ability of our institutions and authorities to deal with the threat."[13]

More specifically, Debbie Nathan proposed that "the ritual abuse scare is a deeply rooted expression of anxieties this culture harbors about unresolved family and sexual issues," related to the influx of women into the workforce and other developments sparked by the women's movement of the late twentieth century.[14]

For some, including Raschke, Satanism has been used as a very elastic category. It is "the name we have conferred, perhaps because of the very eminence of the symbol of God's adversary in Judaeo-Christian history, on the unruly subcurrents of deliberate and ritualized destruction in this late nuclear age."[15] In an attempt to get more concrete, Raschke identified four different types of Satanic activity: the experimental, the occult, the self-styled Satanist, and the traditional Satanist.[16] His attempt at typology, however, is too sloppy to be helpful. It is not entirely clear, for example, why experimentation could not be carried out in any of the other three categories or what separates the traditions observed by so-called traditionalists from those observed by occultists. Raschke's categories quickly collapse into each other, which compromises their usefulness. Other typologies attempt to distinguish atheistic forms of Satanism from theistic ones.[17] A more complex typology, offered on the Web site of the Ontario Consultants on Religious Tolerance, separates religious Satanism in which Satan is either recognized as a deity or life principle, from "gothic Satanism," the imaginary foil created by the medieval Christian Church, and both of them from random dabbling in various types of ritual magic without much concern for forging disparate elements into a coherent system. In addition, the site discusses as "quasi-Satanism" the purported affiliation with forms of Satanism invoked by various criminals, including murderers and child molesters, and the adoption of Satanic symbolism in certain heavy metal musical subcultures.[18] It is clear that polemical uses and lack of rigor in defining categories have made Satanism a fuzzy and highly malleable category. That lack of precision makes it incumbent on any observer to be particularly clear about just what is being described when Satanism is under discussion. The rest of this section will leave behind the impassioned arguments about the pernicious satanic underground conspiracy to focus on the primary institutional forms Satanism has taken in the United States, particularly the Church of Satan founded by Anton Szandor LaVey in San Francisco in 1966 and some of its offshoots.

The Church of Satan and Related Groups

LaVey himself was characteristically blunt about the broadening of Satanism to include all sorts of different characters. He asserted that "there are no categories of Satanists—there are Satanists and nuts."[19] In keeping with his conviction that Satanism was a religious philosophy only for an elite few, LaVey consistently endeavored to distance his church from the masses, be they other Satanists, members of other religious traditions, or even members of other new religions. He stressed, for example, that "the 'Satanic Army' is comprised of individuals, not cultists."[20] LaVey acknowledged that he formulated the ideas for the Church of Satan as "the ultimate conscious alternative to herd mentality and institutionalized thought. It is a studied and contrived set of principles and exercises designed to liberate individuals from a contagion of mindlessness that destroys innovation."[21]

Although he had been interested in the "black arts" for more than a dozen years before that, LaVey formally founded his church on April 30, 1966. The choice of a date had symbolic resonance. It was "the traditional night of the most important demonic celebration of the year, when witches and devils roam the earth, orgiastically glorifying the fruition of the Spring equinox, Walpurgisnacht."[22] Within a few years, LaVey produced the central text of the new church, *The Satanic Bible*. In that text LaVey elaborated his critique of all previous religions. He argued that "past religions have always represented the spiritual nature of man, with little or no concern for his carnal or mundane needs. They have considered this life but transitory, and the flesh merely a shell; physical pleasure trivial, and pain a worthwhile preparation for the 'Kingdom of God.'"[23] Against what he saw as a virtually universal religious denial of fundamental human nature,

LaVey offered his clear-sighted alternative. He proclaimed that "it has become necessary for a NEW religion, based on man's natural instincts, to come forth. THEY have named it. It is called Satanism."[24] LaVey was acutely aware of the context in which he was creating his new church. Emphasizing the symbolic power of his choice of Satan as the primary symbol of the church, he wrote that "Satan represents opposition to all religions which serve to frustrate and condemn man for his natural instincts."[25] Christianity, of course, was chief among the culprits. In direct and vigorous opposition to the oppression of natural human instincts, LaVey called for the exercise of "controlled selfishness."[26] LaVey enshrined the doctrine of the Church of Satan in a set of virtually creedal affirmations, called the Nine Satanic Statements. They are:

1. Satan represents indulgence, instead of abstinence!
2. Satan represents vital existence, instead of spiritual pipe dreams!
3. Satan represents undefiled wisdom, instead of hypocritical self-deceit!
4. Satan represents kindness to those who deserve it, instead of love wasted on ingrates!
5. Satan represents vengeance, instead of turning the other cheek!
6. Satan represents responsibility to the responsible, instead of concern for psychic vampires!
7. Satan represents man as just another animal, sometimes better, more often worse than those that walk on all-fours, who, because of his "divine spiritual and intellectual development," has become the most vicious animal of all!
8. Satan represents all of the so-called sins, as they all lead to physical, mental, or emotional gratification!
9. Satan has been the best friend the church has ever had, as he has kept it in business all these years.[27]

The gratification of the individual ego that is the central focus of those statements also led LaVey to a fundamental assertion about the nature of religion. He wrote that "the Satanist feels: "Why not really be honest and if you are going to create a god in your image, why not create that god as yourself. Every man is a god if he chooses to recognize himself as one."[28] Accordingly, LaVey urged Satanists to celebrate their own birthdays as the most important holidays of the year.[29]

The Satanic Bible lays out in direct fashion the animating ideas behind the creation of the Church of Satan. It also rarely passes up the opportunity to ridicule other religions, particularly Christianity. One of LaVey's most striking forays against Christianity is his direct reversal of the fundamental values of Jesus' Sermon on the Mount in the gospel according to Matthew. Where Jesus praises the poor in spirit, those who mourn, the meek, the merciful, the pure in heart, and the peacemakers, among others, LaVey exalts the strong, the powerful, the bold, the victorious, and the destroyers of false hope and curses those whom Jesus praised.[30] So intent is the Church of Satan in posing itself as an alternative to Christianity that if Christianity didn't exist LaVey would have had to invent it.

Although LaVey devoted a substantial portion of *The Satanic Bible* to an exposition of his ideas about the nature of human beings and the nature of religion, he also emphasized the necessity of ritual and ceremony in the life of a Satanist. LaVey himself claimed a colorful biography and he was not averse to arranging Satanic spectacles for public consumption. LaVey claimed, for example, to have played oboe in the San Francisco Ballet Orchestra, to have been a lion tamer in the circus, and to have worked as a crime scene photographer. He also claimed to have had affairs with both Jayne Mansfield and Marilyn Monroe.[31] Although the details of LaVey's life have been disputed, at the least they demonstrate his flamboyant self-advertisement. In addition to self-dramatization, early on LaVey staged both a Satanic wedding and a Satanic baptism, making sure the press was well represented at both.[32] LaVey enthusiastically endorsed individuals' use of their imagination in ritual, and he supplemented the material on ritual in *The Satanic Bible* with another volume, *The Satanic Rituals*.[33] In his discussions of ritual, LaVey expressed an understanding of magic that was not dissimilar from the one expressed by many Neo-Pagans. He proposed that "your ritual chamber is your fantasy world: harnessing the potent wattage of your emotions, you psychically extend yourself to shape the world beyond the surrounding walls. You impose your magical will, using the metaphors or images you feel most aligned with."[34]

LaVey's message of controlled selfishness and unfettered use of the imagination has continued to draw people to the Church of Satan even though it does not formally solicit members.[35] LaVey himself attributed that success to the consistent message of individual empowerment; he stressed that from the beginning the Church of Satan has "emphasized that each must be his or her own redeemer."[36] Also, on the basis of a survey of contemporary Satanists, James Lewis has observed that "*The Satanic Bible* is still the single most influential document shaping the contemporary Satanist movement" whether or not its readers proceed to formal affiliation with the Church of Satan, in which a lifetime active membership

Anton Szandor LaVey founded the Church of Satan in San Francisco in 1966. ©
Bettmann/CORBIS.

can be secured for a $100 fee.[37] During his life, LaVey experimented with
different organizational forms for his church. For a time it was subdivided
into local groups, called grottoes; in 1975 LaVey discontinued the grotto
system but then reinstated it in the late 1980s. Throughout its history,
however, the Church of Satan has been highly decentralized. LaVey exercised much more intellectual leadership than organizational control.

Because of its emphasis on individuals taking responsibility for their
own lives, the Church of Satan has been able to survive the death of its
founder in 1997, a few days before Halloween. Upon LaVey's death his
acolyte Blanche Barton became the High Priestess of the church; on Walpurgisnacht of 2002 Barton appointed Peggy Nadramia to succeed her as High
Priestess. Nadramia's husband, Peter H. Gilmore, had been appointed High
Priest precisely one year before.[38] The church has resumed publication of its
newsletter, *The Cloven Hoof,* and several of its grottoes and individual
members are active in publishing newsletters, magazines, and other Satanic
literature.[39] Like many other religious movements, the Church of Satan has
taken advantage of the Internet to disseminate its literature.

The Church of Satan has given birth to several other organizations,
both during LaVey's life and since his passing. In 1975 after a dispute with

LaVey over his decision to market initiation into the priesthood in the church for cash, Michael Aquino and a group of other members left the Church of Satan to form the Temple of Set. As with other sectarian movements, the Temple of Set claimed that the Church of Satan had lost its way and departed from its initial principles. When the widespread suspicions about rampant Satanism hit the public media, the Temple of Set saw itself as fighting on two fronts to preserve authentic Satanism. It had "not only to defend authentic Satanism against the shrill screams of the scarecrow-merchants, but also to reject superficial glorification of the scarecrow that would return Satanism's image to nothing more than anti-Christian."[40]

First under the leadership of Aquino and more recently under the direction of Don Webb, the Temple of Set has developed its own distinct theology, produced an extensive collection of its own literature, and moved progressively farther away from its roots in LaVey's Church of Satan. Aquino has even produced a massive revisionist history of the Church of Satan.[41] Though it focuses on the Egyptian deity Set, who was worshiped in ancient Egypt as early as 3200 B.C.E., the group is eclectic in its use of a variety of cultural sources. For members of the Temple, "the 'worship' of Set is thus the 'worship' of individualism" but in conscious opposition to LaVey, the Temple asserts that "glorification of the ego is not enough; it is the **complete** *psyche*—the **entire** self or soul—which must be recognized, appreciated, and actualized."[42] Even more than the Church of Satan, the Temple of Set emphasizes the independence of the individual; it evaluates applications for membership and at least suggests that membership is reserved for a select few. Despite its attempts to maintain a relatively low profile, the Temple of Set has been embroiled in several controversies. In 1986 Aquino, then a lieutenant colonel in the U.S. Army, was implicated in suspicions of child molestation at the day care center at the Presidio Army base in San Francisco but he was never charged; in 1994 he sued a former member who leveled claims that the temple was part of the nationwide Satanic conspiracy that was molesting children and committing murders.[43] Nonetheless, the Temple of Set has weathered both those charges and the transition from Aquino's leadership to that of Don Webb, and, though membership figures are hard to come by, at least maintains a vivid presence on the Internet.

Among the other splinter groups of LaVey's Church of Satan are the First Satanic Church, established by LaVey's daughter Karla in 1999 after acrimonious wranglings with Blanche Barton. Like the Temple of Set, the First Satanic Church sees the Church of Satan as having failed to preserve the legacy of the first years of the Church of Satan. Karla LaVey's group intends to exercise rigorous control over its membership. The group's Web site warns that "acquiring a membership in the First Satanic Church is not a simple task. We do not solicit memberships or accept just anyone. We are the eclectic elite of the Satanic religion and a $100 bill will not buy your way in. To ensure the highest stratum of membership, we find it necessary to screen *all* applicants. Only those who are sincerely interested in Satanism and the occult sciences need apply."[44] The First Satanic Church signals its continuity with the Church of Satan by making it mandatory for all membership applicants to read LaVey's *The Satanic Bible* before applying.

Among the other splinter groups is the First Church of Satan, headquartered in Massachusetts. Its founder, John Dewey Allee (also known as Daimon Egan and Lord Egan), had been an early member of LaVey's Church of Satan and was also associated with Aquino's Temple of Set. In the early 1990s Allee produced a newsletter named *Brimstone* that described itself as the "official organ for the international Ancient Brotherhood of Satan."[45] The magazine billed itself as seeking "true initiates of the left hand path who are not too frightened to explore the dark side of nature" and promised that "together we shall evolve and grow as the most powerful psychic legion anywhere on this planet."[46] The Ancient Brotherhood of Satan appears to have mutated into the First Church of Satan, which retains its predecessor's criticism of LaVey's Church of Satan for having forsaken its roots.[47] The contemporary First Church of Satan is highly critical of the current leadership of the Church of Satan, whom it brands as "hapless."[48] In true sectarian fashion, Allee's group claims that it "has more to do with how the Church of Satan was about at FIRST."[49] Thus, like Karla LaVey's group, the First Church of Satan aims to return to the purity and power of LaVey's original insights, as they were articulated in *The Satanic Bible*. The tension between fidelity to LaVey's original message and the development of new perspectives on what Satanism might entail continues to mark developments in various institutional forms of Satanism in the twenty-first century.

The Church of Scientology

Although the inclusion of the Church of Scientology in Lanning's list of groups that have been described as Satanism may accurately have reflected the opinions of some of its critics, as it presents itself Scientology manifests no direct institutional or doctrinal ties to the Church of Satan and its progeny. Instead, its origins can be traced to the investigations of its founder, L. Ron Hubbard, into the workings of the human mind. Hubbard led a colorful life. Born in Nebraska in 1911, Hubbard moved with his family to Montana, where he became a blood brother in the local Blackfoot tribe at the age of six. As a teenager he went on an extensive summer excursion that took him to Hawaii, Japan, China, the Philippines, and Guam, and he pursued a similar itinerary a year later. He would later lead a scientific expedition to the Caribbean. He enrolled at George Washington University in the fall of 1930 and soon after became an accomplished pilot. Hubbard married in 1933 and never finished his degree. In his early adult years Hubbard turned to writing fiction and he quickly became a popular contributor to a variety of pulp magazines. After working in westerns and a few other genres, he earned his greatest success as a writer of science fiction. Hubbard's writing career was interrupted by World War II, and he served in the navy. Toward the end of the war he was hospitalized and it was then that he turned his mind to detailed contemplation of human psychology. His reflections led him to compose in 1948 a privately circulated paper, "Dianetics: The Original Thesis," and then in 1950 to publish *Dianetics: The Modern Science of Mental Health.*[50]

Hubbard intended his system of Dianetics to provide an accurate diagnosis of the human condition and a therapy that would enable humans to achieve their full potential. He had fond hopes that his discoveries would be welcomed by the medical establishment, but both the American Medical Association and the American Psychiatric Association failed to react with the expected enthusiasm. Dianetics found its strongest partisans elsewhere. John W. Campbell, the editor of *Astounding Science Fiction* which had published some of Hubbard's short stories, became one of his strongest supporters. Joseph Winter, a physician, also became strongly interested in Dianetics and hoped that his colleagues would be attracted by Hubbard's system. *Dianetics: The Modern Science of Mental Health* became a bestseller a month after its publication and quickly gave rise to various groups that attempted to put its prescriptions for mental health into practice.

The fundamental assertion of Dianetics was that the goal of human existence was to survive, and that the human mind functioned to solve problems related to survival. But the drive to survive, Hubbard argued, was complicated by the actions of the mind. In addition to the familiar analytical mind, Hubbard identified what he called the "reactive mind," a vast storehouse of images that when recalled could inhibit the individual's ability to function. Hubbard called the negative images in the reactive mind "engrams" and claimed that they could be reactivated when elements of the whole image of which they were a part were perceived by the individual. Repeated stimulation of the engrams would lead to psychological illness. Through a process of counseling called "auditing," Hubbard proposed, harmful engrams could be recalled and their negative effects on human functioning diminished and eliminated. The individual being counseled could then attain the status of "clear" and establish optimum psychological functioning. Hubbard's analysis was not unprecedented. Roy Wallis has noted that "the process of engram formation resembles the mechanism of repression elaborated by Freud, and Hubbard's distinction between the analytical and the reactive mind loosely fits Freud's distinction of the conscious and unconsciousness."[51] But whatever its sources and similarities to other accounts of human psychology, it is clear that Hubbard's Dianetics became an elaborate and coherent system of its own.

While Hubbard's insights inspired many in the early years of Dianetics, he exercised no organizational control over how his ideas were appropriated and implemented. As a result, Dianetics developed in a number of different directions. One early issue concerned the possibility of reincarnation. In the search for the engrams that kept individuals from achieving their full potential, questions arose about how far back in an individual's history a counseling session could, and should, go. Some, like Dr. Winter, who saw Dianetics as a potentially beneficial addition to contemporary medicine, found the very notion of past lives highly implausible and unscientific. The ensuing disagreements eventually caused a split between Hubbard and some of his most prominent early supporters and led Hubbard to form the Hubbard Association of Scientologists in 1952. Hubbard then began to take his creation in a distinctive new direction, and the proponents of Dianetics whom he left behind were unable to form any substantial and lasting organizations.

With the formation of the first organization of Scientologists, Hubbard moved his attention away from the reactive mind to another dimension of the human being, the spiritual. As an official publication of the Church of Scientology puts it, the breakthrough from Dianetics to Scientology came in the autumn of 1951, after Mr. Hubbard observed many people practicing Dianetics and found a commonality of experience and phenomena which were of a profoundly spiritual nature—contact with past-life experiences. After carefully reviewing all relevant research data, Mr. Hubbard isolated the answer: Man had been misled by the idea that he *had* a soul. In fact, man *is* a spiritual being, who has a mind and a body.[52]

Hubbard called that spiritual being the "thetan," a term that he derived from the Greek letter "theta" and took to mean thought or life.[53] Although Hubbard's identification of the thetan led him to develop a complex cosmology and an elaborate anthropology, his doctrinal system is founded on a few fundamental propositions:

> Man is an immortal spiritual being.
> His experience extends well beyond a single lifetime.
> His capabilities are unlimited, even if not presently realized.[54]

From those propositions, the fundamental practices of the Church of Scientology directly follow.

As with Dianetics, the counseling or auditing session is a central practice. In auditing a trained supervisor guides the person being audited toward the recognition of those images or engrams that are inhibiting the individual's psychological functioning. The church describes auditing as "a precise form of spiritual counseling between a Scientology minister and a parishioner."[55] The auditing process also involves the use of an "e-meter," which measures galvanic skin response and is interpreted as an indicator of how blocked the individual might be. The individual being audited holds two electrodes that are connected to a central console that measures changes in electrical current passing through the electrodes.[56] The actual session consists of a series of brief questions and answers and can involve extensive repetition when the individual being audited is unable to describe adequately the incident that produced the engram. In the official view of the church, "the auditor directs the parishioner's attention to confront aspects of his existence to find the answers to auditing questions, erase the harmful mental and spiritual energy in which the thetan is enmeshed, and thus experience relief from spiritual travail."[57] In this transcript of a brief part of an auditing session the auditor tries to move the individual away from an incomplete memory to the actual incident that lies behind it:

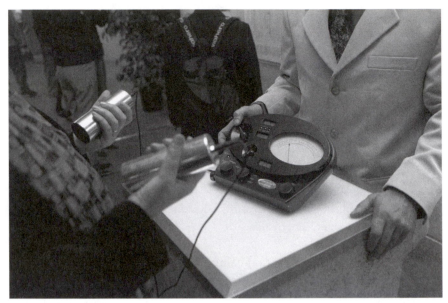

A woman holds two electrodes during a Church of Scientology "auditing" session. ©
Yves Forestier/CORBIS SYGMA.

WOMAN: All I get is "Take her away."
AUDITOR: Go over that again.
WOMAN: Take her away [repeated three times].
AUDITOR: Go over that again.
WOMAN: Take her away.
AUDITOR: Go over that again.
WOMAN: No, no, I won't.
AUDITOR: Go over that again.
WOMAN, I won't, I won't, I won't.
AUDITOR: Go over that again—take her away. Go over the phrase again.
   Take her away.
WOMAN: Take her away [crying] No, no.[58]

The auditing process is designed to help individuals reach the status of
"clear." In the years since auditing was established as a central practice for
Scientology, first Hubbard and then the church have elaborated a series of
additional stages beyond "clear" to which practitioners can aspire. A
chart of the various stages through which an individual can progress is
described as the "Bridge to Total Freedom" and is widely published and
displayed by the Church of Scientology.[59] Periodically, the church has
opened up new levels of the "Operating Thetan" status as it makes known

more of the technology or "tech" that Hubbard had developed. The auditing process thus becomes a continuing ritual for members of the Church of Scientology; their quest to develop their human capacities to the fullest remains open-ended.

For Scientologists auditing is complemented by extensive training, or study of the teachings of Hubbard. Hubbard's writings have the status of scripture within the church he founded and his thoughts are widely circulated in book form and on audio- and videotapes.[60] A full range of life-cycle rituals, including weddings, naming ceremonies, and funeral services, as well as weekly services, is also offered to members of the Church of Scientology by accredited ministers. The church vigorously seeks to interest people in its message and practices and uses a variety of media, including the Internet, to publicize the "successes" experienced by those who have taken up Scientological practice. The church has attracted a substantial number of celebrity members, including actors Tom Cruise and John Travolta, and musicians Chick Corea and Isaac Hayes, among many others, and often uses them in its publicity. Actress Kirstie Alley, for example, has affirmed that "without Scientology, I would be dead. So, I can personally highly recommend it."[61] Similarly, actress Juliette Lewis testified that "I am no longer stuck in the bottomless pit of despair and apathy. Having achieved the state of Clear is the single most important thing that I've done for myself. It has allowed me to experience life in a way I only imagined."[62] But the statements by relatively well-known public figures are also echoed by others. One member of the church wrote that "Scientology is a clean and concise philosophy. It is truth. . . . It helps you become more able."[63] Many of the testimonials from church members emphasize that Scientology simply "works." Some members of the Church of Scientology choose to make a more extensive commitment and sign a billion-year contract (which commits them through their future lives) with the "Sea Org." The "Sea Organization" traces its origins to a period in the late 1960s and early 1970s when Hubbard and the top officials of the church based their operations on a small fleet of ships. The "Sea Org" eventually came ashore but retained its name and it now refers to the most dedicated members of the church who live as a monastic or religious order and serve as staff for the church's management.[64] In addition to nourishing the religious lives of individuals, the church is also involved in an extensive set of social welfare programs, including programs that address drug addiction, criminal behavior, literacy, moral education, religious freedom, and other urgent social problems.[65]

In all of their practices Scientologists are concerned to implement the teachings of Hubbard precisely as he intended them.[66] Primary responsibility for maintaining orthodoxy is vested in the "Religious Technology Center."[67] The church affirms that the "concept of orthodoxy in religious practice is fundamental to Scientology. Thus any attempt to alter or misrepresent the Scripture is regarded as a most severe breach of ecclesiastical ethics."[68] In keeping with that strong commitment, the church has consistently responded vigorously to those it perceived as failing to uphold orthodoxy, as misrepresenting the church and its teachings, or otherwise promulgating false impressions of Scientology belief and practice. Partly as a result of that concern for enforcing orthodoxy, the Church of Scientology has not been a stranger to controversy. Disillusioned former members have published several highly critical books, and the church has often responded with litigation. The tone of those books is suggested by the title of Bent Corydon's *L. Ron Hubbard: Messiah or Madman?* which is also billed on its cover as "the book that survived every attempt to suppress its publication."[69] In his preface, Corydon situates his own work within a series of other exposés of the Church of Scientology and details the efforts of the church to persuade him, through various forms of intimidation, to abandon his project. He claims, for example, that "as of the Spring of 1991, I have been a regular target for Scientology harassment—both 'legal' and otherwise—for over a decade. I have been sued six times. I have countersued twice."[70] Similar in intent is Jon Atack's *A Piece of Blue Sky: Scientology, Dianetics and L. Ron Hubbard Exposed,* which portrays Hubbard as a con-man who delighted in fleecing gullible seekers after salvation.[71]

One of the most notorious controversies in which the Church of Scientology has become embroiled concerned the death of thirty-six-year-old Scientologist Lisa McPherson, who had been a member of the church since she was eighteen, in Clearwater, Florida, in 1995. After being in a minor automobile accident McPherson appeared disoriented and was taken to a local hospital where it was determined that she was physically unharmed but sufficiently upset to be kept for psychological evaluation. Since Scientology is hostile to conventional psychiatry, McPherson left the hospital with fellow Scientologists and moved into a hotel owned by the church. Seventeen days later she died. McPherson's death spawned a tangle of litigation and fueled acrimonious indictments of the church both locally and across the nation.[72] The Church of Scientology, on its part, has responded vigorously in its defense and has impugned the motives of at least some of the partisans who have used the McPherson case as a rallying cry for anticult and anti-Scientology campaigns.[73] The McPherson case remains a primary example of the incendiary emotions that the Church of Scientology has been able to inspire, both against it and on its behalf. Despite the controversy that the Church of Scientology has sparked both in the United States and abroad, it has continued to attract members throughout the world and remains a vital religious organization.[74]

Heaven's Gate

Both in the United States and abroad the 1990s were punctuated by a series of violent events involving new religious movements. The 1993 clash between the Branch Davidians and federal agents of the ATF and FBI claimed more than eighty lives; on March 20, 1995, members of the Japanese group Aum Shinrikyo released deadly sarin gas in the Tokyo subway, killing twelve and injuring more than five thousand; in separate incidents in 1994, 1995, and 1997 in Quebec, Switzerland, and France more than seventy members of the Order of the Solar Temple either committed suicide or were murdered by their fellow members; in March 1997 thirty-nine members of a group that came to be known as Heaven's Gate committed suicide in their home in an exclusive suburb of Rancho Santa Fe, near San Diego. For many in the public those events cemented the necessary connection between membership in cults and violence, and that topic will be taken up again in the following chapter. This section will examine the formation, doctrine, organization, and social interactions of one of those groups, Heaven's Gate.

The origins of Heaven's Gate lie in the religious searches of its two founders, Bonnie Lu Nettles and Marshall Herff Applewhite. Before they even met, Nettles had been interested in Theosophy; Applewhite, the son of a Presbyterian minister, also began to study the works of Madame Blavatsky after he met Nettles. They also had at least a glancing familiarity with Hindu thought.[75] To those early influences they eventually added an elaborate cosmology that posited the existence of "The Evolutionary Level Above Human" or T.E.L.A.H., to which humans should aspire to ascend. Nettles and Applewhite came to see themselves as the "representatives" of T.E.L.A.H., which had entrusted them with the saving knowledge for humanity at the end of this current age. What transformed Nettles and Applewhite from religious seekers to religious leaders was a growing sense that they had been chosen for a mission. Applewhite, for example,

The founders of Heaven's Gate, Marshall Herff Applewhite and Bonnie Lu Nettles. © Bettmann/CORBIS.

reported a vision that he had experienced at the beginning of 1972 in which "a presence had given him all the knowledge of where the human race had come from and where it was going."[76] As their sense of mission deepened, Nettles and Applewhite "consciously recognized that they were sent from space to do a task that had something to do with the Bible, an update in understanding and prophesy fulfillment."[77] For a while, Nettles and Applewhite identified themselves with the "two witnesses" in chapter 11 of the book of Revelation, but an interesting encounter with others who claimed the same status led them in another direction. During a visit to a spiritual center, as Applewhite told the story on a videotape, Nettles and Applewhite allowed that

> "Well, we think that we might be fulfilling the task that was referred to as Two Witnesses in the book of Revelation." And this student just hit the ceiling because her two teachers were the two witnesses. (Laughs) So,

goodness alive, did that do a number on our heads! We thought "Gracious, we don't want to do that again." And it's like, whether we were or not, it was good for us to experience that. And so, from that point on it didn't matter to us what the reality was. Who's going to prove what the reality is, as far as who might be the fulfillment of the application of certain prophecies of individuals?[78]

That encounter demonstrated several prominent characteristics of Nettles and Applewhite's early mission. First, it shows how their roles and claims to authority were not fixed but rather in the process of construction. A whimsical corollary of that flexibility was the sets of names that "the Two" tried on for themselves. For a time, they called themselves "Guinea" and "Pig" to indicate the experimental nature of their investigations; with a nod and a wink to the common image of religious leaders as shepherds of a flock they also called themselves "Bo" and "Peep"; they eventually settled on the musical names of "Do" and "Ti" in part to indicate their harmonious cooperation with each other and with the Next Level. Second, it shows that they were relatively averse to conflict; instead of challenging other claimants to the role of the Two Witnesses, they retreated to a position that affirmed the indeterminacy of prophecy. Third, it suggests that the arenas from which they sought converts or at least interested parties were part of a milieu of spiritual seekers. Finally, it indicates that they would continue to seek to align their conviction that they had been chosen as representatives of the next level, or T.E.L.A.H., with their reading of the Bible.

As Nettles and Applewhite traveled the country, beginning in 1973, they attracted a trickle of converts to their evolving teachings. In early 1975, for example, they attracted two dozen followers from a New Age group in Los Angeles; in September of that year they attracted more than thirty followers after a public presentation in Waldport, Oregon.[79] They also picked up a few converts at other stops along the way. A Wisconsin woman wrote a postcard home to express her joy at having found her religious way: "Mama. Am doing beautifully. Truly feel I am on the path I've searched for. Thank God. Please don't worry. Have faith. I am completely taken care of while I am learning my Father's will always in all ways. P.S. Read Revelation Chapter 11 in the New Testament."[80] In a later letter, the same woman clearly showed how Nettles and Applewhite were reading their message out of the New Testament. She wrote that "the stress of the whole talk was the message given to us almost two thousand years ago by

Jesus, and this is victory over death—ascension. Jesus and his aids [*sic*] are coming into close range of Earth to assist mankind, and we can go through the ascension only through their assistance."[81] Echoing the requirements of Jesus' call to his disciples, the woman asserted that "one must be prepared to leave everything behind" to qualify for ascension.[82]

In the early phases of their mission, then loosely known as Human Individual Metamorphosis, Nettles and Applewhite stressed that the work of preparation for ascension was an individual responsibility. In an interview Applewhite claimed that

> our whole purpose is to tell those who want to hear it how they may go through this metamorphic change and become a member of the next level. . . . This is not done in groups . . . it would never happen as an organization . . . it's only an individual who says "I've had it with this level, and I'm ready for the next . . . and I will sacrifice everything that it requires to make that ascension." For that person, we have a working ground on which to help him with that information.[83]

In those early years, the evolving character of Nettles and Applewhite's message, their virtually constant movement around the United States, and the emphasis on the individual's appropriation of the message combined to limit the number of followers who found and remained with the two teachers. In 1976 Nettles and Applewhite crafted a dramatic response to the relative ineffectiveness of their mission; they ceased their efforts at recruitment and retired with their small band of followers to a secluded life out of the public eye. Their purpose, as it would later be stated, was "not only completing their 'awakening' or adjustment to their human bodies and this primitive civilization," but also to provide a "metamorphic classroom experience of changing over their consciousness and behavior to match with that of their distant culture from whence they had come."[84] In the nearly seventeen years between 1976 and 1992, Nettles and Applewhite turned their loose band of followers into a rigidly organized monastic community devoted to overcoming ties to "mammalian" appetites in order to prepare themselves for their transit to the evolutionary level above human.

Although Nettles died in 1985, Applewhite carried on their teaching work during the years of seclusion.[85] They produced a comprehensive doctrinal system that addressed the course of human history, their own roles in it, the imminent transformation of the world as we know it, and the requirements for moving to T.E.L.A.H. In that system the history of the earth as it is commonly known is portrayed as part of a much larger cosmic process. As one of the group's documents puts it, "*the two* were given to understand that these spacecraft occupants were participants in 'God's creation' of the Earth and had been the participants in relating to Abraham, the Israelites, Jesus, and all of our Bible's record of man's association with God. They also understood that this civilization, since Adam's time until now, is just one planting of Earth's true 'Gardeners.'"[86] Members of T.E.L.A.H. have decided that "this planet is about to be recycled, refurbished, started over" and it will subsequently "have another chance to serve as a garden for a future human civilization."[87] Applewhite and Nettles, Do and Ti, claimed to have been chosen as the representatives of the Next Level to bring the saving knowledge, or gnosis, about the imminent transformation of this world to human beings. On one of his videotapes Applewhite provided the justification for this new revelation. He claimed that "our Father, our Creator, has rules and says 'When I send you Truth, when I send you updates, when I send you information on how you can come into My House, you can't just relate to the information I gave 2000 years ago."[88] Accordingly, Nettles and Applewhite saw themselves as fulfilling the same function in their time that Jesus did in his; like him, they were part of a succession of representatives on this earth who had been commissioned by the Next Level to preach the message of personal metamorphosis.[89]

Do and Ti's attitude to other religions was ambivalent, but largely negative. A June 1994 poster asserted that "all religions were designed as 'prep' for this day," but their dominant message was that "all religions have been spawned from the misinformation (distorted or corrupted truths) propagated by space-alien races ('Luciferians') who, knowingly or unknowingly, look to Lucifer as their god and victimize the humans on this planet."[90] Building on the mentions of Satan as a fallen angel in the book of Genesis, "the Two" developed a extensive account of the cosmic forces that were acting against the interests of the Next Level both on this earth and in the heavens. Do even interpreted rejection of his message as the work of a supernatural adversary, claiming that "the place that Satan has worked the hardest is to have you very reluctant to accept anyone as a Representative of our Father's Kingdom."[91] Despite that reluctance, Do assured his followers that their true identity was more than human. He asserted that "we students and our Teachers are not from this world but from the Level Above Human."[92] Since there is no gender in T.E.L.A.H., "the task of overcoming the human kingdom requires that they overcome human flesh—the genetic vibrations, the lust of the flesh, the desire to reproduce, the desire to cling to offspring, or spouse, or parents, or house, or money, or fame, or job or, or—that could go on and on—overcoming the human flesh and its desires—even its religious desires."[93] As was widely reported in the aftermath of the suicides, some of the male followers of Do had themselves castrated in order to facilitate their renunciation of the flesh, but the less spectacular but more telling indication of monastic discipline is that all members of Heaven's Gate had left families, work, friendships, and the rest of their former lives to form a community dedicated to the implementation of Do's teachings.[94] That they were able to do so was interpreted as evidence that they had activated a "deposit" that had been implanted in them by the Next Level.[95]

Despite their considerable demands on individuals, the teachings of the Two were able to inspire intense commitment from at least a small band of their students. One wrote that "Ti and Do and the Next Level are my life. Without them, there is nothing—literally. Nothing else is real."[96] The formal exit statements made before their suicides by several members of the "crew" or "away team" express similar sentiments. In a statement that echoed Jim Jones' comments on the final night of the Jonestown settlement, one member, "Glnody," wrote that "there is no place for us here. It is time for us to go home—to God's Kingdom, to the Next Level. There is no place for us to go but up."[97] Another student confided that "my more intimate reasons for wanting to leave at this time come not from any sense of hopelessness or despair, as one might suspect. Quite the contrary, it is a profoundly joyous time for me—the fulfillment of everything I have always hoped for—to dwell in the Creator's house and be called by Him, a son."[98] In the end, it was that earnest hope for personal transformation, much more than the accidental correlation of the appearance of the comet Hale-Bopp with the climax of the mission of the Two or extraordinary pressure from external foes, that motivated the group suicide in March 1997. Members of Heaven's Gate who had stuck with Do up until that time were determined to enter another, better world. They had forsaken their attachments to this world as much as possible. Like at least some of the members of the Peoples Temple, they saw suicide as easing a transition to a new world in which their imperfections would vanish and they could achieve a more perfect union with the divine. Death apparently held no fear for them; they saw it simply as part of a necessary transition. In their final press release, the members of Heaven's Gate, who by the time their statement was made public had already departed this world, appealed to the statement of Jesus in the gospel according to John, "Therefore doth my Father love me, because I lay down my life, that I might take it again" (John 10:15). Their final actions provide daunting testimony of the power of religious convictions to transform, and even end, people's lives.

The Raëlians

Heaven's Gate was certainly not the only religious group in U.S. history to have coalesced around the idea of communication with alien beings beyond this world.[99] At the beginning of the twenty-first century the group that attracted the most public attention, particularly with its audacious but unsupported claims to have cloned a human being, was the Raëlian Movement. Like so many other new religious movements, the Raëlians trace their origins to an original visionary experience. In December 1973 the former Claude Vorilhon was walking near an extinct volcano near Clermont-Ferrand, France. As he recalls it, "suddenly in the fog, I saw a red light flashing; then a sort of helicopter was descending towards me. A helicopter, however, makes noise but at that moment, I could hear absolutely nothing, not even the slightest whistle. A balloon maybe? By now the object was about twenty meters above the ground, and I could see it had a somewhat flattened shape. It was a flying saucer."[100] Vorilhon's sighting of the flying saucer led to six days of instructions by an alien being, one of the Elohim who had created life on this earth. The Eloha informed Vorilhon that he had a crucial mission to undertake on earth. He was told that

> you will tell human beings the truth about what they are and what we are. Judging from their reactions we will be able to tell if we can show ourselves freely and officially. Wait until you know everything before you start speaking publicly, so that you can defend yourself properly against those people who will not believe you and so that you can bring them incontestable proof. You will write down everything I will tell you and you will publish the writings in book form.[101]

Vorilhon proceeded to absorb as much as he could in his prolonged tutorial. Much of his instruction consisted of a selective appropriation of and commentary on the Bible. Among its most important elements was the revelation that the "Elohim" mentioned in the creation stories of Genesis actually referred to an advanced race of human beings who were the true creators of life on earth and in many other places in the galaxy. The creation described in Genesis was part of an infinite series of creations that had been conducted by the Elohim in the past and would be performed in the future.[102] Like many others who had a call to found new religious movements, Raël's mission was to awaken human beings to their true identities and restore to them a sense of their true history. Also like many before him, Raël's mission was decidedly urgent. He was informed that "you are the last of the prophets before the Judgment, you are the prophet of the religion of religions, the demystifier and the shepherd of shepherds."[103] Raël's mission was confirmed in a second encounter with the Elohim in July 1975, during which he was whisked away to another planet on which sat the Council of the Eternals, including Yahweh, Abraham, Buddha, Jesus, and Muhammad, enjoying an idyllic existence. Among the things that Raël learned was that "humanity is now arriving at a turning point in its history and its future depends on itself. If it can control its aggressiveness towards itself and its own environment, then it will reach the golden age of interplanetary civilization, universal happiness and fulfillment."[104]

Despite its millennial context, Raël's message is decidedly upbeat; his is a progressive rather than catastrophic millennialism.[105] Raël proclaims that "life is made to be enjoyed. Whether you find pleasure in the diffusion of the Messages of our Creators, or pleasure in contributing to the entry of Humanity into the Golden Age, or pleasure in pleasing yourself by putting yourself in tune with the Infinite, or by any other means."[106] The Raëlians are also enthusiastic about the ability of science and technology to "totally liberate humanity not only from the anxiety of hunger in the world, but also from the obligation to work to live."[107] In that ideal future, humans would be completely free to practice "sensual meditation," "the simplest and most efficient set of techniques for human awakening and fulfillment," a system revealed to Raël by the Elohim themselves.[108] The Raëlian Movement thus promotes an ethic of self-cultivation and individual responsibility. It asserts that "everyone must do as he pleases" but that "each person is totally responsible for his actions" and that "no cause could ever justify inflicting pain or death to a non-violent person, even if the survival of humanity depended on it."[109]

Converts to the Raëlian Movement have cited a variety of reasons for their adherence. Some have claimed that the positive message of Raël has helped them to see through the hypocrisy of established religions. As a Roman Catholic priest who joined the movement put it, "when I had finished reading these first two Messages, I felt very vividly inside of me,

Claude Vorilhon, the spiritual leader of the Raëlians. © Christopher J. Morris/ CORBIS.

the hypocrisy of Christians who pray only from their lips, while the precept of loving their neighbour is almost always forgotten."[110] Others have found the Raëlian account of creation scientifically persuasive. A chemical engineer wrote that "I find everywhere around me confirmation of the messages. It suffices to open our eyes to understand this fabulous story of the coming of the Elohim on the Earth, and the scientific creation of life in laboratories, which we ourselves will soon repeat."[111] Another convert simply said that after hearing Raël speak, "I recognized 'Jesus speaking in his own era.'"[112] Such testimonies are typical of the some sixty thousand members in more than ninety countries that the Raëlian Movement now claims.[113]

The Raëlian enthusiasm for science, as of this writing vividly expressed in a photograph of naked Raëlians arranged to spell out the slogan "I (heart) G M" for their approval of genetically modified foods, is tempered by their objection to the theory of evolution. After inveighing against "the false prophets of our time" who mislead their audiences about the true nature of God, Raël identifies a second category of false prophets as "those people, scientists or not, who claim that life on Earth, and therefore humanity, is the result of successive random chance events which all happened during what they call evolution."[114] For Raëlians, the randomness of evolution would deny human life its direction or goal; they prefer to describe life on earth as the product of a carefully considered and observed experiment by the Elohim.

The Raëlians' distinctive blend of science, religion, and ethics is perhaps best captured in their comments on human cloning. In a somewhat fractured English translation, Raël makes the sweeping assertion that "not only human cloning is not against the wish of what people call god, but it is in our Creators' plan for us to discover and to use it as many other religious leaders claim, and becoming, as it is written in the Bible, equal to our Creators."[115] The Raëlians' goal is nothing short of creating a new civilization "where we can enjoy a life of continual pleasure, where no one has to work, or exhaust themselves doing something they don't want to."[116] As Raëlians work toward that goal they are also trying to build an official embassy where representatives of the Elohim can, at the appropriate time, be received on earth so that humans can enter into formal, and beneficial communication with them.[117]

Although it never matched the notoriety they received with their claims to have cloned human beings, the Raëlians have attracted controversy throughout their history. Some observers found their initial symbol of a swastika within a six-pointed star to have unsavory connotations of anti-Semitism and in 1991 Raël transformed the swastika, which he had viewed as an ancient Hindu and Buddhist symbol, into a swirling representation of a galaxy.[118] Christian opponents of the group have proclaimed its understanding of the Genesis creation stories to be "bizarre" and "unbiblical."[119] It is not yet clear, however, whether the Raëlians' dramatic entry into the contemporary discussions of the morality of cloning will have a substantial effect on the group's ability to attract and retain members.[120] In part that is because the cloning operation is being undertaken by a separate corporation and in part because the Raëlian Movement as a whole does not exercise a strong control over its members' lives. Although Raël remains the undisputed head of the movement, he has not developed institutional structures for the enforcement of orthodoxy to anything like the degree that the Church of Scientology has, for example. The Raëlians remain a loosely knit federation of those who have taken Raël's positive message of human transformation to heart.

Conclusions

Although this chapter has focused on the founding of new religions in the United States during approximately the last half century, such innovative creations have always been part of American history, whether they have gained substantial public attention or not. Spiritualism and Theosophy in the nineteenth century and the "I AM" activity in the years before the Second World War are just a few examples. Whenever they have occurred, new religious movements have faced similar dilemmas. They have had simultaneously to assert their novelty in order to distinguish themselves from established religious traditions and to assert their continuity with the past in order to ease the transition of potential members from their former affiliation to their new commitment. Claude Vorilhon's account of the experiences that transformed him into the prophet Raël provides a good example. His encounters with extraterrestrials were certainly novel, if not entirely unprecedented, experiences, but the wisdom that the Elohim imparted to him focused on casting the familiar creation story of the book of Genesis in a new light. Even Anton LaVey, who announced a complete break with the biblical tradition, depended on a counter-reading of the Bible to achieve legitimacy for his new religious movement.

The Church of Satan and the Church of Scientology also show that new religious movements are themselves as prone to sectarian divisions as more established religions. Even L. Ron Hubbard, despite strenuous attempts to impose and maintain orthodoxy, was unable to prevent the splitting off of rival organizations from the Church of Scientology. LaVey's message of principled individualism at least inadvertently promoted the flourishing of rival teachers and organizations and LaVey himself remained ambivalent about those developments. The Heaven's Gate group's mass suicide forestalled any further developments in or challenges to its organizational structure, but its leaders did experiment with a variety of structures for the group during its brief duration. The relatively loose organization of the Raëlians has not yet spurred any competing interpretations of Raël's experiences with the Elohim or any other claims to have been contacted by the same figures, but those possibilities remain open, particularly when Raël himself passes from this world.

The careers of the four groups discussed in this chapter demonstrate that dramatic religious innovation remains a significant part of the American religious landscape. In the formation of their novel messages, religious leaders have drawn on very diverse sources of inspiration, from encounters with superior figures from beyond this world to painstaking study of human nature and psychology. Each of the groups in this group has found and maintained for some time a small clientele and the Church of Scientology, at least, has had a substantial impact in many societies throughout the world. While the Heaven's Gate group foreclosed on its own future on this earthly plane, the others remain vigorous in proclaiming their messages and accepting, if not systematically seeking, new members. This brief survey of the founding of new religions in the United States gives no indication that such religious innovation will abate or disappear in the near future. New religious movements have always been a part of American religious life and are very likely to continue to be so.

Notes

1. Kenneth V. Lanning, "A Law-Enforcement Perspective on Allegations of Ritual Abuse," in David K. Sakheim and Susan E. Devine, eds., *Out of Darkness: Exploring Satanism and Ritual Abuse* (New York: Lexington, 1992), pp. 109–46, see p. 113. Lanning's essay faithfully follows his original report, the text of which is available at www.religioustolerance.org/ra_repo3.htm.

2. Ibid., p. 145.

3. David Bromley, "Satanism: The New Cult Scare" in James T. Richardson, Joel Best, David G. Bromley, eds., *The Satanism Scare* (New York: Aldine De Gruyter, 1991), pp. 49–72, quotation from p. 68.

4. Carl Raschke, *Painted Black* (New York: HarperCollins, 1990), p. 95.

5. Michelle Smith and Lawrence Pazder, *Michelle Remembers* (New York: Pocket, 1980).

6. Lauren Stratford, *Satan's Underground: The Extraordinary Story of One Woman's Escape* (Gretna, LA: Pelican, 1991).

7. See Debbie Nathan, "Satanism and Child Molestation: Constructing the Ritual Abuse Scare," in Richardson, Best, and Bromley, eds., *The Satanism Scare*, pp. 75–94. See also Debbie Nathan and Michael Snedeker, *Satan's Silence: Ritual Abuse and the Making of a Modern American Witch Hunt* (New York: Basic, 1995).

8. Robert D. Hicks, *In Pursuit of Satan: The Police and the Occult* (Buffalo, NY: Prometheus, 1991), p. 12.

9. Ibid., p. 10.

10. Lanning, "A Law-Enforcement Perspective on Allegations of Ritual Abuse," p. 144.

11. Raschke, *Painted Black*, p. 221.

12. Philip Jenkins and Daniel Maier-Katkin, "Occult Survivors: The Making of a Myth," in Richardson, Best, and Bromley, eds., *The Satanism Scare*, pp. 127–44, quotation from p. 142.

13. Jeffrey Victor, *Satanic Panic: The Creation of a Contemporary Legend* (Chicago: Open Court, 1993), pp. 53–54.

14. Nathan, "Satanism and Child Molestation," p. 88. For a review of the evidence about Satanic ritual abuse from a Christian apologetic perspective, see Bob and

Gretchen Passantino, "The Hard Facts about Satanic Ritual Abuse," available at www.equip.org/free/DO040.html.

15. Raschke, *Painted Black*, p. 135.

16. See ibid., pp. 129–31.

17. See www.religiousmovements.lib.virginia.edu/nrms/satanism/intro.html.

18. See www.religioustolerance.org/satanis3.htm. On Satanic metal music, see Gardell, *Gods of the Blood*, pp. 304–7.

19. As quoted in Blanche Barton, *The Church of Satan* (New York: Hell's Kitchen Productions, 1990), p. 70.

20. www.churchofsatan.com/Pages/MFInterview.html.

21. Anton Szandor LaVey, *The Devil's Notebook* (Venice, CA: Feral House, 1992), p. 9.

22. Barton, *The Church of Satan*, p. 11. See also Anton Szandor LaVey, *The Satanic Bible* (New York: Avon, 1969), pp. 96–97.

23. LaVey, *The Satanic Bible*, p. 48.

24. Ibid. His capitalization.

25. Ibid., p. 55.

26. Ibid., p. 51.

27. Ibid., p. 25.

28. Ibid., p. 96. See pp. 40, 44.

29. Ibid.

30. See ibid., pp. 34–35.

31. For the "official" version of LaVey's life, see Blanche Barton, *The Secret Life of a Satanist: The Authorized Biography of Anton LaVey* (Los Angeles: Feral House, 1990); for a critical view, see Lawrence Wright, "Sympathy for the Devil," *Rolling Stone*, September 5, 1991. See also Gardell, *Gods of the Blood*, pp. 285–89.

32. See Barton, *The Church of Satan*, pp. 15–19.

33. Anton Szandor LaVey, *The Satanic Rituals* (New York: Avon, 1972).

34. Barton, *The Church of Satan*, p. 96.

35. See www.churchofsatan.com/Pages/Affiliation.html.

36. LaVey, "The Church of Satan, Cosmic Joy Buzzer," in Barton, *Secret Life*, p. 250.

37. James Lewis, "The Satanic Bible: Quasi-Scripture/Counter/Scripture," p. 2; available at www.cesnur.org/2002/slc/lewis.htm.

38. See www.churchofsatan.com/home.html.

39. For *The Cloven Hoof*, see ibid., for the publications of the St. Louis "Legion of Loki," see www.home.ix.netcom.com/~ambrosi/; see also www.geocities.com/Athens/Parthenon/2669/devilsdiary.html for other publications.

40. www.xeper.org/pub/lib/xp_FS_lib.htm.

41. See www.xeper.org/maquino/nm/COS.pdf.

42. www.xeper.org/pub/lib/xp_FS_lib.htm; their emphasis.

43. On Aquino's legal difficulties, see www.religiousmovements.lib.virginia.edu/nrms/satanism/tempset.html.

44. www.satanicchurch.com/content/membership.aspx.

45. *Brimstone*, letter to inquirers, April 1, 1991.

46. Ibid.

47. In the summer of 2003 the First Church of Satan was changing again. See www.churchofsatan.org/whyegan.html.

48. www.churchofsatan.org/faq.html.

49. Ibid.

50. A brief account of Hubbard's biography can be found in J. Gordon Melton, *The Church of Scientology* (Salt Lake City, UT: Signature, 2000), pp. 1–7. Although the Church of Scientology has not yet produced an official biography of Hubbard, biographical details are sprinkled throughout its many publications.

51. Roy Wallis, *The Road to Total Freedom: A Sociological Analysis of Scientology* (New York: Columbia University Press, 1977), p. 33.

52. Church of Scientology, *Scientology: Theology and Practice of a Contemporary Religion* (Los Angeles: Bridge, 1998), p. 17.

53. See, for example, Church of Scientology, *What is Scientology?* (Los Angeles: Bridge, 1998), p. 673. For a brief account of how Scientologists explain the concept of the "thetan" in practice, see Harriet Whitehead, *Renunciation and Reformulation: A Study of Conversion in an American Sect* (Ithaca, NY: Cornell University Press, 1987), p. 200.

54. Ibid., p. 635.

55. Church of Scientology, *Scientology: Theology and Practice*, p. 33.

56. See Whitehead, *Renunciation and Reformulation*, pp. 142–58.

57. Church of Scientology, *Scientology: Theology and Practice*, p. 36.

58. As quoted in Wallis, *The Road to Total Freedom*, p. 29.

59. See, for example, Church of Scientology, *What is Scientology?* pp. 179–81.

60. See ibid., pp. 869–89, for a list of materials.

61. Ibid., p. 309.

62. Ibid., p. 31.

63. Ibid., p. 330. In general, see ibid., pp. 307–67. The Church's official Web site also provides multiple accounts of successes; see www.scientology.org/html/en_US/results/index.html, for example.

64. See Melton, *Scientology*, p. 43; Church of Scientology, *What is Scientology?* p. 423.

65. See Church of Scientology, *What is Scientology?* pp. 455–543.

66. See the extensive collection of rituals, sermons, and other materials in Church of Scientology, *The Background, Ministry, Ceremonies, and Sermons of the Scientology Religion* (Los Angeles: Bridge, 1999).

67. See Church of Scientology, *What is Scientology?* pp. 405–9.

68. Church of Scientology, *Scientology: Theology and Practice*, p. 45; see p. 71.

69. Bent Corydon, *L. Ron Hubbard: Messiah or Madman?* rev. ed. (Fort Lee, NJ: Barricade, 1992). Foes of Scientology maintain an extensive presence on the Internet; see, for example, Operation Clambake at www.xenu.net/index.html. Details of "Operating Thetan" levels have been made public at www.b-org.demon.nl/scn/upper-levels/ot1.html. The complete text of Agnes Hadley's *My Life as a Scientologist*, 1998, is available at www.freezone.de/english/reports/e_lastoc.htm.

70. Ibid., p. 13.

71. Jon Atack, *A Piece of Blue Sky: Scientology, Dianetics and L. Ron Hubbard Exposed* (New York: Carol, 1990).

72. See the materials at www.lisamcpherson.org/. See also www.whyarethey-dead.net/room174.html.

73. See the materials collected at www.religiousfreedomwatch.org/.

74. For collections of documents and news articles about Scientology, see www.cesnur.org/testi/se_scientology.htm and www.rickross.com/cgi-bin/htsearch.

75. On the backgrounds of Nettles and Applewhite, see Wessinger, *How the Millennium Comes Violently*, p. 232.

76. As quoted in Hall et al., *Apocalypse Observed,* p. 151.

77. "'88 Update—The UFO Two and Their Crew: A Brief Synopsis," in Representatives from the Kingdom of Heaven, *How and When "Heaven's Gate" (The Door to the Physical Kingdom Level Above Human) May Be Entered* (Denver, CO: Right to Know Enterprises, 1996), sec. 3, p. 3. This anthology produced by Chuck Humphreys, a survivor of the group suicide who eventually took his own life, reproduces many of the Heaven's Gate documents from their original Web site and adds the exit statements of some of those who participated in the group suicide.

78. Ibid., sec. 4, p. 72.

79. See Wessinger, *How the Millennium Comes Violently,* pp. 233–34; Hall et al., *Apocalypse Observed,* pp. 155–56. For the flyer announcing the Waldport meeting, see *How and Why "Heaven's Gate,* sec. 2, p. 3. On the early years of the movement, see Robert W. Balch, "Waiting for the Ships: Disillusionment and the Revitalization of Faith in Bo and Peep's UFO Cult," in James R. Lewis, ed., *The Gods Have Landed: New Religions from Other Worlds* (Albany: State University of New York Press, 1995), pp. 137–66.

80. As quoted in Brad Steiger and Hayden Hewes, *Inside Heaven's Gate: The UFO Cult Leaders Tell Their Story in Their Own Words* (New York: Signet, 1997), pp. 12–13.

81. Ibid., p. 13.

82. Ibid., p. 14.

83. Ibid., p. 83.

84. *How and Why "Heaven's Gate,"* preface, p. vi; sec. 5, p. 4.

85. On Nettles' death, see Wessinger, *How the Millennium Comes Violently,* p. 237; Hall et al., *Apocalypse Observed,* p. 168.

86. *How and Why "Heaven's Gate,"* sec. 3, p. 4.

87. Ibid., addendum sec. 1, pp. 2, 9, respectively.

88. Ibid., sec. 4, p. 13.

89. See ibid., sec. 4, pp. 4, 6, 82; sec. 3, p. 4.

90. Ibid., sec. 6, p. 13; appendix A, p. 29, respectively.

91. Ibid., sec. 4, p. 74.

92. Ibid., appendix A, p. 4.

93. Ibid., addendum sec. 1, p. 10.

94. See Wessinger, *How the Millennium Comes Violently,* p. 237.

95. See *How and Why "Heaven's Gate,"* appendix A, p. 3.

96. Ibid., p. 5.

97. Ibid., addendum appendix A, p. 5. Members of Heaven's Gate all took new names ending in "ody."

98. Ibid., addendum appendix A, p. 7.

99. See the essays collected in Lewis, ed., *The Gods Have Landed* and in Christopher Partridge, ed., *UFO Religions* (New York: Routledge, 2003).

100. Raël (Claude Vorilhon), *The Message Given to Me by Extra-Terrestrials: They Took Me to Their Planet* (Tokyo: AOM, 1986), p. 4. Also published as *The True Face of God* (unknown: The Raëlian Foundation, 1998).

101. Raël (Claude Vorilhon), *The Message Given to Me by Extra-Terrestrials,* pp. 7–8.

102. See Raël (Claude Vorilhon), *Let's Welcome Our Fathers From Space: They Created Humanity in Their Laboratories* (Tokyo: AOM, 1986), p. 41.

103. Ibid., p. 215.

104. Ibid., p. 181.

105. See Wessinger, *How the Millennium Comes Violently,* pp. 16–17, for definitions of those forms of millennialism.

106. Raël (Claude Vorilhon), *Let's Welcome Our Fathers From Space,* p. 61.

107. Raël (Claude Vorilhon), *The Message Given to Me by Extra-Terrestrials,* p. 190.

108. Raël (Claude Vorilhon), *Sensual Meditation: Awakening the Mind by Awakening the Body* (n.p.: Nova Diffusion, 2002), p. 31.

109. Raël (Claude Vorilhon), *Let's Welcome Our Fathers From Space,* pp. 84, 154, 157, respectively.

110. Ibid., p. 180.

111. Ibid., p. 186.

112. Ibid., p. 194.

113. See www.rael.org/english/index.html for the current membership numbers and for a variety of resources, including texts and videos.

114. Raël (Claude Vorilhon), *Let's Welcome Our Fathers From Space,* p. 88.

115. Raël (Claude Vorilhon), *Yes to Human Cloning: Eternal Life Thanks to Science* (Vaduz: Raëlian Foundation, 2001), p. 160. See www.clonaid.com.

116. Ibid., p. 146.

117. See www.rael.org/english/index.html.

118. See, for example, www.rael.yahni.com/.

119. See, for example, www.watchman.org/profile/raelianpro.htm.

120. For a full selection of news articles, see www.rickross.com/groups/raelians.html.

Chapter 8

Themes in the Study
of New Religious Movements

The previous chapters have shown that new religious movements have always been a part of the religious history of the United States. Some have been imported to the United States after taking shape elsewhere, like the Shakers, the Unificationist Movement, the International Society for Krishna Consciousness, and the Raëlians; others have split off from parent bodies in the United States, like the Branch Davidians, the Nation of Gods and Earths, and the Temple of Set; and others have been founded in the United States by individuals claiming extraordinary divine inspiration or unsurpassed insight into the human condition, like the Church of Jesus Christ of Latter-day Saints, the Church of Satan, and the Church of Scientology. Many of the new religious movements that have been active in the United States have attracted an international membership and have established centers of activity in other countries. The Mormon church, for example, maintains a vigorous international mission; Soka Gakkai has attracted adherents throughout the world; and many Neo-Pagans maintain contact with fellow practitioners in England and throughout Europe. The rather amorphous New Age Movement is also worldwide in its scope. Any claim that cults or new religious movements constitute a phenomenon that can be limited to the United States in the later twentieth and early twenty-first centuries is therefore completely undermined by the abundant evidence.[1] New religious movements in the United States have a much longer history, and the United States is by no means the only cultural area to have experienced such religious innovation.

Rarely have new religions escaped creating at least some degree of controversy, primarily because they claim to offer innovative and superior visions of the nature and goals of human life. As David Chidester argued in his study of Jonestown, "any religion is an irreducible experiment in being human."[2] The experiments conducted by new religious movements inevitably challenge more established religions as well as other deeply ingrained social and cultural institutions such as the educational system, the family, and definitions of gender roles. Because they conduct experiments that do not simply replicate established patterns and because they claim results that far surpass what other cultural institutions can offer, new religions often provoke hostile reactions from various protectors of the status quo. Whether their newness is branded as doctrinal deviance or heresy by religious countercultists or as destructive cultism by more secular anticultists, new religions must frequently face challenges to their own legitimacy that are at least vigorous as the challenges that they pose to mainstream religious and cultural institutions. That situation of controversy has pushed several dimensions to the fore of public discussion and indelibly shaped how they are understood by opponents of new religious movements, the news media and law enforcement, interested observers, and even members of new religions themselves. This chapter takes up several of those themes, focusing on the nature of leadership in new religious movements, the processes of entering and exiting new religious groups, the possible connections between new religions and violence, and women and children in new religions.

Cult Leaders

Perhaps the most powerful image that has been constructed by the contemporary anticult movement is that of the eerily powerful cult leader. Margaret Singer has asserted that "in most cases, there is one person, typically the founder, at the top of the cult's structure, and decision making centers in him."[3] She lists these characteristics of the cult leader:

> Cult leaders are self-appointed, persuasive persons who claim to have a special mission in life or to have special knowledge.
> Cult leaders tend to be determined and domineering and are often described as charismatic.
> Cult leaders center veneration on themselves.[4]

Singer's characterization is founded on a rejection of any religious claims that the leader might make. In her view, cult leaders are self-appointed, whether or not they claim to have received a divine calling. Further, they may be described as charismatic, but for Singer that only masks their true, manipulative nature. Cult leaders, as Singer sees it, are in it only for themselves; they want to receive as much honor and other tangible rewards (including money and sex) as possible; any claims to altruism are thereby ruled out. In her critical analysis, "cults basically have only two purposes: recruiting new members and fund-raising."[5] Singer attributes extraordinary power to cult leaders, arguing that "everyone is susceptible to the lure of these master manipulators."[6] Singer's attribution of such overwhelming power to cult leaders leads her to the position that people don't really intentionally join cults, rather they are recruited by deceptive recruiters who manipulate them into membership.[7] Singer's analysis of cult leaders, which is representative of the general approach of anticult activists, amounts to a Great (Bad) Man theory of cult formation. Cunning leaders exercise such irresistible power that those whom they recruit are virtually powerless to resist. In that view, cult recruitment becomes exploitation and members become victims. Responsibility for any damage done to members is lodged firmly with the leader, and individuals who become members of cults are largely exonerated of the consequences of their actions. They have simply been held in thrall by a power greater than their own. In the arguments of Singer and other anticult writers, the image of the cult leader as a powerful and cynical manipulator firmly supports the related argument that individuals who become members of cults have been subjected to a process of brainwashing or coercive persuasion. Before moving to a consideration of those topics, however, it is worthwhile to consider alternative depictions of leadership in new religious movements.

Since Max Weber first articulated three ideal types of legitimate authority, there has been extensive scholarly investigation of charismatic leadership. Weber set charismatic authority in contrast to both rational or bureaucratic authority, which is embedded in institutional forms, and traditional authority, which passes through a defined lineage.[8] Weber argued that charisma, on the other hand, was perceived to be a characteristic of an individual's personality and charismatic authority depended on its recognition by others for its social effectiveness.[9] Put simply, a person might perceive herself or himself to be charismatic, but that perception becomes socially meaningful only when others agree and are willing to act on their agreement. From that perspective, leadership becomes something that is actively constructed through the interactions of claimants to leadership and their audiences. Potential followers have the ability to confirm, dispute, reject, adjust, and transform a leader's claims to authority and thus play a crucial role in the construction of the character and extent of that authority. Religious leadership, from this perspective, is always embedded in an array of social processes that can sustain, augment, or decrease its power, even when it appears to have the support of stable, long-standing institutions. Religious leaders are made, remade, and unmade in their interactions with those whom they seek to recruit and retain as followers.

Two examples will demonstrate how the different approaches to leadership are applied. In the opening of *Cults in Our Midst* Margaret Singer asks "how many more Jonestowns and Wacos will have to occur before we realize how vulnerable all humans are to influence?"[10] As her argument unfolds, it becomes very clear that Singer considers both Jim Jones and David Koresh to be prime examples of the manipulative cult leaders about whom she wants to warn the American public. In Singer's book, however, their conformity to the image of the dangerous cult leader is largely assumed rather than demonstrated. On the surface, at least, the mass murder-suicide of some 922 people on November 18, 1978, in Guyana lends support to Singer's depiction of the Rev. Jim Jones. More detailed analyses of his leadership, however, suggest that the situation was more complex.

After a careful review of how the Jonestown community actually functioned, for example, Mary McCormick Maaga concluded that "in Guyana Jim Jones became more important symbolically as a mascot of cohesion than as a leader in the managerial sense."[11] Maaga argues that by the time the Peoples Temple relocated to Jonestown Jones had become more a liability than an asset because of his increasing drug dependence and paranoia. An inner circle of leaders then took on both the considerable task of managing the daily life of the community and containing the damage done by evidence of Jones' deterioration.[12] Although she acknowledges that it is only a hypothesis, Maaga concludes that "the evidence I have collected suggests that Jones would have either stepped down, been eased out, or died within several months."[13] Maaga's portrait of both Jones and the often ignored other leaders of the Peoples Temple, particularly during its final Jonestown phase, does not conform to the characterization of the cult leader promoted by Singer and other anticult writers. When confronted with Maaga's evidence, it is difficult to see how a debilitated, out-of-touch Jones exercised over his followers the type of control that Singer and her supporters would attribute to the cult leader. Maaga portrays leadership in the Peoples Temple as a much more messy and complicated process. She directs attention to others beyond the founder of the movement who functioned in significant leadership roles and at the same time raises the issue of how commitment was maintained in the virtual absence of the leader. In direct contrast to Singer's assertion that cults are all about the leader, Maaga takes the message of the Peoples Temple seriously as well. Making a potentially crucial distinction, she suggests that "it was not belief in Jim Jones as much as belief in Jonestown that leaders of Peoples Temple were not willing to forsake."[14] Maaga argues, in effect, that Jones' message had a life beyond Jones himself. Once articulated, it became the common property of all who joined the Jonestown experiment. Though Jones attempted to enforce his own brand of orthodoxy on the group, when they came face to face with his own failings and frailties, at least some of the members of the Peoples Temple were able to distinguish the message from the messenger. That separation of the message from the messenger could have provided the germs of an institutionalization of the Peoples Temple after Jim Jones had departed from the scene. But the events of November 1978 forever foreclosed that possibility. The direct introduction of external pressures into an already combustible situation in which the community was barely managing to keep itself alive sparked the deadly "White Night." Maaga's analysis nevertheless shows that Jones' role as leader of the Peoples Temple was much more complex and varied than the stereotypical portrait of the cult leader would indicate.

That impression is confirmed in the case of David Koresh as well. By implying that the destruction of the Mount Carmel Center and the deaths of nearly everyone inside on April 19, 1993, were directly caused by David Koresh, Singer conforms him to the stereotype of the cult leader. Koresh's authority, like Jones', was constructed through much more complicated processes. Because he was part of the Seventh-Day Adventist tradition, Koresh held the Bible as the ultimate authority. He brought to it, however, a distinctive interpretive scheme that was inspired by his own experience. Koresh's conviction that he had been chosen for a prophetic and messianic mission undergirded all of his other claims to authority. It helps to explain how he could see himself in scripture and claim for himself a status that virtually everyone but Koresh's followers would reserve for Jesus. On April 15, for example, Koresh explicitly appropriated two titles intimately associated with Jesus. He told the negotiator, "look. If the seven seals are true, yes, I'm the Lamb of God. Yes, I'm Christ. If the seven seals are true."[15] In a more esoteric reference, Koresh also claimed that he personified the message of the seventh angel of Revelation.[16]

But Koresh also acknowledged, at least superficially, an important check on his claim to ultimate authority, signaled on April 15 by his double reference to the truth of the seven seals. Koresh frequently told his followers and the outside world that his message had to be measured against the evidence of the Bible. He claimed that he was renovating tradition, not creating something wholly new. In fact, those who could not reconcile either Koresh's doctrines or his self-understanding with what they saw in scripture had often left the group.[17] Koresh himself also stated that he tested his own preaching against what he found in the Bible. On March 9 he disclosed to a negotiator that

> the thing of it is is that I can only move on the foundation that God has established. Now, how do I know that the spirit that speaks with me is the true spirit of God, how do I know? Only unless it's perfectly in context with what's been stated beforehand, you know.
> . . . Then how can I believe? Well, especially in the revelation when there's these seven simple steps, seven seals. . . . You know, either we understand them or we do not. If someone says they do, we can't deny it unless we've sat down and honestly, candidly opened up to see what insight this person may or may not have on the subject.[18]

In discussing Koresh with a negotiator during the siege, David Thibodeau, one of the survivors of the April 19 fire, gave a similar explanation. Thibodeau stated that his presence at Mount Carmel "really has nothing to do with David's charisma, . . . it's just opening the book for myself, seeing what it says and saying, wow, is this guy found in the book, you know, and all the Psalms, you, you, really got to sit down and listen to him talk, I mean with the book open."[19] Similarly, commenting on Koresh's refusal to speak with negotiators on April 9, Steve Schneider observed that "unless he can bring in what he is, and that's the Bible, [then he won't speak]. I mean he'll talk about that [leaving] but always in relation to the Bible so you can understand where and why."[20] In the end, Koresh's students may have so thoroughly assimilated his message about the seven seals that they could not use the Bible as an independent source against which to judge what he had to say. Nonetheless, there was at least a theoretical standard, in addition to his personal authority, against which Koresh's pronouncements could be measured. Many of his followers claim to have used that standard; in the judgment of some it led to a strengthening of their faith in the message of the seven seals, but in the judgment of others, it helped them to unmask Koresh as a prophetic pretender.

In the daily life of the Mount Carmel community, David Koresh's status as an authoritative interpreter of the biblical text depended less on his claims to an extraordinary religious experience in Israel in 1985 and more on his repeated ability to make sense of the millennial message of Revelation in his Bible studies. In the view of his students, at least, Koresh's authority was tested every time that he proposed an interpretation of scripture. Like David Thibodeau, they could easily sit before him and check what he had to say against the text itself. On the other hand, every time his students accepted his interpretation of the Bible Koresh's authority was reinforced. The daily Bible studies thus became Koresh's most important tool for maintaining and enhancing his power, authority, and status within the group. Koresh's position as the teacher and prophet of the Mount Carmel community was not an unalterable given. His status as an inspired interpreter of the text was subject to daily renegotiation. It is a measure of his unshakeable confidence in his mission, persuasive ability, and facility with the biblical text that Koresh successfully maintained his position, but it is also a measure of their deep yearning for the thorough social, moral, and religious renovation of the world that the others at Mount Carmel continued to cherish Koresh's teaching about the seven seals and find promised in it the possibility of their eternal salvation.

The anticult activists' characterization of the typical cult leader as an all-powerful manipulator has serious descriptive and analytical flaws. While exaggerating the influence of the leader it diminishes the agency of the followers. It leads directly to over-simplifications that effectively support polemical points but dramatically misconstrue the dynamics of individual groups. Leadership is claimed, exercised, and contested in new religious movements in a variety of specific and fluid contexts; if both their specificity and fluidity are ignored an adequate description, analysis, and interpretation of how leadership functions in new religions cannot be achieved.

Entering and Exiting New Religious Movements

Anticult writers' understanding of conversion to new religious movements is directly tied to their understanding of leadership. If the cult leader is seen to be a powerful and deceptive manipulator, then membership in new religions can only have come about by a process of deceptive recruitment that can be variously described as brainwashing, coercive persuasion, or mind control. From that perspective, the member is a passive dupe; any religious claims are simply lies that cover up the leader's real motivations of self-aggrandizement and self-gratification. Singer describes the process of conversion to cults in this way: "effective cult leaders and recruiters verbally seduce, charm, manipulate, and trick people into taking that first fatal step and then into making increasing commitments to the group. . . . Most recruits have little real knowledge of what will eventually happen to them, and it's rare for a new member to exercise anything like fully informed consent in making the decision to join."[21]

Statements of former members have frequently reinforced that view. In an autobiography whose title, *Crazy for God,* neatly summarizes its position, an early convert to the Unification Church recalled how the persistent warm attention of the group's members led him progressively closer to espousing their cause. Christopher Edwards recalled that "at first I viewed the Heavenly Kingdom as a possibility to be tested, but as the week [spent at the group's farm] progressed I began to accept it much more literally. I embraced what I wanted to believe so badly, the chance to live for something I could die for, to live and die for a love eternal, a love so strong that by its own whim it could command life or death."[22] Edwards subsequently quotes a statement from one of the members of the group that reinforces Singer's worst fears: "just trust us. We'll remake you into a new person. A real heavenly child. Just you wait."[23] In Edwards' recollection of his experience, he succumbed to the irresistible blandishments of the Unificationists that he encountered. At loose ends after his graduation from college and recently disappointed in love, he welcomed the extraordinary attention that was lavished on him and floated into the group on a tide of good feelings. In retrospect, as his autobiography's title suggests, he concluded that he had temporarily lost his mind, that he had not converted but rather been converted, against what at least later he would see as his better judgment.[24]

Testimonies like Edwards' are frequently cited in anti- and countercult literature. They form the basis for conclusions like the one that Christian countercult writer Ronald Enroth provided to talk-show host Oprah Winfrey when she was discussing the cult problem in the aftermath of the Waco disaster. Enroth confidently asserted that "the people who are in cults don't realize that they're being manipulated."[25] Since some former members of new religious movements, like Edwards and Steven Hassan, for example, become active in the anticult movement, their interpretations of their own experience achieve a wider currency than they might otherwise have. The welcome Web page of Hassan's Freedom of Mind Center, for example, identifies him both as a "licensed Mental Health Counselor" and a "former member of the Moon cult."[26] Implicit in such claims is the notion that being a former member guarantees the accuracy of one's observations, that "it takes one to know one." Not all former members, however, view their pasts in the same way. Another former Unificationist chose to portray both her conversion and her exit from the church as conscious decisions rather than as events that she passively experienced. Using the then dominant metaphor for conversion in anticult circles, Barbara Underwood wrote concerning her leaving the church that "my growing consciousness of my own lost integrity was what ultimately deprogrammed me."[27] Similarly, in an interview with Oprah Winfrey, Jeanine Bunds, who had been a member of the Branch Davidians, resisted Winfrey's attempts to characterize her as a passive victim of brainwashing. When Winfrey said, "We all see this as somebody who's taken over your mind," Bunds simply replied, "We didn't." When Winfrey persisted, Bunds repeated her denial.[28] Although she acknowledged the powerful emotional ties that she had with Koresh, Bunds emphasized her own conscious decision to be part of his group of Bible students. In another interview she stated that "I could have walked at any time. I chose to stay. He doesn't keep you. You can leave."[29] From even those few examples it is fair to conclude that the evidence provided by ex-members about the processes by which they entered and exited new religious movements is more complex than is suggested by the anticult stereotype of the irresistible power that the cunning cult leader exercises over passive victims. Without even taking into account the stories told by continuing members, a glaring omission in the anticult literature, the stories of ex-members sketch out a much more complicated situation in which attempts to exercise influence over potential recruits are met with a variety of responses, from willing acceptance through puzzled consideration to outright rejection. A more complex understanding of the phenomenon of conversion is therefore necessary.

Conversion has been a prominent topic in the contemporary study of religion at least since William James made it one of the primary topics in *The Varieties of Religious Experience*. But where James focused on conversion as a type of individual experience, most treatments of conversion to new religious movements view it as a product of social interaction. Stark and Bainbridge, for example, stress that "social networks play an essential role in recruitment to cults, sects, and conventional denominations."[30] More specifically, they argue that "people do not join new religious movements on the basis of theological reflection, but only as they are linked to such movements by interpersonal bonds with group members."[31] From that point of view, the ties that Christopher Edwards formed with his fellow Unificationists or that Jeanine Bunds formed with David Koresh appear to be less the result of devious manipulation and more part of normal social processes of interpersonal interaction. Such a characterization of the conversion process makes both those seeking converts and potential converts themselves active agents in complex social processes. Indeed, after reflecting on a model of conversion that he and Rodney Stark had developed, John Lofland urged students of conversion to turn their attention to "how people go about converting themselves."[32]

The dispute about whether to conceive of the process of affiliation with new religious movements as brainwashing or conversion has dominated both public and scholarly debates about new religious movements and spawned a voluminous literature that cannot be summarized here. Recently, scholars like Benjamin Zablocki and Stephen Kent have tried to rescue brainwashing from scholarly opprobrium and rehabilitate it as a descriptive and analytical category. But their efforts have met with stiff resistance and harsh critiques from other scholars of new religious movements and an impasse remains.[33] The dispute is not merely a squabble over scholarly terminology, however, because the choice of terminology can have practical effects in a variety of legal contexts, such as suits over kidnapping and false imprisonment charges. In a recent review of the state of the dispute, David Bromley has argued that it "centers on individual-group relationships, specifically the appropriate nature and degree of individual embeddedness in religious organizations. Conversion is a symbolic designation that positively sanctions embeddedness while brainwashing negatively sanctions embeddedness."[34] While Bromley is correct to note the political implications of the use of "conversion" to describe the process by which individuals become affiliated with new religious movements, as an analytical category it does have a longer pedigree in the study of religion and can be preserved in its root sense to refer to an individual's turning toward some new religious commitment and consequently turning away from a former commitment. In that sense, conversion is a fundamental part of new religious movements.

Especially in their earlier stages new religions cannot survive without attracting converts; in order to maintain their commitment, they must strive to nourish the religious lives of those converts they do attract, and they must guard against the loss of members through the process of defection or conversion out of the group. Thus, how one views the process of conversion to a new religion determines to a large extent how one views the entire religion. If Christopher Edwards was indeed deceived into joining the Unification Church, then the *bona fides* of the entire organization can rightly come into question. An organization that recruits deceptively is likely to have something to hide, to mask its "real" motives, to be something other than how it presents itself, to be, in short, a fraud. Religious fraud would then be a potentially serious social problem and appropriate action against the group, in order to protect both the gullible and the rest of society, would then be in order. On the other hand, if religious people join religious groups for ostensibly "valid" religious reasons, then their actions would be sheltered under the free exercise clause of the First Amendment to the U.S. Constitution. Then no matter how much outsiders were convinced that the members of a religious group were making fools of themselves or being deceived, the members would be protected from outside interference. It would be entirely up to the individual, as Jeanine Bunds suggested, whether to continue membership or leave the group.

One of the most compelling and firmly grounded arguments against conceiving of the process of affiliation with a new religious movement as brainwashing was presented by Eileen Barker in *The Making of a Moonie: Choice or Brainwashing?* On the basis of interviews, questionnaires, and statistical analyses of people who had encountered the message of the Unification Church, expressed interest in it, and eventually joined the church for some period of time, Barker concluded that "it is also obvious that the Unification environment is not irresistible. Conversion to the movement is the result of a (limited) number of *individual* experiences; it is not the result of a mass-induced hypnosis."[35] In direct contradiction of the prevailing anticult analysis Barker concludes that "most people who are subjected to the Moonies' attempts to recruit them are perfectly capable of refusing to join the movement," which "rules out those explanations which rely totally on Unification techniques of coercion for an explanation of recruitment to the movement. It also rules out any suggestion that the alternative which the Moonies offer is irresistible."[36] Instead, Barker offers, "the personalities and previous experiences which guests 'bring with them' must play a significant role" in determining whether or not they become members of the group. Thus, the second fundamental assertion of the anticult position, that converts are the passive victims of cunning manipulators, proves to be as ill-founded as the caricature of the omnipotent cult leader. Rather than an automatic process to which virtually everyone is susceptible, conversion is instead an individual decision subject to a variety of influences. Careful students of new religious movements are thus well-advised to reject the facile generalizations of anticult activists and seek instead the rich textures of individual lives in their social and religious contexts.

Cults and Violence

The third pillar of the contemporary anticult position is most bluntly summarized by Rabbi Maurice Davis's contention that "the path of the cults leads to Jonestowns."[37] The connection between cults and violence was cemented in the minds of many by a series of incidents in the 1990s that included the 1993 destruction of the Mount Carmel Center of the Branch Davidians, the 1995 Aum Shinrikyo attack on the Tokyo subway, the murders and suicides of members of the Solar Temple in 1994, 1995, and 1997, and the 1997 Heaven's Gate suicides. Because all of those groups were millennialist in one form or another, concerns about cult violence mounted as the year 2000 approached. Concerns about millennial violence, along with worries about potential effects of the turn of the millennium on antiquated computer programs that were not equipped to deal with a year beginning with a "2," led the U.S. Federal Bureau of Investigation to issue a report ominously entitled "Project Megiddo," for the mountain in Israel near which the biblical book of Revelation envisions the climactic battle at the end of the world taking place. The report, which was originally intended to be distributed to U.S. chiefs of police, gives a good indication of how many in law enforcement were viewing the cult problem at the turn of the twenty-first century.[38] "Project Megiddo" seems not only to have been shaped by dramatic events in the 1990s but also by the conclusions that anticult activists drew from them. It cites Singer's characterization of a cultic relationship as one that inculcates near or total dependence and generally adopts Singer's characterization of a cult.[39] As a result, the FBI report ignores the dynamic interaction of leaders and followers that characterizes any social movement and instead endorses the notion of the all-powerful leader that dominates anticult polemics. It claims, for example, that "the potential for violence on behalf of the members of biblically-driven cults is determined almost exclusively by the whims of the cult leader."[40] Anticult arguments may also have shaped the FBI report's taxonomy of groups, which separates "apocalyptic cults" from Christian Identity groups, white supremacists, militias, and Black

Hebrew Israelites.[41] Unfortunately, the largely implicit theoretical frame-work of the report complicates any attempts to investigate potential con-nections between millennialism and violence, though the report's very existence, choices of examples, and rhetoric presume such connections.

Recent scholarship has shown, however, that violence is the product of certain kinds of social interactions rather than being an inherent trait of some groups, especially those identified as "cults." In *Apocalypse Observed* John R. Hall and his co-authors persuasively reject the "cult essen-tialism" that explains everything by reference to supposedly universal internal dynamics of contemporary millennialist groups. In its place they demonstrate the distinctiveness of individual groups and show how the interaction of a movement and its "cultural opponents" is the key to understanding outbreaks of violence. Hall also identifies two different apocalyptic types. The warring sect, under which he classifies the Peoples Temple, the Branch Davidians, and Japan's Aum Shinrikyo, pursues a cli-mactic struggle against the forces of evil. Under a second type, the mysti-cal apocalypse of deathly transcendence, Hall includes both the Order of the Solar Temple and Heaven's Gate. Hall concludes with a caution about how law enforcement itself may contribute to the problem. He observes that "the strong relationship between state-cultural opposition and out-comes of violence underscores how problematic state action becomes in the view of apocalyptic sectarians when it seems to take the side of cultural opponents under the glare of hostile media coverage."[42]

Relying in part on Hall's stress that cultural opponents often catalyze violence between millennialists and the world outside their group, Cather-ine Wessinger identifies three types of millennial groups: fragile, assaulted, and revolutionary. Factors that can make a group fragile include instabil-ity in the leadership, manifest failures to progress toward the millennial goal, and external pressure from opponents; fragile groups may either implode into violence directed against themselves or explode in conflicts with those outside. Assaulted groups either actually are or believe them-selves to be besieged by opponents; they may prepare for what they see as an inevitable conflict and may well fight back if attacked. Revolutionary groups may devise intricate and detailed plans for attacks on their per-ceived enemies, will favor a violent rhetoric, and sometimes may actually act on their plans.[43] Hall and Wessinger share an emphasis on violence as the outcome of specific kinds of interactions, rather than an inherent potential of some groups. For law enforcement cult essentialism is a self-limiting, or even self-defeating, position because it fosters the perception that outsiders are drastically constrained in their ability to alter the course of events. In contrast, the interactionist model described by Hall and Wessinger enlarges the possibilities for positive intervention in any encounter with millennialists, even though recognizing the malleability of the situation in no way guarantees a successful outcome.

Robin Wagner-Pacifici has effectively captured the nuances of conflicts between cults and outsiders in her analysis of the standoff as a social situation. She notes a particular paradox "that while all participants have committed themselves to the situation (with highly variable degrees of freedom), they have, in a profound sense, committed themselves to *different* situations."[44] For example, where anticult activists might see the unconscionable exploitation of gullible individuals, members within a new religious movement will be inclined to see a freely chosen spiritual path. Consequently, Wagner-Pacifici argues that "the action driving the parties of a standoff to a standoff state and out through the other side of it is primarily a project of interpretation."[45] All of the parties in a standoff are involved in interpreting statements and actions, calibrating their responses, and assessing their consequences. While it may appear static, the standoff is actually a very fluid situation. Accordingly, as with interpretations of leadership and conversion, analysis of any individual's or group's potential for violence always needs to be context-specific, deeply attentive to the particular beliefs and convictions at play, fully aware of multiple perceptions of the situation, and cognizant of how matters may change over time. The closer observers come to adopting the view that certain groups are inherently liable to commit violent acts, the further they move away from the kind of nuanced analysis of specific situations that the interactionist model recommends.

Another issue related to the connections between millennialism and violence concerns the relationship of rhetoric to action. The FBI report states that "in light of the enormous amount of millennial rhetoric, the FBI sought to analyze a number of variables that have the potential to spark violent acts."[46] Although the FBI was correct to note that millennial beliefs are very often expressed in dramatically violent language; the extent to which that language has the ability to "spark violent acts" remains to be investigated.[47] Jeffrey Kaplan, for example, has emphasized that most millennial rhetoric is just that. Noting how infrequently violent millennial rhetoric inspires violent actions on the part of millennialists, he suggests that "watching is what millenarians do best," and proceeds to distinguish rhetorical, defensive, and revolutionary forms of violence.[48] In addition, episodic violence is only sometimes related to the programmatic goals of the group, as it was, for example, with the activities of The Order in 1983–84.[49] Defensive violence could occur in either the fragile or the assaulted groups that Wessinger describes. For example, she identifies the Peoples Temple in its final, Jonestown phase as a fragile group that turned its violence inward when it despaired of reaching its millennial goal. In contrast, she sees the Branch Davidians as an assaulted group that reacted violently to a military raid by the Bureau of Alcohol, Tobacco, and Firearms. Kaplan also singles out a factor that can easily be ignored. In his view, the "self-perception as a tiny and powerless band of the faithful acts as a powerful check on the catalyzation of violence. Millenarians are no fools. They are canny judges of the prevailing balance of forces."[50] Taken together, recent scholarly considerations of millennialism and violence, which frequently focus on the activities of new religious movements, provide a much more subtle understanding of millennial language and its relation to action than is evident in the FBI's "Project Megiddo" report.

Children and Women

Another area in which a tendency to act violently has been attributed to new religious movements is their care of children. Allegations of child abuse have rocked the International Society for Krishna Consciousness, touched off the Satanic panic of the 1980s, and been lodged against many leaders of new religious movements, including David Koresh. In the immediate aftermath of the disastrous assault on the Branch Davidians' Mount Carmel, for example, both Attorney General Janet Reno and President Bill Clinton justified the actions of the FBI on the grounds that the federal agents had acted to prevent child abuse. Reno asserted that "we had evidence that babies were being beaten," and Clinton stated that federal officials "had reason to believe that the children who were still inside the compound were being abused significantly as well as being forced to live in unsanitary and unsafe conditions."[51] Dramatic claims of child abuse have also figured prominently in custody cases, where one parent attempts to remove a child perceived to be in danger from the authority of a parent who is a member of a new religious group.

In fact, blanket allegations of child abuse have been leveled against new religious movements so often that James T. Richardson has identified them as a primary device by which society in general has attempted to exert social control over new religions. Richardson identified four major categories into which such claims could generally be sorted: religious home schooling, corporal punishment, low living standards, and sexual abuse.[52] Richardson also notes, however, that efforts to use accusations of child abuse as a broad characterization of the practices of new religious movements have foundered on the very definition of child abuse, the manifold problems with testimony elicited from children, and the lack of fit between legal definitions of child abuse and the ways in which at least some cult opponents have attempted to define child abuse as a constitutive element of the "cultic setting."[53] Examining some of the same issues against the background of U.S. Constitutional law, Michael Homer concluded that "the precarious balance between freedom of religion and the best interests of the child is normally evaluated in the United States on a case-by-case basis with a consideration as to how 'religious practices and beliefs' can and do affect specific children."[54] Homer's cautious observation both implicitly acknowledges the real possibility that unacceptable harm may be done to children in new religious groups, as in many other social settings, while simultaneously steering clear of unsupported sweeping condemnations of all or many new religious movements as sponsors of child abuse. The failure of the late twentieth-century Satanic panic to generate charges of child abuse that could stand up in court indicates that under rigorous examination such accusations do not always prove true; similarly, the exposure of systematic abuse at some of the ISKCON boarding schools lamentably shows that sometimes such accusations are wholly warranted. Each alleged incident, therefore, needs to be carefully scrutinized.

There is, however, more to the topic of children in new religious movements than sordid allegations of abusive behavior. Susan Palmer and Charlotte Hardman have identified four important areas for research: the impact that children have on a young movement, how movements retain and socialize their children, the intersection of socialization practices with broad concerns about religious freedom, and how children in new religions construct religious meaning for themselves.[55] Unless movements determine to grow only by conversion, the socialization of a second generation is crucial to their success. But a quest for socialization that both effectively secures the full participation of children born into a movement and simultaneously respects their rights to make informed choices about their own lives poses an array of institutional dilemmas. The tension between those two impulses has been particularly acute for Neo-Pagans, for example, especially because of their emphasis on individuals' freedom to determine their own religious paths. Some contemporary Pagans have argued against providing any religious instruction to children. One claimed that "by bringing people on the magickal path, as opposed to them finding the path themselves, we run the risk of finding ourselves dealing with an increasingly apathetic magickal community."[56] Others have worried about exposing developing children to the social opposition to their religion, acknowledging, for example, "I'd like to raise my son in the craft ... but I don't want the town bullies to crap on my son for being different."[57] Others who have themselves been socialized into contemporary Paganism have lamented the lack of a regular structure to consolidate and pass on the insights gained by earlier practitioners and chafe at the fact that "everyone comes into Paganism and makes it up all over again."[58] The absence of a well-articulated and far-reaching structure of authority in Neo-Paganism has contributed to the diversity of opinions about whether a second generation of Neo-Pagans should be socialized into the movement, and, if so, how.

The experience of ISKCON in the United States highlights different aspects of the dilemma. The prevalence of abuse in the *gurukulas* effectively undid that experiment in having ISKCON children educated in a wholly separate system. But even before that attendance at a *gurukula* was not an option for all children within the group. Those who had been raised within the communal living arrangements of the Krishna devotees experienced serious culture shock when they entered public schools. One young Krishna woman recalled of her entrance into a public high school that

> I couldn't relate to these kids. I wasn't seeing anything the same way. From age eleven, when we thought of men, we thought of marriage. Nothing was lighthearted and funny. I had to *learn* to laugh, how to have a sense of humor. As a girl we were taught to be chaste—therefore we never learned to ride even a bicycle, and so when I was put into PE class, it was one of the most embarrassing moments for me. I didn't know what third base was or what to do when the ball came to me.[59]

Krishna children who entered public education after having been schooled within their group therefore had to develop an array of coping strategies to respond to the cognitive dissonance and social alienation that resulted from their immersion into a "foreign" culture. Some chose to retreat and emphasize their attachments to their religious group, while others experimented with various ways of fitting in to their new surroundings and with their new associates. But even those of a second generation whose experience of a world beyond their religious group reaffirmed their religious commitments encountered other difficulties. In ISKCON, for example, the chair of the North American Board of Education gave a talk in the early 1990s entitled "All Dressed Up with No Place to Go" that directly confronted the harsh truth that even those who had been thoroughly educated within the movement's school system had little hope of attaining positions within the organization that were commensurate with their training and skills. The organization simply could not absorb all of its younger members into meaningful and challenging positions within the ranks of the movement.

In general, the experience of children in new religious movements is shaped by the particular theology of the group as it is mediated by their parents and other caregivers, by authoritative figures within the group, and by children's own efforts to understand and appropriate it. Consequently, because the theologies of new religious movements vary so widely, so does the experience of children within them. For example, a young member of The Family could say that "there's a secure plan for you: the Lord will bless you when you hold on and if you come through. My teenage friends in The Family have a goal, they seem more fulfilled, but teenagers out there, they're disillusioned with life."[60] For such a person, the clearly articulated ethical system of the group offers a definite alternative to the meaninglessness and lack of direction that he perceives among his peers outside the group. His religious commitment provides his life with structure, meaning, and direction that he believes his peers simply cannot find. Parents involved in the broad New Age Movement, however, espouse a radically different view of child-rearing. One stressed, for example, that "they decide for themselves—I don't decide for them—basic morality is inside them; there are no rules, no strict rules, we all just muddle along; because we have no doctrine, there's nothing to follow—so it's all spontaneous—in the moment."[61] It is impossible to account for such divergent ethics by reference to a putatively uniform experience of children in cults. Those two statements give such divergent views of authority, responsibility, and the nature of human life in the world that they must be accounted for by detailed and painstaking examination of the claims in their appropriate religious and social contexts, rather than by a simple and unreasoned appeal to general characteristics of new religious movements.

Both opponents of new religions and members of the groups have frequently attached great symbolic value to both children and women and emphasized that new religions provide them with roles that offer clear alternatives to what they experience in mainstream society. In the conflict over the Branch Davidians, for example, Reno's and Clinton's concerns about child abuse were countered by David Koresh's intent to sire a group of twenty-four children who would reign in the kingdom of God as the elders prophesied in the book of Revelation.[62]

Similar conflicts mark the discussion of women's roles in new religious movements. If the experience of children within new religious movements is diverse, so certainly is that of women. Susan Palmer has classified women's roles into three broad categories. Groups that advocate sex polarity emphasize the differences between women and men and typically consider men to be the superior sex. Religious groups that endorse sex complementarity regard women and men as possessing different spiritual qualities and emphasize the importance of uniting in order to form a single, complete androgynous being. Groups that promote sex unity see both the body and gender as superficial distinctions that obscure the nature of the true self or spirit. Although Palmer sees groups as being dominated by one of those three views, she readily acknowledges that the implementation or appropriation of a general gender ideology can have different implications for women's access to power in ritual and institutional settings, their modes of conversion to new religious movements, and sexual identities, depending on the context.[63]

Palmer cites both ISKCON and the Rajneesh movement as groups in which sex polarity guides perception of gender roles. She cites a male Krishna devotee as affirming that "in India mothers are regarded with great respect. If you think of every woman as a mother it is impossible to think of them as sex objects. After all, no one is sexually attracted to their mother, although, today in the Kali Yuga you can't even be sure of that!"[64] Palmer finds that an emphasis on the superiority of men pervades the organization and practice of the Krishna Consciousness Movement and that it is also espoused by many female members of the movement. One long-time female devotee, for example, acknowledged that "a man's body is a finer instrument for developing Krishna Consciousness" and that "our ladies are valued and protected because we recognize that a woman needs spiritual protection."[65] The ideology of sex polarity in the Krishna Consciousness Movement has its roots in ancient Hindu patriarchal traditions that were explicitly endorsed by Swami Prabhupada in many instances. Nonetheless, the ISKCON movement in the United States has employed women in positions of serious responsibility, which suggests that, whether due to necessity or design, the movement has not been able to rigidly enforce its Vedic ideals of female subservience.[66] In addition, Palmer suggests, the strict segregation of the sexes into separate *ashrams* and the narrow focus on the role of women as mothers may also have exerted some attraction for women who are striving "to discern a new clarity, integrity, and purity in male-female relationships." Palmer argues that part of the appeal of ISKCON and other new religious movements is that they respond to a social context marked by the increasing fragility of marriage, the weakening of ties between parents and children, and the increased demands upon women who enter the workplace by offering clear and specific "spiritual solutions" that highlight certain roles for women and disregard others.

That was certainly the case in the community founded by Bhagwan Shree Rajneesh, particularly during its tenure in rural Oregon. Among Rajneesh's distinctive innovations was his contention that women were spiritually superior to men. He proposed that "my own vision is that the coming age will be the age of woman" and that "if we can create a few woman Buddhas in the world then woman will be freed from all chains and fetters."[67] Rajneesh's message found an interested audience of middle-aged and upper-middle-class women for whom his message of female empowerment and sexual freedom aligned well with their established way of life. For a time, women also held many of the central positions at Rajneeshpuram in Oregon, but the excesses of Sheela's rule eventually undid that experiment.[68] Rajneesh's exaltation of women was part of his plan to form a new social group that would replace the nuclear family; he averred that "the biological family must be destroyed. Only the spiritual family will remain."[69] In that new spiritual family, women would have equal, if not superior, authority; multiple and fleeting sexual liaisons would be welcomed; and devotees would be bound together by their love for each other and for Rajneesh.

Palmer's category of sex complementarity is clearly evidenced in the Unificationists' conception of themselves as a group of brothers and sisters who are united under a bisexual God who is considered the "One True Parent of Mankind." In Unificationist thought the family plays a crucial role in restoring humanity to the position that God had envisaged for it before the Fall of Adam and Eve. Consequently, marriage is a very important element in the Unificationist view of salvation history. As an official publication of the movement put it

the divine scheme of love and family is laid out in the "four position foundation" . . . God, Husband, wife and child. The pure and perfect relationship with God helps to establish the perfect relationship between husband and wife, and then between parents and children. The spiritual and physical kingdom of God, the total salvation that God intended in sending the Messiah, will be achieved by the ever expanding network of such God-centered families.[70]

Thus, although Unificationist thought attributes distinctive characteristics to both women and men, it also asserts that the goal of life is to form a complementary relationship that can serve as the bases for the individuals' relationships to God and to their eventual children. The resulting "four position foundation" becomes the basis from which Unificationists will usher in the kingdom of God. Sex complementarity thus plays an essential role in the unfolding salvation of humankind.

Palmer argues that an ideology of sex unity is relatively rare in new religious movements, but she finds it expressed by the Raëlians. Even though there are tendencies to replicate the dominant patriarchal gender roles from the surrounding culture, the Raëlians are noteworthy for their openness to homosexuals, transsexuals, and other sexual minorities.[71] Raël wrote that "in as far as sexual contacts are concerned, everything is possible, everything is permitted. I must insist on the word permitted for it does not mean mandatory."[72] At least part of the reason for that attitude of tolerance is the conviction that gender characteristics are more accidental than essential characteristics of human beings. One female "Guide" or priest in the Raëlian Movement expressed the fundamental equality of humans in this way: "they are all considered equal—no discriminations, differences, or favoritism—they're all humans. There are more men guides than women but it's not because they are men, it's because women in our society don't have much chance to expand, but we're getting there! When you reach infinity you don't make differences between man and woman."[73] Especially in the realm of human sexuality, Raël emphasizes the equality of men and women. He asserts that "woman, at last, is truly the equal of man since she can truly enjoy her body without having the fear of enduring alone the undesired consequences of her acts."[74] Thus, on the level of doctrine at least, the Raëlians preach a functional equality and metaphysical unity of women and men. As even their own members emphasize, it has not always been easy to put that doctrine into action, because it runs counter to deeply entrenched expectations about gender roles and patterns of action in the broader society. But the Raëlian emphasis on sex unity at least represents a religiously motivated experiment in transforming both those expectations and patterns of action.

Conclusions

Leadership, conversion, violence, and the roles of women and children are only a few examples of issues that can be pursued in the study of new religious movements. They show in themselves, however, that new religious movements provide a rich and diverse array of data to which a wide range of analytical and interpretive questions can be addressed. Differences among leaders of new religions are potentially as significant as their similarities. It is impossible to assimilate thousands of leaders to a single pattern, such as that of the omnipotent and manipulative cult leader. Similarly, the paths by which people both come to and abandon membership in new religions are quite varied. Only a few claim to have been manipulated or coerced against their will. Many others profess to have embraced their new affiliations with a clear head and an open heart and assert that they have benefitted enormously as a result. The vast majority of people in the United States and throughout its history, however, have remained immune to the attraction of new religious movements. Members of new religious movements still represent a minority of the religious population of the United States. Studying processes of conversion to various new religious movements, then, promises not only to illuminate the actions of individuals but also the social contexts in which they act. With striking frequency, that minority status of new religions has led to clashes between them and their cultural opponents. Fortunately, most of the conflict has remained ideological, a war of words. In a few dramatic instances, however, conflict has flared into actual violence, perpetrated either by the state, members of new religions themselves, or a combination of the two parties. Those cases are important to examine carefully, not for what they reveal about all new religious movements because they are far too few to provide the bases of sweeping generalizations, but for what they might reveal about the specific processes by which violence is catalyzed in certain situations and, therefore, for indications about processes through which violent outcomes might be avoided or at least minimized. Similarly, the diverse approaches to the socialization of children and the construction of gender roles in new religious movements also warrant careful scrutiny, not least for what they reveal about the fondest hopes and deepest worries of individuals as they strive to fashion for themselves coherent, meaningful, and satisfying personal identities.

Beyond those specific issues there are, of course, many more. As the first chapter suggested, the study of new religious movements addresses fundamental questions in the general study of religion such as the nature of religious action, the roles of ritual, myth, and symbol in inspiring and sustaining religious commitment, or the impact of religion on moral convictions, political action, or social activism. If new religious movements can be described as dramatic experiments in specific ways of being human, they also furnish an extraordinary range of vivid examples of human attempts to answer fundamental questions about the origin of the universe, the nature of human beings and the divine, and the goals of human life. Such questions have always been difficult to answer, and specific answers have always produced both insight and controversy. To declare one set of answers unworthy of consideration without seriously considering them, as the dedicated opponents of cults so often have, is simply and needlessly to impoverish the conversation about those fundamental topics.

Notes

1. For an argument about new religious movements as "global cultures" and a particular type of response to modernity, see Irving Hexham and Karla Poewe, *New Religions Movements as Global Cultures: Making the Human Sacred* (Boulder: Westview, 1997). To cast the comparative net even more widely, one could consider new religious movements in other historical periods as well. The ancient Mediterranean world in the period roughly between Alexander the Great (356–323 B.C.E.) and Constantine (ca. 285–337 C.E.) was a hotbed of religious innovation. For a classic treatment, see Arthur Darby Nock, *Conversion: The Old and the New in Religion from Alexander the Great to Augustine of Hippo* (Oxford: Oxford University Press, 1933). Many new religious movements have also sprung up in Africa in the modern period. See David B. Barrett, *Schism and Renewal in Africa: An Analysis of Six Thousand Contemporary Religious Movements* (Nairobi: Oxford University Press, 1968).

2. Chidester, *Salvation and Suicide*, p. 1.

3. Singer, *Cults in Our Midst*, p. 8.

4. Ibid.

5. Ibid., p. 11.

6. Ibid., p. 17.

7. See ibid., p. 24.

8. See Max Weber, "The Pure Types of Legitimate Authority" and "The Nature of Charismatic Authority and its Routinization," in S. N. Eisenstadt, ed., *Max Weber on Charisma and Institution Building* (Chicago: University of Chicago Press, 1968), pp. 46–47, 48–65.

9. See Bruce Lincoln, *Authority: Construction and Corrosion* (Chicago: University of Chicago Press, 1994). Eugene V. Gallagher, "Religion" in George R. Goethals, Georgia J. Sorenson, and James MacGregor Burns, eds., *Encyclopedia of Leadership* (Thousand Oaks, CA: Sage, 2004), pp. 1307–15.

10. Singer, *Cults in Our Midst*, p. 3.

11. Maaga, *Hearing the Voices of Jonestown*, p. 89.

12. See ibid., p. 97, for example.

13. Ibid., p. 113.

14. Ibid., p. 53.

15. Tape 232, April 15, 1993, p. 41. See Tape 72, March 6, 1993, p. 29; Tape 77, March 7, 1993, pp. 8–10.

16. See Howell, "The Identity of the Ancient of Days and the Son of Man" (1985), available at www.home.main.rr.com/waco.

17. Perhaps the most celebrated and important defection was that of Mark Breault, who had once been very close to Koresh. Breault could not accept the so-called New Light revelation that Koresh proclaimed in August 1989, in which Koresh claimed that only he had the right to procreate and that all women within the group should be sexually available to him while all others must practice celibacy. Breault left, along with his wife, Elizabeth Baranyi, and became Koresh's most persistent and effective opponent. Breault tells his own story, in tabloid fashion, with Martin King in *Inside the Cult* (New York: Signet, 1993).

18. Tape 98, March 9, 1993, pp. 12–13.

19. Tape 87, March 7, 1993, p. 26.

20. Tape 201, April 9, 1993, p. 48.

21. Singer, *Cults in Our Midst*, p. 116.

22. Edwards, *Crazy for God*, p. 102.

23. Ibid., p. 135.

24. On the topic of how converts' accounts are shaped by the theology of the groups they enter, see James A. Beckford, "Accounting for Conversion," *British Journal of Sociology* 29 (1978): 249–62; Brian Taylor, "Recollection and Membership: Converts' Talk and the Ratiocination of Commonality," *Sociology* 12 (1978): 316–24. For a thorough contemporary analysis of conversion, see Lewis Rambo, *Understanding Religious Conversion* (New Haven: Yale University Press, 1993).

25. As quoted in Tabor and Gallagher, *Why Waco?* p. 122.

26. See www.freedomofmind.com/.

27. Underwood and Underwood, *Hostage to Heaven*, p. 421.

28. As quoted in Tabor and Gallagher, *Why Waco?* p. 122.

29. As quoted in ibid., p. 137.

30. Stark and Bainbridge, *The Future of Religion*, p. 322.

31. Ibid., p. 325.

32. John Lofland, "Becoming a World-Saver Revisited," in James T. Richardson, ed., *Conversion Careers: In and Out of the New Religions* (Beverly Hills, CA: Sage, 1977), pp. 10–23, quotation from p. 22. The original article by Lofland and Stark, "Becoming a World-Saver: A Theory of Conversion to a Deviant Perspective," appeared in the *American Sociological Review* 30 (1965): 862–74.

33. The essays by Zablocki, Anthony, Bromley, Kent, and Dawson in Zablocki and Robbins, eds., *Misunderstanding Cults,* provide a good orientation to the current state of the dispute.

34. David Bromley, "A Tale of Two Theories: Brainwashing and Conversion as Competing Political Narratives," in ibid., p. 319.

35. Barker, *The Making of a Moonie*, p. 233.

36. Ibid., pp. 233–34.

37. See chapter 1, p. 34, note 21.

38. The text of the FBI's "Project Megiddo" report, along with the texts of similar reports from the Canadian Security Intelligence Service and the Jerusalem Institute for

Israel Studies and a set of scholarly essays, are printed in a special issue of *Terrorism and Political Violence* 14 (2002), edited by Jeffrey Kaplan and published in separate form as Jeffrey Kaplan, ed., *Millennial Violence: Past, Present and Future* (London: Frank Cass, 2002).

39. See FBI, "Project Megiddo," in ibid., pp. 45–46.

40. FBI, p. 4; see p. 29; see also JIIS, p. 7.

41. See ibid., p. 2, for the breakdown of groups.

42. Hall, *Apocalypse Observed*, p. 201.

43. See Wessinger, *How the Millennium*, pp. 12–29. See also Wessinger, "Millennialism With and Without the Mayhem," in Thomas Robbins and Susan J. Palmer, eds., *Millennium, Messiahs, and Mayhem: Contemporary Apocalyptic Movements* (New York: Routledge, 1997), pp. 47–59; and Wessinger, ed., *Millennialism, Persecution, and Violence: Historical Cases* (Syracuse: Syracuse University Press, 2000).

44. Robin Wagner-Pacifici, *Theorizing the Standoff: Contingency in Action* (Cambridge: Cambridge University Press, 2000), p. 7; her emphasis.

45. Ibid., p. 19.

46. FBI, p. 7.

47. For analyses of millennial rhetoric, see Stephen D. O'Leary, *Arguing the Apocalypse: A Theory of Millennial Rhetoric* (New York: Oxford University Press, 1994), and Barry Brummett, *Contemporary Apocalyptic Rhetoric* (New York: Praeger, 1991).

48. See Jeffrey Kaplan, *Radical Religion in America: Millenarian Movements from the Far Right to the Children of Noah* (Syracuse: Syracuse University Press, 1997), p. 168, passage quoted, pp. 55–57, 65, for the types of violence. See also Eugene V. Gallagher, "Cults," in Ronald Gottesman, ed., *Violence in America: An Encyclopedia* (New York: Scribner's, 1999), pp. 364–68 for a distinction between rhetorical, episodic, programmatic, and defensive forms of violence.

49. On The Order, see Kevin Flynn and Gary Gerhart, *The Silent Brotherhood* (New York: Signet, 1990); and Kaplan, *Radical Religion,* pp. 61–67.

50. See Kaplan, *Radical Religion,* p. 171.

51. As quoted in Christopher G. Ellison and John P. Bartkowski, "'Babies Were Being Beaten': Exploring Child Abuse Allegations at Ranch Apocalypse," in Wright, ed., *Armageddon at Waco,* pp. 111–49, quotations from p. 112.

52. See James T. Richardson, "Social Control of New Religions: From 'Brainwashing' Claims to Child Sex Abuse Accusations," in Susan J. Palmer and Charlotte E. Hardman, eds., *Children in New Religions* (New Brunswick, NJ: Rutgers University Press, 1999), pp. 172–86, esp. 175–77.

53. See ibid., pp. 181–82.

54. Michael W. Homer, "The Precarious Balance Between Freedom of Religion and the Best Interests of the Child," in Palmer and Hardman, eds., *Children in New Religions,* pp. 187–209, quotation from p. 203.

55. Susan J. Palmer and Charlotte E. Hardman, "Alternative Childhoods," in Palmer and Hardman, eds., *Children in New Religions,* pp. 1–8, esp. p. 1.

56. As quoted in Berger, *A Community of Witches,* p. 84.

57. As quoted in ibid., p. 85.

58. As quoted in ibid., p. 113; see p. 120.

59. As quoted in E. Burke Rochford, "Education and Collective Identity: Public Schooling of Hare Krishna Youths," in Palmer and Hardman, eds., *Children in New Religions,* pp. 29–50, passage quoted from p. 36.

60. As quoted in Charlotte E. Hardman, "The Ethics of Children in Three New Religions," in Palmer and Hardman, eds., *Children in New Religions*, pp. 227–43, passage quoted from p. 233.

61. Ibid., p. 235.

62. See Tabor and Gallagher, *Why Waco?* pp. 73–76.

63. See Susan Jean Palmer, *Moon Sisters, Krishna Mothers, Rajneesh Lovers: Women's Roles in New Religions* (Syracuse: Syracuse University Press, 1994), pp. 9–10. See also Elizabeth Puttick, *Women in New Religions* (London: Macmillan, 1997).

64. Palmer, *Moon Sisters*, p. 15.

65. Ibid., pp. 16, 17, respectively.

66. See ibid., p. 40. See also Nori Muster's account of her life within ISKCON in *Betrayal of the Spirit*.

67. As quoted in Palmer, *Moon Sisters*, p. 49.

68. See chapter 4, p. 115.

69. As quoted in Palmer, *Moon Sisters*, p. 49.

70. As quoted in ibid., p. 81.

71. See ibid., p. 157.

72. Claude Vorilhon (Raël), *Let's Welcome Our Fathers From Space*, pp. 84–85.

73. As quoted in ibid., p. 179.

74. Claude Vorilhon (Raël), *The Message Given to Me by Extra-Terrestrials*, p. 231.

Timeline

1852	While in prison Mizra Husayn 'Ali Nuri receives a prophetic call from a heavenly maiden and renames himself Baha'u'llah
1857	President Buchanan authorizes military campaign against the Mormons to suppress the practice of polygamy
1863	Baha'u'llah begins his public mission
1875	Theosophical Society founded by Madam Blavatsky and Col. Olcott
	Publication of Mary Baker Eddy's *Science and Health with Key to the Scriptures*
1877	H. P. Blavatsky publishes *Isis Unveiled*
1879	U.S. Supreme Court rules bigamy unconstitutional
July 1879	Charles Taze Russell begins publication of his journal, *The Watchtower and Herald of Christ's Presence*
1888	H. P. Blavatsky publishes *The Secret Doctrine*
late 1800s	Baha'i Movement begins in the United States
1890	President Wilford Woodruff's Manifesto declaring an end to the practice of plural marriage is accepted by the Mormon church
1893	Parliament of the World's Religions in Chicago introduces many to several teachers from Eastern religions
1895	Publication of *The Manual of the Mother Church* by Christian Science
1903	Fillmores found the Unity School of Christianity
1913	Noble Drew Ali founds the first community of what will become the Moorish Science Temple
1920	Swami Yogananda begins speaking tour in the United States
1921	Margaret Murray publishes *The Witch-Cult in Western Europe*, arguing that witchcraft was the pre-Christian religion of Europe
1927	Noble Drew Ali publishes *The Holy Koran of the Moorish Science Temple*

1930	Guy Ballard has his first encounter with the Ascended Master St. Germain
	W. D. Fard appears in Detroit preaching his distinctive Islamic message
	Gerald Gardner claims to have been initiated into a surviving English coven
1930s	Rastafari takes shape in Jamaica
1934	W. D. Fard mysteriously vanishes and Elijah Muhammad becomes the undisputed focal point of the Nation of Islam
1935	Swami Yogananda establishes the Self-Realization Fellowship
Easter 1936	Sun Myung Moon experiences a vision of Jesus
1939	Aidan Kelly's date for the invention of modern witchcraft
1940	Prolonged lawsuit for mail fraud against the I AM Activity begins
1946	Rev. Sun Myung Moon begins public preaching
1948	While in prison Malcolm Little first affiliates with the Nation of Islam
1950	L. Ron Hubbard publishes *Dianetics: The Modern Science of Mental Health*
1950s	Zen Buddhism popularized by Beats and Alan Watts
	Soka Gakkai begins to spread in the United States
1951	English law against witchcraft repealed
1952	Malcolm Little is released from prison and begins his swift rise through the hierarchy of the Nation of Islam
	L. Ron Hubbard forms the Hubbard Association of Scientologists
1955	Rev. Jim Jones founds Peoples Temple in Indianapolis
1958	Mark Prophet founds the Summit Lighthouse
early 1960s	Unification Church missionaries begin to recruit in the United States

1963	Clarence 13X leaves the Nation of Islam and founds the Five Percent Nation of Islam, later the Nation of Gods and Earths
1964	Raymond Buckland founds the first Gardnerian coven in the United States
March 1964	Malcolm X severs ties with the Nation of Islam
1965	Asian Exclusion Act of 1924 rescinded, facilitating immigration from Asia to the United States
	Swami Prabhupada begins the ISKCON mission to the United States
February 21, 1965	Malcolm X is assassinated
April 30, 1966	Anton LaVey founds the Church of Satan
1969	Dwight York's Ansar Pure Sufi Movement becomes the Nubian Islaamic Hebrews, one of its many transformations through the years
	Anton LaVey publishes *The Satanic Bible*
late 1969	Ben Ammi's Black Hebrew Israelites settle in Israel
1970	The former Franklin Jones, now known as Ruchira Avatar Adi Da Samraj, permanently awakens to his new identity
1971	Rev. Moon moves to the United States
1972	Parents Committee to Free Our Sons and Daughters from the Children of God (later FREECOG) formed
1973	Moishe Rosen founds Jews for Jesus
	Stephen McNallen founds the Asatrue Free Assembly
	Marshall Applewhite and Bonnie Lu Nettles begin to recruit members to what would become known later as Heaven's Gate
December 1973	Claude Vorilhon, later Raël, has his first encounter with extraterrestrials
1974	Elizabeth Clare Prophet renames the Summit Lighthouse the Church Universal and Triumphant
	Selena Fox founds the Circle Sanctuary

1975	W. D. Muhammad succeeds his father as head of the Nation of Islam
July 1975	Raël's second encounter with the Elohim
1976	Sen. Robert Dole (R-Kansas) holds hearings on Children of God and cults
February 1977	JZ Knight has her first encounter with Ramtha
1978	Louis Farrakhan, Minister Louis X, splits with W. D. Muhammad, intending to restore the original emphases of the Nation of Islam
November 19, 1978	Nine hundred and fourteen people die at Peoples Temple Agricultural Mission in Jonestown, Guyana
1979	Nation of Yahweh founded by Yahweh ben Yahweh, the former Hulon Mitchell
	Starhawk publishes *The Spiral Dance*
1980	Michelle Smith's memoir, *Michelle Remembers,* sparks fear of Satanic ritual abuse
1981	Bhagwan Shree Rajneesh arrives in the United States and proceeds to set up a utopian community, Rajneeshpuram, in eastern Oregon
1983–93	Peak of "Satanic panic" and widespread fears of Satanic ritual abuse
1985	Bhagwan Shree Rajneesh deported on immigration charges
March 15, 1990	Date on which the Church Universal and Triumphant predicted the end of the world would happen
1991	Lay organization of Soka Gakkai splits with Nichiren priesthood
February 28, 1993	Agents from the U.S. Bureau of Alcohol, Tobacco, and Firearms stage a "dynamic entry" at the Mount Carmel Center of the Branch Davidians; a fifty-one-day siege ensues
April 19, 1993	Mount Carmel Center of the Branch Davidians destroyed by fire, killing seventy-four people

1994, 1995, 1997	Murders and suicides of members of the Order of the Solar Temple in Quebec, Switzerland, and France
1997	Lawkeepers, a Black Israelite group, founded
March 20, 1995	Release of sarin gas by members of Aum Shinrikyo in Tokyo kills twelve and injures thousands
March 27, 1997	Suicides of thirty-nine members of Heaven's Gate group

Glossary

anticult movement—a loose coalition of individuals and groups dedicated to the identification, exposure, and eradication of "dangerous cults"; typically claims to espouse no religious values nor to be antireligious; has been substantially professionalized since its origins in the early 1970s.

apocalypse (apocalyptic, apocalypticism)—from the Greek, meaning "to unveil." More specifically refers to the revelation of the imminent end of the world. Texts and movements or groups can be classified as apocalyptic (e.g., the book of Revelation in the New Testament, or the Branch Davidians) from a variety of perspectives. Some scholars identify apocalypticism as a broad current of thought that may flare up in certain social conditions at different historical periods (e.g., in the strand of early Christianity represented by 1 Thessalonians, Mark 13, and the book of Revelation; in the Millerite and Adventist traditions; in some contemporary "UFO" religions such as Heaven's Gate).

apologetics (apology)—an apology is technically a speech in one's own defense; see Plato's *Apology,* in which Socrates addresses the charges against him; apologetics refers to the defense of the faith by those within a given tradition. Much countercult writing is apologetic in nature.

apostasy (apostate)—departure from a religious movement; one who leaves a movement. Often used from the perspective of the group involved.

Armageddon—a climactic battle to be fought at the end of the world, described in the biblical book of Revelation (16:16) as taking place near Mount (*har*) Megiddo; used broadly to describe a catastrophic end of the world as we know it.

brainwashing—a description and explanation of affiliation with a group that draws either implicit or explicit comparisons to efforts to compel Korean prisoners of war to accept the ideology of their captors. Brainwashing has long been a popular concept in the anticult movement, and anticult arguments often appeal to the work of Robert Lifton. Accusations of brainwashing against new religious movements are sometimes modulated into accusations that they practice "coercive persuasion." As a description of the affiliation process, brainwashing or related concepts can then be used to justify deprogramming, exit counseling, or other efforts to persuade, induce, or compel members to abandon their commitment. Brainwashing is typically rejected as an explanation of affiliation by sociologists and historians of religion, though it continues to be a popular explanation of cult membership.

channel (channeler, channeling)—a conduit through which, either consciously or unconsciously, messages from realms beyond the human can flow; one who channels; the act of channeling.

charisma (charismatic)—literally, from the Greek, a gift (from God), a quality recognized in certain people by certain audiences; used to refer to leadership perceived to be based primarily on personal qualities rather than a position in a bureaucracy or an inherited position; a key element of Max Weber's sociology of forms of legitimate authority, though it is used with less precision in popular discourse.

coercive persuasion—the attempt, through the manipulation of context, language, and other variables, to provoke unwanted change in individuals; used by the anticult movement as an alternative explanation of affiliation with new religious movements.

conversion—a turning away from one set of commitments and allegiances and toward another, different one; used by scholars of religion to describe both affiliation with and disaffiliation from new religious movements.

countercult movement—explicitly religiously motivated attempts to expose the doctrinal errors and unacceptable practices of other religious groups, particularly new and alternative religions.

cult—innovative group introduced to a specific social setting either by being imported from elsewhere or by independent invention. Often used as a pejorative term to indicate that someone views the group in question as suspicious and illegitimate.

deprogramming—an attempt, sometimes forcible, to persuade a member of a religious group to abandon his or her convictions; depends on the assumption that in the first place the member's affiliation had resulted from some sort of programming of his or her mind against his or her better judgment.

esoteric—secret, hidden, preserved only for certain people, especially in reference to a tradition of wisdom that is only periodically brought to light by certain teachers. See also *occult*.

exit counseling—a later development in anticult efforts to effect disaffiliation of members; depends on a counseling model and represents the growing influence of psychologists and social workers on the anticult movement.

gnosis (gnostic, gnosticism)—secret knowledge, often about the possibility of salvation; typically given only to initiates and controlled by a gnostic teacher; having to do with secret knowledge; a religious form or movement that has persisted as an alternative in Western thought for some two thousand years.

guru—originally a Sanskrit term referring to a grave, venerable, or heavy person; in discussions of leaders of new religious movements it is applied to leaders of groups that had their origins in India, but in popular discourse it has also been applied more widely to religious leaders, sometimes with a negative connotation.

hermeneutics—the theory of interpretation; the set of assumptions, often implicit, which an interpreter brings to any text, particularly to scripture or other authoritative religious texts.

medium (spirit medium)—a person through whom disincarnate spirits communicate either verbally or through symbolic actions; the focal points of the Spiritualist Movement.

metaphysics—traditionally, philosophical thought concerning the fundamental nature of reality; though there is some dispute about categorization, New Thought, Christian Science, Theosophy, Spiritualism, and various strands of New Age thought have been described as metaphysical movements.

millennialism (millennium, millennial, millennialist)—the biblical book of Revelation (20:1–10) describes a thousand-year period (a "millennium" from the Latin for "thousand") in which Satan will be imprisoned and resurrected Christian martyrs will reign over the earth with Jesus. In broader terms, millennialism is the expectation of imminent, collective, and earthly salvation. Millennialism often anticipates a catastrophic end to the current order but also can envisage a gradual, progressive movement toward the realization of heaven on earth. Millennialists who expect the catastrophic end of the world as we know it often use violent rhetoric, but rarely undertake violent actions.

occult—literally, hidden, secret, or darkened. Refers to traditions of wisdom that are not part of the mainstream whose practitioners may conceive of themselves as an elite in contact with specially qualified teachers.

orthodoxy—correct thought or doctrine; a concern of the countercult movement; sectarian movements often accuse their parent bodies of having abandoned orthodoxy. *Orthopraxy* refers to correct practice.

sect (sectarian, sectarianism)—group with prior ties to a religious organization from which it has intentionally broken off.

secularization—the process by which various aspects of human life have been removed from religious domination and established as independent spheres of activity with their own particular governing authorities; scholars disagree on the extent to which secularization has been a growing tendency through human history or a self-limiting phenomenon that provokes religious reactions of revival and the formation of new religious groups.

scripture—a text or collection of texts deemed to be authoritative by the members of a specific religious group.

worldview—in the words of cultural anthropologist Clifford Geertz, a "picture of the way things in their sheer actuality are." Worldviews are created, maintained, and communicated by religious groups through their rituals, myths, symbols, and doctrinal statements.

Select Annotated Bibliography

Approaches to the Study of Religion

Books

Berger, Peter. *The Sacred Canopy: Elements of a Sociological Theory of Religion.* Garden City, NY: Doubleday, 1967. A classic sociological analysis of religion.

Burridge, Kenelm. *New Heaven New Earth: A Study of Millenarian Activities.* New York: Schocken, 1969. A very useful theoretical study of the formation of new religious movements and especially the roles of prophets within them.

Durkheim, Emile. *The Elementary Forms of the Religious Life,* trans. Karen E. Fields. New York: The Free Press, 1995. A foundational sociological analysis, from 1912, of religion as a unified system of beliefs and practices relative to sacred things that unites into a single moral community all those who adhere to them, especially through ritual action (see p. 44). Introduces the concepts of religious ideas as collective representations and collective effervescence during ritual.

Freud, Sigmund. *The Future of an Illusion,* ed. and trans. James Strachey. New York: Norton, 1989. A compact and influential analysis of religion as a projection of human wishes.

Geertz, Clifford. "Religion as a Cultural System." In idem, *The Interpretation of Cultures.* New York: Basic, 1973, pp. 87–125. A widely used anthropological definition of religion.

James, William. *The Varieties of Religious Experience.* 1902; rpt. New York: New American Library, 1958. A classic study of religion as "the feelings, acts, and experiences of individual men in their solitude" (p. 42), with a focus on the phenomena of conversion, saintliness, and mysticism.

Paden, William. *Religious Worlds: The Comparative Study of Religion.* Boston: Beacon, 1994. A lucid and accessible introduction to the major structures of religious behavior, including myth, ritual, systems of purity, and gods.

Patton, Kimberley C., and Benjamin C. Ray, eds. *A Magic Still Dwells: Comparative Religion in the Postmodern Age*. Berkeley: University of California Press, 2000. Essays that engage issues in the process of comparison in the study of religion.

Proudfoot, Wayne. *Religious Experience*. Berkeley: University of California Press, 1985. A careful philosophical examination of what can and cannot be known about religious experience.

Taylor, Mark C. *Critical Terms for Religious Studies*. Chicago: University of Chicago Press, 1998. A collection of recent essays by major figures in the field.

Encyclopedias and Dictionaries

Brasher, Brenda, ed. *Encyclopedia of Fundamentalism*. New York: Routledge, 2001. Particularly helpful on sectarian groups.

Cookson, Catherine, ed. *Encyclopedia of Religious Freedom*. New York: Routledge, 2003. Includes many topics relevant to the study of new religious movements.

Glazier, Stephen D., ed. *Encyclopedia of African and African-American Religions*. New York: Routledge, 2001. Includes entries on sectarian, Islamic, and African-inspired groups in the United States.

Jones, Lindsay, ed. *The Encyclopedia of Religion*. 2nd ed. New York: Macmillan, 2004. An updating of the reference work originally edited by Mircea Eliade, with extensive new entries on new religious movements.

Landes, Richard, ed. *Encyclopedia of Millennial Movements*. New York: Routledge, 2000. Includes entries on specific new religious movements as well as general treatments of cults and conversion.

Smith, Jonathan Z., ed. *The HarperCollins Dictionary of Religion*. New York: HarperCollins, 1995. Compiled under the auspices of the American Academy of Religion; includes several entries on new religious movements, as well as on general topics in the study of religion.

Scholarly Journals

Journal for the Scientific Study of Religion. Frequently includes articles and reviews on new religious movements and related topics.

Nova Religio: The Journal of Alternative and Emergent Religions. The preeminent journal for research on new religious movements.

Religion and American Culture. Often includes articles on sectarian groups and new religious movements.

Sociology of Religion. Frequently features articles and reviews on new religious movements and related topics.

Surveys

Books

Ahlstrom, Sidney. *A Religious History of the American People*. New Haven: Yale University Press, 1972. A basic reference work on American religious history, though new religions do not play a prominent role.

Albanese, Catherine. *America: Religions and Religion.* 2nd ed. Belmont, CA: Wadsworth, 1992. An effective attempt to take American religious pluralism seriously.

Barrett, David B. *The New Believers: Sects, "Cults," and Alternative Religions.* London: Cassell, 2001. An accessible survey of new religious movements, with a British focus.

Barrett, David B. *Schism and Renewal in Africa: An Analysis of Six Thousand Contemporary Religious Movements.* Nairobi: Oxford University Press, 1968. An interesting set of data for comparison to the study of new religions in the United States.

Bednarowski, Mary Farrell. *New Religions and the Theological Imagination in America.* Bloomington: Indiana University Press, 1989. A survey of ideas about God, human nature, death, and morality in Mormonism, Christian Science, Theosophy, Scientology, the Unification Church, and New Age thought.

Bromley, David G., ed. *Falling from the Faith: Causes and Consequences of Religious Apostasy.* Beverly Hills, CA: Sage, 1988. Includes essays on the Mormons, the Unification Church, and Peoples Temple.

Bromley, David G., and Phillip E. Hammond, eds. *The Future of New Religious Movements.* Macon, GA: Mercer University Press, 1987. Includes Stark's important essay on how new religions succeed.

Bromley, David G., and James T. Richardson, eds. *The Brainwashing/Deprogramming Controversy.* New York: Edwin Mellen, 1983. An extensive collection of essays on matters at the heart of the contemporary cult controversies.

Dawson, Lorne L. *Comprehending Cults: The Sociology of New Religious Movements.* Oxford: Oxford University Press, 1998. An accessible overview of the topic.

Dawson, Lorne L., ed. *Cults in Context: Readings in the Study of New Religious Movements.* New Brunswick, NJ: Transaction, 1998. A collection of important essays on new religious movements, especially helpful for students.

Deikman, Arthur J. *The Wrong Way Home: Uncovering Patterns of Cult Behavior in American Society.* Boston: Beacon, 1994. A psychiatrist's analysis of cult behavior, based on a case study approach.

Eck, Diana L. *A New Religious America: How a "Christian Country" Has Become the World's Most Religiously Diverse Nation.* New York: HarperCollins, 2001. An important description of the religious context in which contemporary new religious movements exist.

Ellwood, Robert. *Alternative Altars: Unconventional and Eastern Spirituality in America.* Chicago: University of Chicago Press, 1979. Situates contemporary new religious movements in historical context.

Ellwood, Robert. *The Fifties Spiritual Marketplace: American Religion in a Decade of Conflict.* New Brunswick, NJ: Rutgers University Press, 1997. Describes the context of both mainstream religions and religious innovation.

Ellwood, Robert. *The Sixties Spiritual Awakening: American Religion Moving From Modern to Postmodern*. New Brunswick, NJ: Rutgers University Press, 1994. With its companion volume on the 1950s, an essential account of the context for religious innovation in midcentury.

Galanter, Marc. *Cults: Faith, Healing, and Coercion*. New York: Oxford University Press, 1989. An analysis by the author of the American Psychiatric Association's report on cults and new religious movements; includes discussion of the Unification Church and Jonestown under the category of "charismatic groups."

Hall, John R., with Philip D. Schuyler and Sylvaine Trinh. *Apocalypse Observed: Religious Movements and Violence in North America, Europe, and Japan*. New York: Routledge, 2000. Though focused on the topic of violence, this volume provides important theoretical characterizations of new religious movements as well as case studies of the Peoples Temple, the Branch Davidians, Aum Shinrikyo, the Solar Temple, and Heaven's Gate.

Hanegraaff, Wouter J. *New Age Religion and Western Culture: Esotericism in the Mirror of Secular Thought*. Albany: State University of New York Press, 1998. Sets contemporary New Age thought, broadly construed, in the context of Western esoteric traditions from the ancient period to the present.

Hexham, Irving, and Karla Poewe. *New Religions as Global Cultures: Making the Human Sacred*. Boulder, CO: Westview, 1997. An attempt to provide a theoretical framework for understanding new religions cross-culturally.

Jacobs, Janet Liebman. *Divine Disenchantment: Deconverting from New Religions*. Bloomington: Indiana University Press, 1989. Includes discussions of the Divine Light Mission and the International Society for Krishna Consciousness.

Jenkins, Phillip. *Mystics and Messiahs: Cults and New Religions in American History*. Oxford: Oxford University Press, 2000. A lucid and revealing look at the history of new religious movements in the United States that clearly shows that new religions are not simply a phenomenon of the late twentieth and early twenty-first centuries.

Kaplan, Jeffrey. *Radical Religion in America: Millenarian Movements from the Far Right to the Children of Noah*. Syracuse: Syracuse University Press, 1997. Helpful chapters on Christian Identity and Nordic Paganism, and insightful treatments of the interactions between new religions and their opponents.

Kaplan, Jeffrey, and Helene Lööw, eds. *The Cultic Milieu: Oppositional Subcultures in an Age of Globalization*. Walnut Creek, CA: AltaMira, 2002. Essays in response to Colin Campbell's notion of the "cultic milieu," including his original essay.

Lewis, James R., ed. *The Oxford Handbook of New Religious Movements*. New York: Oxford University Press, 2004. A collection of essays by prominent scholars of new religions; includes contributions on new religious movements and the World Wide Web, violence, legal dimensions, conversion, apostasy, millennialism, and the anticult movement.

Melton, J. Gordon. *Encyclopedic Handbook of Cults in America*. Rev. ed. New York: Garland, 1992. An essential resource from the dean of the study of new religions in the United States.

Melton, J. Gordon. *Biographical Dictionary of American Cult and Sect Leaders*. New York: Garland, 1986. Accessible and trustworthy brief accounts of most crucial figures.

Miller, Timothy, ed. *America's Alternative Religions*. Albany: State University of New York Press, 1995. Brief accounts of some forty groups or families of groups. One of the best references and textbooks in print.

Moore, R. Laurence. *Religious Outsiders and the Making of Americans*. New York: Oxford University Press, 1986. Includes chapters on the Mormons and Christian Science.

Noonan, John. *The Lustre of Our Country: The American Experience of Religious Freedom*. Berkeley: University of California Press, 1998. A thorough investigation of issues concerning religious freedom, with extensive consideration of some incidents involving new religions.

Prebish, Charles S., and Kenneth K. Tanaka, eds. *The Faces of Buddhism in America*. Berkeley: University of California Press, 1998. Scholarly essays on the various forms of Buddhism in the United States.

Robbins, Thomas. *Cults, Converts, and Charisma: The Sociology of New Religious Movements*. Beverly Hills, CA: Sage, 1988. Especially important for its overview of the field at the time and for its bibliographical references.

Robbins, Thomas, and Dick Anthony, eds. *In Gods We Trust: New Patterns of Religious Pluralism in America*. 2nd ed. New Brunswick, NJ: Transaction, 1990. A wide-ranging collection of essays, including several specifically on new religions.

Saliba, John A. *Understanding New Religious Movements*. 2nd ed. Walnut Creek, CA: AltaMira, 2003. Includes chapters on the history of new religions in the West, and psychological, sociological, theological, and legal perspectives.

Stark, Rodney, and William Sims Bainbridge. *The Future of Religion: Secularization, Revival, and Cult Formation*. Berkeley: University of California Press, 1985. A major theoretical contribution about the dynamics of sect and cult formation.

Tweed, Thomas A., and Stephen Prothero, eds. *Asian Religions in America: A Documentary History*. New York: Oxford University Press, 1999. A collection of primary sources with insightful commentary.

Wessinger, Catherine. *How the Millennium Comes Violently*. New York: Seven Bridges, 2000. Also focused on the issue of millennialism and violence, but provides extensive treatments of Jonestown and the Branch Davidians, among other groups, as well as a theoretical framework for assessing the potential for violence in any given situation.

Wright, Stuart A. *Leaving Cults: The Dynamics of Defection.* Washington, DC: Society for the Scientific Study of Religion, 1987. A sociological analysis of apostasy; includes recommendations for public policy.

Zablocki, Benjamin, and Thomas Robbins, eds. *Misunderstanding Cults: Searching for Objectivity in a Controversial Field.* Toronto: University of Toronto Press, 2001. A collection of essays on several facets of the contemporary cult controversies.

Web Sites

www.cesnur.org. An extraordinary archive of materials from the Italian Center for the Study of New Religions, under the direction of Massimo Introvigne.

www.clas.ufl.edu/users/gthursby/aar-nrm/. A site maintained by the New Religious Movements group of the American Academy of Religion; includes a bibliography and links to other Web resources.

www.religiousmovements.lib.virginia.edu/. An extensive site, incorporating the work of both students and professors on new religious movements. Includes both general articles and profiles and bibliographies on individual groups.

www.religioustolerance.org. An extensive archive of materials relevant to the study of new religions.

Themes in New Religious Movements

Books

Bromley, David G., ed. *The Politics of Religious Apostasy: The Role of Apostates in the Transformation of Religious Movements.* Westport, CT: Praeger, 1998. Essays on departures from religious movements and their consequences, with several focusing on new religions.

Bromley, David G., and J. Gordon Melton, eds. *Cults, Religion, and Violence.* Cambridge: Cambridge University Press, 2002. Includes some of the most sophisticated theoretical thinking about the possible interrelations of cults and violence.

Gallagher, Eugene V. *Expectation and Experience: Explaining Religious Conversion.* Atlanta: Scholars, 1990. Expositions of different theoretical approaches to conversion, with case studies.

Kaplan, Jeffrey, ed. *Millennial Violence: Past, Present and Future.* London: Frank Cass, 2002. Includes the FBI's "Project Megiddo" report and a range of scholarly essays.

Kent, Steven. *From Slogans to Mantras: Social Protest and Religious Conversion in the Late Vietnam War Era.* Syracuse: Syracuse University Press, 2001. Traces the conversion careers of some who were involved in political protest.

Lincoln, Bruce. *Authority: Construction and Corrosion.* Chicago: University of Chicago Press, 1994. An important theoretical treatment.

Lindholm, Charles. *Charisma.* Oxford: Basil Blackwell, 1990. An important theoretical treatment of charismatic leadership.

Miller, Timothy, ed. *When Prophets Die: The Postcharismatic Fate of New Religious Movements.* Albany: State University of New York Press, 1991. Scholarly essays on how new religions make the transition to the second generation of leadership.

Oakes, Len. *Prophetic Charisma: The Psychology of Revolutionary Religious Personalities.* Syracuse: Syracuse University Press, 1997. A psychological analysis based in part on interviews with leaders; includes discussion of Jim Jones, Bhagwan Shree Rajneesh, and L. Ron Hubbard.

Palmer, Susan Jean. *Moon Sisters, Krishna Mothers, Rajneesh Lovers: Women's Roles in New Religions.* Syracuse: Syracuse University Press, 1994. Identifies three different conceptions of gender roles in new religious movements: sex polarity, sex complementarity, and sex unity.

Palmer, Susan J., and Charlotte E. Hardman, eds. *Children in New Religions.* New Brunswick, NJ: Rutgers University Press, 1999. Essays on a variety of new religious groups.

Puttick, Elizabeth. *Women in New Religions: In Search of Community, Sexuality and Spiritual Power.* New York: St. Martin's, 1997. A thematic approach, including discussions of the master-disciple relationship, sexuality, motherhood, and female leadership.

Rambo, Lewis. *Understanding Religious Conversion.* New Haven: Yale University Press, 1993. A detailed analysis of the phenomenon.

Richardson, James T., ed. *Conversion Careers: In and Out of the New Religions.* Beverly Hills, CA: Sage, 1977. Includes essays on the Unification Church, the early years of the Heaven's Gate group, and the logic of deprogramming.

Robbins, Thomas, and Susan J. Palmer. *Millennium, Messiahs, and Mayhem: Contemporary Apocalyptic Movements.* New York: Routledge, 1997. Includes Wessinger's theoretical essay on catastrophic and progressive millennialism and contributions on the Baha'i, Seventy-day Adventists, Mormons, Christian Identity, and the Branch Davidians.

Stone, Jon R., ed. *Expecting Armageddon: Essential Readings in Failed Prophecy.* New York: Routledge, 2000. A collection of essays engaged with Festinger et al.'s theory of cognitive dissonance.

Storr, Anthony. *Feet of Clay: Saints, Sinners, and Madmen: A Study of Gurus.* New York: The Free Press, 1996. Includes discussions of David Koresh, Jim Jones, and Bhagwan Shree Rajneesh.

Wessinger, Catherine, ed. *Millennialism, Persecution, and Violence: Historical Cases.* Syracuse: Syracuse University Press, 2000. Includes several essays on new religious movements in the United States, including the Branch Davidians.

Encyclopedia

Gottesman, Ronald, ed. *Violence in America: An Encyclopedia.* New York: Scribner's, 1999. Includes entries on several new religions and related topics.

The Anticult Movement

Books

Anonymous. *The Cult Awareness Network: Anatomy of a Hate Group* (no publication data). A special publication of *Freedom* magazine, associated with the Church of Scientology.

Dubrow-Eichel, Stephen K. *Deprogramming: A Case Study* (a special issue of the *Cultic Studies Journal* 6 [1989], published by the American Family Foundation).

Giambalvo, Carol. *Exit Counseling: A Family Intervention: How to Respond to Cult-Affected Loved Ones.* 2nd ed. Bonita Springs, FL: American Family Foundation, 1992. A brief account from a prominent activist.

Hassan, Steven. *Releasing the Bonds: Empowering People to Think for Themselves.* Somerville, MA: Freedom of Mind, 2000. A manifesto for the strategic intervention approach to counseling members of cults.

Lifton, Robert. *Thought Reform and the Psychology of Totalism.* New York: Norton, 1961. A crucial resource of anticult arguments about brainwashing.

Patrick, Ted, and Tom Dulack. *Let Our Children Go!* New York: Dutton, 1976. The autobiography of the first prominent deprogrammer.

Rathbun, Valentine. *An Account of the Matter, Form, and Manner of a New and Strange Religion, Taught and Propagated by a Number of Europeans, Living in a Place Called Nisqueunia, in the State of New-York.* Providence, RI: Bennett Wheeler, 1781.

Shupe, Anson D., and David G. Bromley. *The New Vigilantes: Deprogrammers, Anti-Cultists and the New Religions.* Beverly Hills, CA: Sage, 1980. An early history of the anticult movement.

Shupe, Anson D., and David G. Bromley, eds. *Anti-Cult Movements in Cross-Cultural Perspective.* New York: Garland, 1994. A collection of essays including a history of the anticult movement in the United States; essays on the anticult movements in Canada, France, Germany, Italy, Israel, and the Netherlands, and contributions from anticult activists.

Shupe, Anson D., David G. Bromley, and Donna L. Oliver. *The Anti-Cult Movement in America: A Bibliography and Historical Survey.* New York: Garland, 1984. Materials on the early years of the anticult movement.

Singer, Margaret, with Janja Lalich. *Cults in Our Midst: The Hidden Menace in Our Everyday Lives.* San Francisco: Jossey-Bass, 1995. The fullest statement of the position of the most influential anticult writer.

Article

Melton, J. Gordon. "The Modern Anti-Cult Movement in Historical Perspective," in Jeffrey Kaplan and Helene Lööw, eds., *The Cultic Milieu: Oppositional Subcultures in an Age of Globalization,* Walnut Creek, CA: AltaMira, 2002. Continues the history of the ACM into the 1990s.

Web Sites

www.freedomofmind.com. Steven Hassan's Web site, with a description of his general approach and profiles of several groups.

www.rickross.com. The Web site of anticult entrepreneur Rick Ross, now presented as the work of the Ross Institute. Helpful archives of new articles on many groups.

www.csj.org. An extensive Web site maintained by the American Family Foundation, with excerpts from its publications.

The Countercult Movement

Books

Ankerberg, John, and John Weldon. *Encyclopedia of Cults and New Religions.* Eugene, OR: Harvest House, 1999. Devotes special attention to the Jehovah's Witnesses and Mormons and offers an appendix on Christian doctrine.

Cowan, Douglas E. *Bearing False Witness? An Introduction to the Christian Countercult.* Westport, CT: Praeger, 2003. An analytical treatment by a scholar of new religious movements.

Eisenberg, Gary D., ed. *Smashing the Idols: A Jewish Inquiry into the Cult Phenomenon.* Northvale, NJ: Jason Aronson, 1988. A collection of essays primarily from the perspective of Judaism, including contributions from Rabbi Maurice Davis and Elie Wiesel.

Martin, Walter. *The Kingdom of the Cults.* Rev. ed. Minneapolis: Bethany House, 1997. Perhaps the most influential Christian countercult writer.

Web Sites

www.apologeticsindex.org. Maintained by Anton Hein, provides profiles of various groups deemed to be cults and provides links to countercult literature.

www.equip.org. The site of the Christian Research Institute, led by evangelist Hank Hanegraaff.

www.jewsforjudaism.org. A Jewish countercult ministry.

www.watchman.org. The site of the Watchman Fellowship provides profiles of groups, articles from the *Watchman Observer,* interviews, news updates, and other materials.

Individual Groups/Movements

Baha'i

Primary Text

Baha'u'llah. *The Hidden Words,* trans. Shogi Effendi. Wilmette, IL: Baha'i Publishing, 2002. An accessible collection of aphorisms from the founder.

Books

Cole, Juan R. I. *Modernity and the Millennium: The Genesis of the Baha'i Faith in the Nineteenth-Century Middle East.* New York: Columbia University Press, 1998. A detailed account of Baha'i origins, including a chapter on gender dynamics.

Hatcher, William S., and J. Douglas Martin. *The Baha'i Faith: The Emerging Global Religion.* Rev. ed. Wilmette, IL: Baha'i Publishing, 2002. Covers the history and basic teachings of the faith.

McMullen, Michael. *The Baha'i: The Religious Construction of a Global Community.* New Brunswick, NJ: Rutgers University Press, 2000. Particularly helpful on conversion to the Baha'i; based on the author's fieldwork.

Momen, Moojan. *The Baha'i Faith: A Short Introduction.* Oxford: Oneworld, 1997. An overview of the religion with excerpts from primary texts.

Web Sites

www.bahai.org. The official Web site of the church. Includes excerpts of Baha'i texts, an overview of theology, and other helpful introductory materials.

www.bahai.seeker.net. Designed for those interested in the church, includes excerpts from Baha'i writings.

Black Israelites

Books

Brotz, Howard. *The Black Jews of Harlem.* New York: The Free Press, 1963. Focuses on the Commandment Keepers.

Chireau, Yvonne, and Nathaniel Deutsch, eds. *Black Zion: African American Religious Encounters with Judaism.* Oxford: Oxford University Press, 2000. An essential collection of scholarly essays.

Fauset, Arthur Huff. *Black Gods of the Metropolis: Negro Religious Cults of the Urban North.* Philadelphia: University of Pennsylvania Press, 2001. Includes chapters on the Black Jews and the Moorish Science Temple and excerpts from interviews and testimonies.

Web Sites

www.unnm.com. Official Web site of the United Nuwaubian Nation of Moors, with information about Malachi York in his current persona as a Yamassee Indian chief.

www.illuminopolis.hypermart.net/illiyuwm.html. A site critical of Nuwaubian theology.

www.cogasoc.org. Official site of the Church of God and Saints of Christ, founded by William S. Crowdy; includes texts and audio.

www.churchofgod1896.org. The official site of a splinter group of the Church of God and Saints of Christ.

www.aboutthelambsbookoflife.net/pages/375513/index.htm. Teachings of the prophet Cornelius Owens, within the Crowdy tradition.

www.kingdomofyah.com. Official Web site of the African Hebrew Israelites of Jerusalem, led by Ben Ammi.

www.thelawkeepers.org. Official site of the Lawkeepers, with an extensive archive of texts.

www.members.aol.com/Blackjews/beth1.html. Web site of the Black Hebrew congregation Beth Elohim.

www.yahwehbenyahweh.com. Official Web site of the group led by Yahweh ben Yahweh, with coverage of his legal troubles.

Branch Davidians

Books

Bailey, Brad, and Bob Darden. *Mad Man in Waco: The Complete Story of the Davidian Cult, David Koresh and the Waco Massacre*. Waco, TX: WRS, 1993. Thoroughly informed by anticult arguments.

Breault, Marc, and Martin King. *Inside the Cult: A Member's Chilling, Exclusive Account of Madness and Depravity in David Koresh's Compound*. New York: Signet, 1993. The influential account of Koresh's most dedicated opponent and former follower.

Linedecker, Clifford. *Massacre at Waco, Texas: The Shocking True Story of Cult Leader David Koresh and the Branch Davidians*. New York: St. Martin's, 1993. Another instant book that toes the anticult line.

Madigan, Tim. *See No Evil: Blind Devotion and Bloodshed in David Koresh's Holy War*. Fort Worth: The Summit Group, 1993. Similar to Bailey and Darden, and Linedecker in its treatment.

Moore, Carol. *The Davidian Massacre: Disturbing Questions About Waco Which Must Be Answered*. Franklin, TN: Legacy Communications, 1995; also available at www.firearmsandliberty.com/waco.massacre.html#1. An indictment of government actions against the Branch Davidians by a libertarian activist.

Reavis, Dick J. *The Ashes of Waco: An Investigation*. New York: Simon and Schuster, 1995. A journalist's vivid account of the Branch Davidian tragedy.

Tabor, James D., and Eugene V. Gallagher. *Why Waco? Cults and the Battle for Religious Freedom in America*. Berkeley: University of California Press, 1995. Includes the text of Koresh's unfinished manuscript on the seven seals.

Thibodeau, David, and Leon Whiteson. *A Place Called Waco: A Survivor's Story.* New York: Public Affairs, 1999. Argues forcefully against the contention that those inside Mount Carmel set the fatal fire.

Wright, Stuart A., ed. *Armageddon in Waco: Critical Perspectives on the Branch Davidian Conflict.* Chicago: University of Chicago Press, 1995. A collection of scholarly articles.

Web Sites

www.home.maine.rr.com/waco/. An extraordinary archive of primary materials maintained by Mark Swett.

www.fountain.btinternet.co.uk/koresh/. Provides an introduction to Koresh and the Branch Davidians and links to other helpful sites. Includes primary materials not on the Swett Web site and writings by some of Koresh's followers.

www.sevenseals.com. Devoted to the teaching of the "Chosen Vessel," Jaime Castillo, one of Koresh's students who claims to update and extend Koresh's teaching.

www.start.at/mt.carmel. Provides updates on survivors and other information.

Children of God/The Family

Books

Bainbridge, William Sims. *The Endtime Family: Children of God.* Albany: State University of New York Press, 2002. Discusses the fate of the group both in the United States and abroad.

Chancellor, James D. *Life in the Family: An Oral History of the Children of God.* Syracuse: Syracuse University Press, 2000. Includes primary texts.

Lewis, James R., and J. Gordon Melton, eds. *Sex Slander and Salvation: Investigating The Family/Children of God.* Stanford: Center for Academic Publication, 1994. A collection of essays with special emphasis on the roles of children and sexuality within the family. Includes bibliography of writings in English.

Van Zandt, David E. *Living in the Children of God.* Princeton: Princeton University Press, 1991. Includes some samples of the founder's "Mo Letters."

Williams, Miriam. *Heaven's Harlots: My Fifteen Years as a Sacred Prostitute in the Children of God Cult.* New York: William Morrow, 1998. An insider's account of the group's experiments with sex in recruitment of new members.

Web Site

www.thefamily.org/. The official Web site of the group, with links to an extensive array of materials, including music and videos.

Christian Identity

Books

Barkun, Michael. *Religion and the Racist Right: The Origins of the Christian Identity Movement.* Chapel Hill: University of North Carolina Press, 1994.

Traces current Christian Identity ideas to their roots in British Anglo-Israelism and through the American racist right.

Gayman, Dan. *The Two Seeds of Genesis 3:15*. Self-published, 1977.

Klassen, Ben. *The White Man's Bible*. Billings, MT: Creativity Book Store, 1981.

Christian Science

Primary Texts

Church of Christ, Scientist. *Christian Science: A Sourcebook of Contemporary Materials*. Boston: The Christian Science Publishing Society, 1990. A helpful anthological of analytical and primary materials.

Eddy, Mary Baker. *The Manual of the Mother Church*. 88th ed. Boston: Allison V. Stewart, 1895. A crucial organizational document.

Eddy, Mary Baker. *Science and Health with Key to the Scriptures*. Boston: First Church of Christ Scientist, 1875. The foundational text of Christian Science.

Web Sites

www.mbeinstitute.org. A rich source for Eddy's writings and other materials on Christian Science.

www.tfccs.org. The official site of the First Church of Christ, Scientist; includes links to primary texts and testimonies.

Books

Fraser, Caroline. *God's Perfect Child: Living and Dying in the Christian Science Church*. New York: Metropolitan, 1999. A personal story.

Gill, Gillian. *Mary Baker Eddy*. Reading, MA: Perseus, 1998. A detailed biography of the founder.

Gottschalk, Stephen. *The Emergence of Christian Science in American Religious Life*. Berkeley: University of California Press, 1973. A solid treatment of the origins and growth of Christian Science.

Church of Jesus Christ of Latter-day Saints

Primary Texts

The essential scriptural texts, such as *The Book of Mormon,* the *Doctrine and Covenants,* and the *Pearl of Great Price* are readily available online at www.scriptures.lds.org.

Galbraith, Richard C., ed. *Scriptural Teachings of the Prophet Joseph Smith*. Salt Lake City: Deseret, 1993. A collection of texts from the Prophet.

Hardy, Grant, ed. *The Book of Mormon: A Reader's Edition*. Urbana: University of Illinois Press, 2003. Includes an introduction and notes.

Vogel, Dan, ed. *Early Mormon Documents*. Vol. I. Salt Lake City: Signature, 1996. An important set of documents on Mormon origins.

Secondary Texts

Altman, Irwin, and Joseph Ginat. *Polygamous Families in Contemporary Society.* Cambridge: Cambridge University Press, 1996. Investigates the practice of polygamy among contemporary Mormon dissident groups.

Arrington, Leonard J., and Davis Bitton. *The Mormon Experience: A History of the Latter-day Saints.* 2nd ed. Urbana: University of Illinois Press, 1992. A thorough and trustworthy history.

Barkun, Michael. *Crucible of the Millennium: The Burned-Over District of New York in the 1840s.* Syracuse: Syracuse University Press, 1986. Provides a context for the development of Mormonism and other groups in mid-nineteenth-century New York.

Barlow, Philip L. *Mormons and the Bible: The Place of the Latter-day Saints in American Religion.* Oxford: Oxford University Press, 1991. Particularly helpful on the Mormon use of and the relation of Mormon scriptures to the Bible.

Cross, Whitney R. *The Burned-over District: The Social and Intellectual History of Enthusiastic Religion in Western New York, 1800–1850.* New York: Harper's, 1965. A pioneering work on the context of the development of the Mormon church.

Givens, Terryl L. *By the Hand of Mormon: The American Scripture that Launched a New World Religion.* New York: Oxford University Press, 2002. The genesis, character, and uses of the central Mormon text.

Shipps, Jan. *Mormonism: The Story of a New Religious Tradition.* Urbana: University of Illinois Press, 1985. Convincingly makes the case that the LDS church became an independent religious body, a new religion.

Underwood, Grant. *The Millenarian World of Early Mormonism.* Urbana: University of Illinois Press, 1993. Sets the rise of the Church in the context of nineteenth-century millennialism.

Web Sites

www.lds.org. The official site of the Church of Jesus-Christ of Latter-day Saints.
www.scriptures.lds.org. Provides electronic versions of essential Mormon scriptures.

Church of Satan, Satanism, and Related Groups

Primary Texts

LaVey, Anton Szandor. *The Devil's Notebook.* Venice, CA: Feral House, 1992. Miscellaneous writings and observations from the founder of the Church of Satan.

LaVey, Anton Szandor. *Satan Speaks.* Venice, CA: Feral House, 1998. A collection of short pieces; includes a foreword by musician Marilyn Manson.

LaVey, Anton Szandor. *The Satanic Bible.* New York: Avon, 1969. The fundamental text of the Church of Satan; widely influential beyond the confines of the church.

LaVey, Anton Szandor. *The Satanic Rituals*. New York: Avon, 1972. A compendium of spells and other practices.

LaVey, Anton Szandor. *The Satanic Witch*. Los Angeles: Feral House, 1970. Advice to female practitioners, from LaVey's distinctly nonfeminist perspective.

Books

Baddeley, Gavin. *Lucifer Rising: Sin, Devil Worship and Rock 'n' Roll*. London: Plexus, 1999. Charts the influence of Satanic ideas in popular culture; includes photographs, illustrations, and interviews.

Barton, Blanche. *The Church of Satan*. New York: Hell's Kitchen Productions, 1990. An insider's account of the group's history.

Barton, Blanche. *The Secret Life of a Satanist*. Venice, CA: Feral House, 1990. Written by LaVey's long-time companion; includes pictures, a glossary, and several texts from LaVey.

Ellis, Bill. *Raising the Devil: Satanism, New Religions, and the Media*. Lexington: University Press of Kentucky, 2000. A careful examination of the creation and dissemination of contemporary images of Satanism.

Hicks, Robert. *In Pursuit of Satan: The Police and the Occult*. Buffalo, NY: Prometheus, 1991. Cautious about accepting extraordinary claims about Satanic activity on face value.

Nathan, Debbie, and Michael Snedeker. *Satan's Silence: Ritual Abuse and the Making of a Modern American Witch Hunt*. New York: Basic, 1995. A critical review of claims about satanic ritual abuse.

Raschke, Carl. *Painted Black*. New York: HarperCollins, 1990. An alarmist view of the spread of Satanism from an academic in the study of religion.

Richardson, James T., Joel Best, David G. Bromley, eds. *The Satanism Scare*. New York: Aldine De Gruyter, 1991. Scholarly essays on topics including the history and social context of Satanism, accusations of ritual abuse, Satanism and the law, and the dynamics of accusations about Satanic practice.

Sakheim, David K. and Susan E. Devine, eds. *Out of Darkness: Exploring Satanism and Ritual Abuse*. New York: Lexington, 1992. Essays from the perspective of psychology and counseling; includes Kenneth Lanning's widely cited report.

Smith, Michelle, and Lawrence Pazder. *Michelle Remembers*. New York: Pocket, 1980. An influential memoir of Satanic ritual abuse.

Stratford, Lauren. *Satan's Underground: The Extraordinary Story of One Woman's Escape*. Gretna, LA: Pelican, 1991. A memoir from the perspective of someone who later embraced Christianity.

Victor, Jeffrey. *Satanic Panic: The Making of a Contemporary Legend*. Chicago: Open Court, 1993. A sociological treatment of the formation of rumors about Satanic activity and the underlying causes of the panics they can produce.

Article
Wright, Lawrence. "Sympathy for the Devil." *Rolling Stone,* September 5, 1991.

Web Sites
www.cesnur.org/2002/slc/lewis.htm. A link to James Lewis's study of *The Satanic Bible.*
www.churchofsatan.com. The Web site of LaVey's organization; provides links to Satanic literature, music, and videos.
www.geocities.com/Athens/Parthenon/2669/devilsdiary.html. An extensive collection of writings by "Draconis Blackthorne."
www.xeper.org. The official Web site of the Temple of Set, with an extensive archive of writings by Michael Aquino and Don Webb.
www.satanicchurch.com. The official Web site of The First Satanic Church, founded by LaVey's daughter, Karla.

Church of Scientology

Primary Texts
Church of Scientology. *Scientology: Theology and Practice of a Contemporary Religion.* Los Angeles: Bridge, 1998. An overview of the religion; includes several essays by scholars on how Scientology fits the definition of a religion.
Church of Scientology. *What is Scientology?* Los Angeles: Bridge, 1998. An extensive compendium of Scientological belief and practice.
Church of Scientology. *The Background, Ministry, Ceremonies, and Sermons of the Scientology Religion.* Los Angeles: Bridge, 1999. Includes full texts of sermons and rituals.
Hubbard, L. Ron. *Dianetics: The Modern Science of Mental Health.* Los Angeles: Bridge, 1950. The founding text of the movement, containing the first synthesis of Hubbard's system.

Books
Atack, Jon. *A Piece of Blue Sky: Scientology, Dianetics and L. Ron Hubbard Exposed.* New York: Carol, 1990. An autobiography and bitter indictment from a former member.
Corydon, Bent. *L. Ron Hubbard: Messiah or Madman?* Rev. ed. Fort Lee, NJ: Barricade, 1992. Focuses on Hubbard's character and activities, includes a glossary of Scientological terms.
Melton, J. Gordon. *The Church of Scientology.* Salt Lake City, UT: Signature, 2000. A brief overview, covering events through the 1990s.
Wallis, Roy. *The Road to Total Freedom: A Sociological Analysis of Scientology.* New York: Columbia University Press, 1977. Devotes particular attention to the transition from Dianetics to Scientology. Includes several primary documents in appendixes, including a letter from a Scientology official that critiques the study.

Whitehead, Harriet. *Renunciation and Reformulation: A Study of Conversion in an American Sect*. Ithaca, NY: Cornell University Press, 1987. Focuses on the period up to the early 1970s, and provides informative accounts of the auditing process.

Web Sites

www.scientology.org. The official Web site of the church, with extensive links to Scientology literature, frequently asked questions, and other materials.

www.xenu.net/index.html. The Web site of the anti-Scientology group, "Operation Clambake." Includes texts of exposes, news articles, petitions, and other materials.

www.freezone.de/english/english.htm. An extensive site with personal essays and other materials from dissident Scientologists who maintain that the church lost its way in the early 1980s and departed from Hubbard's original program.

www.lisamcpherson.org. Extensive material on the Lisa McPherson case, on a site critical of the Church of Scientology.

www.religiousfreedomwatch.org. A site that is critical of anticult activists, especially in their interactions with the Church of Scientology.

www.xs4all.nl/~kspaink/index.html. Extensive materials on Scientology, including links to formerly secret teachings and other materials compiled by opponents of Scientology.

Church Universal and Triumphant/"I AM" Movement

Primary Texts

Chanera. *"I AM" Adorations and Affirmations*. Saint Germain Series, vol. 5, pt. 1. Schaumberg, IL: Saint Germain, 1937. Short statements of "I AM" beliefs.

King, Godfre Ray. *Unveiled Mysteries*. Saint Germain Series, vol. I. Schaumberg, IL: Saint Germain, 1934. Guy Ballard's revelations; seventeen other volumes are available.

Prophet, Elizabeth Clare. *The Great White Brotherhood in the Culture, History, and Religion of America*. Livingston, MT: Summit University Press, 1976. An early text that ties CUT directly to "I AM."

Prophet, Elizabeth Clare. *The Lost Teachings of Jesus*, Vol. I. Livingston, MT: Summit University Press, 1986. Three other volumes are available in a series that claims to recover previously unknown teachings of Jesus.

Prophet, Elizabeth Clare. *The Lost Years of Jesus*. Livingston, MT: Summit University Press, 1984. Claims to present documentary evidence that fills in the gaps of the gospels.

Prophet, Elizabeth Clare. *Violet Flame: To Heal Body, Mind and Soul*. Corwin Springs, MT: Summit University Press, 1997. A brief practical introduction to the power of the "violet flame."

Books

Lewis, James R., and J. Gordon Melton, eds. *Church Universal and Triumphant in Scholarly Perspective*. Stanford, CA: Center for Academic Publication, 1994. Essays from a brief study of CUT.

Paolini, Kenneth, and Talita Paolini. *400 Years of Imaginary Friends: A Journey into the World of Adepts, Masters, Ascended Masters, and their Messengers*. Livingston, MT: Paolini International LLC, 2000. A critical account by former insiders.

Whitsel, Bradley C. *The Church Universal and Triumphant: Elizabeth Clare Prophet's Apocalyptic Movement*. Syracuse: Syracuse University Press, 2003. The most detailed scholarly account of CUT yet produced.

Article

Balch, Robert W., and Stephan Langdon. "How the Problem of Malfeasance Gets Overlooked in Studies of New Religious Movements: An Examination of the AWARE Study of the Church Universal and Triumphant." In Anson Shupe, ed., *Wolves Within the Fold: Religious Leadership and the Abuses of Power*. New Brunswick, NJ: Rutgers University Press, 1998. A critique of the study directed by Melton and Lewis.

Web Sites

www.ascendedmaster.org/. A Web site devoted to the teachings of Geraldine Innocente about the ascended Masters.

www.home.gil.com.au/~perovich/Ballards/. A Web site critical of "I AM"; includes extensive excerpts of Gerald Bryan's *Psychic Dictatorship in America*.

www.lawoflife.com/. Teachings of A.D.K. Luk about the ascended Masters.

www.templeofthepresence.org. Offshoot of CUT; includes teaching materials and audio files.

www.tsl.org. The official Web site of the Church Universal and Triumphant group.

Heaven's Gate

Primary Text

Representatives from the Kingdom of Heaven. *How and When "Heaven's Gate" (The Door to the Physical Kingdom Level Above Human) May Be Entered*. Denver, CO: Right to Know Enterprises, 1996. An extensive collection of primary texts from the entire history of the group.

Secondary Texts

Lewis, James R., ed. *The Gods Have Landed: New Religions from Other Worlds*. Albany: State University of New York Press, 1995. A collection of essays, including one on Heaven's Gate.

Partridge, Christopher, ed. *UFO Religions.* New York: Routledge, 2003. Includes an essay on the Heaven's Gate suicides.

Perkins, Rodney, and Forrest Jackson. *Cosmic Suicide: The Tragedy and Transcendence of Heaven's Gate.* Dallas: Pentaradial, 1997. A brief overview, including several primary documents as appendixes.

Steiger, Brad, and Hayden Hewes. *Inside Heaven's Gate: The UFO Cult Leaders Tell Their Story in Their Own Words.* New York: Signet, 1997. Includes important interviews and other primary materials.

Web Site

www.trancenet.org/heavensgate/. A copy of the original Heaven's Gate Web site; reproduces the primary texts.

International Society of Krishna Consciousness

Primary Texts

Prabhupada, A. C. Bhaktivedanta, Swami. *Bhagavad-Gita As It Is.* Los Angeles: Bhaktivedanta Book Trust, 1983. Prabhupada's presentation of the meaning of the Bhagavad-Gita and the central text of his movement.

Prabhupada, A. C. Bhaktivedanta, Swami. *The Science of Self Realization.* Los Angeles: Bhakivedanta Book Trust, 1968. A collection of lectures, interviews, and other short pieces, arranged topically.

Drutakarma dasa et al. *Chant and Be Happy.* Los Angeles: Bhakivedanta Book Trust, 1997. Includes conversations with George Harrison and John Lennon.

Secondary Texts

Rochford, E. Burke, Jr. *Hare Krishna in America.* New Brunswick: Rutgers University Press, 1985.

Shinn, Larry. *The Dark Lord: Cult Images and the Hare Krishnas in America.* Philadelphia: Westminster, 1987. Situates ISKCON in the contemporary cult controversies.

Muster, Nori. *Betrayal of the Spirit: My Life Behind the Headlines of the Hare Krishna Movement.* Urbana: University of Illinois Press, 1997. A personal account of a woman who held various positions of responsibility.

Web Sites

www.introduction.krishna.org. An extensive site with text and audio files.

www.iskcon.com. The official Web site of the movement, with text, audio, and visual materials.

www.krishna.com. The Web site of the Bhaktivedanta Book Trust includes free electronic copies of many ISKCON texts.

www.surrealist.org/gurukula/lawsuit.html. A full collection of materials on the gurukula crisis.

Jehovah's Witnesses

Books

Beckford, James A. *The Trumpet of Prophecy: A Sociological Study of Jehovah's Witnesses*. Oxford: Basil Blackwell, 1975. Sets the Witnesses in historical and social contexts.

Botting, Heather and Gary. *The Orwellian World of Jehovah's Witnesses*. Toronto: University of Toronto Press, 1984. A careful description and critical evaluation of the Witnesses.

Harrison, Barbara Grizutti. *Visions of Glory: A History and a Memory of Jehovah's Witnesses*. New York: Touchstone, 1978. Vivid vignettes of the author's early involvement with the group.

Penton, M. James. *Apocalypse Delayed: The Story of Jehovah's Witnesses*. 2nd ed. Toronto: University of Toronto Press, 1997. A thorough history, with an insider's perspective.

Web Sites

www.members.aol.com/beyondjw/. A Web site run by a former member for those who have left or are contemplating leaving the group.

www.watchtower.org. The official Web site of the Jehovah's Witnesses, with text and video resources.

Jews for Jesus

Books

Telchin, Stan. *Betrayed!* Old Tappan, NJ: Chosen, 1981. A father's story of his Jewish daughter's conversion to Christianity.

Tucker, Ruth A. *Not Ashamed: The Story of Jews for Jesus*. Sisters, OR: Multnomah, 1999. A history of the movement started by Moishe Rosen.

Web Sites

www.exjewsforjesus.org. A Web site maintained by former staff members of Jews for Jesus.

www.jews-for-jesus.com. Includes separate sites for members and for seekers.

www.jewsforjudaism.org. A countercult ministry designed to oppose missionary efforts to convert Jews.

www.outreachjudaism.org. A countercult Web site devoted to refuting the claims of Jews for Jesus.

Nation of Islam and Other Islamic Groups

Primary Texts

Noble Drew Ali. *The Holy Koran of the Moorish Science Temple of America* (n.p., 1927). An interesting text, though it bears little relation to the Qur'an of orthodox Islam.

Elijah Muhammad. *Message to the Blackman in America*. Atlanta, GA: Messenger Elijah Muhammad Propagation Society, 1965. A fundamental text for the Nation of Islam.

Elijah Muhammad. *Our Savior Has Arrived*. Atlanta, GA: Messenger Elijah Muhammad Propagation Society, 1974. A collection of short speeches and articles on a wide range of topics. A helpful index.

Books

Gardell, Mattias. *In the Name of Elijah Muhammad: Louis Farrakhan and the Nation of Islam*. Durham, NC: Duke University Press, 1996. A thorough study of the career of the most well known contemporary figure in the Nation of Islam.

Lee, Martha F. *The Nation of Islam: An American Millenarian Movement*. Syracuse: Syracuse University Press, 1996. Focuses on an interpretation of the Nation's preaching about the "fall of America."

Lincoln, C. Eric. *The Black Muslims in America*. 3rd ed. Grand Rapids, Eerdmans, 1994. A pioneering study, updated through the early 1990s.

Malcolm X, with Alex Haley. *The Autobiography of Malcolm X*. New York: Ballantine, 1964. Provides considerable information about the Nation of Islam as well as Malcolm's life story.

McCloud, Aminah Beverly. *African American Islam*. New York: Routledge, 1995. Provides an historical overview and chapters on family life and women.

Raboteau, Albert J. *Slave Religion: The "Invisible Institution" in the Antebellum South*. Oxford: Oxford University Press, 1978. Includes information about the earliest Muslims in the United States.

Turner, Richard Brent. *Islam in the African-American Experience*. Bloomington: University of Indiana Press, 1997. An instructive survey of Islam in the United States from the time of slavery to the present.

Article

Benyon, Erdmann D. "The Voodoo Cult among Negro Migrants in Detroit." *American Journal of Sociology* 43 (1937). Contains important information about W. D. Fard, Elijah Muhammad, and their first followers.

Web Sites

www.adl.org/main_islam.asp. A Web site of the Jewish Anti-Defamation League that focuses on anti-Semitism in the Nation of Islam.

www.blackapologetics.com/lyrics.html. A collection of hip-hop lyrics that reflect the theology of the Five Percent Nation of Islam.

www.deoxy.org/moorish.htm. The Web site of the very eclectic Moorish Orthodox Church of America.

www.finalcall.com. Official site of the newspaper of the Nation of Islam, with extensive references to the activities of minister Louis Farrakhan.

www.foia.fbi.gov/moortemp.htm. An archive of documents from the FBI's investigation of the Moorish Science Temple.

www.geocities.com/Athens/Delphi/2705/koran-index.html. An electronic version of Noble Drew Ali's *The Holy Koran of the Moorish Science Temple.*

www.geocities.com/Heartland/Woods/4623/. "The Moorish Science Reading Room," an archive of texts, including Noble Drew Ali's *Holy Koran.*

www.members.aol.com/akankem/Declare.htm. Silis Muhammad's 1977 declaration of "spiritual war" against the Nation of Islam.

www.members.aol.com/sidjulview/index52298.html. The Web site of the Moorish American Sid-Jul Mosque.

www.muhammadspeaks.com/. Site of the *Muhammad Speaks* newspaper, with extensive text, audio, and video files.

www.muslimjournal.com. Official site of the weekly newspaper begun by Wallace Deen Muhammad.

www.seventhfam.com/temple/books/black_man/blkindex.htm. An electronic, searchable text of Elijah Muhammad's *A Message to the Blackman in America.*

www.usc.edu/dept/MSA/notislam/? A site maintained by the Muslim Students Association that is critical of the Nation of Islam and several other groups, including the Nation of Gods and Earths.

Neo-Paganism, Wicca, and Related Groups

Primary Texts

Budapest, Zsuzsanna. *The Holy Book of Women's Mysteries.* Berkeley, CA: Wingbow, 1980. Spells, rituals, and observations from an influential feminist witch.

Farrar, Janet and Stewart. *The Witches' Bible: The Complete Witches' Handbook.* Rpt. Blaine, WA: Phoenix, 1985. Rituals and spells in the Gardnerian tradition.

Gardner, Gerald. *The Meaning of Witchcraft.* Thame, England: I-H-O, 2000, reprint of the 1959 edition. A foundational text by the inspiration of the contemporary Pagan revival.

Gardner, Gerald. *Witchcraft Today.* Lake Toxaway, NC: Mercury, n.d. Includes an appreciative introduction by Raymond Buckland and twelve pages of photographs.

Scire (Gerald Gardner). *High Magic's Aid.* Hinton, WV: Godolphin House, 1996. A reprint of Gardner's first, fictional account of witchcraft in 1949.

Murray, Margaret. *The Witch Cult in Western Europe.* Whitefish, MT: Kessinger, 2003, reprint of 1921 ed.; also available at www.sacred-texts.com/pag/wcwe/. An influential contribution to the myth of Wiccan origins.

Ravenwolf, Silver. *Solitary Witch: The Ultimate Book of Shadows for the New Generation.* St. Paul, MN: Llwellyn, 2003. An extensive, eclectic guide for solo practitioners.

Starhawk. *Dreaming the Dark: Magic, Sex and Politics.* Boston: Beacon, 1982. One of the most influential contemporary exponents of the Craft.

Starhawk. *Truth or Dare: Encounters with Power, Authority, and Mystery.* New York: Harper and Row, 1987. Further explorations from a leading figure.

Starhawk. *The Spiral Dance: A Rebirth of the Ancient Religion of the Great Goddess,* special 20th anniversary ed. San Francisco: HarperCollins, 1999. A foundational text for feminist witchcraft.

Valiente, Doreen. *An ABC of witchcraft.* Custer, WA: Phoenix, 1973. An alphabetical guide by an influential early participant in the pagan revival.

Books

Adler, Margot. *Drawing Down the Moon: Witches, Druids, Goddess-Worshippers and Other Pagans in America Today.* Rev. ed. Boston: Beacon, 1986. An influential survey of the neo-Pagan landscape by a practitioner.

Berger, Helen. *A Community of Witches: Contemporary New-Paganism and Witchcraft in the United States.* Columbia: University of South Carolina Press, 1999. Accounts of ritual based on fieldwork, with particular attention devoted to the transition to a second generation in the contemporary pagan movement.

Berger, Helen, Evan A. Leach, and Leigh S. Shaffer. *Voices from the Pagan Census: A National Survey of Witches and Neo-Pagans in the United States.* Columbia: University of South Carolina Press, 2003. The fullest collection of data about Pagans in the contemporary United States.

Bonewits, Isaac. *Real Magic.* Rev. ed. York Beach, ME: Samuel Weiser, 1989. Both scholarly and practical, from a major voice in Paganism.

Buckland, Raymond. *Witchcraft from the Inside: Origins of the Fastest Growing Religious Movement in America.* 3rd ed. St. Paul, MN: Llwellyn, 1995. A Gardnerian's account of the movement he helped to shape in the United States.

Clifton, Chas S., ed. *Witchcraft Today,* Book One: *The Modern Craft Movement.* St. Paul, MN: Llwellyn, 1992. The first of four collections of essays. Other volumes address "Rites of Passage," "The Shamanic Connection," and "Living Between Two Worlds."

Davis, Philip G. *Goddess Unmasked: The Rise of Neopagan Feminist Spirituality.* Dallas: Spence, 1998. A critique of the claims that contemporary worship of the goddess is in continuity with ancient practices.

Eller, Cynthia. *Living in the Lap of the Goddess: The Feminist Spirituality Movement in America.* New York: Crossroad, 1993. Sets Neo-Paganism in the broader context of women's spirituality.

Eller, Cynthia. *The Myth of Matriarchal Prehistory: Why an Invented Past Won't Give Women a Future.* Boston: Beacon, 2000. A critical review by a sympathetic observer.

Gardell, Mattias. *Gods of the Blood: The Pagan Revival and White Separatism.* Durham, NC: Duke University Press, 2003. A thorough treatment of the intersections between the contemporary revival of Nordic Paganism and white racism.

Harvey, Graham. *Contemporary Paganism: Listening People, Speaking Earth.* New York: New York University Press, 1997. A broad survey with helpful chapters on basic rituals and on the interactions of Pagans with other religions.

Hutton, Ronald. *The Triumph of the Moon: A History of Modern Pagan Witchcraft.* Oxford: Oxford University Press, 1999. Focuses on the pagan revival in Britain, with chapters on Gerald Gardner.

Kelly, Aidan. *Crafting the Art of Magic, Book I: A History of Modern Witchcraft, 1939–1964.* St. Paul, MN: Llwellyn, 1991. A painstaking review of the "paper trail" of the creation of contemporary Paganism.

Lewis, James R., ed. *Magical Religion and Modern Witchcraft.* Albany: State University of New York Press, 1996. A collection of essays featuring both practitioners and scholars.

Luhrmann, T. M. *Persuasions of the Witch's Craft: Ritual Magic in Contemporary England.* Cambridge, MA: Harvard University Press, 1989. An anthropological study, with important analysis of the development of the Neo-Pagan revival in England.

Pike, Sarah M. *Earthly Bodies, Magical Selves: Contemporary Pagans and the Search for Community.* Berkeley: University of California Press, 2001. Based on extensive fieldwork; focus on festivals as sites for the creation of Pagan identities.

York, Michael. *Pagan Theology: Paganism as a World Religion.* New York: New York University Press, 2003. An attempt to situate contemporary Paganism as a legitimate spiritual perspective that is practiced throughout the world.

Article
Gallagher, Eugene V. "A Religion Without Converts? Becoming a Neo-Pagan." *Journal of the American Academy of Religion* 62 (1994). A critical review of the notion that no one converts to Paganism.

Web Sites
www.asatru.org. Official site of the Asatru Alliance, includes reports on Althings, the by-laws of the organization, primary texts, and other resources.

www.asatru-u.org. The site for on-line learning about Asatru.

www.celticcrow.com. The Web site of the Witches' League for Public Awareness, dedicated to dispelling false impressions of witches, Pagans, and other practitioners of the craft.

www.circlesanctuary.org/. The site of the Circle Sanctuary, including links on the activities of the Lady Liberty League in defense of Pagan religious freedom.

www.cog.org. The Web site of the Covenant of the Goddess organization, with links to resources about children and Neo-Paganism and links to other organizations.

www.doreenvaliente.com. A Web site dedicated to Valiente that includes some of her writings, a biography, and "video tributes."

www.geraldgardner.com. Includes an archive of difficult-to-find documents and essays on Gardner.

www.hrafnar.org. The site for a Berkeley, California Nordic group led by Diana L. Paxson; includes essays and information about rituals.

www.neopagan.net. Isaac Bonewits's homepage; includes a guide to evaluating whether groups are cults.

www.runestone.org. Official site of the Asatru Folk Assembly; includes basic information about the group, articles, audio files, and links to other resources.

www.sacred-texts.com/pag/index.htm. Electronic versions of several early texts, including a version of Gardner's *Book of Shadows*.

www.thetroth.org. Extensive resources for the worshipers of the gods of the Northlands, including an electronic copy of "Our Troth," guidelines for clergy, and an array of essays by practitioners.

www.thornecoyle.com. Thoughtful essays from a pagan activist, writer, and musician.

www.witchvox.com/. The Web site of "The Witches' Voice," including essays, news, and other resources.

New Age/Channeling

Books

Brown, Michael. *The Channeling Zone: American Spirituality in an Anxious Age.* Cambridge, MA: Harvard University Press, 1997. An anthropologist's analysis.

Ferguson, Duncan S. *New Age Spirituality: An Assessment.* Louisville: Westminster/John Knox, 1993. Includes essays by New Age practitioners and evaluations by Christian theologians.

Harner, Michael. *The Way of the Shaman.* 10th ed. San Francisco: Harper, 1990. An account from an contemporary advocate of shamanic practices.

Heelas, Paul. *The New Age Movement.* Oxford: Basil Blackwell, 1996. A comparative survey that focuses on the New Age notion of self.

Lewis, James R., and J. Gordon Melton, eds. *Perspectives on the New Age.* Albany: State University of New York Press, 1992. A collection of essays that provides scholarly and historical perspectives.

MacLaine, Shirley. *Out on a Limb.* New York: Ballantine, 1983. A popular account of the author's various interactions with New Age practitioners.

Melton, J. Gordon. *Finding Enlightenment: Ramtha's School of Ancient Wisdom.* Hillsboro, OR: Beyond Words, 1988.

Ramtha. *The Plane of Bliss: On Earth as it is in Heaven.* Yelm, WA: JZK, 1997.

Web Sites

www.jzkpublishing.com. Site for the publisher of Ramtha's revelations, channeled through JZ Knight; includes a brief introduction to Ramtha.

www.lazaris.com. Includes articles, transcripts of tapes, and excerpts from books of the Lazaris material, a schedule of Jach Pursel's appearances, and links to other resources including audio and videotapes.

www.ramtha.com. The official site of Ramtha's School of Enlightenment; includes downloadable texts and streaming video on "Ramtha TV."

www.shamanicstudies.com. The Web site of the Foundation for Shamanic Studies, founded by Michael Harner, with a collection of articles and a schedule of workshops.

Peoples Temple/Jonestown

Books

Chidester, David. *Salvation and Suicide: An Interpretation of Jim Jones, the Peoples Temple, and Jonestown.* Bloomington: Indiana University Press, 1988. Includes careful analysis of the American public's reaction to the Jonestown tragedy.

Hall, John R. *Gone from the Promised Land: Jonestown in American Cultural History.* New Brunswick, NJ: Transaction, 1987. A thorough examination of the history and theology of Peoples Temple.

Kahalas, Laurie Efrein. *Snake Dance: Unravelling the Mysteries of Jonestown.* New York: Red Robin, 1998. A former member's personal account.

Layton, Deborah. *Seductive Poison: A Jonestown Survivor's Story of Life and Death in the Peoples Temple.* New York: Doubleday, 1998. An insider's critical account.

Maaga, Mary McCormick. *Hearing the Voices of Jonestown: Putting a Human Face on an American Tragedy.* Syracuse: Syracuse University Press, 1998. Focuses on the roles of women, especially in leadership positions, in Peoples Temple. Includes a transcript of the "Death Tape."

Mills, Jeannie. *Six Years with God: Life Inside Rev. Jim Jones's Peoples Temple.* New York: A & W, 1979. A critical view from a former insider.

Moore, Rebecca. *In Defense of Peoples Temple, and Other Essays.* Lewiston, NY: Edwin Mellen, 1988. Essays from a major figure in the documentation and analysis of the Peoples Temple.

Moore, Rebecca. *A Sympathetic History of Jonestown: The Moore Family Involvement in Peoples Temple.* Lewiston, NY: Edwin Mellen, 1985. A history that relies on personal experience with Jonestown and its members.

Moore, Rebecca, Anthony B. Pinn, and Mary R. Sawyer, eds. *Peoples Temple and Black Religion in America.* Bloomington: Indiana University Press, 2004. A set of scholarly essays investigating the interactions between Jim Jones' congregations and African American religion.

Article

Smith, Jonathan Z. "The Devil in Mr. Jones." In *Imagining Religion: From Babylon to Jonestown*. Chicago: University of Chicago Press, 1982, pp. 102–20. A provocative comparative essay by an historian of religions.

Web Site

www.jonestown.sdsu.edu/. An extraordinarily rich archive of materials on Peoples Temple maintained by Rebecca Moore and Fielding McGhee. An essential starting point for research on the group.

Raëlians

Primary Texts

Vorilhon, Claude (Raël). *Let's Welcome our Fathers from Space: They Created Humanity in Their Laboratories*. Tokyo: AOM, 1986. Answers questions about Raël's two encounters and provides testimonies from Raëlian converts.

Vorilhon, Claude (Raël). *The Message Given to Me by Extra-Terrestrials*. Tokyo: AOM, 1986. Details Raël's encounters with the "space brothers."

Vorilhon, Claude (Raël). *Sensual Meditation: Awakening the Mind by Awakening the Body*. n.p., Canada: Nova Diffusion, 2002. Details the basis for Raëlian practices of sensual meditation.

Vorilhon, Claude (Raël). *Yes to Human Cloning*. Vaduz, FL: Raëlian Foundation, 2001. Provides the argument for cloning humans.

Web Site

www.rael.org. The official Web site of the organization; includes both audio and video materials.

Bhagwan Shree Rajneeesh/Osho

Primary Text

Bhagwan Shree Rajneesh. *The Book of Wisdom*, Volume I: *Discourses on Atisha's Seven Points of Mind Training*. Rajneeshpuram, OR: Rajneesh Foundation International, 1983. A collection of the guru's discourses.

Books

Appleton, Sue. *Bhagwan Shree Rajneesh: The Most Dangerous Man Since Jesus Christ*. No city, West Germany: Rebel, 1987. An appreciative account that laments the Bhagwan's mistreatment at the hands of authorities.

Carter, Lewis F. *Charisma and Control in Rajneeshpuram: The Role of Shared Values in the Creation of Community*. Cambridge: Cambridge University Press, 1990. A careful analysis of the community in Oregon, based on fieldwork.

Fox, Judith M. *Osho Rajneesh*. Salt Lake City: Signature, 2000. An accessible short introduction.

Goldman, Marion S. *Passionate Journeys: Why Successful Woman Joined a Cult.* Ann Arbor: University of Michigan Press, 1999. Investigates the conversion process based on extensive interviews.

Hamilton, Rosemary. *Hellbent for Enlightenment: Unmasking Sex, Power, and Death with a Notorious Master.* Ashland, OR: White Cloud, 1998. A forthright account of one follower's odyssey.

Palmer, Susan J., and Arvind Sharma, eds. *The Rajneesh Papers: Studies in a New Religious Movement.* Delhi: Motile Banarsidas, 1993. Includes essays and interviews with devotees.

Web Sites

www.oshocom/. The online *Osho Times,* with information about the Osho retreat center, the "multiversity," and links to audio Webcasts.

www.oshoworld.com. Includes a biography of Osho and other primary texts.

www.sannyas.net. An extensive site maintained by the "friends of Osho"; includes news, photographs, excerpts from texts, words and chords for Osho music, and a section of children's resources.

Santeria/Rastafari/Vodou

Books

Bodin, Ron. *Voodoo: Past and Present.* Lafayette: The Center for Louisiana Studies, 1990. Focuses on New Orleans and its environs and includes an interview with a convert to Vodou.

Brown, Karen McCarthy. *Mama Lola: A Vodou Priestess in Brooklyn.* Berkeley: University of California Press, 1991. A vivid biography of a priestess.

Desmangles, Leslie. *The Faces of the Gods: Vodou and Roman Catholicism in Haiti.* Chapel Hill: University of North Carolina Press, 1993. Pays particular attention to the interaction of African, indigenous, and Roman Catholic elements in Vodou.

Edmonds, Ennis Barrington. *Rastafari: From Outcasts to Culture Bearers.* New York: Oxford University Press, 2003. A thorough survey of Rastafarian beliefs and practices.

Glassman, Sallie Ann. *Vodou Visions: An Encounter with Divine Mystery.* New York: Villard, 2000. The author has appropriated Vodou into her own eclectic spiritual practice.

Murphy, Joseph M. *Santeria: An African Religion in America.* Boston: Beacon, 1988. Focuses on the practice of Santeria in immigrant communities.

Murrell, Nathaniel Samuel, William David Spencer, and Adrian Anthony McFarlane, eds. *Chanting Down Babylon: The Rastafari Reader.* Philadelphia: Temple University Press, 1998. Includes some discussion of the attraction exerted by Rastafari on Caucasian Americans.

Web Sites

www.church-of-the-lukumi.org. The site of the Santeria church in Hialeah, Florida, whose practices were upheld in a landmark U.S. Supreme Court case.

www.jahworks.org. Focused on Caribbean music and culture, with record, concert, and film reviews, and a guide to reggae radio on the Web.

www.rastafaritimes.com. Includes news articles, "reasonings," and extensive links to Rastafarian materials.

www.rastafarispeaks.com. Includes articles, essays on history, poetry, and selected speeches of Haile Selassie.

www.web.syr.edu/~affellem/index.html. An extensive archive of Rastafari materials and links to Rastafari and reggae sites.

Seventh-Day Adventists

Primary Text

White, Ellen. *The Great Controversy Between Christ and Satan: The Conflict of the Ages in the Christian Dispensation.* Mountain View, CA: Pacific Press Publishing Association, 1950. A complete account of White's theological system.

Books

Bull, Malcolm, and Keith Lockhart. *Seeking a Sanctuary: Seventh-day Adventism and the American Dream.* New York: Harper & Row, 1989. Reviews the history, theology, and practice of the Church.

Numbers, Ronald L., and Jonathan M. Butler, eds. *The Disappointed: Millerism and Millenarianism in the Nineteenth Century.* Knoxville: University of Tennessee Press, 1993. Provides an account of the origins of the church and some primary materials.

Web Sites

www.adventist.org. The official site of the Seventh-Day Adventist Church, with a collection of documents and audio and video materials.

www.sdanet.org. An extensive collection of materials on Adventism, with a searchable index going back to 1990.

Shakers

Primary Texts

www.passtheword.org/SHAKER-MANUSCRIPTS/. An extensive collection of primary texts from the early days of the movement.

Books

Campion, Nardi Reeder. *Mother Ann Lee: Morning Star of the Shakers.* Hanover, NH: University Press of New England, 1990. A biography of the founder.

Stein, Stephen J. *The Shaker Experience in America*. New Haven: Yale University Press, 1992. A full and compelling account of the origins and history of the Shakers.

Web Site

www.discernment.org/some.htm. A countercult comparison between the Shakers and the contemporary Signs and Wonders Movement.

Soka Gakkai

Primary Text

Ikeda, Daisaku, et al. *The Wisdom of the Lotus Sutra: A Discussion*, vol. I. Santa Monica, CA: World Tribune, 2000. A chapter-by-chapter interpretation of the central text of the movement. For a list of his writings, see www.sgi.org.

Books

Dobbelaere, Karel. *Soka Gakkai: From Lay Movement to Religion*. Salt Lake City: Signature, 2001, ET. A compact introduction and overview.

Hammond, Phillip, and David Machacek. *Soka Gakkai in America: Accommodation and Conversion*. Oxford: Oxford University Press, 1999. A sociological study of Soka Gakkai in the United States.

Hochswender, Woody, Greg Martin, and Ted Morino. *The Buddha in Your Mirror: Practical Buddhism and the Search for Self*. Santa Monica: Middleway, 2001. A popular presentation of the message of Soka Gakkai.

Web Sites

www.sgi.org. The Web site of Soka Gakkai International; includes the texts of speeches and essays by Daisaku Ikeda and a full list of his books.

www.sgi-usa.org/. The official site of Soka Gakkai in the United States; includes text, audio, and video resources, and some materials for children.

www.toda.org. Founded by Daisaku Ikeda to honor the second president of Soka Gakkai, Josei Toda.

Spiritualism

Books

Braude, Ann. *Radical Spirits: Spiritualism and Women's Rights in Nineteenth-Century America*. Boston: Beacon, 1989. Details the intersections of spiritualism with women's activism.

Moore, R. Laurence. *In Search of White Crows: Spiritualism, Parapsychology, and American Culture*. New York: Oxford University Press, 1977. Sets spiritualism in its cultural contexts and examines its conflicts with debunkers.

Article

Braude, Ann. "The Perils of Passivity: Women's Leadership in Spiritualism and Christian Science." In Catherine Wessinger, ed. *Women's Leadership in Mar-*

ginal Religions: Explorations Outside the Mainstream. Urbana: University of Illinois Press, 1993. An informative treatment of gender and leadership.

Theosophy

Books

Campbell, Bruce F. *Ancient Wisdom Revived: A History of the Theosophical Movement.* Berkeley: University of California Press, 1977. A lucid, accessible history of the movement.

Cranston, Sylvia. *HPB: The Extraordinary Life and Influence of Helena Blavatsky, Founder of the Modern Theosophical Movement.* New York: G. P. Putnam, 1993. An extensive positive account of HPB, rich with detail.

Ellwood, Robert. *Theosophy: A Modern Expression of the Wisdom of the Ages.* Wheaton, IL: Quest, 1986. A brisk, sympathetic survey by one of the foremost students of new religious movements.

Johnson, K. Paul. *The Masters Revealed: Madame Blavatsky and the Myth of the Great White Lodge.* Albany: State University of New York Press, 1994. Provides biographical sketches of the various adepts with whom HPB came into contact.

Johnson, K. Paul. *Initiates of Theosophical Masters.* Albany: State University of New York Press, 1995. Surveys prominent Theosophical teachers.

Washington, Peter. *Madame Blavatsky's Baboon: A History of the Mystics, Mediums, and Misfits Who Brought Spiritualism to America.* New York: Schocken, 1993. A critical account of the cultural context in which Theosophy developed.

Article

Wessinger, Catherine. "Democracy vs. Hierarchy: The Evolution of Authority in the Theosophical Society." In Timothy Miller, ed., *When Prophets Die: The Postcharismatic Fate of New Religious Movements.* Albany: State University of New York Press, 1991.

Web Sites

www.theosociety.org. The Web site of the Theosophical Society headquartered in Pasadena, California; includes links to full texts by Madame Blavatsky and other key figures in Theosophical history.

www.theosophy.org/Library.htm. Links to a vast library of electronic texts about Theosophy.

Unification Church

Primary Texts

Anonymous. *Divine Principle.* New York: The Holy Spirit Association for the Unification of World Christianity, 1973. The fundamental scriptural text of the movement.

Anonymous. *Outline of the Principle, Level 4*. New York: The Holy Spirit Association for the Unification of World Christianity, 1980. A frequently used text by Unificationists.

Lewis, James R., ed. *The Unification Church III: Outreach*. New York: Garland, 1990. Texts and other documents.

Mickler, Michael, ed. *The Unification Church I: Views From Outside*. New York: Garland, 1990. Includes a variety of primary texts, some very difficult to get elsewhere.

Mickler, Michael, ed. *The Unification Church II: Inner Life*. New York: Garland, 1990. More primary texts.

Books

Barker, Eileen. *The Making of a Moonie: Brainwashing or Choice*. London: Blackwell's, 1984. A magisterial treatment of the issue of conversion that includes a capsule portrait of the church.

Bromley, David G., and Anson D. Shupe, Jr. *"Moonies" in America: Cult, Church, and Crusade*. Beverly Hills, CA: Sage, 1979. A complete history of the early years of the movement in the United States.

Chryssides, George D. *The Advent of Sun Myung Moon: The Beliefs and Practices of the Unification Church*. London: Macmillan, 1991. Good attention to both doctrine and the ritual life of Unificationists.

Edwards, Christopher. *Crazy for God*. Englewood Cliffs, NJ: Prentice-Hall, 1979. An influential apostate's account of life in the church.

Hong, Nansook. *In the Shadow of the Moons: My Life in Reverend Sun Myung Moon's Family*. Boston: Little, Brown, 1998. An exposé of life behind the scenes by the ex-wife of one of Rev. Moon's sons.

Introvigne, Massimo. *The Unification Church*. Salt Lake City: Signature, 2000. A brief introduction that covers the period through the 1990s.

Mickler, Michael. *A History of the Unification Church in America 1959–1974: Emergence of a National Movement*. New York: Garland, 1993. A history of the early years by a church official.

Underwood, Barbara and Betty. *Hostage to Heaven*. New York: Clarkson N. Potter, 1979. A nuanced and subtle account of what led a young woman into and ultimately out of the Unification Movement, written in alternating chapters by a mother and daughter.

Articles

Lofland, John. "Becoming a World-Saver Revisited." In James T. Richardson, ed. *Conversion Careers: In and Out of the New Religions*. Beverly Hills: Sage, 1978. Revisits the influential account of conversion to the Unification Church.

Lofland, John, and Rodney Stark. "Becoming a World-Saver: A Theory of Conversion to a Deviant Perspective." *American Sociological Review* 30 (1965). Focuses on the earliest group of converts in the United States.

Web Sites

www.geocities.com/Athens/4623/. Includes links to full texts of many Unificationist publications and links to a variety of other Web sites about the church.

www.unification.org. The official Web site of the Unification Movement.

Index

About the Author

EUGENE V. GALLAGHER is the Rosemary Park Professor of Religious Studies and Faculty Fellow of the Center for Teaching and Learning at Connecticut College. He is the co-author (with James D. Tabor) of *Why Waco? Cults and the Battle for Religious Freedom in America* (1995) and the author of *Expectation and Experience: Explaining Religious Conversion* (1990).